FASCISM, VULNERABILITY, AND THE ESCAPE FROM FREEDOM

Fig. 1. Detail from Hieronymus Bosch, *Ship of Fools* (1490–1500)

First published in 2022 by punctum books, Earth, Milky Way.
https://punctumbooks.com

ISBN-13: 978-1-68571-080-4 (print)
ISBN-13: 978-1-68571-081-1 (ePDF)

DOI: 10.53288/0392.1.00

LCCN: 2022947239
Library of Congress Cataloging Data is available from the Library of Congress

Book design: Vincent W.J. van Gerven Oei
Cover photograph: Daniel Delogu, Yellow Vest protest in Toulouse, France, March, 2019.

p. punctumbooks

spontaneous acts of scholarly combustion

HIC SVNT MONSTRA

C. Jon Delogu

Fascism, Vulnerability, and the Escape from Freedom

Readings to Repair Democracy

p.

Contents

For Rose and Daniel, in memory of J. Hillis Miller, and to my students in the 2015, 2017, 2018, and 2019 seminars that laid the groundwork for this book.

Ik heb een sterk uitkomende karaktertrek die iedereen die me langer kent moet opvallen, en wel mijn zelfkennis. Ik kan mezelf bij al mijn handelingen bekijken, alsof ik een vreemde was. Helemaal niet vooringenomen of met een zak verontschuldigingen sta ik dan tegenover de Anne van elke dag en kijk toe wat die goed en wat ze slecht doet. Dat 'zelfgevoel' laat me nooit los en bij elk woord dat ik uitspreek weet ik dadelijk als het uitgesproken is: 'Dit had anders moeten zijn', of 'Dat is goed zo als het is'. Ik veroordeel mezelf in zo onnoemelijk veel dingen en zie steeds meer hoe waar dat woord van vader was: 'Ieder kind moet zichzelf opvoeden'. Ouders kunnen alleen raad of goede aanwijzingen meegeven, de uiteindelijke vorming van iemands karakter ligt in zijn eigen hand. Daarbij komt nog, dat ik buitengewoon veel levensmoed heb, ik voel me altijd zo sterk en tot dragen in staat, zo vrij en zo jong! Toen ik dat voor het eerst opmerkte was ik blij, want ik geloof niet, dat ik gauw zal buigen voor de slagen die ieder moet opvangen.

I have one outstanding character trait that must be obvious to anyone who's known me for any length of time: I have a great deal of self-knowledge. In everything I do, I can watch myself as if I were someone else. I can stand across from the everyday Anne and, without being biased or making excuses, watch what she's doing, both the good and the bad. This self-awareness never leaves me, and every time I open my mouth, I think immediately upon hearing my own words, "You should have said that differently" or "That's fine the way it is." I condemn myself in so many ways that I'm beginning to realize the truth of Father's adage: "Every child has to raise itself." Parents can only advise their children or point them in the right direction. Ultimately, people shape their own characters. In addition, I face life with an extraordinary amount of courage. I feel so strong and capable of bearing burdens, so young and free! When I first realized this, I was glad, because it means I can more easily withstand the blows life has in store.

 — Anne Frank, *Diary*, Saturday, July 15, 1944
  (translation by Susan Massotty, modified)

Il est tentant de se débarrasser du fardeau exigeant de sa personnalité ! Il est tentant de se laisser englober dans un vaste mouvement d'enthousiasme collectif ! Il est tentant de croire, parce que c'est commode, et parce que c'est suprêmement confortable !

It's tempting to get rid of the demanding burden of one's personality! It's tempting to allow oneself to be sucked into a vast all-encompassing movement of collective enthusiasm! It's tempting to believe, because it's convenient, and because it's supremely comfortable!

— Roger Martin du Gard, *Les Thibault*
(Épilogue, 1940; translation by the author)

Introduction

It is a truth universally acknowledged that the Covid-19 pandemic tested every regime around the world — at local, regional, and national levels — severely punishing people who live under those operating with pride, prejudice, and distrust, while treating less harshly the citizens of countries that hew to the truth, transparency, and a spirit of solidarity when approaching problems and projects. Though biological in origin, the pandemic was a human-made disaster, a cascade of bad choices that confirmed the old saying "You reap what you sow"[1] and the wisdom that says to get out of a hole one must first stop digging it deeper.[2]

I started writing this book in the winter semester of 2020 while teaching my seminar on "Tocqueville and Democracy in the Internet Age." As the seriousness of the new coronavirus

---

1   On the Biblical dimension of the Covid-19 pandemic within a broader American crisis, see David Marchese, "Rev. William Barber on Greed, Poverty and Evangelical Politics," *The New York Times,* December 28, 2020. https://www.nytimes.com/interactive/2020/12/28/magazine/william-barber-interview.html.

2   For a twenty-minute summary focused on US incompetence in response to the coronavirus pandemic, see *The New York Times* video by Johnny Harris, Nicholas Kristof, and Adam B. Ellick, "America Wrote the Pandemic Playbook, Then Ignored It," September 29, 2020, https://www.nytimes.com/video/opinion/100000007358968/covid-pandemic-us-response.html.

became apparent, my students and I debated whether democracies or authoritarian regimes would respond best to a pandemic. Events over the following months demonstrated that the worst performing countries were neither the straight up authoritarian regimes like China, nor the healthy democracies such as South Korea or New Zealand, but instead countries where democracy is broken or hobbled due to authoritarianization — a process that substitutes authoritarian for democratic rule all the while preserving a façade of democratic practices and people power.[3] Such countries typically make use of fascist rhetoric to mask the fact that the people have surrendered or been robbed of their sovereignty. Meanwhile, as Tocqueville already observed in Andrew Jackson's day, they ruthlessly and legally punish their enemies while rewarding their friends.[4] Today those deceitful countries include Brazil, India, the Philippines, Russia, and the United States. It's not surprising that these countries failed the Covid-19 test since the hallmarks of authoritarianization — a reliance on deceptive propaganda and mythologies, a concen-

---

3   For an account of authoritarianization in the aftermath of the US Senate's vote not to remove President Trump from office after he was impeached by the House of Representatives in 2019, see Adam Serwer, "The First Days of the Trump Regime," *The Atlantic*, February 19, 2020, https://www.theatlantic.com/ideas/archive/2020/02/trump-regime/606682/: "Modern authoritarian institutions diligently seek to preserve the appearance of democratic accountability." For a general introduction referenced by Serwer, see Erica Frantz, *Authoritarianism: What Everyone Needs to Know* (New York: Oxford University Press, 2018).

4   See Alexis de Tocqueville, *Democracy in America; and, Two Essays on America*, trans. Gerald Bevan (London: Penguin Books, 2003), vol. 1, part 2, ch. 10, subsection "The Present State and Probable Future of the Indian Tribes which Populate the Territory of the Union." On contemporary techniques in Florida, Hungary, and elsewhere, see Kim Lane Scheppele, "What Donald Trump and Ron DeSantis Are Learning About the Politics of Retribution," *The New York Times*, May 24, 2022, https://www.nytimes.com/2022/05/24/opinion/trump-desantis-viktor-orban.html. For a profile of Orbán and his supporters in Hungary and the United States, see Andrew Marantz, "Does Hungary Offer a Glimpse of Our Authoritarian Future?" *The New Yorker*, July 4, 2022, https://www.newyorker.com/magazine/2022/07/04/does-hungary-offer-a-glimpse-of-our-authoritarian-future.

tration of wealth and power, and a division between deserving loyalists and unworthy "enemies of the people" — are inimical to both scientific method and democratic institutions which believe in reality-based decision-making, value knowledge and respectful national and international debates and the free circulation of verifiable information, and regularly practice aggregating and sifting the experience, expertise, and opinions of many individuals and groups from all walks of life with the aim of implementing better practices and achieving healthier outcomes that advance the general public good and repair past mistakes.[5] If responding to Covid-19 was a trial run for the larger challenge of stopping global warming, man's inability on both fronts to "unite behind the science," as Greta Thunberg has so often demanded, raises doubts about the prospects for our survival under any regime.[6]

I grew up in Maine, did all my studies in New England, and moved to France in 1992. I have worked in the English department of three tuition-free French state universities and regularly return to the US to teach and translate. Over my lifetime I have witnessed expanding inequality of social conditions and the weakening of democracy in the United States across the ethically compromised Republican presidencies of Richard Nixon (Watergate), Ronald Reagan (Iran-Contra), George W. Bush (fake WMD and real torture), and Donald Trump (abuse of

---

5   See Zeynep Tufekci, "Where Did the Coronavirus Come From? What We Already Know Is Troubling," *The New York Times,* June 25, 2021, https://www.nytimes.com/2021/06/25/opinion/coronavirus-lab.html, and "How Millions of Lives Might Have Been Saved from Covid-19," *The New York Times,* March 11, 2022, https://www.nytimes.com/2022/03/11/opinion/covid-health-pandemic.html; Lawrence Wright, *The Plague Year: America in the Time of Covid* (New York: Alfred A. Knopf, 2021).

6   On the need for a future "progressive globalism," see Adam Tooze, "What If the Coronavirus Crisis Is Just a Trial Run?" *The New York Times,* September 1, 2021, https://www.nytimes.com/2021/09/01/opinion/covid-pandemic-global-economy-politics.html. On the difficulty of uniting behind the science, see Jay S. Kaufman, "Science Alone Can't Heal a Sick Society," *The New York Times,* September 10, 2021, https://www.nytimes.com/2021/09/10/opinion/covid-science-trust-us.html.

public office for personal gain) — presidencies which, however, were all successful at concentrating wealth and power, sowing or worsening social divisions, and reasserting America's plutocratic, oligarchic, imperial norm after three generations of a more egalitarian, social-democratic trend that lasted from Teddy Roosevelt's Progressive Era to Franklin Delano Roosevelt's New Deal to Lyndon B. Johnson's Great Society.[7] I have also witnessed smart, decent, Democratic presidents (Jimmy Carter, Bill Clinton, Barack Obama) unable or unwilling to slow the return of authoritarian political and economic practices that advance with the sly help of global capitalism no matter which party is in power.[8] I've witnessed the conservative campaign to take over the courts,[9] and I've seen the capture of state governments by conservative ideologues such as Sam Brownback in Kansas, Scott Walker in Wisconsin, and Paul LePage in Maine.[10] But I have also seen democratic pushback in Maine which instituted ranked-choice voting to avoid governance by mere plurality, circumvented somewhat the anti-democratic Electoral College with the District Method of vote apportionment, and replaced a demagogue with a Democrat, Janet Mills, who has been one of the more successful governors when it comes to flattening

---

7   On the current crisis of US democracy as a "relapse" and not a "collapse," see Jon Grinspan, "What We Did the Last Time We Broke America," *The New York Times*, October 29, 2021, https://www.nytimes.com/2021/10/29/opinion/normal-politics-gilded-age.html.

8   See Nancy MacLean, *Democracy in Chains: The Deep History of the Radical Right's Stealth Plan for America* (New York: Viking, 2017), and Sheldon S. Wolin, *Democracy Inc.: Managed Democracy and the Specter of Inverted Totalitarianism* (Princeton: Princeton University Press, 2010).

9   See Linda Greenhouse, "The Supreme Court, Weaponized," *The New York Times*, December 16, 2021, https://www.nytimes.com/2021/12/16/opinion/supreme-court-trump.html, a condensed version of her argument in *Justice on The Brink: The Death of Ruth Bader Ginsburg, the Rise of Amy Coney Barrett, and Twelve Months That Transformed the Supreme Court* (New York: Random House, 2021).

10   For a profile of one of many regional attacks on labor unions and democracy, see Dan Kaufman, "Scott Walker's Wisconsin Paved the Way for Donald Trump's America," *The New York Times*, July 6, 2021, https://www.nytimes.com/2021/07/06/opinion/wisconsin-act-10-trump.html.

the curve of coronavirus infections and rekindling a sense of compassion and citizen solidarity which remain dismally low in much of the country.[11]

In France, a country that mostly ignored its greatest specialist on democracy for over a century and still counts a number of royalists and Empire nostalgics, democracy has made progress. I have seen career politicians forced to question their longstanding preference for authority, hierarchy, and deference; heard inclusive, left-wing populist calls for "participatory democracy" (the implication being that France's Fifth Republic has often been democracy in name only); and watched the nation make strides to live up to its revolutionary motto, *Liberty, Equality, Solidarity.* France affirmed the importance of accountability and the principle that no one is above the law by allowing courts to prosecute two former presidents (Jacques Chirac and Nicolas Sarkozy) and a prime minister (François Fillon), all eventually convicted of wrongdoing.[12] Also, from late 2018 and through all of 2019 there was wide support for a sixty-week string of Saturday afternoon public protests by lower-middle-class "Yellow Vests" opposed to unequal burden-sharing of a shift to ecology politics, disinvestment in public services, and working longer for smaller retirement benefits. I have witnessed the rise of a nationalist far-right party in France, but also its leveling off (for now) at around 25 percent of the electorate — far short of being

---

11 Thomas Friedman, "America 2022: Where Everyone Has Rights and No One Has Responsibilities," *The New York Times,* February 8, 2022, https://www.nytimes.com/2022/02/08/opinion/spotify-joe-rogan-covid-free-speech.html. Maine is home to some creative, energized Democrats committed to reviving compassion and problem-solving directed at the rural US instead of writing it off. See Chloe Maxim and Canyon Woodward, "What Democrats Don't Understand About Rural America," *The New York Times,* May 2, 2022, https://www.nytimes.com/2022/05/02/opinion/democrats-rural-america.html.

12 On the importance of accountability in a democracy, see Michelle Goldberg, "After Trump, America Needs Accountability for His Corruption," *The New York Times,* August 13, 2020, https://www.nytimes.com/2020/08/13/opinion/trump-corruption.html. On Chirac's 2011 conviction, see my book, *Tocqueville and Democracy in the Internet Age* (Ann Arbor: Open Humanities Press, 2014), 254–56.

able to take power but powerful enough to be normalized and participate as one party among others so long as they accept to play by democracy's rules and norms.[13] In short, with eddies and countercurrents, I've watched my birth country become less democratic and less egalitarian over the last forty years and my second country become more democratic and somewhat more respectful of ordinary people despite lingering racism, prejudice, and xenophobia.[14]

Because I have witnessed directly the inverse political and cultural evolution of two proud countries which for long have each been the bad conscience of the other, and also because I have a background in comparative literature, an interdisciplinary field devoted to narratology and rhetorical analysis and one that embraced *intersectionality* before the term even existed, I believe this book provides a more complete account than other studies offer of the push and pushback between authori-

---

13 Observers inside and outside France often repeat that the far-right has gained considerable strength since 2002, but the numbers do not line up to support that claim. In 2022, Marine Le Pen lost the presidential election for the third time. While there may be strong support for her party in the more sparsely populated northeast, southeast, and other rural pockets of France, her national total in the April 24, 2022 second-round runoff (after finishing second with 23 percent in the first round on April 10) was still only 41.5 percent to Emmanuel Macron's 58.5 percent; and her losing share shrinks to 27 percent if one factors in the blank and absent voters who represented together sixteen million or 32.5 percent of all registered voters in 2022. During President Macron's first five-year term, Marine Le Pen and seven others of her far-right party held eight of 577 seats in France's legislative body, the Assemblée nationale — their number rose to eighty-nine (or 15.5 percent) after legislative elections in 2022. As of 2020, roughly a dozen mayors (out of 34,955) belong to Marine Le Pen's neofascist party, Le Rassemblement National.

14 Although an optimist by temperament, I notice many fear that democracy in America is dying or dead. For an assessment compiled two years after I drafted this Introduction, see Thomas B. Edsall, "How to Tell When Your Country Is Past the Point of No Return," *The New York Times,* December 15, 2021, https://www.nytimes.com/2021/12/15/opinion/republicans-democracy-minority-rule.html. More warnings, including of civil war or a negotiated breakup of the country, were published around the first anniversary of the January 6 Capitol riot.

tarianism and democracy. The importance of this book *now* is its focus on the seductiveness of fascism, euphemized today as "right-wing populism," and the impulse to escape from freedom (and duck responsibility) in times of high vulnerability.

The argument of this book is that vulnerability — exposure to attack or hurt, either physically or in other ways — causes freedom to be perceived as something negative and threatening which in turn leads people to go along with a hijacking of democracy in the direction of fascism and authoritarianism. Acute or chronic feelings of vulnerability, especially about real or perceived loss and lack, trigger various insecurities and fears, including fear of freedom. Freedom or liberty, we can take the two as synonyms here, is then no longer experienced as something precious, for some as precious as life itself ("Give me liberty or give me death"); it is no longer experienced as positive individual opportunity or free agency ("freedom *to*"[15]), but instead as vertigo-inducing; in other words, part and parcel of a dizzying and embarrassing lack of self-trust, confidence, and potency to the point of existential crisis. The only viable escape from this dire predicament — or so these panicky individuals come to believe — is to turn away from the bricolage of open-ended, participatory democracy and their personal role in that collaborative social experiment, and to adopt instead, to the point of dissolution and fusion, the clarity, order, and rules of a fascist movement or the bleak regimentation of an authoritarian or totalitarian regime. Fascism is an escape from freedom.

This surrender of selfhood and personal sovereignty and the acceptance of "voluntary servitude" (Étienne de La Boétie) is the hallmark of the aptly named *chain of command*; in other words, the extremely bonded group behavior that one observes in military units but also in some religious cults, corporate cultures, athletic teams with fanatical fans and extreme team spirit, po-

---

15 For a presentation of Isaiah Berlin's "Two Concepts of Liberty," freedom from and freedom to, see the entry with helpful links to Berlin's essay and other related documents, *Stanford Encyclopedia of Philosophy,* s.v. "Positive and Negative Liberty," https://plato.stanford.edu/entries/liberty-positive-negative/.

litical parties, clubs, mafia organizations, including large bossy family gatherings, and — our focus here — fascism. Fascism is not the dismantling or abandonment of democracy so much as its radical redirection, when caught off guard or in a weakened state — hence the hijack metaphor. It draws people and energy away from horizontal popular sovereignty of, by, and for the Many toward a largely unregulated and unaccountable vertical system managed by (and mostly for) a select Few under the direction of a charismatic usually male leader protected by loyal "bland fanatics" (Reinhold Niebuhr and Pankaj Mishra). This leader claims to have the support of the people and therefore to be a democratic leader, even though in reality the regime he sits atop is only a "zombie democracy,"[16] sometimes called a "managed democracy,"[17] "democracy in name only,"[18] or "democracy without democracy."[19] Fascism, according to a longtime expert on the subject, the historian Robert O. Paxton, is "a phenomenon of failed democracies."[20] In the very first sentence to the Introduction of his authoritative *Anatomy of Fascism* (2004), Paxton writes, "Fascism was the major political innovation of the twentieth century, and the source of much of its pain."[21] The pain takes the form of mental and physical violence, including

16 "Zombie," as noun and adjective, is recurrent in the opinion writings of Paul Krugman, see *Arguing with Zombies: Economics, Politics, and The Fight for a Better Future* (New York: W.W. Norton & Co., 2020). See Kenneth Roth, "The Age of Zombie Democracies," *Foreign Affairs,* July 28, 2021, https://www.foreignaffairs.com/americas/age-zombie-democracies.

17 Sheldon Wolin and others; also "guided democracy," principally in reference to Russia and Indonesia.

18 Madeleine Rosen, "Democracy in Name Only," *Amor Mundi,* December 22, 2017, https://medium.com/amor-mundi/democracy-in-name-only-c0e8aa5a661a.

19 Richard Bellamy, "Democracy without Democracy? Can the EU's Democratic 'Outputs' Be Separated from the Democratic 'Inputs' Provided by Competitive Parties and Majority Rule?" *Journal of European Public Policy* 17 (2010): 2–19.

20 Paxton is relaying a claim made by the exiled Italian socialist turned Harvard professor, Gaetano Salvemini. Robert O. Paxton, *The Anatomy of Fascism* (New York: Alfred A. Knopf, 2004), 216.

21 Ibid., 3.

often a "murderous frenzy"[22] that is visited upon designated "enemies of the people" as the fascist movement, fueled by rule-or-perish impulses, carries out its hijacking of democracy, or, stated less metaphorically, its *authoritarianization* of democracy.[23]

If a research project, in whatever field, seeks to understand the pain caused by a particular problem with the aim of reducing that pain, then a crucial step in explaining the problem explored in this book is to account for how it happens that a painful situation (e.g., feeling vulnerable and anxious) deranges the judgment of the pained individual or group to such an extent that it causes them to inflict more pain on themselves and others (e.g., by embracing fascistic thinking and behaviors) instead of pursuing alternative strategies with a higher probability of actually reducing pain. This is the problem Paxton invites his reader to grapple with by asking, alongside Gaetano Salvemini, "why 'Italians felt the need to get rid of their free institutions' at the very moment when they should be taking pride in them, and when they 'should step forward toward a more advanced democracy.'"[24] After pointing out this paradoxical behavior, Paxton follows up with a useful distinction between fascism and "classical tyranny."

Fascism, for Salvemini, meant setting aside democracy and due process in public life, to the acclamation of the street. It

---

22 Ibid., 212. In the United States, this would be "the violent defense of whiteness," as Kathleen Belew states. "The Long Game of White-Power Activists Isn't Just About Violence," *The New York Times,* May 17, 2022, https://www.nytimes.com/2022/05/17/opinion/buffalo-shooting-replacement-theory.html, is an editorial published after the Buffalo, New York shooting by a white, male 18-year-old who killed ten Black people, a murderous frenzy many see as enabled by conservative politicians and media, not a random act.

23 On authoritarianization, see Amanda Taub using the research of Yale political science professor Milan Svolik, "How Autocrats Can Triumph in Democratic Countries," *The New York Times,* April 18, 2017, https://www.nytimes.com/2017/04/18/world/europe/how-autocrats-can-triumph-in-democratic-countries.html.

24 Paxton, *The Anatomy of Fascism,* 216.

is a phenomenon of failed democracies, and its novelty was that, instead of simply clamping silence upon citizens as classical tyranny had done since earliest times, it found a technique to channel their passions into the construction of an obligatory domestic unity around projects of internal cleansing and external expansion. We should not use the term *fascism* for pre-democratic dictatorships. However cruel, they lack the manipulated mass enthusiasm and demonic energy of fascism, along with the mission of "giving up free institutions" for the sake of national unity, purity, and force.[25]

As useful as Paxton's *Anatomy of Fascism* is, and we shall return to it later, it will be necessary to go beyond the narratives of historians and listen also to psychologists, sociologists, memoirists, and creative writers if we are to understand the paradoxical behavior of those in great pain who harm themselves further rather than seek genuine help to alleviate that pain. Evidence of such behavior (choosing self-harm over self-care, stepping backward instead of forward while perhaps thoroughly convinced one is stepping forward) can be seen everywhere: in the cycle of addiction, be it to alcohol, opioids, oil, or screen time; the trap of exploitive relationships (cults and clubs, abusive marriages, toxic work environments); the destructiveness of impulsive and compulsive behaviors (cutting, eating disorders, and the dark routines within narcissistic-codependent dyads); or the ultimate destruction of (mass) murder or suicide.[26]

We all know examples of "throwing fuel on the fire," all those behaviors that lead from bad to worse, and we all know that it's standard advice to avoid doing so. There's a reason why, for example, it is commonly recommended that after a big trauma, such as a death or divorce, one should not make major life de-

---

25 Ibid.

26 Covid-19-induced isolation and dislocation has greatly magnified these problems. See the addiction specialist Maia Szalavitz, "Opioids Feel Like Love, That's Why They're Deadly in Tough Times," *The New York Times,* December 6, 2021, https://www.nytimes.com/2021/12/06/opinion/us-opioid-crisis.html.

cisions in the first year following the event. Why not? Because one is particularly vulnerable, and hence not in one's right mind: "Move to Patagonia? Are you out of your mind?" Short answer: *Yes*. In that vulnerable state, one is susceptible to harming oneself further and thereby compounding one's problems — "digging the hole deeper," as it's often called — instead of following the stock advice: "Stop digging!" Of course, that's easier said than done, which means the same advice gets repeated and ignored over and over.[27]

The goal of this book is twofold: first, to give as full an account as possible of its main claim which is that vulnerability provokes fear of freedom and a misguided embrace of fascism; and second, to reduce vulnerability in order to decrease the likelihood of that destructive choice. This was also Paxton's goal: "Contemplating fascism, we see most clearly how the twentieth century contrasted with the nineteenth, and what the twenty-first century must avoid."[28] Agreed. However, I believe we shall see more clearly still if, in addition to the insights provided by the historians of German and Italian fascism, and of later "functional equivalents" of fascism, we also make use of the work of philosophers and psychologists — the first because they are specialists of logic and rhetoric, including the twisted logic of specious arguments; and the second because they are specialists when it comes to understanding the workings of the unconscious and the odd logic of seemingly irrational behavior. I have found the writings of the philosophy professors Jason Stanley (*How Propaganda Works*, 2015; *How Fascism Works*, 2018) and Martha Nussbaum (*The Monarchy of Fear*, 2018) particularly helpful. I am most indebted, however, to the work of the well-known but often overlooked psychologist Erich Fromm, especially his 1941 classic *Escape from Freedom*. The third term in my title signals that debt. My title is meant to function as a deliberate echo of Fromm's argument that a friend helped him

---

27 A quick internet search reveals countless websites on this topic, such as the free advice at verywellmind.com.

28 Paxton, *The Anatomy of Fascism*, 21.

encapsulate when he convinced Fromm to use *Escape* — with no article — for the English edition which he wrote himself. Fromm's English title can be read as a devilish provocation: (You must) *Escape from Freedom!* The title holds off on naming the origin of that commanding drive, *fear,* which appears in the German, French, and Spanish titles of the book. In those translations, Fear (*Die Furcht vor der Freiheit, La peur de la liberté, El miedo a la libertad*) is preceded by a definite article that signals a more traditional work of definition and exposition of *The Fear of Freedom.*[29] But Fromm's book is more than a description or diagnosis. It is a manifesto, a call to a higher action: *to escape from the escape from freedom.*

As noted above, Paxton defines fascism among a given people as a "technique" to "channel their passions"; and twice — early and late in his *Anatomy* (pages 42 and 219) — he offers a list of the "mobilizing passions" of fascism, also memorably termed "the emotional lava that sets fascism's foundations." He also makes the offhand comment, "Perhaps it is the fascist publics rather than their leaders who need psychoanalysis."[30] Therefore it's somewhat odd that nowhere does Paxton mention Fromm who famously attempted to do that very thing. Even though Paxton acknowledges that "visceral feelings"[31] are more characteristic of fascism than articulating an ideology or doctrine, he is surprisingly dismissive of "psycho-historical explanations of fascism."[32] Far from dismissing such approaches, this study

---

29 Erich Fromm (1900–1980), a German Jewish immigrant in the United States, wrote the book in English as a personal challenge and as a show of thanks to the country and culture that gave him a new start in life. See Lawrence J. Friedman, *The Lives of Erich Fromm: Love's Prophet* (New York: Columbia University Press, 2013). There exist English editions of Fromm's book entitled *The Fear of Freedom,* for example the 1942 Routledge & Kegan Paul edition, but I will be discussing Fromm's original *Escape from Freedom* from 1941, reprinted many times by Henry Holt and Company and with a new forward by Fromm added in 1965.

30 Paxton, *The Anatomy of Fascism,* 208.

31 Ibid., 219.

32 Ibid., 208. Paxton does however mention the *Ungleichzeitigkeit* theories of Ernst Bloch concerning the uneven mixture of modernization blended

shall combine Paxton's thorough history and useful inventory of fascism's emotional lava with Stanley, Nussbaum, and Fromm's explanations of how and why that lava burns so hot.

I am convinced that the only way to prevent the pain of fascism — which may without exaggeration or poetic whim be considered to operate like a virus or cancer preying on unsuspecting social organisms with weak or vulnerable immune systems — is to examine the three interrelated factors that make up what epidemiologists, and lately an array of social scientists across many fields, call the *epidemic triangle*; in other words, the relationships between *pathogen, host,* and *environment*.[33] For this work, it stands to reason that a comparative, multidisciplinary, and transnational approach will be more productive than any single method or solitary example. Fromm is a model of such an open approach, since *Escape from Freedom* makes use of an array of political and religious histories from the Middle Ages to modern times, as well as insights taken from philosophy, psychology, literature, and popular culture to construct a compelling explanation of the impulse to flee democratic free-

---

with nostalgia and tradition; the resentment hypothesis of Seymour Lipset, *Political Man: The Social Bases of Politics* (Garden City: Anchor Books, 1963); the theories of Talcott Parsons from 1942, one year after Fromm's *Escape from Freedom,* about how "fascism emerged out of uprooting and tensions produced by uneven economic and social development"; and Hannah Arendt's theory of the new rootless mob resulting from "an atomized mass society in which purveyors of simple hatreds found a ready audience unrestrained by tradition or community" (209–10).

33 I wrote the first draft of this Introduction in January 2020 during the early stages of the coronavirus epidemic. I am thankful to Dan Werb's editorial in *The New York Times* from January 30, 2020, "To Understand the Wuhan Coronavirus, Look to the Epidemic Triangle," https://www. nytimes.com/2020/01/30/opinion/wuhan-coronavirus-epidemic.html. The key sentence for our purposes is this: "Every single epidemic — be it the flu, cholera, or even behavioral epidemics like drunken driving — is the result of a dynamic shift in one of these points of the epidemic triangle, which then causes a domino effect leading to a sudden explosion of new cases." Behavioral epidemics that may be studied with this model include school shootings, gang violence, suicide, and, I am claiming, the spread of modern-day fascism, often euphemistically called "right-wing populism" or simply, though inaccurately, "populism."

doms and embrace codependency, "automaton conformity," and far-right nativism. In a later chapter we shall pair Fromm's eighty-year-old observations about the sadism and masochism intertwined in the "Psychology of Nazism" with the recent social scientific experiments recounted and analyzed by Keith Payne in his 2017 bestseller *The Broken Ladder.* In a way entirely consistent with Fromm's observations about unhealthy power relations, Payne demonstrates how extreme inequality can lead the most vulnerable toward reckless, self-destructive behaviors (i.e., masochism); or, though it's not his main focus, toward extremes of sadistic rage, resentment, and revenge directed by the powerful or less vulnerable toward the more vulnerable. Payne's book is an eye-opening account of the emotional cost of the extreme income and wealth inequality that has developed since roughly 1980 in the US and elsewhere. As such, it is a useful supplement to Fromm's analysis of the vulnerable and painful conditions that existed in America and Europe before and during World War II and afterwards in peacetime during the "glorious," "happy days" of the 1950s and '60s which were in truth more unhappy times for vulnerable and persecuted groups.

This study will also make use of literary genres to gain further insight into the emotional lava of fascism. These include memoir (Leslie Jamison's *The Recovering: Intoxication and Its Aftermath,* 2018), diary (*The Journal of Hélène Berr,* 2008), narrative nonfiction (Erik Larson, *In the Garden of Beasts: Love, Terror, and an American Family in Hitler's Berlin,* 2011), and the novel (Margaret Atwood, *The Handmaid's Tale,* 1985; Philip Roth, *The Plot against America,* 2004; Sally Rooney, *Conversations with Friends,* 2017). Jamison tells the story of her submission to a tyrant (alcohol) and her long freedom journey to independence. She blends her story with an insider's close reading of other addiction memoirs and with the oral testimonies of fellow addicts she encountered along the way. In 1942 Hélène Berr was a young, Jewish college student trying to make her way in occupied Paris. Her sensitive and insightful diary, unknown outside her family circle until it was published for the first time in 2008, was an irritating bestseller during France's debates over veil laws and charges of French intolerance toward a different minority sixty years after Auschwitz: Muslims. Erik Larson tells the story of the United States ambassador to Germany appointed the same year Adolf Hitler comes to power and how this genteel professor and his authoritarian-loving daughter gradually come to recognize the evil of the Nazi regime. The three novels discussed — *The Handmaid's Tale, The Plot against America,* and *Conversations with Friends* — were all bestsellers and adapted for television. All three have served as prostheses to help vulnerable, shell-shocked citizens, Americans and others, reflect on the many threats to democracy, freedom, and their children's future that carried over into the post-Cold War Internet Age. The three chief threats are 1) climate change and its consequences, especially climate migration that will likely sharpen hostility toward immigrants and "people from away"; 2) the insidiousness of us-versus-them fascist politics, euphemistically called "right-wing populism" and soft-pedaled as "alt-right" or "alternative," "illiberal" democracy; and 3) fascism's non-identical twin, the soul-crushing brute force of underregulated global capitalism in the age of monopolistic Big Tech and low accountability. These longstanding threats were compounded in 2020 by the coronavirus pandemic and associated fears that only made Big Tech bigger. They were also exploited by some autocrats to augment their power and by others to accelerate deregulation and thereby block oversight, investigations, and accountability. As people felt their daily reality becoming more "dystopian" starting in 2016, calls multiplied to "Make Margaret Atwood Fiction Again" and to have conversations with friends in real life again.

If the goal of everyone, except for the autocrat and his circle, is to fend off one-party authoritarianization, embrace decency, and invent healthy forms of dignity-based democracy better suited to meeting the basic needs of ordinary people, it is not enough to "never forget," nor is the act of remembering always easy, healthy, or productive.[34] Histories of fascism and explana-

---

34 See Andrew Higgins, "Bound by a Sense of Victimhood, Serbia Sticks with Russia," *The New York Times,* March 30, 2022, https://www.nytimes.

tions of how fascism works, though valuable and necessary, are not adequate tools for explaining why fascism works, who is especially susceptible to fascism, and who is more immune.[35] For this we need to become familiar with the actual circumstances of vulnerable people; in other words, the stories of "hosts" exposed to the pathogen of fascism in their day to day lives. This study will listen to the testimony of novelists, memoirists, and the findings of social scientists, psychologists, and journalists with a view toward *building* compassion and empathy and *reducing* vulnerability, burnout, and backlash. The two actions must go together because "I feel your pain" rings hollow if crippling injustice (racial, social, economic) goes unaddressed. Justice not charity (William Sloane Coffin) is the motive behind the retelling and commentary of these stories of vulnerable people. The idea is that doing so will help slow or stop fascism's divisiveness and its annihilation of the dignity, life, and memory of those it dehumanizes and deems undeserving of full personhood.

A virus can be combatted with an energetic deployment of testing, contact tracing, quarantine, social distancing, masks, handwashing, and eventually gene-mapping and vaccine development. However, stopping the pain and destruction of fascism — and I include here the contemporary "pandemic" of exclusionary, right-wing nationalist populisms from Brazil to Budapest — requires a more sophisticated and sustained approach. That approach involves two main tasks. The first is eliminating or at least reducing some vulnerabilities by reducing

---

com/2022/03/30/world/europe/ukraine-serbia-russia.html. The misuse of "never forget" can lead to "cults of victimhood," "dialogues of the deaf," and more "digging the hole deeper."

35 On the threat to democracy of a new wave of history censorship via "memory laws," see Timothy Snyder, "The War on History Is a War on Democracy," *The New York Times,* June 29, 2021, https://www.nytimes.com/2021/06/29/magazine/memory-laws.html. On the shuttering of the research and human rights organization Memorial, see Masha Gessen, "The Russian Memory Project That Became an Enemy of the State," *The New Yorker,* January 6, 2022, https://www.newyorker.com/news/newsdesk/the-russian-memory-project-that-became-an-enemy-of-the-state. In the US, see debates around the 1619 Project and Critical Race Theory.

inequality and building a more level playing field and a better social safety net for the twenty-first century. This would have the effect of reducing the fascist's apocalyptic siege mentality with the desperate zero-sum thinking that believes "It's them or me" — an attitude that often leads to vengeful cruelty and violence. The second task involves transforming or reimagining some perceived vulnerabilities and seeing them instead as opportunities, just as crises can sometimes be recast as chances for transformative personal growth or collective recovery and future prosperity. This healing work, which is emphatically not mere TED-talk boosterism about how an individual ought to lean into their vulnerability, will be returned to in the chapters on *The Recovering* and *The Broken Ladder,* and in the Conclusion.

❦

The idea for this book grew out of a seminar in 2015 whose syllabus was sketched out months before Trump, Bolsonaro, or Brexit came on the scene. The class was entitled "Fascism and the Escape from Freedom." It was intended as an opportunity for me to think out loud about Paxton and Fromm whom I had discovered shortly after publishing the results of another seminar, *Tocqueville and Democracy in the Internet Age* (2014), devoted to examining the pros and cons of democracy as advanced by its sympathizers and skeptics since 1776.

In his monumental two-volume study *Democracy in America* (1835, 1840), the French travel writer, sociologist, elected representative, and foreign affairs minister Alexis de Tocqueville was of two minds about democracy in America, and he wondered what might go wrong with the American experiment in popular (Caucasian) sovereignty.[36] Trained as a lawyer, Tocqueville

---

36 See Greg Grandin, "Caucasian Democracy," in *The End of the Myth: From the Frontier to the Border Wall in the Mind of America* (New York: Macmillan, 2019), ch. 3. Tocqueville was not blind to the fact that white "freedom to" in Andrew Jackson's United States was achieved by denying those same freedoms to Native Americans (via genocide, predatory debt, and

had a deep intellectual as well as personal interest in the topic since he had lost family members during France's democracy-run-amok period known as the Reign of Terror (1793–94). He was born in 1805, one year after Napoleon's self-crowning as emperor. Tocqueville's childhood spanned the time of the Battle of Waterloo and Europe's revulsion and exhaustion with "*assez de Bonaparte*."[37] He then witnessed the gradual asphyxiation of individual liberty and rights across a succession of centralized constitutional monarchies (Louis XVIII, Charles X, Louis-Philippe), before finally lamenting the hijacking of semi-democratic republicanism in 1851 with the rise to supreme power of the elected populist Napoleon III. This Second Empire as it was called, after a coup that ended the Second Republic, exercised more total administrative control over people's lives than did the Old Regime that existed before the French Revolution of 1789. That first French experiment in popular sovereignty was later ruined or saved, depending on one's point of view, by the original Napoleon, Louis Napoleon's uncle, starting in 1799. Being himself physically vulnerable — Tocqueville would eventually die of tuberculosis, like Thoreau and so many others of his generation, in 1859 — and yet remarkably resilient and hard-working, this Norman aristocrat with democratic sympathies was attuned to the strengths and weaknesses of the societies he observed and a keen student of their governing institutions and the personalities of the governors themselves.

The single most quoted chapter from the highly quotable *Democracy in America* has to be chapter 6 of part 4, volume 2:

---

deportation) and to Black people (via slavery, torture, and terror). Jamelle Bouie uses the terms "competitive authoritarianism" and "herrenvolk democracy," to name the restriction of democratic practices to certain persons and the exclusion of others which has been the norm throughout most of United States history, in "Can Only Republicans Legitimately Win Elections?" *The New York Times*, January 5, 2021, https://www.nytimes.com/2021/01/05/opinion/trump-georgia-senate-elections.html.

37 Emerson uses this expression, "enough of Bonaparte," in his essay on Napoleon in *Representative Men* (1850). See "Napoleon; or, the Man of the World," in *The Portable Emerson*, ed. Jeffrey S. Cramer (New York: Penguin, 2014), 354–71.

"What Sort of Despotism Democratic Nations Have to Fear." Therefore, I was not surprised to find Paxton featuring three sentences from it near the very beginning of his introductory first chapter devoted to "The Invention of Fascism." Paxton claims Tocqueville was one of the few pre-World War I thinkers who glimpsed the future possibility of a "dictatorship against the Left amidst popular enthusiasm."[38] "Although Tocqueville found much to admire on his visit to the United States in 1831," Paxton writes, "he was troubled by the majority's power in a democracy to impose conformity by social pressure, in the absence of an independent social elite."[39] Then come these words of Tocqueville in the Mansfield & Winthrop translation Paxton chose to use:

> The kind of oppression with which democratic peoples are threatened will resemble nothing that had preceded it in the world; our contemporaries would not find its image in their memories. I myself seek in vain an expression that exactly reproduces the idea that I form of it for myself and that contains it; the old words despotism and tyranny are not suitable. The thing is new, therefore I must try to define it, since I cannot name it.

Rereading these lines in Paxton from Tocqueville's meticulous research into the history and future prospects of democracy, I felt as though I'd picked up right where I had left off. As for Fromm's *Escape from Freedom*, I first came to it by chance, a recommendation by a childhood friend, Miriam Goldfarb, and was struck by the book's comparative approach and the urgent yet calm exposition of its argument. Fromm was centrally concerned with how the rise of capitalism and protestantism out of premodern feudal catholicism brings mixed results: empowering some who can embrace creativity and entrepreneurship, while rendering others vulnerable and insecure, and therefore ready to fall in line behind charismatic leaders (first Luther and

---

38 Paxton, *The Anatomy of Fascism,* 3.
39 Ibid., 4.

Calvin, later Hitler) each promising a refuge from the destructive side of more freewheeling social arrangements in a post-feudal, competitive modern capitalist society. Fromm never quotes Tocqueville, and I have yet to determine if he had read him, but he was a careful reader of Karl Marx, and Marx had read Tocqueville, and both of these nineteenth century thinkers were keen students of France's social upheavals in 1789, 1799, 1815, 1830, 1848, and 1851, which were all struggles between democratic and authoritarian preferences.

In that first edition of my seminar, Paxton provided the comprehensive historical narrative — the what, when, where, and how of fascism that I wanted to get to know better, especially since far-right populism was then gaining ground in France under a gruff female leader, Marine Le Pen. Fromm provided an intriguing hypothesis about the *why* of fascism; especially "Why in Germany?" — Fromm's civilized homeland — and why, ominously, perhaps maybe in the United States, Fromm's second home which he had escaped to, like so many Jews fleeing persecution, in order to be free from Nazi Germany. Was fascism possible in *Amerika*?, asks Fromm from the relative safety of New York in 1940 where he writes *Escape from Freedom* in English in the heat of the moment, so to speak, before the release of the iconic escape adventure movie *Casablanca,* after Kristallnacht but before Auschwitz and the German genocide of Europe's Jews becomes common knowledge, before the United States has even entered the war against Japan and Nazi Germany, and long before the publication of more dispassionate postwar accounts of the origins of totalitarianism and the authoritarian character by two other German ex-pats, Hannah Arendt and Theodor Adorno.

Fromm was writing in urgency in 1940 from inside a country with a long history of white protestant supremacy that had been openly flirting with fascism for decades and was then on the verge of war against his homeland, Germany, that seemed to fully support its fascist *Führer,* Adolph Hitler, who himself was an admirer of American white supremacy politics. Sixty years later, an elderly Robert Paxton, who had nothing to prove professionally since making his scholarly reputation with his paradigm-altering study *Vichy France: Old Guard and New Order 1940–1944* (1972), took up his pen in the wake of George W. Bush's unusual rise to power and the double catastrophe of 9/11 and America's response to it. Paxton drops several hints that he was disturbed by signs and symbols of a new Orwellian patriotism at the start of the new century and especially by popular support for restricting civil liberties, a disregard for human rights, and fascistic jingoism during the presidency of George W. Bush.[40] In other words, both of their books — just like Tocqueville's sociology and Orwell's fables — were not only about faraway places and times; Fromm and Paxton were also commenting on the present and possible future of the places their readers were living in. I wanted my students in 2015 to pick up on that and think seriously about this "presence of the past," as Sheldon Wolin called it (following William Faulkner).

In 2016, while on leave in the United States, I watched the election results come in on the night of November 8 after having voted for Hillary Clinton and other Democrats earlier in the day. The next morning, 9/11 for Europeans, Donald J. Trump was declared the forty-fifth president of the United States thanks to about 80,000 key votes in Florida, Pennsylvania, Michigan, and Wisconsin that clinched for him the electoral college victory despite losing the popular vote by a margin of nearly three million.[41] Given that rather odd and unexpected outcome, democracy in America seemed to many observers, both inside and outside the country, to be truly broken. Journalists, academics, and others spent the next weeks and all of Trump's first year in office trying to figure out how it happened. Millions

---

40 Ibid., 202. In a later chapter we shall also examine Philip Roth's *The Plot against America,* published the same year as Paxton's *Anatomy,* 2004, and also written by a senior man of letters who had nothing to prove and yet manifestly felt the need to write that book in the aftermath of 9/11, the Patriot Act, and the runup to George W. Bush's war of choice in Iraq that started in 2003 while both authors were busy writing their responses.

41 In 2000, George W. Bush also lost the popular vote to Al Gore by roughly 500,000 votes.

marched in protest the day after his inauguration. Many hoped Trump would be quickly impeached for violating the Emoluments Clause or for some other high crime or misdemeanor. Others cheered on his brash, confrontational style of governing, applauded the dozens of conservative judges he nominated at every opportunity, and participated directly or indirectly in the nonstop, in-your-face rallies Trump orchestrated for himself and his fervent supporters — his and their fountain of youth and power — thus extending a permanently combative, fiercely partisan campaign mode to his administration without even a pretense of being "a president for all Americans."[42]

I was grateful to be able to teach my "fascism seminar" again in 2017 after returning to my post in Lyon one month after the Charlottesville riots.[43] Enrollment had doubled because students were still processing the now "undemonized" far-right populist presidential candidate Marine Le Pen, even if she lost to the center-right candidate Emmanuel Macron in the spring of 2017. They also wanted to know, like so many others, how an unhinged, kitschy TV celebrity with no governing experience could be president of the United States. I promised that reading Paxton and Fromm and some others would help them find answers. In 2018, with the US mid-term elections looming, there was added drama during the third edition of the seminar which I renamed, adding the middle term *vulnerability,* since it had become the general consensus that Trump's success with certain voters (like that of Jair Bolsonaro in Brazil, Narendra Modi in India, Vladimir Putin in Russia, and far-right leaders and candidates across Europe) was linked to complicated feelings of

---

42 A phrase used by Joe Biden and nearly every candidate and president. On crowds and permanence, see Elias Canetti, "Hitler, According to Speer: Grandeur and Permanence," in *The Conscience of Words,* trans. Joachim Neugroschel (New York: Continuum, 1979), 145–70.

43 Back in Lyon, I read up on the French connection to the Charlottesville riots and discussed it with my students. Thomas Chatterton Williams, "The French Origins of 'You Will Not Replace Us,'" *The New Yorker,* December 4, 2017, https://www.newyorker.com/magazine/2017/12/04/the-french-origins-of-you-will-not-replace-us.

vulnerability, fear, unavowable envy, status anxiety, and open resentment, despite frequent reports of a stronger economy (but for whom?) ten years after the housing crash and Great Recession of 2008.[44]

In the fall of 2019, as details about Donald Trump's "drug deal"[45] with Ukraine brought questions of presidential abuse of power, accountability, and the rule of law back into focus, I taught the course for the fourth time, again under the title "Fascism, Vulnerability, and the Escape from Freedom." The list of suggested readings had become longer (Madeleine Albright, Masha Gessen, Levitzky and Ziblatt, Martha Nussbaum, Keith Payne, Timothy Snyder, Jason Stanley), but I retained the central core around Paxton and Fromm. I told this group of students that I would not be teaching the seminar again in 2020 because I would be returning to America for the year. But I said I planned to turn the course into a book, and I promised I would dedicate it to them and to their classmates from the three earlier years. That book is what you are reading now — the fruit of much labor, but also good luck and the goodwill of my students who had the patience and curiosity to listen to me feel my way into this material, especially during the first two years. Their written work and oral presentations allowed me to learn from their perspectives and concerns and pushed me to be as clear and convincing as possible. To them I say, *thank you.* I am also grateful to the authors whose work is featured in these chapters — you have taught me so much — and to the writers referenced in footnotes who added supporting evidence to my argument. Having access to quality journalism and research confirms the importance of a free press and open universities for building and preserving individual liberty, rights, and dignity.

---

44 The Covid-19 crisis adds further legitimacy to giving central importance to the notion of vulnerability, as the title of this early collective volume attests: *Vulnerable: The Law, Policy and Ethics of Covid-19,* eds. Colleen M. Flood et al. (Ottawa: University of Ottawa Press, 2020).

45 The term used by then National Security Advisor John Bolton to describe Trump's bribery or quid pro quo that Congressman Adam Schiff described as "a classic mafia-like shakedown."

To be clear, this is not a scholarly treatise on fascism obeying the questionable academic ideology of disinterestedness; nor is it an exhaustive history of the subject for the very good reason that fascism, in one stage or another, is still happening. This book is a comparative study addressed to curious readers concerned about the shaky health and prospects of democracy and, perhaps, about their own vulnerability. These interlocking essays go beyond the usual focus on strongmen and major turning points to consider the personal suffering and moral choices of vulnerable individuals whose stories are often left out of account in standard histories of fascism. Sharing information, thoughts, and feelings from a variety of sources spurs further thinking and raises awareness about problems and solutions that the citizens of democratic lands, who are ultimately responsible for their own destiny, can debate and put to good use. Following the inspiring example of Kenneth Burke, a contemporary of Fromm and the author of "The Rhetoric of Hitler's 'Battle'" (1939), I hope readers of this book will find it to be useful equipment for living better lives.

I

The History and Psychology
of Fascism

1

Using History to Prevent Fascism Today

Robert Paxton, *The Anatomy of Fascism* (2004)

This examination of Paxton's *The Anatomy of Fascism*,[1] as with all the chapters that will follow, does not intend to be a digest that would replace reading the book itself. My aim is to convince the reader that it is genuinely worth taking the time to read the whole book — something Paxton and his publisher have made very easy since the complete text is free and downloadable in PDF form. Such generosity is rare and commendable, especially in a context where other "content providers" would seek to cash in on the mix of enthusiasm and anxiety that surrounds fascism and populism in recent years.[2] How and why Paxton and Ran-

---

1   Robert O. Paxton, *The Anatomy of Fascism* (New York: Alfred A. Knopf 2004). Hereafter cited parenthetically throughout this chapter.

2   In his 1939 essay on Hitler's *Mein Kampf* (reprinted as "The Rhetoric of Hitler's 'Battle,'" in *The Philosophy of Literary Form: Studies in Symbolic Action,* 3rd edn. [Berkeley: University of California Press, 1973], 191–220), Kenneth Burke objected to opportunistic critics he termed "vandalistic" for "cashing in" on the tense historical situation. See Garth Pauley, "Criti-

dom House came to this open access agreement are not matters I'm privy to, but we can conjecture that the author, a senior professor at a prestigious university, had enough clout to convince his publisher to profit from the symbolic capital that would accrue by releasing the book into the public domain, *pro bono*. He may also have been eager to have his *Anatomy* reach the widest possible audience, including the increasing number of people who either cannot or will not buy or borrow books these days. If fascism is mass politics from the Right, then it stands to reason — following the logic of fight fire with fire — that it cannot be effectively opposed except by mass, not elite, politics from the Left. Paxton may also share the historian's credo formulated by George Santayana and paraphrased by Winston Churchill and countless others that "those who cannot remember the past are condemned to repeat it" — a fate that is all the more certain when history and other humanities departments are facing declining enrollment, libraries have budgets and operating hours cut, and new history books may be priced beyond the budgets of the Many. Because *The Anatomy of Fascism* is free and downloadable, my students had no excuse for not reading Paxton since all it cost them was some time and attention.

At 220 pages, in smallish type, and with an additional thirty-page annotated bibliography, plus fifty pages of footnotes, one gets the impression that Paxton has read everything on the subject, and not just in English but also in German, French, Italian, and Spanish. The one exception is the curious absence of any mention of Erich Fromm, a direct witness of German fascism whose psychologist's eye-view and sense of urgency and duty offers a valuable supplement to Paxton's external witness approach.[3] However, other than that omission, Paxton's book offers a comprehensive and tightly organized treatment of the

cism in Context: Kenneth Burke's 'The Rhetoric of Hitler's "Battle".'" *KB Journal* 6, no. 1 (Fall 2009), https://www.kbjournal.org/content/criticism-context-kenneth-burkes-rhetoric-hitlers-battle.

3 Both studies are wartime testimonies — World War II for Fromm, the Second Iraq War for Paxton.

subject, even if the chapter "Other Places, Other Times" would now need to be expanded to take into account all that has happened since its first publication in 2004 — a hole filled by Jason Stanley's *How Fascism Works* (2018), which is the focus of the last chapter of this book.

Paxton's *Anatomy of Fascism* makes a three-part argument: first, that "fascism was the major political innovation of the twentieth century, and the source of much of its pain" (3); second, that the twenty-first century "must avoid" (21) repeating the twentieth century's painful experiments with fascism; and third, that "We stand a much better chance of responding wisely" to the fascist temptation "if we understand how fascism succeeded in the past" (220, Paxton's closing words).[4]

Understanding fascism — both its success and the pain and destruction it caused in the past and may cause again — is best achieved, Paxton argues, if one avoids two types of misguided thinking. First, a "nominalist" approach, which refuses to recognize fascism as a knowable general phenomenon and prefers instead to speak of Fascism, with a capital F, as a proper noun in exclusive reference to the Italian case, and then of nazism or Hitlerism, Stalinism, Peronism, down to Trumpism, Putinism, and so forth as an open-ended list of unique cases. Paxton nicknames this the "bestiary." The second mistake is the "ideal type" approach that would seek to identify some fascist essence. As a historian understandably inclined to favor a diachronic over a synchronic view, Paxton rejects both these approaches for being overly static and insensitive to the fact that fascism is a protean, opportunistic, political innovation that evolved differently in different contexts over time. Therefore, Paxton recommends, "Let us instead watch fascism in action, from its beginnings to its final cataclysm, within the complex web of interaction it forms with society. Ordinary citizens and the holders of political, social, cultural, and economic power who assisted, or failed

---

4   This view of fascism and authoritarianism as a permanent temptation remains current. See, for example, Anne Applebaum, *Twilight of Democracy: The Seductive Lure of Authoritarianism* (New York: Doubleday, 2020).

to resist, fascism belong to the story. When we are done, we may be better able to give fascism an appropriate definition" (21–22). Paxton agrees that providing a general definition of fascism is crucially important; however, in his view it needs to be arrived at after reviewing the relevant histories, not posited beforehand with the history serving as mere confirmation or illustration of some "theory." That a historian should give primacy to history is hardly surprising, but this is not, in Paxton's case, mere professional bias. Instead it's argued and persuasive, which is why the biology metaphor mobilized in the title, *The* Anatomy *of Fascism,* suggests an intermediate "third way" sufficiently supple to account for both the diachronic and synchronic realities and their mutual interaction.

If Paxton's rejection of the "fascist essence" approach is largely because it is anti-historical (and therefore intellectually dishonest with a tendency to ignore distinguishing facts such as how Italian fascism "showed few signs of anti-Semitism until sixteen years after coming to power," [9]), his rejection of the "bestiary" approach also has a broader moral dimension that is clear from this description of two symmetrical flawed images of fascism:

> Everyone is sure they know what fascism is. The most self-consciously visual of all political forms, fascism presents itself to us in vivid primary images: a chauvinist demagogue haranguing an ecstatic crowd; disciplined ranks of marching youths; colored-shirted militants beating up members of some demonized minority; surprise invasions at dawn; and fit soldiers parading through a captured city.
>
> Examined more closely, however, some of these familiar images induce facile errors. The image of the all-powerful dictator personalizes fascism, and creates the false impression that we can understand it fully by scrutinizing the leader alone. This image, whose power lingers today, is the last triumph of fascist propagandists. It offers an alibi to nations that approved or tolerated fascist leaders, and diverts attention from the persons, groups, and institutions who helped him. We need a subtler model of fascism that explores the

interaction between Leader and Nation, and between Party and civil society.

The image of chanting crowds feeds the assumption that some European peoples were by nature predisposed to fascism, and responded enthusiastically to it because of national character. The corollary of this image is a condescending belief that the defective history of certain nations spawned fascism. This turns easily into an alibi for onlooker nations: It couldn't happen here. Beyond these familiar images, on closer inspection, fascist reality becomes more complicated still. For example, the regime that invented the word fascism — Mussolini's Italy — showed few signs of anti-Semitism until sixteen years after coming to power. (9)

Each false image provides a convenient alibi: the image of the all-powerful dictator lets his enablers off the hook ("the devil made me do it"); while the essentialist notion of a fascist national character lets people who happen not to have Italian or German ancestry off the hook while unfairly casting a shameful evil stain and endless suspicion on those who do, or on all present-day Italians and Germans or Serbians or Japanese or any other group one wants to stigmatize as innately inclined toward authoritarianism.

After pointing out these traps to be avoided, Paxton makes the historian's case for approaching the subject in chronological order across five major stages of development that fascism may traverse, and did in the cases of Germany and Italy, while in others the fascist temptation — or "virus" or "cancer" if one likes — stopped at stage one or two. This division into five incremental stages — "creating fascist movements," "taking root," "getting power," "exercising power," and "the long term: radicalization or entropy?" — allows Paxton to dive into the historian's main task, reality-based storytelling, without the burden of having to conform to a restrictive one-size-fits-all definition of fascism that would either be misleading or require an endless series of qualifying statements and thus unravel the definition.

The reason for giving primacy to the historical approach, Paxton explains, is that fascism gained force in the wake of World War I by challenging all -isms, especially conservatism, liberalism, and socialism, that had been elaborated and argued for by rational-minded children of the Age of Reason such as Edmund Burke, John Stuart Mill, Charles Fourier, Alexis de Tocqueville, and Karl Marx and Friedrich Engels. For these *thinkers,* a title they wore proudly, political *science* and social *science* were not only possible but, if done properly on the model of the physical sciences, the surest road to lasting peace and prosperity. Early fascist movements, noting Reason's slip-ups and doubting its preeminence, opportunistically exploited rivalries between those confident, established -isms, critiquing their positions, track records, and plans while, as the new outsider with no record or established principles, fascists could themselves elude similar critiques. It is therefore misleading, Paxton argues, to think of the political innovation of fascism as a new -ism. It would be more accurate to think of it instead as the corrosive (fascists would say "cleansing") anti -ism or counter-ideology best grasped via its actions and not from a stable set of beliefs. This does not mean that fascist movements did not have goals, but those goals were largely related to amassing and retaining power — mostly for itself, not in the service of some higher goal, though grandiose vaguely worded projects were often promised, perhaps even believed in by some for a time. This is why the analogy to a virus or cancer is tempting when talking about fascism because just as there is not a Marxist or Liberal cancer cell or virus strain — each just "wants" to reproduce and take control of its host — there is little evidence of any fascist movement thinking beyond its own acquisition and exercise of power toward any sustainable larger vision and succession principle.[5] This is why Paxton begins his account of stage five, "The Long

---

5   Paxton uses the metaphor "fascist virus" (68) at the beginning of his evocation of France's unsuccessful fascism after World War I. "Succession principle" is a term I borrow from Timothy Snyder's *The Road to Unfreedom: Russia, Europe, America* (New York: Tim Duggan Books, 2018), 37–38 et passim.

Term: Radicalization or Entropy?" with the assertion, "Fascist regimes could not settle down into a comfortable enjoyment of power" (148).[6]

The suspicion that fascism's unseemly thirst for power is akin to vampirism and necrophilia may explain many people's aversion to the very word and a decided preference for the euphemism *right-wing populism* or simply, and more sneakily, the shorter label *populism*. The blanket term *populism* obscures the crucial distinction between inclusivity (e.g., the goal of MLK and Stacey Abrams-style populism) and exclusionary right-wing populism (i.e., brothers versus others). Before getting elected, candidate Donald Trump was the focus of a barrage of commentary asking whether he might be a fascist; however, President Trump did not face equal scrutiny until the Portland "riots" of 2020 and the assault on the US Capitol in January 2021. During his presidency he was usually labeled a populist, often alongside Hungary's Victor Orbán and Brazil's Jair Bolsonaro. With each on a different continent, the Trump, Orbán, Bolsonaro grouping lends a global air to populism's resurgence but one that is difficult to measure since the term *populism* conflates pro-democracy movements (Black Lives — and votes — Matter too) and anti-democratic movements like Trump's fascist Make American Great Again messaging that always only favored "real Americans."

Rather than getting bogged down in a discussion of trends, principles, and essences, Paxton invites his reader to focus more on the real actions of fascists and populists over time and to notice what fascism *did* more than what it *said* it stood for or claimed it did or would do. In condensed form, but with ample footnotes to allow the reader to further explore any number of events between March 23, 1919 (fascism's official birthday) and May 8 and 9, 1945 (the end of World War II), Paxton notes that

---

6   This restlessness despite outward success recalls one of the many paradoxes Tocqueville identifies in his *Democracy in America, and, Two Essays on America,* trans. Gerald Bevan (London: Penguin Books, 2003), vol. II, part 2, ch. xiii, section "Why Americans are So Restless in the Midst of Their Prosperity," 622–26.

fascism — both the movements in several countries and the Italian and German regimes that actually exercised power — did many things. Fascism redrew the boundaries between public and private; it redistributed social, political, and economic power; it unleashed aggressive emotions; it brought politics from closed salons and studies to streets and stadiums; it operated with energy, force, speed, and "visceral feelings" that made all ideas, values, and thinkers become instrumentalized and disposable; it degraded the value of truth and weaponized lying, today's "alternative facts"; and it blurred the distinction between secular and religious spheres and championed unmediated direct contact between leader and led that would bypass both secular and sacred representatives — congress and clergy — in a transcendent fusion of Church and State, *Volk* and *Führer* as savior. Once Paxton has retold the story of fascism's worming its way into weakened, post-World War I European societies in his first chapter, "Creating Fascist Movements," he offers his list of the "mobilizing passions" mentioned earlier in a set of nine bullet points that constitute the "emotional lava" of fascism:

— a sense of overwhelming crisis beyond the reach of any traditional solutions;

— the primacy of the group, toward which one has duties superior to every right, whether individual or universal, and the subordination of the individual to it;

— the belief that one's group is a victim, a sentiment that justifies any action, without legal or moral limits, against its enemies, both internal and external;

— dread of the group's decline under the corrosive effects of individualistic liberalism, class conflict, and alien influences;

— the need for closer integration of a purer community, by consent if possible, or by exclusionary violence if necessary;

— the need for authority by natural leaders (always male), culminating in a national chief who alone is capable of incarnating the group's destiny;

— the superiority of the leader's instincts over abstract and universal reason;
— the beauty of violence and the efficacy of will, when they are devoted to the group's success;
— the right of the chosen people to dominate others without restraint from any kind of human or divine law, right being decided by the sole criterion of the group's prowess within a Darwinian struggle. (41)

It is these same bullet points that are repeated when Paxton finally offers his definition of fascism on the book's third to last page:

> Fascism may be defined as a form of political behavior marked by obsessive preoccupation with community decline, humiliation, or victimhood and by compensatory cults of unity, energy, and purity, in which a mass-based party of committed nationalist militants, working in uneasy but effective collaboration with traditional elites, abandons democratic liberties and pursues with redemptive violence and without ethical or legal restraints goals of internal cleansing and external expansion. (218)

Between the shorter definition of fascism as a particular "form of political behavior" and the longer description of fascism's "emotional lava," Paxton states his middle-of-the-road answer to the question of whether fascism valued ideas and actually believed in something versus the view, assigned to Franz Neumann, that National Socialism's ideology was "constantly shifting. [...] It has certain magical beliefs — leadership adoration, supremacy of the master race — but [it] is not laid down in a series of categorical and dogmatic pronouncements" (219). Paxton's view is that fascist ideology was "proclaimed as central, yet amended or violated as expedient[, ...] fascism consisted neither of the uncomplicated application of its program, nor of freewheeling opportunism" (219). This neither/nor position allows Paxton to insist on the all-important factor of human choice.

Like Tocqueville and Ralph Waldo Emerson, Paxton is a liberal who takes an agnostic middle position on the question of freewill versus determinism.[7] The history he tells is neither exclusively about impersonal Forces that ineluctably shape human affairs, nor does it see Great Men as shaping those affairs more or less single-handedly. "To be sure," begins Paxton, so as to tip the reader toward his point of view, "political behavior requires choices, and choices — as my critics hasten to point out — bring us back to underlying ideas" (218). He keeps silent about the names of his critics; however that he alludes to their existence this one time before crossing his finish line is, I think, a useful reminder for the reader that *The Anatomy of Fascism,* like all history writing, is not value-neutral but, like political behavior, includes choices that "bring us back to underlying ideas" as well as to *beliefs,* some perhaps unverifiable or unfalsifiable or unavowable, and to *temperament,* as William James insisted in his 1907 manifesto on pragmatism.

There is no need to retell Paxton's entire story of the five stages of fascism. Instead we can quote a representative sample in the last three paragraphs of his chapter "Getting Power." They recount the tipping point between fascism's candidacy and its actual taking power and presiding. Here Paxton is at his most eloquent and open about the underlying beliefs that shape his practice as a historian:

It is a worthwhile exercise of the historical imagination to recall the other options open to the fascists' principal allies and accomplices. In that way, we can do what historians are supposed to do: restore the openness of the historical moment with all its uncertainties. What else could the political elite of Germany and Italy do? In Italy, a coalition of the social Catholic Popolari and the reformist socialists would have assured a parliamentary majority. It would have taken a lot

---

7   Emerson's position is presented in his essay "Fate"; Tocqueville's is in vol. 2, pt. 1, ch. 20 of *Democracy in America* devoted to how history gets made and how it gets (re)told — a distinction that also interests Philip Roth.

of persuasion and cajolery, since issues of Church-state relations and religious education separated the two. We know that it was not tried, and it was not wanted. In Germany, a parliamentary government with the social democrats and the centrist parties was an arithmetic possibility, but a real possibility only with strong presidential leadership. A workable alternative in both countries might have been a government of technicians and nonparty experts, to deal in a nonpartisan way with the crisis of government authority and of institutions. This, too, was never tried. If constitutional government had to be abandoned, we know today that we would prefer a military authoritarian government to Hitler. But the army did not want to do that (unlike in Spain), and chose to support the fascist alternative. The Italian army would not oppose fascism in Italy because its leaders feared the Left more.

In each case, it helps to see that political elites make choices that might not be their first preferences. They proceed, from choice to choice, along a path of narrowing options. At each fork in the road, they choose the antisocialist solution.

It works better to see the fascist seizure of power as a process: alliances are formed, choices made, alternatives closed off. High officials, possessing some freedom of maneuver, choose the fascist option over others. Neither Hitler's nor Mussolini's arrival in power was inevitable. Our explanatory model must also leave room for luck — good or bad, depending on one's point of view. Mussolini could have been turned back in October 1922 or removed in June 1924 if the king, Establishment political leaders, and the army had resolutely taken actions within their legal competence. Mussolini's luck was that the king exercised a choice in his favor. Hitler also had some lucky breaks. The Führer benefitted from the rivalry for office of von Papen and Schleicher, and the refusal of German conservatives to accept reformist socialists as fellow citizens. It was von Papen who took the decision to make Hitler chancellor, as the best way to form a majority that would exclude both his rival Schleicher and the moderate Left. Crises of the political and economic system made a

space available to fascism, but it was the unfortunate choices
by a few powerful Establishment leaders that actually put the
fascists into that space. (117–18)

"They proceed, from choice to choice, along a path of narrowing
options." This sentence aptly describes the position of historians
like Paxton who want to affirm that no outcome is guaranteed
in advance and that it could have been otherwise. Paxton insists
that neither Hitler's nor Benito Mussolini's taking power was inevitable, though it can easily look that way on casual inspection
after the fact. But it is precisely the historian's self-assigned duty
to not rest with such a passive, deterministic view of the matter.
Paxton's claim that crises "made a space available to fascism" and
"unfortunate choices by a few powerful Establishment leaders
[…] put the fascists into that space" undercuts the commonly
held belief in strong fascist agency and self-fashioning. Neither
Hitler nor Mussolini arrived in power with an electoral majority or by coup d'état or through a solo triumph. They were invited to become heads of government by President Hindenberg
and King Victor Emmanuel III, respectively, amid conditions of
extreme volatility (96–97). Paxton's knowledge of the historical
record allows him to then dissect a dozen other unsuccessful
fascisms, notably the case of France from 1924 to 1940.

France, the country Paxton has studied the most, did not
go from stage two (taking root) to stage three (getting power),
because those elected to power in 1932 and reelected in 1936,
namely the Third Republic's center-left majority under Jewish
prime minister Léon Blum, did not allow it. Also, Blum took
the decisive step of banning paramilitary leagues in June 1936,
something Paxton points out the German chancellor Heinrich
Brüning did *not* do four years earlier, thus allowing Germany's
dual state arrangement to strengthen. Despite all the revolutionary talk, then coming from both Left and Right, Paxton argues
that France's fascist elements, including François de la Roque's
Parti Social Français, calmed down between 1936 and 1940 and
became integrated within an "aggressively anti-Semitic" (9) tra-

ditional Right that the German invasion and Armistice would allow to hold power during the Vichy years from 1940 to 1944.

According to Paxton's extensive research on the topic, the social, economic, and political crisis of the 1920s and '30s was less severe in the French case, and therefore the Right was unable to peel away enough popular support from the Left. Paxton notes that the Depression was less severe in France, the Third Republic's institutions were not paralyzed and still getting things done (ensuring harvests would feed the cities, for example), mainstream conservatives did not feel threatened by communists or anything else to the point where they were willing to make common cause with fascists, and there was no standout charismatic French fascist willing or able to do the deal-making that Mussolini and Hitler achieved (71). In a word, French people felt less vulnerable than Italians or Germans and were therefore less willing to abandon their republican *Liberté, Égalité, Fraternité* ideals for some untried Brand X.

However, just because a fascist government did not take power in France does not mean that fascist politicians (or right-wing populists, if one prefers), then and now, have not exerted a certain influence from off-stage, so to speak. The problem of the democracy-sapping rightward tilt of mainstream conservatives (from Action Française in the 1930s to Jean-Marie Le Pen's influence on President Nicolas Sarkozy in the early 2000s, or the Tea Party wing within the United States's Republican Party, or the AfD in Germany, or Vox in Spain) is real and really mischievous. Paxton's history reminds the reader that in the 1920s, '30s, and every subsequent decade, there have been sizeable numbers of people, in France and elsewhere, who were democracy skeptics — people for whom *Liberté, Équalité, Fraternité* was fine as a motto over school entrances but who temperamentally were not democrats but instead republicans à la Plato who favored rule by elites (especially, under the Fifth Republic, by graduates of France's top governing school, the *École Nationale d'Administration*). Then as now, the tacit motto of this ruling elite has been *Authority, Hierarchy, Deference* (22).

Paxton shows how starting in the 1920s and constantly there-after, fascism, like a bully on the playground, would wait and watch for opportunities to peel away voters from their tradi-tional sympathies with mainstream parties on the Left or the Right, and lead them to take a chance on a neither/nor new-comer party that would use nationalism to take over the renewal and emancipation rhetoric from the traditional Left while also taking over the traditionalism and law and order rhetoric from the traditional Right. Fascism had a sneaky way of casting itself as both radical and conservative, and conflating going forward with going backward. In normal times, or at least non-crisis times, the illogical fusion of polar opposites, such as backward and forward, could not attract a serious following (or even pass the laugh test). But in social situations with large numbers of unemployed, aggrieved veterans, as well as nervous, moneyed classes or small property holders worried about losing it all overnight, such as directly after World War I and, ten years later, during the Great Depression,[8] Paxton shows how fascism could topple an already fragilized confidence in Enlightenment reason and progress (the shared foundation of nineteenth-century lib-eralism, conservatism, and socialism). Fascism would lead fear-ful, vulnerable people to lower their guard and go along with an alternative pseudoscientific, social Darwinist script of end-less struggle between the strong and the weak. It allowed them the chance to join a winning team complete with spiffy apparel,[9]

---

8   Or the Great Recession. Though Paxton's book pre-dates the implosion of the housing bubble by four years, his analysis of how vulnerability opened the door to fascism in the 1920s and '30s is transposable to the situations of the Great Recession in America (2008–10) and its aftermath. The end of the housing bubble caused shock waves in Europe that were compounded by the Greek debt crisis and the Syrian civil war that led to a destabilizing influx of immigrants, especially in 2015 — a perfect storm of events that were skillfully exploited by far-right populists across Europe.

9   On the link between extremism and dressing up, see William Golding *Lord of the Flies* (London: Faber and Faber 1954) and the observations of fashion critic Vanessa Friedman in "Why Rioters Wear Costumes," *The New York Times,* January 7, 2021, https://www.nytimes.com/2021/01/07/style/capitol-riot-tactics.html.

inspiring songs and slogans, and a low bar for entry so long as one was not identified with some demonized out-group (e.g., Jews, Roma, communists). Fascisms offered the perfect haven for overwhelmed individuals who found themselves on the losing end within traditional meritocracies where, in peacetime at least, winning depended on family connections, good test results and diplomas, or real-world superior skill in some area of industry or commerce. Taking a cue from the tactics of Napoleon III who was the first to use mass suffrage to gain and retain power, fascist leaders realized that the bar to play the democracy game was actually very low — all that mattered was winning the election, by hook or by crook. Like a topsy-turvy Mardi Gras or Christmas atmosphere where servants could mock or bully their masters, and ordinary rules and decorum would be suspended, fascism in Italy and Germany offered for a time an alternate fantasy reality where losers could be winners. But instead of only lasting the duration of an evening of bossy caroling ("O, bring us some figgy pudding!") or wistful, revolutionary singing (such as with "Beasts of England" in George Orwell's *Animal Farm*); an hour of feel-good reading or radio; or rapturous listening at some afternoon or evening rally, the fascist alternate reality in Italy and Germany lasted for twenty and twelve years, respectively. This was a short time as a percentage of the twentieth century, but long enough, as Paxton notes, to be "the source of much of its pain."

Thankfully, as Paxton shows in his chapter "Other Times, Other Places," a fascist generational revolt of youth against elders has rarely gone beyond stage two since 1945. Recall that Mussolini and Hitler were fairly young at 39 and 44 years old when they came to power.[10] Regimes that are often labeled fascist (Vichy France, Franco's Spain, Perón's Argentina, and so forth) were actually, Paxton argues, authoritarian regimes which may

---

10 The leaders of the American war of independence against the British — John Adams, Alexander Hamilton, Thomas Jefferson, George Washington, and the rest — were all fairly young in 1776. Hamilton, born in 1757, was only 19; Washington was 44.

have found it useful to borrow some of the fascist "decor" and its youthful spirit to camouflage their advancing age.[11] A "murderous frenzy" is more likely to be carried out when an exclusionary populist movement is led by "young Turks" with nothing to lose instead of aging Proud Boys.

Twentieth-century authoritarian regimes also caused much pain, as do many now in the twenty-first century; therefore, it may be instructive, though hardly consoling, to be told that certain regimes are not *really* fascist but *only* authoritarian. What's the difference? Paxton makes this distinction in an early footnote to his introduction and then elaborates in a subsection of his final chapter entitled "Boundaries":

> Authoritarian dictatorships govern through preexisting conservative forces (churches, armies, organized economic interests) and seek to demobilize public opinion, while fascists govern through a single party and try to generate public enthusiasm. (253, n. 34)

Paxton elaborates in this meticulous paragraph:

> The boundary separating fascism from authoritarianism is more subtle, but it is one of the most essential for understanding. I have already used the term, or the similar one of traditional dictatorship, in discussing Spain, Portugal, Aus-

---

11 "Local dictators tended to adopt the fascist decor that was the fashion of the 1930s, while drawing Depression remedies as much from Roosevelt's New Deal as from Mussolini's corporatism" (192). When asked if it would be accurate to categorize Donald Trump as a fascist, Paxton replied in a *Harper's* magazine piece from May 2017 that despite having some of the fascist trappings, he most resembles a plutocrat. Trump's much-vaunted "base" consists primarily of voters aged 45 to 60, and within government his key supporters are white senators from the South, Appalachia, and West whose average age is 62. Trump was born in 1946, the same year as his first Attorney General Jeff Sessions. Another Trump collaborator, Republican Senate Majority Leader Mitch McConnel, was born in 1942. Some may prefer to see Trumpism as an authoritarian gerontocracy and not as fascism.

tria, and Vichy France. The fascist-authoritarian boundary was particularly hard to trace in the 1930s, when regimes that were, in reality, authoritarian, donned some of the decor of that period's successful fascisms. Although authoritarian regimes often trample civil liberties and are capable of murderous brutality, they do not share fascism's urge to reduce the private sphere to nothing. They accept ill-defined though real domains of private space for traditional "intermediary bodies" like local notables, economic cartels and associations, officer corps, families, and churches. These, rather than an official single party, are the main agencies of social control in authoritarian regimes. Authoritarians would rather leave the population demobilized and passive, while fascists want to engage and excite the public. Authoritarians want a strong but limited state. They hesitate to intervene in the economy, as fascism does readily, or to embark on programs of social welfare. They cling to the status quo rather than proclaim a new way. (216–17)

But in one of three footnotes to this paragraph, Paxton admits that the distinction is blurry (306). And as he also documents, fascists and fascistic authoritarians may change policies and preferences according to changing political winds as they seek to outfox their opponents — something Orwell satirized in both *Animal Farm* and *1984* by having political alliances absurdly and cynically shift all of a sudden over the course of those stories.

Paxton makes other distinctions in his discussion of "Boundaries." Since fascism arises within democracies that are perceived as weak, failed, or dysfunctional and is marked by the people's voluntary surrender or signing over of its free institutions and agency to a trusted leader ("Napoleon is always right," says Boxer in *Animal Farm*), he believes the term fascism should not be applied to regimes of "classical tyranny," "pre-democratic dictatorships," or "military dictatorships" that have never known democracy in the first place. The latter are all authoritarian regimes that do not want to stir public excitement, or only do so very occasionally for ceremonial anniversaries, and do not seek to "reduce the private sphere to nothing." So, if it does seek to meld private and public life, is *fascism* synonymous with *totalitarianism*? For many it is, but not for Paxton because even though the Italian and German fascists may have professed a desire for unifying totality, and even displayed signs and symbols of it here and there, other words and deeds of theirs go in the opposite direction toward a toleration or even exploitation of private, personal, or group autonomy (211). There's something off about equating fascism with totalitarianism since Stalin's communist Soviet Union is usually considered an example of totalitarianism, which then requires accepting the strange "horseshoe logic" that says political extremes meet. But then why were German fascists opposed to communists if they had so much in common? Paxton accepts that nazism and communism used similar mechanisms of control and both inflicted enormous suffering; but the social situations and professed aims of Hitler and Stalin were very different, although both desperately wanted to control Ukraine, as Timothy Snyder insists in *Bloodlands* (2010).[12]

Without reproducing Paxton's entire discussion, it may be useful to quote his impatience with a mostly frivolous "exercise in comparative moral judgment"; and then his observation of how that indulgence masks the disorderly aspects of fascist rule, a type of disorder that for a time at least may have contributed to keeping the fascists on top by keeping everyone else continuously off balance.

> Treating Hitler and Stalin together as totalitarians often becomes an exercise in comparative moral judgment: Which monster was more monstrous? Were Stalin's two forms of mass murder — reckless economic experiment and the paranoid persecution of "enemies" — the moral equivalent of Hitler's attempt to purify his nation by exterminating the medically and racially impure?

---

12   Timothy Snyder, *Bloodlands: Europe Between Hitler and Stalin* (New York: Basic Books, 2010).

The strongest case for equating Stalin's terror with Hitler's is the famine of 1931, which, it is alleged, targeted Ukrainians and thus amounted to genocide. This famine, though indeed the result of criminal negligence, affected Russians with equal severity. Opponents would note fundamental differences. Stalin killed in grossly arbitrary fashion whomever his paranoid mind decided were "class enemies" (a condition one can change), in a way that struck mostly at adult males among the dictator's fellow citizens. Hitler, by contrast, killed "race enemies," an irremediable condition that condemns even newborns. He wanted to liquidate entire peoples, including their tombstones and their cultural artifacts. This book acknowledges the repugnance of both terrors, but condemns even more strongly Nazi biologically racialist extermination because it admitted no salvation even for women and children.

A more pragmatic criticism of the totalitarian model complains that its image of an efficient all-encompassing mechanism prevents us from grasping the disorderly character of Hitler's rule, which reduced government to personal fiefdoms unable to discuss policy options and choose among them rationally. Mussolini, assuming multiple cabinet ministries himself but unable to impose orderly priorities on any of them, did no better. The totalitarian image may evoke powerfully the dreams and aspirations of dictators, but it actually obstructs any examination of the vital matter of how effectively fascist regimes managed to embed themselves in the half-compliant, half-recalcitrant societies they ruled. (212–13)

To those for whom Hitler and Stalin have become distant cartoons (for example, the makers and consumers of the movies *The Death of Stalin* [2018] and *Jojo Rabbit* [2019]), this discussion may seem less interesting than what Paxton has to say about the present or future possibility of totalitarianism or a "functional equivalent of fascism" in Europe, America, or somewhere else.

Obviously in 2004 Paxton could not know what was ahead.[13] However, before concluding this review of his field guide to fascism, it's important to consider what he did know in 2004 and the tools he left his readers for facing fascisms and fascistic authoritarian regimes in the future. That Paxton wants his book to be used as a guide to recognize and ward off painful politics and policies is clear from the concluding paragraph of his thorough and temperate "Other Times, Other Places" chapter:

> Armed by historical knowledge, we may be able to distinguish today's ugly but isolated imitations, with their shaved heads and swastika tattoos, from authentic functional equivalents in the form of a mature fascist-conservative alliance. Forewarned, we may be able to detect the real thing when it comes along. (205)

The key trauma in Paxton's day — the analog to the destruction and dislocation provoked by World War I, the "Spanish Flu" pandemic, and the Depression that all set the stage for 1920s and '30s fascist experiments — was the death and destruction caused by the terrorist attacks of September 11, 2001. As bad as those attacks were, however, it's important not to see false equivalency, because death tolls in the thousands (2,996) are not the same as death tolls in the millions. Also, the republics of the twentieth century were relatively young, inexperienced, and filled with democracy skeptics; unlike today's republics which have weathered many storms and count more democracy sympathizers among their ranks. That reminder is important, and yet there is little doubt that September 11 reignited prejudice and nativ-

---

13   I have in mind the ongoing authoritarianization in Russia, Turkey, Hungary, Poland, and Brazil occurring as I wrote the first draft of this chapter two weeks after Trump's acquittal by Senate Republicans on February 5, 2020. Also, going back a few years, the worldwide shocks caused by the Great Recession of 2008–10; the Tea Party takeover of the US House of Representatives in 2010; and expansions of executive authority that attract less attention, such as the rollbacks and deregulation imposed by Trump's executive orders.

ism in the US and Europe.[14] In the "Other Times, Other Places" chapter Paxton discusses fascist thinking and behavior in many countries on every continent; however, his observations are particularly shaped by turn-of-the-century events in the United States, France, and Serbia.

Serbia is important in Paxton's history because at the time Europe seemed to have safely evaded a "functional equivalent" of fascism, fueled by nationalism and religion, on its eastern flank. Slobodan Milošević (1941–2006) was no longer in power in 2004, and the rule of law — symbolized by the International Criminal Court in The Hague where Milošević was put on trial in 2002 and 2004 for genocide, crimes against humanity, violations of the customs of war, and grave breaches of the Geneva Convention — seemed to have triumphed. After the faraway genocide in Rwanda (1994), some American and European leaders belatedly came to regret not doing more to prevent it.[15] Therefore the 1999 mobilization of NATO forces to prevent "ethnic cleansing" of non-Serbs and non-Christians in the vast multi-ethnic territory in eastern Europe known then as Yugoslavia was critically important to European security but had even greater significance for Europe's moral standing and self-esteem as it demonstrated its ability to do the right thing and live up to the post-Auschwitz promise of "never again."

France is also important at the time Paxton is writing his *Anatomy of Fascism* because it too offers a consoling narrative. Only two years before, in 2002, the French electorate, with Left

---

14 That the American army was going to teach those "towel heads" a lesson in 2003 was not a new or rare sentiment in the United States's white supremacist history as Greg Grandin documents in *The End of the Myth: From the Frontier to the Border Wall in the Mind of America* (New York: Macmillan, 2019).

15 On April 16, 2015, Colin Keating, president of the UN Security Council in 1994, apologized publicly for "the Council's refusal to recognize and halt the slaughter, in which up to one million lives were lost." Per Liljas, "An Apology for the Rwandan Genocide, 20 Years Later," *Time Magazine,* April 17, 2014, https://time.com/66095/rwanda-genocide-keating-apology/.

and Right united for once,[16] voted massively against the far-right candidate Jean-Marie Le Pen. To most people's surprise, Le Pen got to the second round of the presidential election by beating out the sitting prime minister (the center-left, *gauche caviar* socialist Lionel Jospin) who was running against the president he was serving alongside (the center-right incumbent Jacques Chirac). Blocking the extreme-right's path to power — *barrer la voie à l'extrême droite* — was considered a moral necessity; and a solid majority of French citizens, some "holding their noses," did what they saw as their duty in voting for Chirac. Thus, these two test cases are taken by Paxton as healthy signs that the European "inoculation" against the far-right — preventing it from getting beyond stage two ("taking root") to stage three ("getting power") — was still effective in 2004.

But those two pieces of good news do not prevent Paxton from doubting the long-term effectiveness of that inoculation which he calls "inherently temporary." Given recent concerns about the rise of anti-Semitic and anti-immigrant violence throughout Europe and of the far-right AfD in Germany, especially in the province of Thuringia where Hitler had his first electoral successes,[17] this paragraph is particularly resonant:

The inoculation of most Europeans against the original fascism by its public shaming in 1945 is inherently temporary.

---

16 In a sense, France's center-left and center-right are always united — a hallmark of France's centrism that some admire and others bemoan. What was unusual in 2002 was that socialists, communists, and conservatives from both rural and urban areas voted for President Jacques Chirac to give him a landslide victory in the second round, 82 percent versus 18 percent, though for many it was really a vote against Le Pen.

17 In the days when I was completing the first draft of this chapter, German Chancellor Angela Merkel was objecting to her party's coalition-building in a Thuringia parliamentary election with the far-right Alternative für Deutschland (AfD) party, essentially calling for a do-over, and two weeks later she was lamenting the "poison" (*Gift*) of hate and racism following a mass shooting in Hanau, near Frankfurt, where a 43-year-old radicalized German man killed nine foreign-looking people in two cafés before killing his mother and himself at their home.

The taboos of 1945 have inevitably faded with the disappear-ance of the eyewitness generation. In any event, a fascism of the future — an emergency response to some still unimag-ined crisis — need not resemble classical fascism perfectly in its outward signs and symbols. Some future movement that would "give up free institutions" in order to perform the same functions of mass mobilization for the reunification, purification, and regeneration of some troubled group would undoubtedly call itself something else and draw on fresh symbols. That would not make it any less dangerous. (174)

In the next paragraph Paxton goes on to note with Orwell's help that "there is no sartorial litmus test for fascism"; on the con-trary, "new fascisms would probably prefer the mainstream pa-triotic dress of their own place and time," and the stigmatized, enemy out-group does not need to be Jews. Paxton did not see then as we do now the perfect fit of Trump's red MAGA baseball hat within the "make America great again" campaign, but he does speculate about who the future "enemies of the people" in various contexts are likely to be:

An authentically popular American fascism would be pi-ous, anti-black, and, since September 11, 2001, anti-Islamic as well; in western Europe, secular and, these days, more likely anti-Islamic than anti-Semitic; in Russia and eastern Europe, religious, anti-Semitic, Slavophile, and anti-Western. (174)

Obsessed with "homeland security," some saw the United States as a crucible for neofascism in 2004.[18] First, because of the ero-sion of civil liberties post-9/11 with the rushed passage in Oc-tober 2001 of the unconstitutional Patriot Act that expanded the federal government's power to spy on private citizens. The Patriot Act (and the Total Information Awareness program that grew out of it in 2003), though not mentioned by name in Pax-

---

18 See Herman and Julia Schwendinger, *Homeland Fascism: Corporatist Government in the New American Century* (Earth: punctum books, 2016).

ton's book, looks like a prime example of a democracy giving up free institutions — a key component for any passage from stage-two to stage-three fascism. Secondly, President George W. Bush was campaigning in 2004 (with pre-social media dirty tricks[19] against the distinguished senator and Vietnam war veteran John Kerry) to consolidate the shaky hold on power that he obtained thanks to a 5-to-4 Supreme Court decision that decided the 2000 presidential election in his favor, despite having lost the popular vote.[20] Superficially at least, 9/11 can look like Bush's Reichstag fire; in other words, a conveniently timed catastrophe that will allow Bush to play the righteous avenging superhero capable of healing a wounded United States and leading the country — like a latter-day Woodrow Wilson, F.D.R., Harry S. Truman, and Dwight Eisenhower rolled into one — through its trauma and its retaliation in the form of a just "war on terror" against designated evil-doers until once again the world is made safe for democracy.[21] The third reason is that the Second Iraq War, which started in 2003, showed signs early on of being an Orwellian forever war waged as much to defeat Democrats ("internal enemies") in upcoming elections as it was to defeat terrorists "over there" on the ground.

---

19 For an up-to-date explanation, see Steven Levitsky and Daniel Ziblatt, "Why Republicans Play Dirty," *The New York Times,* September 20, 2019, https://www.nytimes.com/2019/09/20/opinion/republicans-democracy-play-dirty.html. For an unapologetic explanation by Mark McKinnon, Bush's lead campaign strategist, of "persuasive" storytelling, see *The New York Times* Op-Doc by Sarah Klein and Tom Mason, "How to Win an Election," February 18, 2016, https://www.nytimes.com/2016/02/18/opinion/how-to-win-an-election.html. Of course, one person's persuasive is another person's manipulative.

20 See Jeffrey Toobin, *Too Close to Call* (New York: Random House, 2001).

21 It has often been observed that Bush's performance would have been more convincing and effective had he called on all Americans to pull together in combined military and civilian national service in a spirit of solidarity and shared sacrifice, instead of inviting them to continue living as before and "to go shopping more."

After a brief review of the United States's "legacy fascisms" of the stage-one or -two variety from the Ku Klux Klan[22] to Huey Long, Father Coughlin, and Gerald L.K. Smith, Paxton makes some passing observations that loom larger now, especially his use of the word "resentment." He then adds one more paragraph, at once a backward glance and a look ahead, where an early use of the term "polarization" is likely to jump out at the reader with 20–20 hindsight.[23]

---

22 Near the end of his chapter on "Creating Fascist Movements," Paxton convincingly argues that the post-Civil War Ku Klux Klan (banned in 1871) was the first fascist movement: "It may be that the earliest phenomenon that can be functionally related to fascism is American: the Ku Klux Klan. Just after the Civil War, some former Confederate officers, fearing the vote given to African Americans in 1867 by the Radical Reconstructionists, set up a militia to restore an overturned social order. The Klan constituted an alternate civic authority, parallel to the legal state, which, in the eyes of the Klan's founders, no longer defended their community's legitimate interests. By adopting a uniform (white robe and hood), as well as by their techniques of intimidation and their conviction that violence was justified in the cause of their group's destiny, the first version of the Klan in the defeated American South was arguably a remarkable preview of the way fascist movements were to function in interwar Europe. It should not be surprising, after all, that the most precocious democracies — the United States and France — should have generated precocious backlashes against democracy" (49). That last remark is central to Paxton's conception of fascism as political behavior which is exploiting the weaknesses of democratic institutions. On page 227 of his bibliographical essay, Paxton insists again on this point and praises an early "how democracies die" book from forty years before Levitsky and Ziblatt: "An essential precondition for the fascist achievement of power is the opening up of a space brought about by the failure of democracy, a subject too often overlooked because so many assume that the fascist leader did everything himself. A rare and valuable study is Juan J. Linz and Alfred Stepan, eds., *The Breakdown of Democratic Regimes: Europe* (Baltimore: Johns Hopkins University Press, 1978)." What Paxton's Klan reference does not take into account is that the semi-clandestine return of the Ku Klux Klan during the Jim Crow era would become the fascist-conservative alliance that locked in decades of authoritarianism across the southern United States. For a short summary that sees Trump's closest autocratic analogs to be as American as baseball, and not European, see Jamelle Bouie, "The Authoritarian Stamp of Jim Crow," *The New York Times,* January 21, 2020.

23 Though Cass R. Sunstein published his "Law of Group Polarization" in 1999, in 2004 the term was not yet the household word it has since become

Today a "politics of resentment" rooted in authentic American piety and nativism sometimes leads to violence against some of the very same "internal enemies" once targeted by the Nazis, such as homosexuals and defenders of abortion rights.[24]

Of course, the United States would have to suffer catastrophic setbacks and polarization for these fringe groups to find powerful allies and enter the mainstream. I half expected to see emerge after 1968 a movement of national reunification, regeneration, and purification directed against hirsute antiwar protesters, black radicals, and "degenerate" artists. I thought that some of the Vietnam veterans might form analogs to the Freikorps of 1919 Germany or the Italian Arditi, and attack the youths whose demonstrations on the steps of the Pentagon had "stabbed them in the back." Fortunately I was wrong (so far). Since September 11, 2001, however, civil liberties have been curtailed to popular acclaim in a patriotic war upon terrorists. (202)

Why Paxton does not mention the Patriot Act by name is a bit odd given his usual precision. Perhaps he saw that law's curtailment of civil liberties to expand the surveillance state as simply one worrisome symptom among many. Also of note is the parenthetical "so far." Paxton tells the reader that the nightmare scenario of a far-right backlash against the 1968 anti-war movement; that is, against the un-American, back-stabbing, degenerate liberals who opposed the war, was on his mind in the early 1970s while he was researching and writing his paradigm-

---

in the writings of Jonathan Haidt, among journalists, and on social media.
24 In a footnote that appears here, Paxton references Alan Crawford's
    Thunder on the Right: The "New Right" and the Politics of Resentment
    (New York: Pantheon, 1980), an important reminder that the line between
    Nixon's Southern Strategy and Trump's weaponization of the Tea Party
    passes through Ronald Reagan and Lee Atwater, his aggressive campaign
    manager. See Rick Perlstein, *Reaganland: America's Right Turn, 1976–1980*
    (New York: Simon & Schuster, 2020).

changing study of the Vichy government. But that nightmare has still not happened, he sighs in relief, so far.[25]

Nonetheless, Americans may want to ask the question posed most recently by an early commentator of polarization, Cass R. Sunstein: *Can it happen here?*[26] Paxton's short answer would seem to be: *Not unless things get much worse.* But what things? His scrutiny of all the cases around the world leads him to identify the favorite enemies that far-right groups like to target for their anti-political politics. They include cosmopolitans, multiculturalists, environmentalists, and of course incompetent politicians. Naturally there are no bad politicians in their own ranks which are composed entirely of true patriots, resolute deciders, and stable geniuses doing a great job. Since the end of the Cold War and the collapse of the Soviet Union, Paxton notes that some far-right groups have gone from the margins to the mainstream. They have become normalized in France, the Netherlands, Austria, Italy, and recently in Spain and Germany. But the flow of influence, when they come in contact with mainstream politics and media, cuts both ways. Far-right groups are hyperaware of optics, symbolism, and connotation because there is still generally a visceral objection to any recycling of the fascist decor of the 1920s and '30s — especially displays of mass physical violence (as in Myanmar, for example).[27] Therefore the rhetoric, such as the dog-whistles of coded speech, has had to

---

25 Some are not so sure. See Henry A. Giroux, *American Nightmare: Facing the Challenge of Fascism* (San Francisco: City Lights, 2018). Many more shared Giroux's concerns after the riot at the US Capitol on January 6, 2021.

26 Cass R. Sunstein, ed., *Can It Happen Here? Authoritarianism in America* (New York: Dey St., 2018) — a collection of nineteen essays, including one by Jon Elster on the rise to power of Napoleon III, a fascist *avant la lettre*, so to speak. Elster is the author of many books including Alexis de Tocqueville, *The First Social Scientist* (Cambridge: Cambridge University Press, 2009), which I discuss in my own Tocqueville book.

27 On Myanmar and the weaponization of social media, see Evan Osnos, "Can Mark Zuckerberg Fix Facebook before It Breaks Democracy?" *The New Yorker,* September 10, 2018, https://www.newyorker.com/magazine/2018/09/17/can-mark-zuckerberg-fix-facebook-before-it-breaks-democracy.

become subtler in recent years, just as the targeting of messages has become more sophisticated in the internet age.[28]

After listing off the enemies of the new post-Cold War fascist movements, Paxton usefully reminds his reader that far-right groups do not have such a novice set of democracies to doubt and belittle as Hitler could against the Weimar Republic. They also cannot point to levels of dysfunction that compare to the post-World War I context with bombed out cities, the lingering "Spanish Flu," economic devastation, and broken infrastructure. Today's democracies, while far from perfect, are not exactly "failed states."[29] They are getting things done: garbage is being collected, firemen are putting out fires, disaster relief gets delivered, schools educate, hospitals treat the sick, and roads and bridges get built and repaired. Could all of those activities be better funded and run better? Of course they could. My point is that sometimes critics on the Left can unwittingly do the work of the far-right by painting an overly bleak picture of dysfunction. Laudable idealism can lead some to forget that "perfect is the enemy of good." Since far-right groups thrive on disorder and a perception of dysfunction, lack, and vulnerability, you can be sure they will seize every opportunity, no matter who the content provider is, to magnify everything negative.[30] Only

---

28 For a comprehensive and incisive study of the rhetoric of Marine Le Pen's normalized far-right party in France, the Front National, now renamed the Rassemblement National, see Cécile Alduy and Stéphane Wahnich, *Marine Le Pen prise aux mots: décryptage du nouveau discours frontiste* (Paris: Seuil, 2015).

29 Noam Chomsky, *Failed States: The Abuse of Power and The Assault on Democracy* (New York: Metropolitan Books, 2006).

30 In the left-leaning daily *Libération,* democracy sympathizer and Collège de France member Pierre Rosanvallon's harsh criticism of French President Emmanuel Macron, though perhaps factually correct, seems rather tone deaf and tactically misguided if it ends up doing the demolition work of the far-right in its place. Pierre Rosanvallon, "Emmanuel Macron est devenu la figure centrale de la droite française," *Libération,* March 30, 2022, https://www.liberation.fr/idees-et-debats/pierre-rosanvallon-emmanuel-macron-est-devenu-la-figure-centrale-de-la-droite-francaise-20220330_HPVFRPUZIJC5TO3S2QW6E32WCQ/. Reading this piece, the expression "with friends like that who needs enemies?" comes to mind… as well as

by getting large numbers of people to see the glass half empty or worse (by repeating over and over the word "carnage," for example) will fascists be able to succeed in peeling voters away from democratic institutions and the democracy game in general. Bad news is good news for fascists and authoritarians so long as they can make it look as though democracy and liberalism are to blame for the dysfunction. Bots and trolling on social media can then spread those negative perceptions until they become a self-fulfilling prophecy.[31]

The good news in 2004, Paxton points out, is that Europe's new far-right parties are less extreme than their Italian and German forebears. In Europe between 2000 and 2022 there was no widespread attack on the rule of law, though there was plenty to the east in Russia and by Russia on its direct neighbors.[32] On the contrary, far-right parties have been (zealous) champions of law and order. With the possible exception of Orbán's Hungary, there is no open promotion of a one-party state; instead many are eager to join multi-party coalitions and to claim that their electoral successes were won fair and square. There is also no regulatory impulse toward central control of the economy, but

the wisdom of Shakespeare: "striving to better, oft we mar what's well" (*King Lear,* Act I, scene 4, line 369).

31 See Andrew Marantz, "Free Speech Is Killing Us," *The New York Times,* October 4, 2019, https://www.nytimes.com/2019/10/04/opinion/sunday/free-speech-social-media-violence.html, an extract from his book *Antisocial: Online Extremists, Techno-Utopians, and the Hijacking of the American Conversation* (New York: Penguin Books, 2019). See also *The New York Times* documentary on Russian meddling, *Operation InfeKtion,* 2018.

32 Terrorist attacks such as those in France in 2015 or the 2020 Hanau mass shooting that killed nine foreign-looking people in German cafés may be on the increase, but they are condemned by all political parties, including the AfD. More worrisome are reports such as Katrin Bennhold and Melissa Eddy, "'Politics of Hate' Takes a Toll in Germany Well Beyond Immigrants," *The New York Times,* February 21, 2020, https://www.nytimes.com/2020/02/21/world/europe/germany-mayors-far-right.html, which states that 1,240 politically motivated attacks occurred in 2019 in Germany against elected officials criticized for being not anti-immigrant enough. There is also concern that far-right members exist within the German military.

often a (zealous) desire for deregulation and a worship of markets and so-called free trade. The trouble with authoritarianization, however, is that displays of respect for freedom, law, and the democracy game may be insincere, opportunistic, one-sided, and temporary, hence the need for vigilance by a free press, engaged citizenry, and evidence-based research.

In all, Robert Paxton's *Anatomy of Fascism* is still a valuable book for understanding fascism and authoritarianization — a word that was not current in 2004 but has gained circulation in the work of Erica Frantz, Milan Svolik, and others.[33] But detecting "the real thing when it comes along" is only half the battle. One must go further than understanding how fascism happens and actually build *empathy* for both the cruel pain that fascists inflict on vulnerable groups and, yes, for the pain endured by the fascists themselves — suffering, whether self-inflicted or coming from elsewhere, that their misguided amateur remedies not only fail to eliminate but actually magnify and cause to spread.[34] To understand those paradoxes and ironies with compassion and without demonization, and eventually become an effective pain reducer, one must go beyond the toolbox of the rational, open-eyed historian and make use of what can be learned from experienced observers of the complex workings of the human mind, especially its seemingly irrational and less visible unconscious aspects. The writings of Erich Fromm, especially his 1941 multi-million copy bestseller *Escape from Freedom,* are a good place to start.

---

33 Amanda Taub, "How Autocrats Can Triumph in Democratic Countries," *The New York Times,* April 18, 2017, https://www.nytimes.com/2017/04/18/world/europe/how-autocrats-can-triumph-in-democratic-countries.html; Adam Serwer, "The First Days of the Trump Regime," *The Atlantic,* February 19, 2020, https://www.theatlantic.com/ideas/archive/2020/02/trump-regime/606682/; Erica Frantz, *Authoritarianism: What Everyone Needs to Know* (Oxford: Oxford University Press, 2018); and Milan W. Svolik, *The Politics of Authoritarian Rule* (Cambridge: Cambridge University Press, 2012).

34 We will return in a later chapter to empathy — the practice of love, what Fromm called "the art of loving" — as a prerequisite for wanting to reduce vulnerability and the pain it causes individually and collectively.

2

Understanding the Emotional Lava of Fascism, Then and Now

Erich Fromm, *Escape from Freedom* (1941)

« Il n'y a rien de plus dur que l'apprentissage de la liberté ».
[Nothing is harder than learning to be free.]
        — Alexis de Tocqueville, *Democracy in America* (I, 2, vi)

Since first reading *Escape from Freedom* in 2014,[1] I used it in the four iterations of my seminar, "Fascism, Vulnerability, and the Escape from Freedom," where, combined with Paxton's *Anatomy,* it formed the "dual-core processor" for the whole course. Over those years, 2015–19 — a time period that has seen a clear increase of both aspirations for democracy on every continent but also of authoritarian hijackings of democracy — I was watching to see if anyone out there was making use of Fromm's writings as part of either their diagnosis or remedy for what ails democracy. Despite having sold more than five million copies since its publication in early 1941, and despite having been translated into twenty-eight languages, hardly anyone has even

---

1   Erich Fromm, *Escape from Freedom* (New York: Henry Holt, 1969). Hereafter cited parenthetically throughout this chapter.

mentioned Fromm.[2] This chapter will claim that this omission is not a matter of chance but instead a symptom of the central issue alluded to in the book's very title: in times of high vulnerability, when "economic, social and political conditions [...] do not offer a basis for the realization of individuality" (35), many people register freedom as a burden — even as an existential threat — instead of as an opportunity. But since those may be considered shameful, unavowable feelings, it's easier to ignore the messenger (in this case Fromm) who has the nerve to claim that large numbers of people living in presumptively open, democratic societies in "the free world" are really afraid of freedom, actively flee freedom in myriad ways, and submit to unfreedom — including fascist thinking and deeds — every day. In other words, I am claiming that there is widespread resistance to Fromm today, not least among those considered *serious people.* While this is not new, traditional academia never embraced Fromm even during his heyday in the 1960s and '70s,[3] it is especially regrettable now because his diagnosis of the "Psychology of Nazism" and of the mechanisms of *Escape from Freedom* — 1) Authoritarianism; 2) Destructiveness; 3) Automaton Conformity — could be particularly valuable in the contemporary context; if, that is, enough people still think that democracy offers more real advantages to more people than empire or authoritarianism or any other vertically and centrally organized regime can deliver.

If it's a pity that Paxton did not mention Fromm, it's remarkable but actually quite wonderful that Fromm never mentions Alexis de Tocqueville since it then looks as though the French-

---

2   An exception is Masha Gessen who made a favorable allusion to Fromm — "my favorite social psychologist" — in a June 22, 2020 interview with *The New Yorker* editor David Remnick on the occasion of the publication of her book *Surviving Autocracy* (New York: Riverhead Books, 2020). A second exception comes within the study of American fascist tendencies by Matthew C. MacWilliams, *On Fascism: 12 Lessons from American History* (New York: St. Martin's Press, 2020).

3   Tocqueville was also mostly shunned by his countrymen for a century after his death.

man and the German were working like two distant laboratories on the same problem — *the grandeur and vulnerability of the free individual in modern society.* And, lo and behold, independently and roughly a century apart in 1840 and 1940, they both come up with the same diagnosis, share many of the same concerns, articulate some of the same paradoxes, and trail off with the same guarded optimism, not unlike Paxton's or my own. Fromm and Tocqueville both believe that individual *liberté,* Tocqueville's preferred Latinate term, and *freedom,* Fromm's Anglo-Saxon preference, in German *Freiheit,* will prevail, "and that government of the people, by the people, for the people, shall not perish from the earth," as Lincoln declared, also with guarded optimism, in 1863 — a year roughly equidistant from the eras of both Tocqueville (1805–59) and Fromm (1900–80).

Lawrence J. Friedman's intellectual biography *The Lives of Erich Fromm: Love's Prophet* (2013) is the indispensable guide to every stage of Fromm's education, professional activities as an analyst and teacher of psychoanalysis, and his four decades of writings. It's entirely fitting that Friedman devotes an entire chapter to *Escape from Freedom,* Fromm's breakthrough book. And since I want this chapter to be a supplement and not a substitute for reading Fromm and Friedman, I will be brief about his life and concentrate on Fromm's argument.

Fromm was a Jew raised in Frankfurt and his education encompassed three important traditions: Talmudic studies; the German philosophical canon from Emmanuel Kant to Georg W.F. Hegel to Karl Marx; and the emergent discourse of psychology. Fromm's birth year, 1900, is also the year of the dissemination of Sigmund Freud's all-important *Traumdeutung, The Interpretation of Dreams.* One could say Fromm becomes a native speaker of that new discourse, Freudianism, just as we say those born after 1989 are digital natives. Fromm fled Nazi Germany in 1934 roughly one year after Hitler became chancellor. He was able to secure himself a position within the Frankfurt Institute for Social Research at Columbia University which he had been partly responsible for founding. New York City had by then surpassed London and Paris as the world's literary, cultural, and intellectual center, in part thanks to large numbers of talented and motivated European immigrants. With a foothold in New York, Fromm soon thrived, taking full advantage of the open doors and wallets that allowed him to pursue a dense schedule of clinical practice, teaching, reading and writing, and enjoyment of New York's art scene.[4] Fromm overcame early social awkwardness and with the encouragement of circles of friends and colleagues grew in confidence over the following decades. He took pride, for example, at being able to write directly in English, the first language of his adopted country, though he would also learn Spanish and spend important years training analysts in Mexico.

My page references will be to the Holt paperback edition of *Escape from Freedom* from 1969 that contains the valuable Foreword II that Fromm wrote in 1965 to accompany the twenty-fifth anniversary edition published the following year in 1966. It's important to keep in mind that the book was first written in urgency, outlined by Fromm in March 1939, six months before the start of World War II, and then worked on intensively, according to Friedman, through 1940 and eventually published in March 1941. However, Fromm did not believe the emergency it was addressing was over on Victory in Europe Day in 1945. The second foreword is not celebratory; it is instead a renewal of Fromm's call for vigilant engagement to solve a persistent problem.[5] Also worth noting on the cover of the Holt edition is how the font choice for the letters of the author's name and the title recalls those often used in modernist Vienna around

---

4   Lawrence J. Friedman, *The Lives of Erich Fromm: Love's Prophet* (New York: Columbia University Press, 2013), ch. 3, "The Americanization of a European Intellectual," 65–96.

5   Here too there is a similarity with Tocqueville who published his *Old Regime and the Revolution* (1856) not as a declaration of victory and progress but as a reiteration, this time more directly focused on France and Europe, of his worries about the threats to liberty posed by a centralized government's total administration over weak and isolated individuals — a problem he had first articulated twenty-one years earlier in *Democracy in America*.

1900. Those words are set within a blue rectangle at the bottom of which is a sentence of high praise from *The Washington
Post*: "Fromm's thought merits the critical attention of all concerned with the human condition and its future." Agreed. Looking closely, one sees that this rectangle of author, title, and blurb
copy, in descending order, is centered over a light-brown, half-
tone image of what seems to be a crowd of people in a tight circle
with upraised arms and hands reaching out for something. The
cover design, credited on the back flap to one Raquel Jaramillo,
deftly combines clarity and mystery. There's both an anchor to
a certain orderly pre-democratic Western civilization, with the
allusion to pre-war imperial Vienna, and a striving or aspiration, symbolized by the dynamic representation of the mass
of outstretched upwardly reaching arms and hands and a few
heads that can also be distinguished. Is it a wild mob or a wise
crowd? The representation of collective and individual striving, not saluting (Robert Paxton and Jason Stanley's publishers
both chose to represent that fascist cliché), successfully creates
intrigue and an invitation. The same is true for the title. Notice
it is not promising *the* or *an* escape from freedom but stating
simply *Escape from Freedom,* as though this were a command or
imperative. But who would want to escape from freedom? And
why? And to go into what state of *unfreedom* and, once there,
to do what? The mid-1960s, the zenith of Fromm's popularity,
was a time when many people around the world were pushed or
pulled by hot and cold wars to ask big societal questions such as
one finds in Rachel Carson's *Silent Spring* (1962), *The Port Huron
Statement* (1962), or Martin Luther King Jr.'s *Where Do We Go
From Here: Chaos or Community?* (1967). Fromm's four decades
of writings from the 1940s through the '70s are a leading example of that "counter-culture" age of introspection and activism,
and conservative backlash, that is commonly associated with
"the sixties."[6]

---

6   For a look back from the age of MAGA and BLM to the age of SDS (Students
    for a Democratic Society) and FSM (the Free Speech Movement), see Louis
    Menand, "The Making of the New Left," *The New Yorker,* March 22, 2021,

Fromm states the thesis of *Escape from Freedom* early and often. The first formulation comes near the beginning of the first foreword:

> It is the thesis of this book that modern man, freed from the bonds of pre-individualistic society, which simultaneously gave him security and limited him, has not gained freedom in the positive sense of the realization of his individual self; that is, the expression of his intellectual, emotional, and sensuous potentialities. Freedom, though it has brought him independence and rationality, has made him isolated and, thereby, anxious and powerless. This isolation is unbearable and the alternatives he is confronted with are either to escape from the burden of his freedom into new dependencies and submission, or to advance to the full realization of positive freedom which is based upon the uniqueness and individuality of man. (x)

More succinctly, his thesis is that modern man as an individual has achieved *freedom from* many past constraints, but the *freedom to* pursue an infinite number of possibilities is often experienced as a burden instead of an opportunity. This causes the isolated-feeling individual to wish to *escape from freedom* via some mode of voluntary servitude rather than push forward as a free agent constructing a personal project related to the world. Directly after stating his thesis, Fromm adds that he is offering "an analysis rather than a solution." But he claims that his analysis is necessary because "the understanding of the reasons for the totalitarian flight from freedom" are the indispensable guide to "any action which aims at the victory over the totalitarian forces" (xi). Therefore, *Escape from Freedom* is first of all a German Jewish immigrant's contribution on the American home

---

https://www.newyorker.com/magazine/2021/03/22/the-making-of-the-new-left, adapted from Menand's book, *The Free World: Art and Thought in the Cold War* (New York: Farrar, Straus and Giroux, 2021). See also Todd Gitlin, *The Sixties: Years of Hope, Days of Rage* (New York: Bantam Books, 1987).

front to the war effort that is then mobilizing between 1939 and 1941 to oppose the spread of destructive forces unleashed in his country of origin, principally against people like him, Jews. In other words, *Escape from Freedom* is personal.[7]

In Foreword II, Fromm gives the first indication that his analysis is based on his understanding of "the breakdown of the Medieval World."[8]

> *Escape from Freedom* is an analysis of the phenomenon of man's anxiety engendered by the breakdown of the Medieval World in which, in spite of many dangers, he felt himself secure and safe. [...] [Y]et, as the analysis in *Escape from Freedom* attempts to show, modern man still [in 1965] is anxious and tempted to surrender his freedom to dictators of all kinds, or to lose it by transforming himself into a small cog in the machine, well fed, and well clothed, yet not a free man but an automaton. (xiii–xiv)

Anxiety and willingness to become an automaton have increased in developed countries, Fromm claims in 1965, due to 1) the use and proliferation of the atomic bomb; 2) computers; and 3) life-saving modern medicine and the population explosion (xiv–xv). At the same time he notes certain triumphs that offer hope for man's capacity to meet future challenges: 1) the disappearance of the dictatorships of Hitler and Stalin; 2) the fortitude and resilience of the US in resisting the spread of totalitarianism within its borders; and 3) the political and social lib-

---

7   Here is another similarity with Tocqueville, who, Adam Gopnik has noted, was preoccupied with how one creates a regime of popular sovereignty serving the needs of the Many that does not degenerate into a terror machine killing off members of your family. See "The Habit of Democracy," *The New Yorker*, October 8, 2001, https://www.newyorker.com/magazine/2001/10/15/the-habit-of-democracy.

8   This is another similarity with Tocqueville who saw the emergence of democracy in America as the culmination of seven hundred years of expanding equality of social conditions; that is, since the "Renaissance of the 12th century."

eration of "Negroes."[9] "Yet," Fromm adds, "all these reassuring facts must not deceive us into thinking that the dangers of 'escape from freedom' are not as great, or even greater today than they were when this book was first published" (xv). Not only must freedom and democracy be reconquered and reinvented by each generation anew, since nearly every person lives within a quasi-autocratic regime — one's own family — for the first two decades of one's life; but also, Fromm claims, the intellectual development of the human species outstrips its emotional development: "Man's brain lives in the twentieth century; the heart of most men lives still in the Stone Age" (xvi).

Despite his certain knowledge of Freud's warning against "wild psychoanalysis" that would try to cure neurosis by imparting knowledge in a way similar to responding to someone's hunger by showing them a menu, Fromm's prescription relies heavily on the Enlightenment era's faith in the emancipatory powers of "objectivity," "awareness," and "reason":

> How can mankind save itself from destroying itself by this discrepancy between intellectual-technical over-maturity and emotional backwardness?
>
> As far as I can see there is only one answer: increasing *awareness* of the most essential facts of our social existence, an awareness sufficient to prevent us from committing irreparable follies, and to raise to some small extent our capacity for *objectivity* and *reason*." (xvi, emphasis added)

Notice the goal is not a total cure. Fromm seems to concede that to be impossible which shows a healthy recognition of the power of resistance to the Enlightenment's hyperbolic liberation doctrine. Instead, the aim is to prevent "irreparable follies" — a

---

9 This second foreword is written at the time of the passage of the landmark Civil Rights Act (1964) and Voting Rights Act (1965) by the US Congress and signed into law by President Lyndon Johnson — a major step in the direction of a re-democratization of the South which had been operating under authoritarian Jim Crow rules for nearly a century after the formal end of Reconstruction in 1877.

more realistic, achievable goal that again puts Fromm close to Tocqueville who listed among the real advantages of democracy its capacity to make repairable mistakes (*fautes réparables*).[10]

At the start of chapter 1, "Freedom — A Psychological Problem?," Fromm reiterates the victory of man's *freedom from*: "Modern European and American history is centered around the effort to gain freedom from the political, economic, and spiritual shackles that have bound men" (1). The principal victories of human freedom are overcoming domination by 1) nature; 2) the Church; and 3) the absolutist state. World War I was at first thought to have been the final victory, but less than twenty years later, "new systems" of domination emerged.[11]

> [N]ew systems emerged which denied everything that men believed they had won in centuries of struggle. For the essence of these new systems, which effectively took command of man's entire social and personal life, was the submission of all but a handful of men to an authority over which they had no control. (2)

Fromm next dismisses fallacious explanations of authoritarianism's return: 1) madness of a few individuals; 2) lack of training in democratic governance specific to Italians and Germans; 3) Hitler and his kind were first cunning then ruthless users of force and fraud, and therefore the whole population was alleged to be a "will-less object of betrayal and terror" (3). This list is similar to the list of responsibility-ducking explanations that Paxton also denounces. Fromm then cites John Dewey to say that the true explanation for the crisis of democracy has to do with something as yet untreated within ourselves: "The serious threat to our democracy," says Dewey, "is not the existence of

---

10 For more on the limits of psychoanalysis and "the talking cure," see Janet Malcolm's two-part essay from the year of Fromm's death, "The Impossible Profession," *The New Yorker,* November 24 and December 1, 1980.

11 On the emergence of these new systems for command and control, see Yves Cohen, *Le siècle des chefs: une histoire transnationale du commandement et de l'autorité, 1890–1940* (Paris: Editions Amsterdam, 2014).

foreign totalitarian states. It is the existence within our own personal attitudes and within our own institutions of conditions which have given a victory to external authority, discipline, uniformity and dependence upon The Leader in foreign countries. The battlefield is also accordingly here — within ourselves and our institutions."[12] This shift in focus from "over there" (e.g., Europe, Vietnam, the Middle East) to "here — within ourselves and our institutions" aligns Fromm, following Dewey, with the domestic social justice and liberation movements of the sixties, notably the Civil Rights Movement of James Baldwin, Angela Davis, John Lewis, Malcolm X, Martin Luther King, Jr., Rosa Parks, and many others.

Fromm says he intends to supplement the account of the economic and social preconditions for fascism, ably provided in other studies such as Paxton's, with an account of "dynamic factors in the character structure of modern man, which made him want to give up freedom in Fascist countries and which so widely prevail in millions of our own people" (4). Next comes a dense bramble of questions that the Virgil-like Fromm lays out as a set of guiding topics for the inquiry he invites the bewildered Dante-like reader to pursue in his company:

These are the outstanding questions that arise when we look at the human aspect of freedom, the longing for submission, and the lust for power: What is freedom as a human experience? Is the desire for freedom something inherent in human nature? Is it an identical experience regardless of what kind of culture a person lives in, or is it something different according to the degree of individualism reached in a particular society? Is freedom only the absence of external pressure or is it also the presence of something — and if so, of what? What are the social and economic factors in society that make for the striving for freedom? Can freedom become

---

12 Fromm is quoting from Dewey's *Freedom and Culture* (New York: Putnam, 1939). Dewey was born the year Tocqueville died, 1859, and lived to be nearly 100, dying in 1952, and thus may have read *Escape from Freedom*.

a burden, too heavy for man to bear, something he tries to escape from? Why then is it that freedom is for many a cherished goal and for others a threat?

Is there not also, perhaps, besides an innate desire for freedom, an instinctive wish for submission? If there is not, how can we account for the attraction which submission to a leader has for so many today? Is submission always to an overt authority, or is there also submission to internalized authorities, such as duty or conscience, to inner compulsions or to anonymous authorities like public opinion? Is there a hidden satisfaction in submitting, and what is its essence?

What is it that creates in men an insatiable lust for power? Is it the strength of their vital energy — or is it a fundamental weakness and inability to experience life spontaneously and lovingly? What are the psychological conditions that make for the strength of these strivings? What are the social conditions upon which such psychological conditions in turn are based? (4–5)

Central to this list of questions, and located in the approximate middle of the above quotation, is the paradox that there may be both "an innate desire for freedom" and "an instinctive wish for submission." Recognition of this paradox, a sort of enigma or riddle, may be one of the pathways for building the empathy that I am claiming is necessary for getting beyond mere blaming and shaming of fascist behavior and actually reducing the willingness and likelihood of falling into fascist co-dependencies. Also of note in these early pages is that Fromm names only Freud, Marx, and Friedrich Nietzsche as harbingers of the danger of capital-F Fascism. He makes no mention, as Paxton would sixty years later, of Tocqueville's warning in *Democracy in America* (vol. 2, part 4). Perhaps it was a gap in his reading.[13]

---

13 The centenary of *Democracy in America* in 1935 spurred a revival of interest in Tocqueville; but Fromm's neglect of that anniversary can be excused since he had just arrived in America the year before and under more strained circumstances than those that had brought Tocqueville and Gustave de Beaumont to the US in 1831.

Fromm's analysis is based on the conviction that man and society mutually shape each other; there is not a static "human nature" and on the other side "society as something apart from him" (10). The "character structure" of man, Fromm claims, has been changed by particular circumstances, and then in turn shapes those circumstances: "man is not only made by history — history is made by man" (11–12). For example, a "burning ambition for fame," admiration for "the beauty of nature," and an "obsessional craving to work" are three specific human character features that arise in particular circumstances; they have not existed throughout human history, and, who knows, they may pass out of human history (11). Those features may result from social conditions, but they in turn "become *productive forces, molding the social process*" (12). This circular vision of social history where effects in turn become causes is also to be found in Tocqueville's writings.

Fromm next introduces the notion of adaptation, and he is especially interested in *dynamic* adaptation whereby the individual's character is altered as a result of the pursuit of a primary need of self-preservation and the avoidance of what he calls "moral aloneness." Fromm describes a domineering father-son relationship[14] worth citing at length:

> By dynamic adaptation we refer to the kind of adaptation that occurs, for example, when a boy submits to the commands of his strict and threatening father — being too much afraid of him to do otherwise — and becomes a "good" boy. While he adapts himself to the necessities of the situation, something happens in him. He may develop an intense hostility against his father, which he represses, since it would be too dangerous to express it or even to be aware of it. This repressed hostility, however, though not manifest, is a dynamic factor in

---

14 Parallels may be drawn to the curious case of Donald J. Trump and his father Fred as presented by Trump's niece, the psychologist Mary L. Trump in *Too Much and Never Enough: How My Family Created the World's Most Dangerous Man* (New York: Simon & Schuster, 2020).

his character structure. It may create new anxiety and thus lead to still deeper submission; it may set up a vague defiance, directed against no one in particular but rather towards life in general […] this kind of adaptation creates something new in him, arouses new drives and new anxieties. Every neurosis is an example of this dynamic adaptation; it is essentially an adaptation to such external conditions (particularly those of early childhood) as are in themselves irrational and, generally speaking, unfavorable to the growth and development of the child. Similarly, such socio-psychological phenomena as are comparable to neurotic phenomena (why they should not be called neurotic will be discussed later), like the presence of strong destructive or sadistic impulses in social groups, offer an example of dynamic adaptation to social conditions that are irrational and harmful to the development of men. (13–14)

This behavior of the son is part of a set of behaviors linked to bodily self-preservation. Of special note is a young person's relation to *work* which is always conditioned by the economic system in which one finds oneself at birth:

When man is born, the stage is set for him. He has to eat and drink, and therefore he has to work; and this means he has to work under the particular conditions and in the ways that are determined for him by the kind of society into which he is born. Both factors, his need to live and the social system, in principle are unalterable by him as an individual, and they are the factors which determine the development of those other traits that show greater plasticity.

Thus the mode of life, as it is determined for the individual by the peculiarity of an economic system, becomes the primary factor in determining his whole character structure, because the imperative need for self-preservation forces him to accept the conditions under which he has to live. This does not mean that he cannot try, together with others, to effect certain economic and political changes; but primarily his

> personality is molded by the particular mode of life, as he has already been confronted with it as a child through the medium of the family, which represents all the features that are typical of a particular society or class. (16–17)

Fromm then turns to another category of adaptations that have to do with *mental* self-preservation, and first among these is avoiding both physical isolation and "moral aloneness": "To feel completely alone and isolated leads to mental disintegration just as physical starvation leads to death" (17).[15] Fromm lists a variety of forms of spiritual relatedness that may serve the basic need of fending off moral isolation.

> This lack of relatedness to values, symbols, patterns, we may call moral aloneness and state that moral aloneness is as intolerable as the physical aloneness, or rather that physical aloneness becomes unbearable only if it implies also moral aloneness. The spiritual relatedness to the world can assume many forms; the monk in his cell who believes in God and the political prisoner kept in isolation who feels one with his fellow-fighters are not alone morally. Neither is the English gentleman who wears his dinner jacket in the most exotic surroundings nor the petty bourgeois who, though being deeply isolated from his fellow men, feels one with his nation or its symbols. The kind of relatedness to the world may be noble or trivial, but even being related to the basest kind of pattern is immensely preferable to being alone. Religion and nationalism, as well as any custom and any belief however absurd and degrading, if it only connects the individual with others, are refuges from what man most dreads: isolation. (17–18)

---

15   See Atul Gawande on the mental breakdown of prisoners placed in solitary confinement — a practice that some seek to ban, claiming it is a form of inhumane torture: "Hellhole," *The New Yorker,* March 23, 2009, https://www.newyorker.com/magazine/2009/03/30/hellhole.

Man dreads isolation.[16] It is worth noting here that Fromm makes use of literary sources — Honoré de Balzac, John Milton, Daniel Defoe — to get his point across. We can share a portion of his use of *Robinson Crusoe* since the desert island story of the eponymous character is familiar to most people:

> Any attempt to answer the question why the fear of isolation is so powerful in man would lead us far away from the main road we are following in this book. However, in order not to give the reader the impression that the need to feel one with others has some mysterious quality, I should like to indicate in what direction I think the answer lies.
>
> One important element is the fact that men cannot live without some sort of cooperation with others. In any conceivable kind of culture man needs to co-operate with others if he wants to survive, whether for the purpose of defending himself against enemies or dangers of nature, or in order that he may be able to work and produce. Even Robinson Crusoe was accompanied by his man Friday; without him he would probably not only have become insane but would actually have died. Each person experiences this need for the help of others very drastically as a child. On account of the factual inability of the human child to take care of itself with regard to all important functions, communication with others is a matter of life and death for the child. The possibility of being left alone is necessarily the most serious threat to the child's whole existence. (19)

Fromm's choice of example proves his point well. However, in addition to the strong desire to cooperate with others so as to increase one's chances of survival, there is also, he notes, the

---

16 Isolation and loneliness have worsened in the internet age. See Jacqueline Olds and Richard S. Schwartz, *The Lonely American: Drifting Apart in the Twenty-First Century* (Boston: Beacon Press, 2009). On loneliness and Trumpism, see Michelle Goldberg, "Loneliness Is Breaking America," *The New York Times,* July 19, 2021, https://www.nytimes.com/2021/07/19/opinion/trump-covid-extremism-loneliness.html.

use one makes of others and of the natural world to know that one is distinctly oneself: an individual. He calls this "the fact of subjective self-consciousness" (19). But, he adds, the individuation process will likely be accompanied by ambivalent feelings ranging from positive pride ("I *am* somebody," as Jesse Jackson intoned) to negative dread that one is no more than "a particle of dust" (20). Hence man's drive to "relate himself to any system which would give meaning and direction to his life" (20). At the end of chapter 1 Fromm restates the main theme of his book. It is the first of many summaries that prevent the reader from getting lost. Indeed, Fromm uses the attention-getting words "to sum up" five times. This improves his chances of getting through to a mass readership about a vital if somewhat complicated subject: the "ambiguous gift" of freedom.

> Before we proceed, it may be helpful *to sum up* what has been pointed out with regard to our general approach to the problems of social psychology. […] This discussion will always be centered around the main theme of this book: that man, the more he gains freedom in the sense of emerging from the original oneness with man and nature and the more he becomes an "individual," has no choice but *to unite himself with the world in the spontaneity of love and productive work or else to seek a kind of security by such ties with the world as destroy his freedom and the integrity of his individual self.* (20–21, emphasis added)

In chapter 2 Fromm presents his theory of "The Emergence of the Individual and the Ambiguity of Freedom." Basic to his vision is the idea of the "primary ties" with one's parents or other primary caregivers, ties which are gradually severed after the first ten or so years of one's life. Here again Fromm makes use of a literary source, Richard Hughes's *A High Wind in Jamaica* (1932), to make his point about the shock that accompanies the sudden awareness of one's own individuality. This complicated fact is what makes so-called coming of age stories from *The Adventures of Huckleberry Finn* to Anne Frank's diary to Charlie

Brown to *Jojo Rabbit* such perennially popular subject matter across many genres, time periods, and cultural contexts.[17] Fromm was clearly quite taken by Hughes's novel with its focus on a certain Emily, for he quotes extensively from it before zeroing in with italics on the lesson he wants his reader to retain:

[O]ne side of the growing process of individuation is the growth of self-strength. […] The other aspect of the process of individuation is *growing aloneness* […] the child […] becomes aware of being alone, of being an entity separate from all others. (28)

"What's the problem?" someone who has forgotten their 10-year-old self might ask. Fromm has the answer:

This separation from a world, which in comparison with one's own individual existence is overwhelmingly strong and powerful, and often threatening and dangerous, creates a feeling of powerlessness and anxiety. As long as one was an integral part of that world, unaware of the possibilities and responsibilities of individual action, one did not need to be afraid of it. When one has become an individual, one stands alone and faces the world in all its perilous and overpowering aspects. (28–29)

What happens next in the child's life is uncertain and will depend on a variety of factors, among them feelings of vulnerability and anxiety versus security and confidence. Here we can see that Fromm is another liberal who believes in choices. But many choices are harmful coping strategies, or even self-sabotage, while only some provide genuine long-term benefits. The

---

17   While preparing the first draft of this chapter, I had the chance to see both *Jojo Rabbit* (2020) and a more somber coming of age story, *La Cravate* (2019, *The Necktie*), a documentary about the young Bastien Régnier and his work on behalf of France's far-right Front National party up to and including Marine Le Pen's defeat in the 2017 presidential election. These two films would be fascinating to teach back-to-back to older teenagers.

following passage expands on the father-son dynamic Fromm sketched in the previous chapter.

> Impulses arise to give up one's individuality, to overcome the feeling of aloneness and powerlessness by completely submerging oneself in the world outside. These impulses, however, and the new ties arising from them, are not identical with the primary ties which have been cut off in the process of growth itself. Just as a child can never return to the mother's womb physically, so it can never reverse, psychically, the process of individuation. Attempts to do so necessarily assume the character of submission, in which the basic contradiction between the authority and the child who submits to it is never eliminated. Consciously the child may feel secure and satisfied, but unconsciously it realizes that the price it pays is giving up strength and the integrity of its self. Thus the result of submission is the very opposite of what it was to be: submission increases the child's insecurity and at the same time creates hostility and rebelliousness, which is the more frightening since it is directed against the very persons on whom the child has remained — or become — dependent.
>
> However, submission is not the only way of avoiding aloneness and anxiety. The other way, the only one which is productive and does not end in an insoluble conflict, is that of *spontaneous relationship to man and nature,* a relationship that connects the individual with the world without eliminating his individuality. This kind of relationship — the foremost expressions of which are love and productive work — are [sic] rooted in the integration and strength of the total personality and are therefore subject to the very limits that exist for the growth of the self. (29)

To sum up, Fromm claims that there is first a loosening of primary ties — but then what? One cannot climb back into the womb, so other ties to the world are needed if one is to avoid moral aloneness. "Impulses arise" — but which kind? Destructive or productive ones? There is no single answer, but clearly (the feeling of) vulnerability, S, M, L, or XL, will be a factor. The choices made will be either healthy or unhealthy over the long-term, either ultimately destructive of the self (while perhaps initially grasped at for some real or imagined short-term benefit[18]) or genuinely productive of a new, larger self that will be connected by doing and making with people, places, and things in the larger world. One will not become "one with the universe" — that's as impossible while alive as returning to the womb — but instead a unique someone, a conscious artistic agent, operating in the universe.[19] The healthy path is best described late in Fromm's chapter 7, "Freedom and Democracy":

If the individual realizes his self by spontaneous activity and thus relates himself to the world, he ceases to be an isolated atom; he and the world become part of one structuralized whole; he has his rightful place, and thereby his doubt concerning himself and the meaning of life disappears. This doubt sprang from his separateness and from the thwarting of life; when he can live, neither compulsively nor automatically but spontaneously, the doubt disappears. He is aware of himself as an active and creative individual and recognizes that *there is only one meaning of life: the act of living itself.* (261)

But before Fromm gets to this exuberant declaration of the meaning of life, he has to walk the reader through a series of

---

18 In the documentary *La Cravate,* Régnier speaks of having joined a group of skinheads as a teenager because he was both intimidated by them — not knowing what violent acts they had done and were capable of — and reassured by them since, after joining the group, he became confident that he had them as allies, not threats.

19 One may think of William Wordsworth's poem and the force that "rolls through all things" (from "Tintern Abbey," 1798). A complex recent example treating similar themes is Lea Ypi's memoir about growing up in Albania, *Free: Coming of Age at the End of History* (London: Allen Lane, 2021). See also Vincent W.J. van Gerven Oei, "Lea Ypi and the Rehabilitation of Albanian Fascism," *Exit,* July 30, 2022, https://exit.al/en/2022/07/30/lea-ypi-and-the-rehabilitation-of-albanian-fascism/.

regrettable though understandable errors: the Lutheran and Calvinist Reformation movements; the cover-up of capitalism's cruel sorting into winners and losers via rationalizing gestures of Renaissance and Modernist aesthetic ideology and Social Darwinism; the enormously destructive psychology of nazism, an offshoot of colonialist paternalism and condescension regarding "the white man's burden"; and after the war, the sixties-era temptation to lose oneself in the false glories of consumerism, technological utopianism, and other "artificial paradises" (Charles Baudelaire). This 500-year tragedy is told by Fromm in six chapters.

Tragedy here is not a literary flourish, it is the name for the core paradox of grandeur and vulnerability at the heart of human existence, as Fromm sees it. Man's weakness at birth — weaker and more vulnerable than so many other species who fend for themselves much better and earlier — "is the basis from which human development springs; *man's biological weakness is the condition of human culture*" (32). Fromm recalls man's status as *Homo Faber,* the toolmaker.

> He invents tools and, while thus mastering nature, he separates himself from it more and more. He becomes dimly aware of himself — or rather of his group — as not being identical with nature. It dawns upon him that his is a tragic fate: to be part of nature, and yet to transcend it. He becomes aware of death as his ultimate fate even if he tries to deny it in manifold phantasies. (32–33)

Fromm then goes on to retell the story of Adam and Eve in the Garden of Eden. Eating from the tree of knowledge of good and evil is Adam's transgression of God's orders, and thus from the standpoint of the Church, notes Fromm, it is "essentially sin." "From the standpoint of man, however, this is the beginning of human freedom. Acting against God's orders means freeing himself from coercion […] The act of disobedience as an act of freedom is the beginning of reason" (33). Fromm lets the second shoe drop, so to speak, on the next page:

The myth emphasizes the suffering resulting from this act. To transcend nature, to be alienated from nature and from another human being, finds man naked, ashamed. He is alone and free, yet powerless and afraid. The newly won freedom appears as a curse; he is *free* from the sweet bondage of paradise, but he is not free to govern himself, to realize his individuality. (34)

The problem is that "'Freedom from' is not identical with positive freedom, with 'freedom to'" (34). Fromm calls this non-identity a "lag" and later a "disproportion." It is this lag or gap that provides the opening for the charismatic fascist leader and all other sirens of far-right populism:

Primary bonds once severed cannot be mended; once paradise is lost, man cannot return to it. There is only one possible, productive solution for the relationship of individualized man with the world: his active solidarity with all men and his spontaneous activity, love and work, which unite him again with the world, not by primary ties but as a free and independent individual.

However, if the economic, social and political conditions on which the whole process of human individuation depends, do not offer a basis for the realization of individuality in the sense just mentioned, while at the same time people have lost those ties which gave them security, this lag makes freedom an unbearable burden. It then becomes identical with doubt, with a kind of life which lacks meaning and direction. *Powerful tendencies arise to escape from this kind of freedom into submission* or some kind of relationship to man and the world which promises relief from uncertainty, even if it deprives the individual of his freedom. (35, emphasis added)

The lag represents in fact a double danger, Fromm will insist on the following page, since it opens not only the possibility of "panicky flight from freedom" but also of "complete indifference" (36); in other words, on the one hand über-engagement and on the other total disengagement, abstention, passivity, slow effacement to the point of suicide (today's "deaths of despair"[20]).

> European and American history since the end of the Middle Ages is the history of the full emergence of the individual. It is a process which started in Italy, in the Renaissance, and which only now seems to have come to a climax. It took over four hundred years to break down the medieval world and to free people from the most apparent restraints. But while in many respects the individual has grown, has developed mentally and emotionally, and participates in cultural achievements in a degree unheard-of before, the lag between "freedom from" and "freedom to" has grown too. The result of this disproportion between freedom from any tie and the lack of possibilities for the positive realization of freedom and individuality has led, in Europe, to a panicky flight from freedom into new ties or at least into complete indifference. (36)

Once Fromm has completed his story of "The Emergence of the Individual and The Ambiguity of Freedom," the next four chapters are fairly straightforward and hardly need to be quoted from at length, as we have done so far, because they provide a chronological account of the by now familiar bullying and predatory behavior of mostly white, Christian, and male leaders and organizations. These are individuals and groups who have exploited the vulnerability of the weak and cowed them into thinking they, the leaders, are serving the greater good, or even doing God's will. But whatever the sincerity, high or low, of their stated intentions, they are most certainly consolidating their personal hold on power and laying up for themselves treasures upon earth.[21] His concluding chapter 7, "Freedom and Democ-

---

20 Anne Case and Angus Deaton, *Deaths of Despair and the Future of Capitalism* (Princeton: Princeton University Press, 2020). Fromm's argument allows one to see the US opioid epidemic, late capitalism, and Trumpism as interrelated facts.

21 On earthly versus heavenly treasure, see Matthew 6:19–20.

racy" constitutes Fromm's guardedly optimistic conclusion in which he hopes for a pivot from other-directed infantilizing authoritarianism to self-directed adult democracy, and yet the last paragraph is punctuated by a series of "only if" statements that underscore how hard the road may be.

Chapter 3, "Freedom in the Age of the Reformation," begins by sketching the stable, pre-individualistic Medieval world where man's leading preoccupation was salvation not status; and childhood primary ties could extend across one's whole life because individuation of children from parents then was hardly what it would later become. The idea is that humans were more like squirrels or other animal or plant species back then — "a rose is a rose is a rose." The fact that many people were named after their occupation (e.g., Baker, Cooper, Miller) speaks to the more limited individuality in premodern times of all but those at court and in the higher clergy. In other words, it was a markedly different social set up compared to the more individualized world of *David Copperfield, Madame Bovary,* or *I, Tonya.* The late Middle Ages and Renaissance see the emergence of capitalism and with it a more diversified society of distinct social classes. The lower classes were mostly still an anonymous mass of peasants but among the upper middle and higher classes there were individuals. The portraits of self-aware merchants and makers painted by Lucas Cranach (1472–1553) can serve as an emblem of this breaking away of very important people from the struggling middle classes and peasant masses. Those portraits are also emblems of what Fromm considers to have been the distinctive change in human psychology that coincides with capitalism's more wide-open competition: namely the emergence of anxiety about one's social standing and consequently man's "passionate craving for fame" — in other words, status or "good standing" or what Thorstein Veblen called "a race for reputability."[22] The race intensifies when capitalists, who are now

---

22 Thorstein Veblen, *The Theory of the Leisure Class* (New York: Modern Library, 2001), 25. See, more generally, chapter 2 "Pecuniary Emulation" and chapter 6 "Pecuniary Canons of Taste." In *The Broken Ladder: How In-*

making money effortlessly from investments, attempt to lord it over those still only making money from selling their labor. It's an endless competition that leads to endless anxiety and with it the intensification of the related emotions of fear, envy, anger, and resentment.

We have reasons to doubt whether the powerful masters of Renaissance capitalism were as happy and as secure as they are often pictured. It seems that the new freedom brought two things to them: an increased feeling of strength and at the same time an increased isolation, doubt, skepticism, and — resulting from all these — anxiety. It is the same contradiction that we find in the philosophic writings of the humanists. Side by side with their emphasis on human dignity, individuality, and strength, they exhibited insecurity and despair in their philosophy.

This underlying insecurity resulting from the position of an isolated individual in a hostile world tends to explain the genesis of a character trait which was, as Burckhardt has pointed out, characteristic of the individual of the Renaissance and not present, at least in the same intensity, in the member of the medieval social structure: his passionate craving for fame. If the meaning of life has become doubtful, if one's relations to others and to oneself do not offer security, then fame is one means to silence one's doubts. It has a function to be compared with that of the Egyptian pyramids or the Christian faith in immortality: it elevates one's individual life from its limitations and instability to the plane of indestructibility; if one's name is known to one's contemporaries and if one can hope that it will last for centuries, then one's

---

equality Affects the Way We Think, Live, and Die (New York: Viking, 2017), the focus of my Chapter 10, Keith Payne discusses why we "crave status" and the unhealthy consequences of those cravings in a regime of extreme inequality. See also the harm of envy examined in Martha Nussbaum's *The Monarchy of Fear: A Philosopher Looks at Our Political Crisis* (New York: Simon & Schuster, 2018), ch. 9.

life has meaning and significance by this very reflection of it in the judgments of others. (48–49)

The above passage nicely dovetails with Tocqueville's explanation of "Why Americans are so Restless in the Midst of Their Prosperity."[23] This is one of the many chapters in *Democracy in America* that offer independent confirmation of what Fromm says about the paradox of "individualism," a term coined by Tocqueville some say, and the ambiguity of freedom for modern individualized man: the liberating *freedom from* versus the burdensome, when not actionable, *freedom to*. For the upper middle and higher classes there is hustling and striving with enough victories that one may even aspire to be remembered after death for one's achievements — perhaps with one's name on a school, bridge, street, library, hospital, bank, or book. But what about everyone else?

It is obvious that this solution of individual insecurity was only possible for a social group whose members possessed the actual means of gaining fame. It was not a solution which was possible for the powerless masses in that same culture nor one which we shall find in the urban middle class that was the backbone of the Reformation. (49)

For all the working stiffs, Fromm explains for the remainder of the chapter, there is the consoling Reformation ideology of Martin Luther (1483–1546) and John Calvin (1509–64).[24]

Luther and Calvin's doctrines have two distinct sides, Fromm writes, and understandably the more positive side, as seen from the winner's circle, has been stressed in countries where protes-

---

23 Alexis de Tocqueville, *Democracy in America; and, Two Essays on America*, trans. Gerald Bevan (London: Penguin Books, 2003), vol. II, part 2, ch. 2, xiii.

24 And of a third figure, Théodore de Bèze (1519–1605), a Frenchman who became Calvin's right-hand man in Geneva and who over a long career energetically extended Calvinist teachings across Europe and the British Isles.

tantism has been influential and praised; namely the idea that the Reformation breaks up the Roman Catholic Church's monopolistic authority, distributes power over religious matters to worthy individuals, inculcates personal responsibility, and teaches the notion of salvation through faith. But *faith*, precisely, is the troublesome notion, Fromm argues, because "Psychologically, faith has two entirely different meanings":

> It can be the expression of an inner relatedness to mankind and affirmation of life; or it can be a reaction formation against a fundamental feeling of doubt, rooted in the isolation of the individual and his negative attitude towards life. Luther's faith had that compensatory quality.
>
> It is particularly important to understand the significance of doubt and the attempts to silence it, because this is not only a problem concerning Luther's and, as we shall see soon, Calvin's theology, but it has remained one of the basic problems of modern man. (78)

The first kind of faith — call it the "free to be" belief in one's self, one's abilities, and one's relatedness to the world — is entirely healthy and receives Fromm's ringing endorsement many times.[25] However the second faith is, he says, a "reaction formation," in other words "a defense mechanism in which emotions and impulses which are anxiety-producing or perceived to be unacceptable are mastered by exaggeration of the directly opposing tendency."[26] Faith as a reaction formation, then, would be an *escape from freedom* into submission and service to an external or internal authority. These two meanings of faith allow a protestant leader to send different messages to different groups. Affirmative "Yes, we can" messages are sent to the upwardly mo-

---

25 This faith in self-worth and agency is repeated several times as a person's "realization of his individual self; that is, the expression of his intellectual, emotional, and sensuous potentialities." Fromm, *Escape from Freedom*, x.

26 Quoted from *Wikipedia*, s.v. "reaction formation," https://en.wikipedia.org/wiki/Reaction_formation.

bile strivers.[27] Consoling "when the saints go marching in" messages — sometimes called "the opium of the people" — are sent to wage slaves, actual enslaved people, and lower-middle-class workers anxious about losing out as winner-take-all capitalism becomes more omnipotent and omnipresent. Protestantism's mass appeal rested on the latter messaging that consoled the Many for their lack of economic, political, or social freedom. In other words, in exchange for low fulfillment of the basic human needs for power, agency, love, belonging, and fun in "this world of trouble," protestantism extended *hope* in a bountiful, future Promised Land that one reaches by "crossing over Jordan" — "And when you reach the other side, you shall be free."[28]

Since Fromm's book is devoted mainly to explaining how freedom can be perceived by the weak and vulnerable as scary and dangerous rather than a cheerful creative enterprise, he focuses primarily on the aggravating mischief, to put it lightly, that Luther and Calvin's fear-mongering lessons have caused by constantly insisting on man's innate wickedness, his depravity, his predestination as damned or saved, and how good works are of no avail in his salvation. Fromm claims that Lutherans and the many protestant denominations influenced by the theological orientation of Calvinism deny fundamental human equality and thereby nullify any basis for solidarity beyond a tribal level.[29] As such, they give rise to "differentialist" societies, to borrow the vocabulary of the French demographer Emmanuel Todd, where rankings and racism are basic defining features of the system when one believes that all men are created unequal,

---

27 The allusion is to the campaign slogan of President Barack Obama, author of the memoir, *A Promised Land* (New York: Crown, 2020).

28 For a recording with lyrics of "Crossing over Jordan — Redeemed Quartet," *ZionLyrics,* https://zionlyrics.com/redeemed-quartet-crossing-over-jordan-lyrics.

29 See Fromm, *Escape from Freedom*, 89: "Calvin's theory of predestination has one implication[, …] the principle of the basic inequality of men[, …] the equality of mankind is denied in principle. Men are created unequal. This principle implies also that there is no solidarity between men, since the one factor which is the strongest basis for human solidarity is denied: the equality of man's fate."

not bugs or aberrations in that system. In such societies, vertically organized authoritarianism is natural and egalitarian democracy is suspect.[30] While lip-service may be paid to freedom, and actually exercised by a powerful Few, what really matters in protestant-dominant areas is unswerving submission to God, country, company, or all three. Similarly, under protestantism, "Love thy neighbor" gets downgraded to "love thy neighbor who resembles you" — when it's not "beat out your neighbor" or "beat up your neighbor." "We are all in this together" is not what Calvinists believe. With basic equality out the window, one has an easy rationalization of "tough love," overt tribalism, "crusades," and unrestrained cruelty.

Given the more or less direct line Fromm traces from Luther and Calvin to Hitler,[31] it's a wonder how the book ever sold five million copies, and hardly surprising that sales and attention have fallen off in the post-1960s, protestantism-fueled era of "greed is good" and "fear of falling" in a broken American society

---

30 See Katherine Stewart, *The Power Worshippers: Inside the Dangerous Rise of Religious Nationalism* (New York: Bloomsbury, 2020). Stewart summarizes her argument in this editorial, "Trump or No Trump, Religious Authoritarianism Is Here to Stay," *The New York Times,* November 16, 2020, https://www.nytimes.com/2020/11/16/opinion/trump-religion-authoritarianism.html, and repeats it one year after the Capitol riot, "Christian Nationalism Is One of Trump's Most Powerful Weapons," *The New York Times,* January 6, 2022, https://www.nytimes.com/2022/01/06/opinion/jan-6-christian-nationalism.html. Stewart's argument would be strengthened by citing Fromm or some other authority to underscore the rejection by Christian nationalists of the American civil religion's founding precept that "all men are created equal."

31 Fromm sees "moral indignation" — a combination of hostility, resentment, and envy — as "characteristic for the lower middle class from Luther's time to Hitler's," Fromm, *Escape from Freedom,* 96. Fromm's lineage claim receives further confirmation from Paxton's observations, acknowledged by others since, that Hitler was inspired by the American Protestant-inspired hate group, the Ku Klux Klan. See James Q. Whitman, *Hitler's American Model: The United States and the Making of Nazi Race Law* (Princeton: Princeton University Press, 2017). "Moral indignation" is clearly a main ingredient in the "emotional lava" of fascism as described in bullet points by Paxton in his introduction and conclusion.

of extreme inequality.[32] It's easy to see how Fromm's calm denunciation of these two founding protestant leaders as prime examples of the "authoritarian character"[33] — plagued by self-hatred, adoration of the powerful, and contempt for the weak[34] — would be a turnoff for both Goldwater–Reagan–Bush–Trump Republicans *and* for centrist Democrats. Both camps tend to only recognize the character-building, "bootstrap"-pulling dimension; in other words, the ultimately comforting and consoling side of their brand of Christianity.[35] They overlook its crazy-making dimension that pits the middle classes against each other and

---

32 I am referring to Gordon Gekko's speech as delivered by Michael Douglas in the movie *Wall Street* (1987) and to the Barbara Ehrenreich book *Fear of Falling: The Inner Life of the Middle Class* (New York: Pantheon, 1989) — two classics from the later Reagan years by which time individualistic protestant striving had reasserted itself after shoving aside the push for universalism, egalitarianism, and collaborative striving that characterized one side of "the sixties." On America's "broken" society, see Frank Rich, "In 2008, America Stopped Believing in the American Dream," *New York Magazine,* August 5, 2018, https://medium.com/new-york-magazine/in-2008-america-stopped-believing-in-the-american-dream-2d493c7ae7f3.

33 The authoritarian character was also later studied by Fromm's Frankfurt School colleague Theodor Adorno, *The Authoritarian Personality* (London: Verso, 2019). On Luther's "authoritarian character," see "Luther as a person was a typical representative of the 'authoritarian character'," (ibid., 66) and "This simultaneous love for authority and hatred against those who are powerless are typical traits of the 'authoritarian character'" (83). Fromm's discussion of this notion is expanded in ch. 5, "Mechanisms of Escape," and is the central concern of Fromm's chapter 6, "Psychology of Nazism." See also the research of Karen Stenner, *The Authoritarian Dynamic* (Cambridge: Cambridge University Press, 2005).

34 Fromm, *Escape from Freedom,* 95: "Luther and Calvin portray this all-pervading hostility. Not only in the sense that these two men, personally, belonged to the ranks of the greatest haters among leading figures of history, certainly among religious leaders; but which is more important, in the sense that their doctrines were colored by this hostility and could only appeal to a group itself driven by an intense, repressed hostility."

35 While I was drafting this chapter, Jon Meacham plugged his new book, *The Hope of Glory: Reflections on the Last Words of Jesus from the Cross* (New York: Convergent Books, 2020), with the editorial, "Why Religion Is the Best Hope against Trump," *The New York Times,* February 25, 2020, https://www.nytimes.com/2020/02/25/opinion/christianity-trump.html. The editorial's subtitle testifies to the author's faith in faith: "Evangelicals

pushes them toward becoming their own slave-drivers; in other words, hyper-organized, multi-tasking, time-conscious, anger-repressing workaholics constantly looking over their shoulder and at their neighbor's driveway — all to please an Angry God or twisted "conscience," or to serve some other fetishized idea such as Nation or Excellence or Competitiveness or Productivity or Growth.

Fromm's point is that the Reformation ideology responds to the needs of the vulnerable and largely powerless masses who end up anxiously struggling in the rough-and-tumble capitalism game that replaces the more tranquil, medieval social order. However, it responds to those needs in ways that generally worsen their problems — on account of the *freedom to* being denied or deferred, and because the unavowable hostility about that denial of self-realization then gets repressed, acted out, or taken out on bystanders such as spouses, children, or other defenseless subordinates (people of color, queers, immigrants, Jews, Muslims, or other scapegoats). The sad truth, if one accepts Fromm's account, is that Luther and Calvin are con artists who, with extraordinary powers of suggestion over the weak and isolated, get their marks to surrender willingly to structures of what we now refer to as *codependency,* a theory first developed by one of Fromm's colleagues, Karen Horney, also in the early 1940s.[36] Correspondingly, among the lucky and well-off and the ever-anxious middle class, Luther and Calvin's protestantism becomes a rationale and fertilizer for hate groups and racist moralizers who camouflage their sadism and mean-spiritedness under nostrums about "self-sufficiency," "personal responsibility," and "character building" so as to have a good conscience while blocking the vulnerable from becoming a "public charge"

---

may support an amoral president. But faith can still offer hope for liberation and progress."

36 See Susan Quinn, A *Mind of Her Own: The Life of Karen Horney* (New York: Da Capo, 1988). For a summary of codependency, see Linda Exposito, "6 Signs of a Co-dependent Relationship," *Psychology Today,* September 19, 2016, https://www.psychologytoday.com/us/blog/anxiety-zen/201609/6-signs-codependent-relationship.

instead of helping them become less vulnerable and dependent.[37] Fromm uses the terms sadism and masochism to analyze the narcissist-codependent "symbiosis" (157). The malignancies of those exploitive relationships become the focus of the next two chapters, "The Two Aspects of Freedom for Modern Man" and "Mechanisms of Escape" after which Fromm conducts his most detailed case study of the authoritarian character in chapter 6, "Psychology of Nazism."

In the chapter devoted to modern man, Fromm demonstrates the consequences on the social order of the psychological changes brought about by the Protestant Reformation which itself resulted from a changed social order when Western society passes out of the relatively stable medieval world into the hubbub of competitive capitalism. This is consistent with Fromm's circular view of circumstances making a new man, and then new men making new circumstances — another important similarity he has with Tocqueville who often observed that growing equality was the generating fact (*le fait mère*) that allowed for democratic institutions, and then those institutions shape a new democratic man whose new mores (*mœurs*) make him markedly different from men who had grown up in aristocratically organized lands. The biggest difference is the development and aftereffects of individualism. Tocqueville noted its development as well as many of its contradictory side-effects, including the mind-scrambling role played by envy, for example, that could lead democratic voters to select mediocre leaders.[38] However Fromm, as one would expect given his training and years of experience in individual and social psychology, has a more detailed account of this tension. For Fromm, individualism expands for the next 400 years after the Reformation. As modern

---

37 This blocking tactic became evident in the early weeks of the spread of Covid-19 in the US. See, the Editorial, unsigned, "With Coronavirus, 'Health Care for Some' Is a Recipe for Disaster," *The New York Times*, March 6, 2020, https://www.nytimes.com/2020/03/06/opinion/coronavirus-immigrants-health.html.

38 Envy will be discussed further in Chapter 9, devoted to Nussbaum's *The Monarchy of Fear*.

individual man emerges, his individualism may be the happy expression of one's "intellectual, emotional, and sensuous potentialities" in either personal projects or collective efforts, such as within trade unions. However, there is very often, though not always, an unhealthy reaction-formation consequent to the *thwarting* (a favorite Fromm word) of those potentialities. A further complication is that this opposing force may come from the *outside* — from an individual, group, or "the market" — or from the *inside* via the individual's self-surrender, and it may be difficult to tell which is which. The upshot is the divided character of modern man which results from these "two aspects of freedom":

> [T]he structure of modern society affects man in two ways simultaneously: he becomes more independent, self-reliant, and critical, and he becomes more isolated, alone, and afraid. The understanding of the whole problem of freedom depends on the very ability to see both sides of the process and not to lose track of one side while following the other. (104)

In the "Two Aspects" chapter, Fromm is adamantly not opposed to capitalism as such. He simply points out, like so many observers before and since, that its great contribution to freeing man from "traditional bonds" of mostly a material kind lead in turn to emotional complications for the vast majority of individuals; namely, unbearable feelings of insignificance and powerlessness as well as barely contained anger against liberals (in the British sense) and libertarians who dare crow that man is "free to choose."[39] Fromm's account of how modern man becomes "a

---

39 It is noteworthy that Milton Friedman's influential "personal statement," *Free to Choose,* was published the year Fromm died, 1980. For an account of what became a sort of bible in the Reagan era and the neoconservative movement of the past forty years, see Elton Rayack, *Not So Free to Choose: The Political Economy of Milton Friedman and Ronald Reagan* (New York: Praeger, 1987). See also Paul Krugman's classic counter-manifesto (in reply to the arch conservative Barry Goldwater), *The Conscience of a Liberal: Reclaiming America from the Right* (New York: W.W. Norton & Co., 2007).

cog in the vast economic machine" (110) will be familiar to older readers who grew up watching *The Jetsons* and who have experienced modern "alienation" first hand. But it is worth rereading by younger generations as they prepare to sell themselves in the labor market as *employees* under the direction of an *employer*:

Modern man's feeling of isolation and powerlessness is increased still further by the character which all his human relationships have assumed. The concrete relationship of one individual to another has lost its direct and human character and has assumed a spirit of manipulation and instrumentality. In all social and personal relations, the laws of the market are the rule. It is obvious that the relationship between competitors has to be based on mutual human indifference. [...]
The relationship between employer and employee is permeated by the same spirit of indifference. The word "employer" contains the whole story: the owner of capital employs another human being as he "employs" a machine. They both use each other for the pursuit of their economic interests; their relationship is one in which both are means to an end, both are instrumental to each other. It is not a relationship of two human beings who have any interest in the other outside of this mutual usefulness. The same instrumentality is the rule in the relationship between the businessman and his customer. The customer is an object to be manipulated, not a concrete person whose aims the businessman is interested to satisfy. The attitude towards work has the quality of instrumentality; in contrast to a medieval artisan the modern man-

---

For an assessment of the Friedman doctrine written in the middle of the 2008 mortgage crisis, see Peter S. Goodman, "A Fresh Look at the Apostle of Free Markets," *The New York Times,* April 13, 2008, https://www.nytimes.com/2008/04/13/weekinreview/13goodman.html. For a backward glance during the Covid-19 pandemic, see Andrew Ross Sorkin, "A Free Market Manifesto That Changed the World, Reconsidered," *The New York Times,* September 11, 2020, https://www.nytimes.com/2020/09/11/business/dealbook/milton-friedman-doctrine-social-responsibility-of-business.html.

ufacturer is not primarily interested in what he produces; he produces essentially in order to make a profit from his capital investment, and what he produces depends essentially on the market which promises that the investment of capital in a certain branch will prove to be profitable.

Not only the economic, but also the personal relations between men have this character of alienation; instead of relations between human beings, they assume the character of relations between things. But perhaps the most important and the most devastating instance of this spirit of instrumentality and alienation is the individual's relationship to his own self. Man does not only sell commodities, he sells himself and feels himself to be a commodity. (118–19)

Those three paragraphs are enough to give the reader the flavor of the bleak picture Fromm paints of modern man's predicament in a capitalist system of cogs greased by protestantism. In the remaining pages he multiplies the examples from everyday life but also from the canons of philosophy (Søren Kierkegaard), literature (the journals of Julian Green and Franz Kafka's *The Castle*), and popular escapist entertainment such as the chase narratives of Mickey Mouse cartoons. All depict a helpless individual, "torn and tormented by doubts," facing powerful, hostile enemies with little chance of overcoming the gap between *freedom from* and *freedom to*. In the era of Big Tech, sometimes personified as GAFAM (Google, Apple, Facebook, Amazon, Microsoft), these pages do not seem to have aged, and may even startle contemporary readers with their up-to-date diagnosis.[40] The founders of famous internet companies may have taken inspiration in their teenage years from the 1960s incitement to create and innovate and be their own person — Steve Jobs turned thirteen in 1968 — and yet the second generation of their

---

40 See David Leonhardt, "The Monopolization of America," *The New York Times,* November 25, 2018, https://www.nytimes.com/2018/11/25/opinion/monopolies-in-the-us.html, in which he references the arguments of Tim Wu in *The Curse of Bigness: Antitrust in the New Gilded Age* (New York: Columbia Global Reports, 2018).

inventions has largely freighted everyone else with the problems of gigantism and alienation that their originators were trying to escape from. The irony that those who developed addictive technologies kept their inventions away from their own children is the opening hook in the captivating story Adam Alter tells in *Irresistible: The Rise of Addictive Technology and the Business of Keeping Us Hooked.*[41] But irony-awareness, like 1960s-era consciousness raising, is only a first step in problem-solving, and a lot easier than actually forging programs that durably reduce addiction. The takeaway from this chapter is Fromm's insistence that understanding fascism and the automatizing of man in modern democracies requires paying attention to both psychological mechanisms and social and cultural conditions. This approach is quite different from Paxton's *Anatomy of Fascism,* which favors body over spirit. After acknowledging the importance of choices and the existence of "emotional lava," Paxton mostly ignores the unconscious with its half-mysterious, half-knowable drives, rationalizations, projections, compulsions, obsessions, and transfers — not Fromm.

The "Mechanisms of Escape" chapter is Fromm's effort to make the unconscious strategies to *escape from freedom* comprehensible to the general reader who has no background in psychology or psychoanalysis. This chapter is the crux of the whole book and it either flies or flops based on how persuasive one finds its claims, reasons, and evidence. Even though its arguments would be familiar to anyone who has read a book on narcissism[42] or browsed the website of *Psychology Today,* it still makes for instructive and engaging reading here in the

---

41 Adam Alter, *Irresistible: The Rise of Addictive Technology and the Business of Keeping Us Hooked* (New York: Penguin Books, 2017).

42 For example, Stephanie Donaldson-Pressman and Robert M. Pressman, *The Narcissistic Family: Diagnosis and Treatment* (San Francisco: Jossey-Bass, 1994); Patrick J. Carnes, *The Betrayal Bond: Breaking Free of Exploitive Relationships* (Deerfield Beach: Health Communications, 1997); E.D. Payson, *The Wizard of Oz and Other Narcissists: Coping with the One-Way Relationship in Work, Love, and Family* (Royal Oak: Julian Day, 2009); and Albert J. Bernstein, *Emotional Vampires: Dealing with People Who Drain You Dry* (New York: McGraw Hill, 2012).

internet age because the mechanisms described in its seventy pages — Authoritarianism, Destructiveness, and Automaton Conformity — seem not to have changed, nor have the major culprits. The bully-sadist is still the opportunist who has a feral sixth sense to detect the susceptibility for masochism in his victim because he himself is, like the masochist, insecure, weak, and self-hating.[43] In a prime example of the adage "it takes one to know one," the narcissist, often a bully, also knows who to recruit as their Echo because they were once the needy Echo coerced to "love" a self-absorbed, domineering parent, boss, or other authority figure at an earlier point in time.[44] Inversely, the masochist, vulnerable and alone, is primed and ready to submit and serve the one playing the sadist because the masochist shares the defining feature of the authoritarian character: fear of freedom and a misguided belief that their needs will be served, rather than crushed, by the Führer they have enabled to gain power — mistakenly believing that the Führer loves his followers when actually he can barely hide his contempt for such weaklings and losers. "Bait and switch" is the favorite technique of the sadist to first bond the masochist and then disappoint, over and over, such that both parties cement in place their shared love of "fate," the past, and eternity thinking — "it was ever thus" — and seamlessly rationalize their willingness to submit to TINA think-

---

43 "Millions are impressed by the victories of power and take it for a sign of strength. [...] But in a psychological sense, the lust for power is not rooted in strength, but in weakness. It is the expression of the inability of the individual self to stand alone and live. It is the desperate attempt to gain secondary strength where genuine strength is lacking." Fromm, *Escape from Freedom*, 160.

44 Fromm explains well the narcissist's domination as counterfeit love. Describing the narcissist's relation to the codependent twin, he writes, "He bribes them with material things, with praise, assurances of love, the display of wit and brilliance, or by showing concern. He may give them everything — everything except one thing: the right to be free and independent." Ibid., 145.

ing: "there is no alternative."[45] The latter is also the tragic mind-set of the battered woman who remains with her tormentor.

The three mechanisms of *Escape from Freedom* correspond to three types of authority — external, internal, and anony-mous — that sway the individual in modern society to varying degrees. External authority is most evident in the behavior of the authoritarian character which manifests itself in the sym-biotic, codependent relationship between sadist and masochist. This codependency is the transposition to the world of psychol-ogy of the master-slave allegory familiar to readers of Hegel's philosophy. The mostly unconscious goal of both sides is "to fuse one's self with somebody or something outside of oneself in order to acquire the strength which the individual self is lack-ing" (140). The masochist, feeling himself weak and alone, sub-mits to the authority and protection of the sadist, and the sadist "needs the person over whom he rules, he needs him very badly, since his own feeling of strength is rooted in the fact that he is the master over someone. This dependence may be entirely unconscious" (144). Regrettably his strength does not derive from self-confident feelings about his own abilities and agency. Fromm underscores the typical *illusion* of both love and power in these relations.[46] In fact, says Fromm, the love is phony since the relations are not based on mutual respect and equality, but on asymmetrical power relations; and the power is also phony since the sadist is actually terrified of his impotence — his fear that he's unable to create or make — for which his domination over another (a substitute maker and doer who will carry out his orders) is the flawed solution: "Power, in the sense of domi-nation, is the perversion of potency, just as sexual sadism is the

---

45 See *Wikipedia,* s.v. "There is no alternative," https://fr.wikipedia.org/wiki/There_is_no_alternative. The French *Wikipedia* entry is more informative than the English version because it discusses the expression's afterlife in France and elsewhere. See also Mark Fisher, *Capitalist Realism: Is There No Alternative?* (Hants: Zero Books, 2009).

46 See Patrick J. Carnes, *Don't Call It Love: Recovery from Sexual Addiction* (New York: Bantam, 1991) and his more broadly encompassing study, *The Betrayal Bond.*

perversion of sexual love" (161). In other words, the so-called love is really *power over*; and the power is really a mask or substitute for powerlessness, an acting out of a real or perceived lack of *power to*. In the age of predators such as Donald Trump, Harvey Weinstein, and Jeffrey Epstein this all may seem completely obvious, but it has the merit of being clearly stated by Fromm in 1941, many decades before the Hollywood Access tape and #MeToo — and it stands a chance of being impactful for younger readers with 20–20 hindsight.

As so often with explanations that affirm the existence of unconscious motivations and compulsions, those who are most in need of reading such accounts are precisely the ones least likely to do so. Furthermore, that resistance and denialism can receive intellectual cover from exclusively rational-minded figures such as the doctor and therapist Alfred Adler (whom Fromm politely criticizes in the "Mechanisms" chapter, 148–49), the philosopher Karl Popper who called out the unfalsifiable dimension of the theory of the unconscious, and the historian Paxton who is manifestly unwilling to follow Fromm, for whom "Nazism is a psychological problem." Fromm's whole argument is based on a *cause-to-effect-to-cause* filiation that he first states in the introduction, repeats in the "Freedom in the Age of the Reformation" chapter, and again in the "Psychology of Nazism" chapter that we cite here:

In our opinion none of these explanations [the same ones Paxton decries: the myth of the all-powerful dictator, the myth of a flawed national character] which emphasize political and economic factors to the exclusion of psychological ones — or vice versa — is correct. Nazism is a psychological problem, but the psychological factors themselves have to be understood as being molded by socio-economic factors; Nazism is an economic and political problem, but the hold it has over a whole people has to be understood on psychological grounds. What we are concerned with in this chapter [six] is this psychological aspect of Nazism, its human basis. This suggests two problems: the character structure of those

people to whom it appealed, and the psychological characteristics of the ideology that made it such an effective instrument with regard to those very people. (206)

The authoritarian character receives fuller treatment in chapter 6 and was already the longest of the three sections in the
"Mechanisms of Escape" chapter. But this is completely understandable when one recalls that Fromm's book was written in
urgency at the start of World War II and published in March
1941. In comparison, the sections on destructiveness and automaton conformity may seem to be of secondary importance;
but that would be a mistaken interpretation, resulting perhaps
from forgetting that points can only be made sequentially and
never all at once. All three mechanisms are related to the same
inability to overcome the "lag" between *freedom from* and *freedom to,* and consequently to the unhealthy tendency to replace
primary ties with secondary ties that aggravate rather than solve
the problem of one's fear of freedom — one's fear of being, yes, a
free individual person.

Those in the 1930s, '40s, '60s, or now who may think they are
very advanced and sufficiently wised up — and would therefore
never be swayed by an external authority ostentatiously deploy-
ing or recycling the fascist decor and repeating white supremacist clichés that date from nineteenth-century colonialism and
KKK *revanchisme* — may still pause over Fromm's descriptions
of internal and anonymous authority in the second and third
sections of chapter 5. There Fromm evokes more subtle mechanisms which infiltrate the unconscious and may disrupt one's
confidence that one is really acting as oneself instead of obeying
a script or suggestions. Here Fromm's earlier discussion of the
Reformist ideology is useful for explaining how in a first phase
modern man is led to give orders to himself via the notions of
"conscience" and "duty"; and then how those internal authorities eventually yield to the still subtler anonymous authority
of "common sense, science, psychic health, normality, public
opinion" (166). This yielding, called *Gleichschaltung* in the Nazi
context, is on display in Donald Trump's hypnotic tagline "a lot

of people are saying."[47] Fromm's pages about internal and anonymous authority contain plausible explanations of "burnout" and "deaths of despair."[48] They also affirm modern man's general reluctance to acknowledge the "manufactured" quality of what

---

47 Russell Muirhead and Nancy L. Rosenblum, *A Lot of People Are Saying: The New Conspiricism and the Assault on Democracy* (Princeton: Princeton University Press, 2020). Commentators of Donald Trump's language have noticed his frequent tendency to lead or follow with "A lot of people are saying," "I've heard people say," "that's what people say" — all formulas that worm their way into becoming his followers' anonymous authority while practically erasing all trace of their provenance from the hypnotic-like power of "Agent Orange." Trump's mastery of Twitter and other brief performative speech acts is recognized by both his admirers and opponents. For an insightful early rhetorical analysis of candidate Trump by the film critic and fellow New Yorker David Denby, see "The Plot against America: Donald Trump's Rhetoric," *The New Yorker,* December 15, 2015, https://www.newyorker.com/culture/cultural-comment/plot-america-donald-trumps-rhetoric. Denby asks, "Is he a Fascist?" — capital F — and answers, "Whether we call him a Fascist or a right-wing demagogue, Trump's acts and words remain the same. It makes sense that, in America, an insurgent movement would grow out of the media and entertainment, that it would issue from enormous prior celebrity, and not from an obscure rural corner, the world of militias and white nationalists." Denby says Roth's *The Plot against America* is "worth another reading." The same could be said of Denby's pieces on Trump's rhetoric. A second Denby piece on Trump's "anti-rhetoric," "The Three Faces of Trump," appears in the August 12, 2015 issue of the magazine, https://www.newyorker.com/culture/cultural-comment/the-three-faces-of-trump. Denby's insights are consistent with Fromm's analysis of the insidious charm of the authoritarian personality: "Yet Mussolini and Trump share something: They appeal to an appreciation, even love, of overwhelming ego strength and extreme machismo, however crass in expression — in fact, the crasser and more preposterous the better (shame doesn't exist for some public men). Those who are drawn to such strength nestle under it." The relationship Denby describes so well with that "nestle under it" image is what Fromm calls *symbiosis* (Fromm, *Escape from Freedom,* 157) and others *codependency.*

48 The economists Anne Case and Angus Deaton have studied "deaths of despair." For a summary, see David Leonhardt and Stuart A. Thompson, "How Working-Class Life Is Killing Americans, in Charts," *The New York Times,* March 6, 2020, https://www.nytimes.com/interactive/2020/03/06/opinion/working-class-death-rate.html, and also Jonathan Malesic, "How Men Burn Out," *The New York Times,* January 4, 2022, https://www.nytimes.com/2022/01/04/opinion/burnout-men-signs.html.

he prefers to believe is "fate" and the eternal "order of things."[49] Therefore these pages will likely resonate with those familiar with Edward S. Herman and Noam Chomsky's *Manufacturing Consent*[50] or with any treatise on the techniques of modern advertising or propaganda.[51] The questions Fromm raises here are nicely summarized in the title of Sheldon S. Wolin's last major publication, *Democracy Inc.: Managed Democracy and The Specter of Inverted Totalitarianism.*[52] Wolin's argument in this post-Bush, pre-Trump warning, published at the dawn of the supposedly liberal, enlightened, and progressive Obama years, echoes Fromm's concerns about Automaton Conformity and the emergence of an essentially fake, hollow, or zombie democracy, the very sort that Tocqueville described in one of the final chapters of *Democracy in America* as a distinct possibility.

A reader sympathetic or at least open to Fromm's dual approach, which pays attention to both outer historical events and inner psychological predispositions and tendencies, will find the chapter "Psychology of Nazism" a compelling account of German fascism that actually coheres with Paxton's five-stages model and the latter's insistence on the importance of human choices, including the choice to believe that choice does not ex-

---

49 On the seductiveness of fate, see Fromm, *Escape from Freedom,* 168 and 169: "The authoritarian character loves those conditions that limit human freedom, he loves being submitted to fate" and "The authoritarian character worships the past. What has been, will eternally be. To wish or to work for something that has not yet been before is crime [sic] or madness. The miracle of creation — and creation is always a miracle — is outside of his range of emotional experience." For more on the "politics of eternity" and the "politics of inevitability," see Timothy Snyder's *On Tyranny: Twenty Lessons from the Twentieth Century* (New York: Tim Duggan Books, 2017), 117–26, and *The Road to Unfreedom: Russia, Europe, America* (New York: Tim Dougan Books, 2018), 7–8 et passim.

50 Edward S. Herman and Noam Chomsky, *Manufacturing Consent: The Political Economy of Mass Media* (New York: Pantheon, 1988).

51 From Edward L. Bernays, *Propaganda* (Brooklyn: ig Publishing, 2014), first published in 1928, to Jason Stanley, *How Propaganda Works* (Princeton: Princeton University Press, 2015).

52 Sheldon S. Wolin, *Democracy Inc: Managed Democracy and the Specter of Inverted Totalitarianism* (Princeton: Princeton University Press, 2008).

ist. Fromm's account offers an explanatory model that can be transposed to Italian fascism or to any number of other fascist experiments and trends in "other times, other places," including our own. This relatability and transferability derive from his underlying belief in universalism, the idea that in the aggregate, humans in similar conditions behave in similar ways.

For Fromm, the lower middle class is the "nucleus" of the Nazi movement at the critical, stage-two moment of "taking root." Hitler's initial success stems from the fact that he himself could so perfectly channel that vulnerable group's desires and grievances because, says Fromm, "He was the typical representative of the lower middle class, a nobody with no chances or future. He felt very intensely the role of being an outcast" (215). But in writing *Mein Kampf* he first teaches himself and then others how to literally paper over those insecurities with a barrage of projections and rationalizations. In evidence-based pages that the historian Paxton could only admire, I should think, Fromm recalls how the lower middle class was the "most defenseless" and the "hardest hit" in the aftermath of World War I (212). First, inflation wiped out savings they could least afford to lose causing many to suffer material and psychological status loss. Second, the downfall of the monarchy rattled "the little man" who had most "identified himself in his subaltern manner with all of these institutions" (213) and now felt lost without the Kaiser; whereas the working class could say "good riddance," while Germany's industrialists and Junkers could absorb the loss and adapt, confident they would retain the upper hand in any new regime. Also, given the boost to working class prestige provided by the recent success of Russia's communist revolution, "the prestige of the lower middle class fell in relative terms. There was nobody to look down upon anymore, a privilege that has always been one of the strongest assets in the life of small shopkeepers and their like" (213). A third factor underlined by Fromm is the particular resentment felt by the lower middle class toward the overturning of the traditional patriarchal family structure. His observations about the family are worth quoting at length since they bear a strong resemblance to the 1960s-era rebellion of the "hip" and the "cool" against their "square" parents, as well as to more recent tensions between digital natives and their tech-challenged Boomer caregivers — and because the family is the crucial portal between outer public life and inner private life:

> In addition to these factors, the last stronghold of middle-class security had been shattered too: the family. The post-war development, in Germany perhaps more than in other countries, had shaken the authority of the father and the old middle-class morality. The younger generation acted as they pleased and cared no longer whether their actions were approved by their parents or not.
>
> The reasons for this development are too manifold and complex to discuss here in detail. I shall mention only a few. The decline of the old social symbols of authority like monarchy and state affected the role of the individual authorities, the parents. If these authorities, which the younger generation had been taught by the parents to respect, proved to be weak, then the parents lost prestige and authority too. Another factor was that, under the changed conditions, especially the inflation, the older generation was bewildered and puzzled and much less adapted to the new conditions than the smarter, younger generation. Thus the younger generation felt superior to their elders and could not take them, and their teachings, quite seriously any more. Furthermore, the economic decline of the middle class deprived the parents of their economic role as backers of the economic future of their children. (213–14)

Psychology skeptics ought to be required to come up with a better explanation instead of simply rejecting this resentment-to-revenge narrative which plausibly explains not only the rise of nazism in Germany in 1933, but also how an aging, insecure United States elects "morning again in America" Ronald Reagan after the serial failure (from the aggrieved lower-middle-class, white perspective) of Lyndon B. Johnson (Texas traitor), Richard Nixon (Watergate "crook"), Gerald Ford (fumble, stumble), and Jimmy Carter (President "Malaise" who was said to have mishandled the Iran hostage crisis and who led a pullout from the 1980 Moscow Olympic Games that many found misguided). And how it later chooses "make America great again" Trump — and may elect another demagogue down the road since the children of today's Trump supporters may share their parents' mindset.

Another similarity between Fromm and Paxton's accounts is how both agree there is a bandwagon effect exerted by peer pressure starting in 1933. Once a certain tipping point has been passed, key figures who may have been uncomfortable with Hitler at earlier stages cave in and back him, at least passively, rather than risk being labeled bad Germans or suffering more severe retribution.[53] Fromm's 1941 remarks on this matter speak to the difficulty of dislodging a leader with fascist tendencies once the movement that person is leading has reached Paxton's stage three, "getting power" and especially stage four, "exercising power":

However much a German citizen may be opposed to the principles of Nazism, if he has to choose between being alone and feeling that he belongs to Germany, most persons will choose the latter. It can be observed in many instances that persons who are not Nazis nevertheless defend Nazism against criticism of [i.e., *by*] foreigners because they feel that an attack on Nazism is an attack on Germany. The fear of isolation and the relative weakness of moral principles help any party to win the loyalty of a large sector of the population once that party has captured the power of the state. (208)

---

53 This is related to the "continuum of destruction" evoked by Holocaust survivor Ervin Staub in discussing the Rwandan genocide. "Reconciliation after Genocide, Mass Killing, or Intractable Conflict: Understanding the Roots of Violence, Psychological Recovery, and Steps toward a General Theory," *Political Psychology* 27, no. 6 (December 2006): 867–94. The momentum of nazism is discussed in this volume's Chapter 3 on *In the Garden of Beasts: Love, Terror, and an American Family in Hitler's Berlin* (New York: Crown, 2011).

And yet at the end of the chapter's twenty-page examination of "Hitler's personality, his teachings, and the Nazi system" and how they made "a powerful appeal to those parts of the population that were — more or less — of the same [authoritarian] character structure" (219), Fromm predicts that German fascism will eventually collapse. Why? Because, despite appearances in 1941 — and Fromm grants that the projections, rationalizations, and the emotional satisfaction of "sadistic spectacles" (219) can go a long way toward extending self-deception — nazism does not fulfill the genuine emotional needs of a population composed, whether they like it or not, of individuals living after the destruction of the medieval world, after the industrial and communications revolutions, and after the invention of democratic institutions. That some, perhaps even occasionally a plurality or majority, want to give up those democratic institutions and the freedom that is both their precondition and byproduct, does not, in Fromm's view, remove the basic reality that "man will remain an individual" (236) unless by some unlikely turn of events the entire course of history of the last five hundred years is "destroyed and changed to the preindustrial level" (236). In short, the individual "cat" is too far out of the proverbial bag for fascism to succeed, Fromm claims; however, it does cause lots of pain and destruction along the way to its own self-destruction.

The authoritarian character, whether expressed as sadism or masochism, believes that the only happiness possible lies in blind submission to a higher authority. However, in the book's final chapter "Freedom and Democracy," Fromm sketches a healthy alternative to the *escape from freedom*. This better alternative for Germany, his homeland, and for the United States, his second home — and ultimately for the whole world — requires the individual's affirmation of self through spontaneous, creative activity; in other words, as he said from the start, the expression of one's intellectual, emotional, and sensuous potentialities. Only by actively affirming one's place in the world can a person pass from early primary ties to healthy, sustainable secondary ties and overcome the lag or gap between *freedom from* and *freedom to.* Fromm's concluding paragraph is uplifting but also cautionary with four repetitions of "only if":

> *Only if* man masters society and subordinates the economic machine to the purposes of human happiness, and *only if* he actively participates in the social process, can he overcome what now drives him into despair — his aloneness and his feeling of powerlessness. Man does not suffer so much from poverty today as he suffers from the fact that he has become a cog in a large machine, an automaton, that his life has become empty and lost its meaning. The victory over all kinds of authoritarian systems will be possible *only if* democracy does not retreat but takes the offensive and proceeds to realize what has been its aim in the minds of those who fought for freedom throughout the last centuries. It will triumph over the forces of nihilism *only if* it can imbue people with a faith that is the strongest the human mind is capable of, the faith in life and in truth, and in freedom as the active and spontaneous realization of the individual self. (274, emphasis added)

We have now learned, from two able guides, how an *escape from freedom* leads to fascism. In the following chapters, I will argue that "the victory over all kinds of authoritarian systems" will never be achieved or endure without first acknowledging and then actually reducing the real pain and suffering caused by vulnerability. These chapters, grouped into three genres of three examples each, may be called "vulnerability studies." However this should not be confused with the epithet "victim studies" which was the belittling term used by some US conservatives starting a generation ago to disparage progressive-minded, cross-disciplinary, intersectional programs in the humanities such as women's studies, Black studies, Holocaust studies, and the like.[54]

---

54 "Victim studies" is also today a degree program about crime victims and victim counseling offered by colleges and universities including Sam Houston State University, Anna Maria College, and the University of

The first of these nine stories is a retelling of the experience and testimony of the US ambassador to Germany, William E. Dodd, who was appointed by Franklin Roosevelt the same year both the United States president and Adolf Hitler take office — 1933.

Massachusetts at Lowell. For an example of right-wing disparagement of "victim studies" in the Allan Bloom tradition, see Bruce Bawer, *The Victims' Revolution: The Rise of Identity Studies and the Closing of the Liberal Mind* (New York: Broadside Books, 2012).

II

Nonfiction Narratives

3

Waking Up to Fascism or Sleeping with Fascists

Erik Larson, *In the Garden of Beasts: Love, Terror, and an American Family in Hitler's Berlin* (2011)

Erik Larson (1954–) is best known for his wildly successful tale of construction and destruction, *The Devil in the White City* (2002), however for our purposes his most important book is *In the Garden of Beasts: Love, Terror, and an American Family in Hitler's Berlin* (2011).[1] It will be the first of the nine "vulnerability studies" appended to the two previous theoretical chapters, and the first in this Part 2 devoted to nonfiction narratives.[2]

Erik Larson is a serious independent scholar and a talented storyteller. The first attribute is clear from the seventy-five pages of footnotes, bibliography, and helpful index at the end

---

1 Erik Larson, *In the Garden of Beasts: Love, Terror, and an American Family in Hitler's Berlin* (New York: Crown, 2011). Hereafter cited parenthetically throughout this chapter.
2 I thank my friend Karin Jackson for putting me onto this book during a conversation at her home in Cundy's Harbor in 2016 when she asked me what I had been teaching lately and I described my fascism seminar to her.

of the volume; the second is clear from the very first sentence: "Once, at the dawn of a very dark time, an American father and daughter found themselves suddenly transported from their snug home in Chicago to the heart of Hitler's Berlin" (xvii). Larson's euphonious opening built on consonances and tro-chees (dawn/dark; father/daughter; father/found/from; them-selves/their snug; home/heart/Hitler's) and the shrewd, incipit "Once," which both suggests and avoids the fairy tale opening "once upon a time," make this a very engaging beginning to a nearly 400-page bestseller that marvelously and efficiently bal-ances instruction with entertainment, business with pleasure, Great Man history with an inside story of the emotional lives of ordinary individuals. From the start the reader is given the arc of the whole narrative: Chicago to Berlin — a doubling of Larson's journey between his "White City" and the darkness of 1930s Germany. The "two primary subjects" are identified: a father-daughter pair, thus two different generations forty years apart and different sexes. In the second sentence we are told that the essential time period to be covered will be roughly one year: summer 1933 to summer 1934. So the classical dramatic unities of time, place, and action are fulfilled and the reader is oriented and ready to dive into this intimate history of "an American family in Hitler's Berlin." Larson, as Virgilian guide to the hubris and vulnerabilities of 1933–34, will tell of "arms and the man" and retrace the narrative arc from naïve "wishful thinking" to "lost illusions" of both the professor father and his princess daughter.

Larson clearly states the motive that led him to research and write this book, but he does not say if the specific timing of his project in the first decade of the twenty-first century had any-thing to do with the dark shadows of George W. Bush's post-9/11 Patriot Act presidency.

> I have always wondered what it would have been like for an outsider to have witnessed firsthand the gathering dark of Hitler's rule. How did the city look, what did one hear, see,

and smell, and how did diplomats and other visitors interpret the events occurring around them? Hindsight tells us
that during that fragile time the course of history could so
easily have been changed. Why, then, did no one change it?
Why did it take so long to recognize the real danger posed by
Hitler and his regime? (xvii)

It will take Larson a few years and several hundred pages to answer those questions, but a short answer comes in the one-liner
by Upton Sinclair (1878–1968) who lived through the return of
the Ku Klux Klan and the rise of fascism: "It's difficult to get a
man to understand something when his salary depends upon
his not understanding it."[3] If we expand "salary" to include "way
of life," "value system," or "worldview," that's a pretty good summary of the "I-was-blind-and-now-I-see" conversion narrative
that this tragic tale of deferred irony will tell.

On June 8, 1933, after several others had already turned
down the job, a 64-year-old history professor at the University
of Chicago, William E. Dodd, is asked by President Franklin D.
Roosevelt, who had been sworn into office on March 4, 1933,
to become the new United States ambassador to Germany,
where Hitler was in power since January 30, 1933. Dodd accepts
with the idea, as he sees it, of serving his country by defending United States liberalism, but with the parallel idea that he
shall be able to return to the happy place of his student days
(i.e., Leipzig circa 1900) and have the peace and quiet away from
university responsibilities to advance on his magnum opus, a
multi-volume study of *The Rise and Fall of the Old South* that he
is anxious to complete as the capstone to his scholarly life. His
wife, son, and daughter do not object to going to Berlin. The
twenty-something-aged children especially, having no burning

---

3   The quip circulates in different wordings, but it seems to have originated
    in Sinclair's 1935 memoir *I, Candidate for Governor, and How I Got Licked*
    (Berkeley: University of California Press, 1994). See *Quote Investigator*:
    https://quoteinvestigator.com/2017/11/30/salary/.

career prospects, view it as an adventure and a way to ditch routines and dead ends.

Anyone who compares Larson's *In the Garden of Beasts* with, say, the Wikipedia entry for William Dodd[4] can see that while the latter contains more facts, Larson's "novelistic history," as the *New York Times* calls it, provides the emotional intelligence one needs to formulate the most compelling answer to Larson's basic question: Why did it take so long for the Americans to wise up to "the real danger posed by Hitler and his regime"? Without mentioning either Paxton or Fromm, Larson's *In the Garden of Beasts* offers a subtle synthesis of the approaches of both authors: a factual account combined with suggestive portraits of the psychological makeup — especially the authoritarian character — of the German leadership and people and also of their United States counterparts, especially State Department officials, Ambassador Dodd, and his daughter.[5]

In the early chapters Larson reviews the main external factors that give a more or less rational explanation of the mix of ignoring and downplaying of Hitler's racist, belligerent, and genocidal ambitions, despite having been clearly stated years earlier in his prison book *Mein Kampf* (1925). These factors include the post-World War I resurgence of isolationism with 95 percent of Americans wishing to avoid another war (19) and the $1.2 billion in German bonds that sat on the books of prominent banks, a powerful lobby for bending the US government to play nice lest the German government halt payments and cause further economic chaos (19). A third factor was the garden variety anti-Semitism of many ordinary Americans at the time, including Martha Dodd ("We sort of don't like the Jews anyway," 88) and her father who shared in a meeting with Hitler his widely held view that "over-activity of Jews in university or official life made trouble" but was capable of being dealt with in more civi-

---

4   *Wikipedia,* s.v. "William Dodd (ambassador)," https://en.wikipedia.org/wiki/William_Dodd_(ambassador).

5   See also Robert Dallek, *Democrat and Diplomat: The Life of William E. Dodd* (Oxford: Oxford University Press, 2012).

lized ways than those Hitler was implementing. This last item is the most delicate since it crosses the line from external fact to personal conviction. As fact, anti-Semitism can be documented in the textual events of German laws passed and implemented to deprive Jews, little by little, of basic civil rights and the right to make a living down to the ultimate suppression of their right to live at all. The laws are well known, especially the exclusion from many professions and the implementation of Aryan versus Jewish apartheid symbolized by the infamous yellow star.

Larson also underscores the importance of the less well-known anti-immigrant US law of 1930 signed by President Hoover. It incorporates language from the earlier 1917 Immigration Act, and "barred entry to all would-be immigrants considered 'likely to become a public charge'" (31). This "LPC clause," as it was called, revived by the Trump administration for similar exclusionary purposes, was perfectly consistent with the anti-immigrant sentiment in post-1929 America where, Larson reports, "two-thirds of those surveyed favored keeping refugees out of the country." Therefore low quotas per country were set, but overzealous and anti-Semitic members of the State Department exploited the "public charge" exclusion even further by misinforming Ambassador Dodd about the number of available slots for German citizens, thus causing him in effect to turn away perfectly acceptable visa applicants such as the Jewish chemist Fritz Haber and how many others (77–78).

Larson also exposes, without exculpation or blame, the contradictions that extended to President Roosevelt who, we can see now, sent mixed signals to his new ambassador. On the one hand he says to Dodd on the day he offers him the job, "I want an American liberal in Germany as a standing example" (20); but when it comes to the Jews, he tells Dodd over lunch:

> The German authorities are treating the Jews shamefully and the Jews in this country are gravely excited. […] But this is also not a governmental affair. We can do nothing except for American citizens who happen to be made victims. We must protect them, and whatever we can do to moderate the gen-

eral persecution by unofficial and personal influence ought to be done. (32)

Larson then leaves a caesura of several blank lines to let that sink in: in 1933 and for years afterwards little *official* influence would be marshalled by Roosevelt's administration to "moderate the general persecution" of Jews, and Dodd, like so many others, goes along with that for the duration of his service as ambassador to Germany which lasts until December 29, 1937.

An additional external factor that Larson barely touches on is that Dodd, Roosevelt, and other liberal, northern Democrats knew they could hardly be lecturing Hitler about civil rights for minorities at a time when, to get elected, they had in effect made a devil's bargain with their illiberal southern counterparts who also called themselves Democrats but in actuality had instituted throughout Dodd's dear Old South a racist authoritarian regime with fascistic elements such as terror via lynching and cross burnings, forced expulsions, expropriations of African American property, segregation, and voter-suppression techniques — all of which served Hitler as a sort of toolbox or template that he would adapt to the lands under his authority.[6] Fas-

---

6 For an example in Georgia from 1912 that combines all these techniques, see Patrick Philips, *Blood at the Root: A Racial Cleansing in America* (New York: W.W. Norton, & Co., 2016). On Hitler's borrowing from racist American authoritarianism, see James Q. Whitman, *Hitler's American Model: The United States and The Making of Nazi Race Law* (Princeton: Princeton University Press, 2018). On "race riots" and lynching, especially the East St. Louis riot of 1917, see Jamelle Bouie's newsletter entitled (quoting Marcus Garvey), "This Is a Crime against the Laws of Humanity," *The New York Times*, April 2, 2022, https://www.nytimes.com/2022/04/02/opinion/anti-lynching-law-east-st-louis.html 2 — a piece timed in proximity to Joe Biden's March 29, 2022 signing into law of the Emmett Till Anti-Lynching Act making lynching a federal crime after a century of obstruction by Congress to pass such legislation. Bouie references Amy Louise Wood's comprehensive study, *Lynching and Spectacle: Witnessing Racial Violence in America, 1890–1940* (Chapel Hill: University of North Carolina Press, 2009) and the research of Charles L. Lumpkins, *American Pogrom: The East St. Louis Race Riot and Black Politics* (Athens: Ohio University Press, 2008).

cist leaders, as Paxton demonstrates, are not original thinkers or thinkers at all; they are shameless plagiarists, opportunists, feral intuitionists, and exploiters of the desires, fears, contradictions, and moral turpitude of their allies and enemies. Hitler surely knew that the sympathetic Woodrow Wilson biography which made Dodd's scholarly reputation and got him noticed by leading Democratic politicians retold the life of a white supremacist.[7] Wilson claimed he wished to "make the world safe for democracy," but he also tolerated the resurgence of the Ku Klux Klan and exclusionary Jim Crow practices in the southern half of the country he presided over. Wilson also invited an apologist for the Lost Cause, D.W. Griffith, the most influential moviemaker of his day, to organize a private showing of his racist film *The Birth of a Nation* at the White House.[8] In short, Dodd, Roosevelt, and the 1930s Democratic leadership knew they would be exposing themselves to withering charges of hypocrisy by foreign governments should they lift a finger to lecture the Nazis about human rights, all men being equal, or liberty and justice for all.[9] Larson accurately notes that "For Roosevelt,

---

7 William E. Dodd, *Woodrow Wilson and His Work* (Garden City: Doubleday, 1920).

8 Melvyn Stokes, *D.W. Griffith's "The Birth of a Nation"* (Oxford: Oxford University Press, 2008).

9 As early as the Scottsboro trial in 1931, Soviets published examples of American racism internationally, Jelani Cobb reminds his reader in a profile of Derrick Bell, "The Man Behind Critical Race Theory," *The New Yorker,* September 13, 2021, https://www.newyorker.com/magazine/2021/09/20/the-man-behind-critical-race-theory. At the time many Democrats were conservative in temperament. Near the end of the introduction to his *Anatomy of Fascism,* Paxton recalls the attraction-repulsion between conservatives and fascists: "Conservatives wanted order, calm, and the inherited hierarchies of wealth and birth. They shrank both from fascist mass enthusiasm and from the sort of total power fascists grasped for. They wanted obedience and deference, not dangerous popular mobilization, and they wanted to limit the state to the functions of a 'night watchman' who would keep order while traditional elites ruled through property, churches, armies, and inherited social influence. More generally, conservatives in Europe still rejected in 1930 the main tenets of the French Revolution, preferring authority to liberty, hierarchy to equality, and deference to fraternity. Although many of them might find fascists useful,

FASCISM, VULNERABILITY, AND THE ESCAPE FROM FREEDOM

this was treacherous ground" (28), but he is talking about "Nazi treatment of the Jews" not white America's treatment of people of color. Larson accurately identifies half the problem lower down on the same page:

> But Roosevelt understood that the political costs of any public condemnation of Nazi persecution or any obvious effort to ease the entry of Jews into America were likely to be immense, because American political discourse had framed the Jewish problem as an immigration problem. (28)

One can understand that at the time many Americans barely recovering from joblessness and financial ruin after the Depression were protectionist and therefore anti-immigrant; but then why not have the American political discourse frame the "Jewish problem" as a human rights issue instead?[10] One reason is that the human rights movement was still about thirty years in the future and that in the 1930s the language, and will, did not yet exist to frame the problem in that way.[11] Another unavowable answer is that doing so would have required 1930s America to first acknowledge and then dismantle the systematic human rights violations by the fascistic authoritarian regime that had consolidated power throughout the southern United States and the everyday racism that infected the northern states

---

or even essential, in their struggle for survival against dominant liberals and a rising Left, some were keenly aware of the different agenda of their fascist allies and felt a fastidious distaste for these uncouth outsiders." Robert O. Paxton, *The Anatomy of Fascism* (New York: Alfred A. Knopf, 2004), 22.

10 See David S. Wyman, *The Abandonment of the Jews: America and the Holocaust 1941–1945* (New York: Pantheon, 1984), xv: "Franklin Roosevelt's indifference to so momentous an historical event as the systematic annihilation of European Jewry emerges as the worst failure of his presidency."

11 The *Universal Declaration of Human Rights* (1948) laid the foundation, but it took twenty more years for the idea of human rights to gain acceptance and become a legal lever for positive change. See Mike Chinoy, *Are You With Me? Kevin Boyle and the Rise of the Human Rights Movement* (Dublin: The Lilliput Press, 2020).

as well.[12] The expansion of full personhood and thus human rights to Black people (or to Jews, homosexuals, the disabled, or women) was not in the cards in the 1930s. Such an acknowledgement would only begin first thirty years later in the 1960s and then, with renewed conviction, sixty more years later after the awakening provoked by the controversial 2016 US presidential election. Ironically, the human rights movement got a boost thanks to President Trump's rekindling of the regressive desire — following Goldwater, Nixon, and Reagan's backlash against the progressive liberation movements of the sixties — to make America more like the 1930s, '40s, and '50s again, a time when the "pretty good club" (35) of white Anglo-Saxon, protestant (WASP), manly men was firmly in power and there were no "women's libbers" or "perverts" or racial and religious minorities prating about their rights.[13]

---

12 Larson references the potentially "embarrassing position" for Roosevelt when a State Department memorandum written by a friend of Dodd, R. Walton Moore, anticipates that Germans would call out American mistreatment of "negroes" were the American president or US Senate to speak out against Jewish persecution. Larson, *In the Garden of Beasts,* 241.

13 I am thankful to many of Jamelle Bouie's winter 2020 columns in *The New York Times* for opening my eyes wider to the authoritarian character of Jim Crow. See, for example, "Where Might Trumpism Take Us?" February 21, 2020, https://www.nytimes.com/2020/02/21/opinion/trump-authoritarian-jim-crow.html: "It's not just that we have had moments of authoritarian government — as well as presidents, like John Adams or Woodrow Wilson, with autocratic impulses — but that an entire region of the country was once governed by an actual authoritarian regime. That regime was Jim Crow, a system defined by a one-party rule and violent repression of racial minorities. The reason this matters is straightforward. Look beyond America's borders for possible authoritarian futures and you might miss important points of continuity with our own past. Which is to say that if authoritarian government is in our future, there's no reason to think it won't look like something we've already built, versus something we've imported." See also, "The Republican Party Has Embraced Its Worst Self," February 7, 2020, https://www.nytimes.com/2020/02/07/opinion/sunday/senate-impeachment-acquittal.html. This excerpt develops Bouie's claim that authoritarianization and democratization are constantly opposing forces throughout American history: "If the story of the American republic is the story of democratic decline as much as it is of democratic expansion — if backlash shapes our history as much as progress does — then the

None of this civil rights or human rights history seems to matter much in Larson's *In the Garden of Beasts* — after all, the focus is a white American family's first year in Hitler's Berlin. And yet he does include a teachable moment when Martha, who practically brags about the families of both her parents having once owned slaves, is scolded by her Russian communist lover Boris:

Though it took a good deal of effort, she told Boris that her parents were both offspring of old southern landowning families, "each as well ancestored as the other, and almost pure British: Scotch-Irish, English, and Welsh."

Boris laughed. "That's not so pure, is it?"

With an unconscious note of pride in her voice, she added that both families had once owned slaves — "Mother's about twelve or so, Father's five or six."

Boris went quiet. His expression shifted abruptly to one of sorrow. "Martha," he said, "surely you are not proud that your ancestors owned the lives of other human beings."

He took her hands and looked at her. Until this moment the fact that her parents' ancestors had owned slaves had always seemed merely an interesting element of their personal history that testified to their deep roots in America.

---

current moment is easy to understand. We are living through a period of democratic erosion, in which social and political reaction limits the reach and scope of past democratic victories. In this way of looking at the present, we're living through a period of institutional deterioration, during which American government ceases to function in the face of polarization, zero-sum conflict and constitutional hardball. […] If the acquittal of Trump shows us anything, it's a Republican Party free of pretense or artifice, ready to embrace its worst self without shame or embarrassment." I also thank Lissette Mariez who sent me a quotation from Albert Camus while I was working on the first draft of this chapter: "Be on your guard, when a democracy is sick, fascism comes to its bedside, but it's not to ask How are you feeling today?" ["Faites attention, quand une démocratie est malade, le fascisme vient à son chevet mais ce n'est pas pour prendre de ses nouvelles."]

Now, suddenly, she saw it for what it was — a sad chapter to be regretted.

"I didn't mean to boast," she said. "I suppose it sounded like that to you." She apologized and immediately hated herself for it. She was, she conceded, "a combative girl."

"But we do have a long tradition in America," she told him. "We are not newcomers."

Boris found her defensiveness hilarious and laughed with unrestrained delight. (124)

This little morality play is a good example of the poetic license that Larson's novelistic history allows, since really what does he know of Boris's laughter or of Martha's unconscious or her true degree of regret? Her regret may be an inference from the diary entry "I didn't mean to boast"; but isn't that just Larson's generous interpretation, and moreover one that her self-description as "a combative girl" — someone unapologetically fond of dominating and winning — undermines? Other details that are revealing of Martha's character, and representative of her time, are the preoccupation with pure bloodlines and a family history of dominating others that goes back several generations: "We are not newcomers." The accidental phonemic similarity of *Martha* and *master* locks in the identity of Professor Dodd's daughter as a power-hungry descendant of people used to being on top and taking liberties, even if it came at the expense of others' vulnerability, submission, unfreedom, or enslavement. It's hardly surprising therefore that she enjoys having sex with Nazis and other powerful people.

We will return to Martha later, but we should first sum up the four external factors that explain why it took so long for America to denounce "the real danger posed by Hitler and his regime." First there was the resurgence of isolationism after World War I and the Great Depression; second, the sizable bank loans that Germany could use to in effect blackmail the US government to keep quiet; next there was the anti-Semitism within the WASP-dominated State Department and the anti-Jewish sentiment in the country at large that didn't mind seeing Jews taken down a

peg or two; and finally there was the highly embarrassing inability of the US government to denounce human rights abuses
abroad when for over a generation it had turned a blind eye to
similar mistreatment of African Americans and other second-
class citizens at home. This last contradiction is so taboo that
even Larson, who publishes *In the Garden of Beasts* in President Obama's America, can only treat it glancingly, such as in
the above passage, and again on page 241, and in the final concluding pages where he recounts that, in retirement, Professor
Dodd was involved in a hit-and-run car accident in which he
seriously injured a young girl. Larson's choice of words is kind
to Dodd: "*his car* struck a four-year-old black girl named Gloria
Grimes" (352, emphasis added). After first pleading innocent,
Dodd changed his plea to guilty, Larson informs the reader. After first having his driver's license and right to vote taken away
as a result — "an especially poignant loss for so ardent a believer
in democracy" — we learn on the next page, "The governor of
Virginia restored his right to vote, explaining that at the time of
the accident Dodd was 'ill and not entirely responsible.'" I imagine that Larson, who, like many historians and literary types, is
endlessly intrigued by irony's wheel of fortune, carefully crafted
these lines and every paragraph in the curtain-lowering last
chapter he entitled "As Darkness Fell." However, a few more observations are in order before we leave Larson's bestiary.

***

In addition to the four external factors, Larson provides elements that add weight to Erich Fromm's hypothesis: widespread
pursuit or at least toleration (inside and outside Germany) of
nazism and its sadistic persecution of a targeted out-group, the
Jews, was due to real or perceived vulnerability among the lower
middle class in the wake of World War I and the Great Depression. That base of support dovetailed with the "authoritarian
character" of many wealthier, established individuals as well as
other middle-class descendants of Luther and Calvin desirous

of protection and willing to support a system of white supremacist domination by the "fittest" led by a strong leader-savior.

A first element is that Dodd has another reason for accepting
the Berlin job: "He also saw in this adventure an opportunity
to have his family together one last time" (22). Professor Dodd
seems to have had a traditional view of the family that places a
high value on vertical arrangements where the husband-father
leads, the wife-mother follows, and the children obey. It's a bit
odd that at twenty-four and twenty-eight, respectively, Martha
and Bill Jr. (beware of fathers who do not give their male offspring first names of their own) have not been able or perhaps
allowed to leave this patriarchal nest and are instead nestling
in it. In the language first developed by Karen Horney, we may
have here an example of codependency between a domineering father-husband and the submissive spouse and children. In
the language of Fromm, Martha and Bill Jr. have not successfully severed their primary ties. Although manifestly adult-aged
individuals, they seem unable to behave as independent adults
powerful enough to construct life projects of their own. From
Larson's account, it would seem the faux-rebellious Bill Jr. is
only interested in parties and joy riding in the family Chevro-
let that Ambassador Dodd insisted on shipping to Germany.
Meanwhile Martha spins her wheels, so to speak, by playing at
becoming a writer and serially sleeping with Nazis. Both sets of
actions, consorting with established literati and powerful men,
are degraded versions ("acting out" that is half imitation-as-
homage, half vengeful antithesis) of her father's distinguished
career as an influential professor and author, and now public
servant.

Larson leaves Bill Jr. in the shadows, perhaps for economy
and because he kept no diary; but probably also because Martha's infatuation with nazism and Nazis is so titillating and illus-
trative of the blindness and seduction that he believes is crucial
for explaining why exclusionary right-wing populism (i.e., fascism) was such a tempting alternative to liberal democracy in the
1920s and '30s in Europe and America. But Larson is not claiming that this temptation is simply a female weakness: "Martha's

cheery view of things was widely shared by outsiders visiting Germany and especially Berlin" (55). Moreover, he repeatedly states that many of Dodd's Waspy male collaborators in the State Department, with the exception of George Messersmith,[14] were willing followers of Hitler's National Socialist experiment and may have even favored it over Roosevelt's big-tent, New Deal politics that had a whiff of the same class betrayal that his cousin Teddy Roosevelt was accused of a generation earlier during the so-called "Progressive Era."[15] It's clear that Dodd's coworkers are not particularly qualified for their jobs — unlike Dodd who knows German, Germany, and a lot of history — but they have the right pedigree, social codes, and enough money to project power through a lavish lifestyle that can mask their actual impotence; in other words their inability to actually do or think for themselves.[16] This makes them perfect apologists for Hitler, "a nobody with no chances or future,"[17] who is playing a similar

---

14 Messersmith, a career diplomat who worked under Dodd in Berlin, had a dim view of the Nazi leaders: "There are so many pathological cases involved that it would be impossible to tell from day to day what will happen any more than the keeper of a madhouse is able to tell what his inmates will do in the next hour or during the next day." George Messersmith, quoted in Larson, *In the Garden of Beasts*, 159.

15 One of the ironies of American history is that the Progressive Era coincides with the rise of Jim Crow and that one of its supposed proponents was Teddy Roosevelt (1858–1919) who rose to prominence during the racism and murderous frenzy of the Spanish–American war of 1898. See Greg Grandin, *End of Myth: From the Frontier to the Border Wall in the Mind of America* (New York: Macmillan, 2019), ch. 8, "The Pact of 1898."

16 See Erich Fromm, *Escape from Freedom* (New York: Henry Holt, 1969), 170: "The authoritarian character does not lack activity, courage, or belief. But these qualities for him mean something entirely different from what they mean for the person who does not long for submission. For the authoritarian character activity is rooted in a basic [unavowable] feeling of powerlessness which it tends to overcome. [...] The authoritarian character wins his strength to act through his leaning on superior power. [...] He lacks an 'offensive potency' which can attack established power without first feeling subservient to another and stronger power." The point is that knowing some things, both facts and skills, arms Dodd to stand up to Papen and Hitler in ways that his State Department colleagues were unprepared, unwilling, and unable to do.

17 Ibid., 215.

masquerade. It also makes them highly allergic to someone like Dodd whose plain clothes, used car, and penny-pinching habits must be constantly mocked, since his actual qualifications for the job of foreign diplomat and adherence to basic American values of liberty and justice for all, as well as his reality-based moral compass, were all unassailable. In a characteristic declaration from January 1934, by which time Dodd had made up his mind about the destructiveness of nazism and was trying to convince the leaders in the State Department of that fact, a diary entry reads, "I do, however, think facts count; even if we hate them" (216). In other words, he and his colleagues and the whole world may have *wished* for Hitler's National Socialist party to succeed so long as it played by the rules of liberal democracy; but a year later that is manifestly not happening, hence Dodd's advocacy starting in early 1934 for a firmer line against the one-party German state with its mounting persecution of Jews and bellicose attitude toward neighboring states. It's true, Larson relates, that after a July 15, 1933 meeting with the German foreign affairs minister Konstantin von Neurath, who "believed he could help control Hitler and his party," Dodd was able to write to a friend, "Hitler will fall into line with these wiser men and ease up on a tense situation" (66). But Dodd's aspirational, wishful thinking about Hitler's capacity to see reason comes to a halt, especially after the phony parliamentary elections Hitler supervised on November 12, 1933 with only one party on the ballot. Many after this date remain lenient and are still willing to play ball with Hitler. Not Dodd. This comparatively precocious change of heart from a man who had also written in a letter to Roosevelt, "Give men a chance to try their schemes,"[18] may be why Dodd is portrayed as a flawed but heroic figure — the "Cassandra of American diplomats" (350).

---

18 The quote comes from a letter Dodd sent to Roosevelt: "[…] fundamentally, I believe a people has a right to govern itself and that other peoples must exercise patience even when cruelties and injustices are done. Give men a chance to try their schemes." William Dodd, in a letter to Franklin Roosevelt, August 12, 1933, quoted in Larson, *In the Garden of Beasts,* 82.

Regrettably, the Wikipedia conclusion to the entry on "William Dodd (ambassador)" misrepresents both Larson and Dodd, almost as though it were written by one of the descendants of the Waspy members of the Pretty Good Club of career State Department officials that Larson says were constantly undermining "*der gute* Dodd," as Hitler condescendingly referred to the ambassador (235):

Dodd and his family's time in Nazi Germany are the subject of Erik Larson's bestselling 2011 work of popular history, *In the Garden of Beasts,* which portrays Dodd as well-meaning but naive and unprepared, believing as a historian that all national leaders are ultimately rational actors, and rendered helpless when he realizes that Hitler may in fact be completely irrational.

"Naïve and unprepared," except where sex was involved, accurately describes the faux-innocent Martha, but not her German-speaking, history professor father. Dodd was well-acquainted with Edward Gibbon's *History of the Decline and Fall of the Roman Empire* (1776), and he knew even more intimately because his own family lived it, "The Rise and Fall of the Old South." Dodd may have wished, like all descendants of Locke, Madison, and Mill, that national leaders would be rational actors; however, just like the Founding Fathers who did their level best to construct an idiot-, traitor-, and tyrant-proof Constitution, Dodd knew the historical record was littered with examples of leaders who were neither angels nor rational actors, nor all that bright. Indeed, this was the whole thrust of his allegorical public history lesson delivered in the banquet hall of the Adlon Hotel to the Berlin branch of the American Chamber of Commerce on Columbus Day, October 12, 1933. Whoever authored that portion of the Wikipedia entry was either inattentive or deliberately misrepresenting Dodd since Larson devotes six pages to the ambassador's carefully crafted Columbus Day speech and its reception. The speech cemented Dodd's reputation as a hero to many and as a thorn in the side of his fascist-leaning American colleagues and an annoyance to Hitler and his propaganda chief Joseph Goebbels who did everything in his power to block its publication and circulation. After drawing on ancient examples of corruption, Dodd, an experienced lecturer to half-educated undergraduates, drives his point home in terms that would be recognizable to anyone with ears to hear. In other words, Larson's account shows Dodd to be anything but a naïve or unprepared public speaker:

> He stepped into the deep past to begin his allusive journey with examples of Tiberius Gracchus, a populist leader, and Julius Caesar. "Half-educated statesmen today swing violently away from the ideal purpose of the first Gracchus and think they find salvation for their troubled fellows in the arbitrary modes of the man who fell an easy victim to the cheap devices of the lewd Cleopatra." They forget, he said, that, "the Caesars succeeded only for a short moment as measured by the test of history. […] In conclusion," he said, "one may safely say that it would be no sin if statesmen learned enough history to realize that no system which implies control of society by privilege seekers has ever ended in any other way than collapse." (149)

Larson does not speculate about the Cleopatra reference being possibly inspired by his daughter's promiscuous behavior, which surely had not escaped Dodd's attention, but I will. Martha is Larson's foil whose naïve, unprepared, and reckless ways contrast vividly with Dodd's, and thus make her a stand-in for the erratic, self-serving, and delusional United States foreign policy establishment of the time. Martha is a combative narcissist taking sadistic pleasure at shocking her perhaps overcontrolling, smothering, and no doubt "square" parents, in other words, the standard teen revenge plot in the bohemian, flapper tradition of the preceding decades. (It's almost too novelistic to be true that she eventually ends up living in gilded exile in, yes, Czechoslovakia where the original Bohemian Slavs came from.) Martha craves status and the attention of ambitious, power-hungry men. Her words and deeds correspond exactly to the authoritarian character described by Fromm in *Escape from Freedom.* Being five foot-three, female, with no skills or achievements to speak of, and knowing only baby German and living a long way from home, Martha would be understandably vulnerable and insecure. But admitting or accepting powerlessness is not in her DNA, so to speak, and therefore she makes the most of the assets she has, namely sex appeal and the advantage of being the US ambassador's daughter. She goes right to work and sensitive souls — especially writers, aristocrats, and rising Nazi stars — are her favorite bedmates. She seems to have an insatiable appetite and to enjoy creating jealousy among her suitors. (Larson does not go into how she avoided sexually transmitted infections and unwanted pregnancies — or if she did.) Her top conquests, we learn, are the Gestapo director Rudolph Diels (1900–1957) and a rather obscure Soviet spy, Boris Winogradov. These are codependent sado-masochistic relations of power — not love.[19] There is also a German Harvard man, Ernst Hanfstaengl, nicknamed "Putzi," a fast-talking maven who gets Martha to fantasize about becoming mistress to the Führer himself. Alas, her speed-dating encounter with Hitler at a fancy restaurant did not, it seems, lead to bigger things. But Larson gets a lot of mileage out of retelling every detail of their encounter. It may be this *frisson,* passed down from Martha to Larson to the reader, that accounts for half of the book's popularity.

Besides the lurid and lewd, however, there is of course the learned, serious side of the story, and sometimes these two come together as when Martha, for so long contemptuous of the weak and admiring of the strong, belatedly comes around to seeing that Diels and his violent associates are in fact beasts; however not always large and terrifying, but sometimes weak "like a frightened rabbit" (244), or strangely both at once because the

---

19 Here too, Fromm's pages on fake love and sado-masochistic symbiosis in both *Escape from Freedom,* 114–16 and 140–77, and in his very popular, shorter book *The Art of Loving* (New York: HarperCollins, 2006) are helpful for deciphering Martha's Cleopatra complex.

paranoia could turn to violent rage or vicious revenge in a split second. This became clear during the Night of the Long Knives episode, described in chapters 46 to 51, when Hitler's purge of his rivals resulted in somewhere between 100 and 1000 extrajudicial killings on June 29–30, 1934. It is the culminating event of the book and one that clinches Martha's "final disillusionment" (328). In the end, it takes her twice as long as her father, but she finally "gets it":

> "By the spring of 1934 what I had heard, seen, and felt, revealed to me that conditions of living were worse than in pre-Hitler days, that the most complicated and heartbreaking system of terror ruled the country and repressed the freedom and happiness of the people, and that German leaders were inevitably leading these docile and kindly masses into another war against their will and their knowledge."
>
> She was not willing, however, to openly declare her new attitude to the world. "I still attempted to keep my hostility guarded and unexpressed." (274)

This is a very different Martha from the young woman, who, on a road trip to Nuremberg with her brother and a friend in August 1933, witnessed the rowdy humiliation of a young woman who is paraded through the town with a placard around her neck stating, "I have offered myself to a Jew" (97). That younger Martha was able to rationalize and argue that this incident was not representative of all the actual good that was going on in Germany (98). Yet even in the above passage one notices that a year later, or whenever she wrote it, she is somehow forgetful of the mocking laughter and frenzy of that Nuremberg mob, and thus commits what Paxton calls one of the "facile errors"[20] that lets nazism's many enablers off the hook by claiming that "docile and kindly masses" were duped by an all-powerful dictator. True mourning, as Paul de Man once noted, is less deluded.

---

20 Robert O. Paxton, *The Anatomy of Fascism* (New York: Alfred A. Knopf, 2004), 9.

Diels, Martha's principal teacher, was closer to the mark, from a psychological point of view, in this 1934 declaration to a British embassy official:

"The infliction of physical punishment is not every man's job, and naturally we were only too glad to recruit men who were prepared to show no squeamishness at their task. Unfortunately, we knew nothing about the Freudian side of the business, and it was only after a number of instances of unnecessary flogging and meaningless cruelty that I tumbled to the fact that my organization had been attracting all the sadists in Germany and Austria without my knowledge for some time past. It had also been attracting unconscious sadists; i.e., men who did not know themselves that they had sadist leanings until they took part in a flogging. And finally it had been actually creating sadists. For it seems that corporeal chastisement ultimately arouses sadistic leanings in apparently normal men and women. Freud might explain it." (252)

We could call the evolution Diels describes as the power of *Gleichschaltung,* a term Larson translates as "coordination" (56), which means getting everyone locked on the same channel, in sync, what Fromm called "automaton conformity," and teenagers know as peer pressure. Once started, impressionable people like Martha, a veritable infant when she arrives in Germany with no German in 1933, will carry it on themselves, a process known as *Selbstgleichschaltung,* "self-coordination," just to fit in and appear normal.[21]

Chapter 31, "Night Terrors," is particularly effective at conveying how this process worked both on native Germans — Jews and non-Jews — and on foreigners like the Dodds.

---

21 This coordinated conformity was at work in the cruel mass violence of the Hutu against the Tutsi in Rwanda, as reported by Philip Gourevitch, Jean Hatzfeld, Ervin Staub, and in other legal and governmental investigations.

The lives of the Dodds underwent a subtle change. Where once they had felt free to say anything they wished within their own home, now they experienced a new and unfamiliar constraint. In this their lives reflected the broader miasma suffusing the city beyond their garden wall. […] It was Rudolf Diels who first conveyed to Martha the unfunny reality of Germany's emerging culture of surveillance. One day he invited her to his office and with evident pride showed her an array of equipment used for recording telephone conversations. […] As time passed the Dodds found themselves confronting an amorphous anxiety that infiltrated their days and gradually altered the way they led their lives. The change came about slowly, arriving like a pale mist that slipped into every crevice. (223–25)

In this chapter, and especially with the "pale mist" metaphor, we can see that the slow creep of *Gleichschaltung* is related to the strategy of gaslighting, a form of psychological manipulation that destabilizes people by exploiting their vulnerabilities and insecurities in order to better control and "coordinate" them. Both techniques attempt to destroy one's perception of reality and lock in another set of truthy truths or "alternative facts." These techniques are especially important to right-wing populists who face the challenge of spreading to at least 50 percent of the people, if they are to take power democratically, the idea that a more or less arbitrarily chosen out-group (Jews, "Blacks," Mexicans, Muslims, "Arabs," "queers," "retards") do not deserve the same human rights as everyone else. In other words, one must achieve a rationalization of dehumanization and persecution, a way to make unfairness seem fair, the unjust just. Dodd witnessed this propaganda but did not succumb to it:

Dodd had been struck again and again by the strange indifference to atrocity that had settled over the nation, the willingness of the populace and of the moderate elements in the government to accept each new oppressive decree, each new act of violence, without protest. It was as if he had entered the dark forest of a fairy tale where all the rules of right and wrong were upended. He wrote to his friend Roper, "I could not have imagined that outbreak against the Jews when everybody was suffering, one way or another, from declining commerce. Nor could one have imagined that such a terroristic performance as that of June 30 would have been permitted in modern times." (328)

Looking at the lives of William and Martha Dodd as portrayed in *In the Garden of Beasts,* it would seem that resisting *Gleichschaltung* and gaslighting is easier if one is somewhat educated, has lived abroad for a bit, and has a steady job that pays a living wage. William Dodd knew his history and had lived in Leipzig in the Kaiser's Germany, but he was also a tenured professor and the US president's ambassador. Therefore he does not fear for his life or his livelihood when he refuses to attend the Nuremberg rally or speaks his mind at dinner parties and in public. What's more, he already had a history of taking unpopular stances, such as when he objected to one-sided theories about the causes of World War I or to the Lost Cause ideology that discounted slavery's evil and endorsed a glorious "heritage" of the antebellum South.[22] That independent, contrarian spirit is what made Dodd's reputation before, during, and after his Berlin years. In short, Dodd was his own man from start to finish, and therefore it was easier for him to see the limitations of cliques, clubs, and exclusionary right-wing populisms and embrace instead the basic tenets of liberalism: the idea of a democratic republic based on welcoming everyone's talents and hard work in a collaborative spirit of equality under the law, basic individual rights and freedoms to construct and pursue one's life projects with dignity, and a level playing field that gives everyone a fair chance at opportunities regardless of skin color, gender, religion, background, and so forth. Dodd may have gone into the Berlin job with "rudimental anti-Semitism," as Larson calls it (167), but I

---

22 These non-fatal political stands are mentioned in the *Wikipedia* entry, not by Larson.

believe Dodd when he says, "I am no race antagonist" (166). Did his own father's semi-literate, impoverished condition, mentioned in the Wikipedia entry, combined with the persecution of Jews that he witnessed firsthand in Germany grant him more emotional intelligence, greater empathy for the vulnerable, and spur him to champion freedom all the more loudly after his return to the United States? Maybe, though the triggers of empathy, sympathy, and antipathy can often remain mysterious.

Martha, truly "naïve and unprepared," had to learn things the hard way. After an exaggerated period of infatuation and denialism, she eventually sheds her enthusiasm for nazism but only to fall for another authoritarian regime, Soviet communism, until many years later, Larson tells us, "Martha grew disillusioned with communism as practiced in everyday life. Her disenchantment became outright disgust during the 'Prague Spring' of 1968, when she awoke one day to find tanks rumbling past on the street outside her house during the Soviet invasion of Czechoslovakia" where she lived in exile with her last sugar daddy, Alfred Stern (362). Martha's inner sexual politics and her outer political views were of a piece. She had trapped herself in the "betrayal bond," to use the term of Patrick J. Carnes, and only broke free of exploitive relationships in the later years of her long exile in Prague where, according to her own account, she lived closer to "fruit trees, lilacs, vegetables, flowers, birds, and insects" (361) than to other human beings — more a beast in her garden than a free human being in the world.

4

Not Sorry to Bother You

Hélène Berr, *Journal* (2008)

Comparison is helpful, until it isn't. Saying X is like Y can il-
luminate; however, as with flashlights, analogies can also dis-
tort or leave what's outside the bright circle rather dark and
neglected. In other words, because they both open and close,
comparisons can be instructive, but one should not overdo it.
With that in mind, I would like to make two claims right away
to clarify things about Hélène Berr (1921–45) and her *Journal*
(2008).[1] First, Hélène Berr was not and is not "the French Anne

---

1   Hélène Berr, *Journal* (Paris: Éditions Tallandier, 2008). Hereafter cited par-
    enthetically throughout this chapter. I shall write *Journal* when referring
    to the Tallandier paperback publication from 2009 with a preface by Nobel
    Prize-winning author Patrick Modiano and appendices written and edited
    by Mariette Job. All page references are to this edition. I use the common
    noun "journal" or "diary" when referring to the object itself.
        I am again thankful to Karin Jackson for recommending Berr's *Journal*
    to me. I also thank Christine and Charles Hadley with whom I lived for
    parts of 2018 and 2019 at 1, avenue Berthelot in Lyon for introducing me
    to the nearby Center for the History of the Resistance and Deportation
    (CHRD) situated at 14, avenue Berthelot. It was there as part of a temporary
    exhibit devoted to growing up during World War II, "Génération 40: les
    jeunes et la guerre," that I saw a page of Hélène Berr's journal — a loose

Frank." And second, for those acquainted with *The Great Gatsby* (1925) and *A Room with a View* (1908) — two novels that Hélène Berr could have read but there is no evidence that she did — it may serve as a helpful transition from Martha Dodd's Berlin to Hélène Berr's Paris to say that Martha Dodd is to Daisy Buchanan as Hélène Berr is to Lucy Honeychurch. In addition, the rhythmic symmetry of this ratio and proportion makes it easy to remember. Martha Dodd is to Daisy Buchanan as Hélène Berr is to Lucy Honeychurch.

Like Lucy, Hélène Berr loved Beethoven. She also loved the English Romantic poets. She hoped to write a dissertation on John Keats and there are signs in the *Journal* that it might have been a strong piece of work had she been able to carry out that project. Her language skills and literary sensitivity were apparently fairly well-known in Paris's bookish circles, since one day out of the blue, but unfortunately less than two months before she and her parents are arrested, someone had offered her the chance to be the French translator of Percy Bysshe Shelley's *Defense of Poetry* — one of the most important texts in the entire English canon — and not as a personal favor or with some ulterior motive, nor as an act of charity, but, it seems, because he thought Hélène Berr, a young bright Jewish woman, was capable of doing a good job. Imagine that!

Nothing summarizes Martha Dodd's reckless life better than Nick Carraway's description of Tom and Daisy Buchanan in *The Great Gatsby*: "They were careless people — Tom and Daisy — they smashed up things and creatures and then retreated back into their money or their vast carelessness or whatever it was that held them together, and let other people clean up the mess they had made." Thanks to her US passport, political connections, and Aryan status, Martha could effortlessly escape Hitler's Berlin when things got too uncomfortable by boarding a ship or perhaps by then a plane to fly over Hélène Berr's Paris, cross the Atlantic, and land — a reverse Lindy hop! — in

piece of grid paper, roughly 15 × 20 cm, covered with a fairly small but not tiny handwriting in blue ink with very little crossing out.

New York, the city then taking over from Berlin, London, and Paris as the Western world's cultural capital, in part due to talented refugees from France (Marcel Duchamp), Germany (Erich Fromm), and other European countries. If Martha Dodd's escape from Germany is just one more instance of her "escape from freedom," Hélène Berr, when faced with the choice between fight or flee, remain or leave, decides "to continue to bother." In the parlance of our times, "she persisted." Her stubborn decision takes shape at the beginning of July 1943 when her father, detained at the Drancy prison about fifteen kilometers northeast of central Paris, is told he can be set free if he agrees to make a ransom payment but also leave Paris. Hélène Berr writes out her thinking of what this means:

> But with Papa disappearing into the Free Zone, the whole thing is calmed down, flattened out, that's their wish. They don't want any heroes. They want to make all contemptible, they don't want to incite any admiration for their victims.
>
> Well, if that's how it is, I make the wish to continue to bother them with all my force [*je fais le voeu de continuer à les gêner de toutes mes forces*].[2] (92)

That action verb *gêner* — to bother, annoy, irritate — captures well the major difference between the wartime lives of Hélène Berr and Anne Frank. The heroism of each of these "little women" is real but also quite different: Anne Frank writes while toughing it out in hiding; Hélène Berr writes as a witness from inside the lion's den, which is why it is simply unfair and misleading to call Hélène Berr the French Anne Frank. What's more, such a comparison, even if the intention is to praise and lift Hélène Berr and her *Journal* into public notice by associating her with the world-famous icon Anne Frank, risks backfiring if a hurried person who hears or reads that analogy thinks, "Why

---

2   I have translated this and other quotations from the journal myself, but there does exist a published English translation by David Bellos, *The Journal of Hélène Berr* (New York: Weinstein Books, 2008).

should I bother with a copy?" — in which case both Hélène Berr and her journal fall back into the oblivion where they had been lying for over sixty years; "A youth to Fortune and to Fame unknown."

Hélène Berr and her parents, Raymond and Antoinette, do not go into hiding until the winter of 1944 when sudden arrests of French Jews of all ages, not just foreign Jews on French soil, are becoming a near daily occurrence. And even when they do hide (Hélène Berr stays at the home of the family cook, Andrée Bardiau), the urge to sleep again in their own beds in their own apartment on March 7 — because, well, it *is* their home — leads to their arrest on the morning of March 8, the transfer to Drancy, and the deportation to Auschwitz on March 27, 1944, Hélène Berr's twenty-third birthday. Anne Frank was fifteen at that time and still hiding in the "secret annex"; Martha Dodd was thirty-six, based in New York, and had already published her own memoir, *Through Embassy Eyes* (1939), another book that Hélène Berr might have read had she but world enough and time.

So who is Hélène Berr and why did she keep a journal? Before answering, let me first say that I am going to keep calling her Hélène Berr because according to Nadine Heftler who knew her at Auschwitz, this is how she referred to herself. Heftler's testimony can serve as a first glimpse of the sort of person we're dealing with:

> What most struck me was the combination of tranquility and life force that she tried to pass on to us all. What would she say? She was always giving us encouragements. She managed to transport us out of the camp and our bottomless misery solely with the magic of her words. She also had this moral elegance and class that was entirely natural. She's the only person whose family name I remember, because Hélène liked to say that her name was Hélène Berr. (304)[3]

---

3   In line with Hélène Berr's own preferences, she is referred to by her full name throughout this chapter.

Why did she call herself Hélène Berr? Who knows, but my guess is that by always repeating both her names, as though it were a hyphenated first name like Jean-Charles, she reaffirmed her dual identity as both herself, a unique individual, and a link within wider circles of existence and concern, starting with the Berr family, a large, hard-working, fun-loving, and successful tribe with a long history of achievements and service to others and to France.[4] Besides being fluent in music, Hélène Berr studied both English and German as was the custom for people of the educated classes before, during, and after the war until about 1990 and, given her spirited love of languages, I like to think she may have been tickled that her family name sounded like the English word bear, first because her own mother had some of the protective, nurturing characteristics of a mother bear — Antoinette Berr née Rodrigues-Ély being one of many sturdy, accomplished, and kind women in the family.[5] And also because she is wildly enthusiastic about *Winnie-the-Pooh* (1926) to the point of wanting to read passages out loud to her mother and sister and get them as excited about that loveable literary bear as she was — and thereby momentarily shut out the horrible news of the deportations of friends and acquaintances that was raining down on them in mid-November 1943 (239–40). Hélène

---

4 I will not go into the details which are available online. Suffice it to say, her father graduated from France's most prestigious engineering school, École Polytechnique (1907), fought bravely in World War I, and rose to become one of the top directors of the important French chemical company Kuhlmann, now Péchiney. The family of Hélène Berr's mother also had a distinguished history. Both parents were beneficiaries of the Enlightenment-era values of reason, science, and toleration that gained traction in France's post-revolutionary meritocracy across two empires and three republics from 1789 to 1940. As assimilated Jews, not unlike the family of Alfred Dreyfus, Hélène Berr's family tree was somewhat cosmopolitan and had been fertilized by European romanticism, which explains the family's love of both German classical music and English literature.

5 Hélène Berr's awareness of the burdens borne by women in her family comes through in this remark from the entry for February 1, 1944: "La verité est que tout le souci et la fatigue de cette vie vont retomber sur Maman, toujours sur la femme" [The truth is that all the cares and fatigue of this life are going to fall on Mother, always on the woman] (286).

Berr would also know the homonyms of her animal name: *bear* as a verb meaning to support or put up with; *bear* also meaning to produce, create, or bring forth, as in to bear fruit; and *bare* meaning to reveal, but also *bare* as an adjective meaning stripped, naked, exposed, vulnerable. That her first name alludes to the Hellenistic period of Greek history, for many the cradle and summum of Western civilization from which the Nazi regime was an abominable falling off, requires no commentary. It is not impossible that Hélène Berr knew the adage attributed to Plautus, nomen est omen. In any case the *Journal* certainly confirms the unique fit between this person's life and her name.

For those interested in birth order and timing, it's worth noting that Hélène Berr is the fourth daughter of five children, the last being a boy, Jacques Berr (1922–98). Her oldest sister Jacqueline died of scarlet fever in 1921, the year Hélène Berr was born. Her two other older sisters, Yvonne and Denise, were born in 1917 and 1919, respectively. Yvonne and Jacques receive only passing references in the *Journal* because by then they are both living in the southern *Zone libre* (104). Hélène Berr, who played violin, was close to her sister Denise who played piano, probably taught by her mother, and it's clearly a loss to her, musically and emotionally, when Denise marries François Job on August 12, 1943 and moves out of the family apartment. Denise survives the war thanks to more successful hiding that started in 1944. It's Denise's daughter, Mariette Job, who will be the impetus behind the eventual publication of her aunt's diary, some of which had circulated informally among family members while the complete manuscript remained in the private possession of Hélène Berr's boyfriend of the time, Jean Morawiecki (1921–2008), who received it from the cook Bardiau after the war.[6]

It's worth taking a moment to consider two factors that may have impacted Hélène Berr's idea of herself starting around age

---

6 The cook can be commended for not throwing the journal away. For Mariette Job and Morawiecki, who both, for different reasons and in different ways, could have suffered from a certain survivor's guilt vis-à-vis Hélène Berr, the publication of the *Journal* may have helped them to have their "conscience calmed."

10 or 11 — the time, according to Fromm, of "the emergence of the individual and the ambiguity of freedom."[7] First, she in a sense replaced her oldest sister coming along as she did the same year Jacqueline died. Second, she may have wondered if her birth — *It's a girl!* — was perhaps greeted with murmurs of disappointment — *What? Again!?* — given the renewed efforts and eventual "success" of Antoinette and Raymond to produce a male heir, frère Jacques,[8] the following year in 1922. Perhaps these bothersome facts intensified Hélène Berr's determination, as though her family's stellar CV weren't enough, to become somebody, to make her own mark — *I'll show you!* — and yet remain mindful of life's transpersonal dimension that "you are not your own" (Alan Noble). She seeks to become a proficient violin player, in effect an original repeater of notes written by someone else, a translator (ditto), and, more daringly, a writer — a journalist or literary critic, and perhaps one day a poet and storyteller like Paul Valéry or A.A. Milne. By keeping a diary, she hits on the chance to give birth to herself, a second spiritual self that can live alongside her material, biological self, and perhaps survive the thousand natural shocks that her flesh will be heir to. She was fully acquainted with Hamlet's famous "to be or not to be" soliloquy (255) and many other canonical works. This rebirth is eventually what her niece and boyfriend together fully achieve in 2008, the same year Morawiecki dies, coincidentally; but the process was started by Hélène Berr herself with the very first words of her journal that could not be more perfect: "*Je reviens…,*" I'm returning.

So what is this *Journal* anyway? It is almost three hundred pages of dated entries, some as short as two or three lines, others two or three pages long, that span the time period from 4 p.m. April 7, 1942 to 7:15 p.m. on Tuesday February 15, 1944. There are

---

7   Erich Fromm, *Escape from Freedom* (New York: Henry Holt, 1969), 36.
8   Given the specter of the dead older sister Jacqueline, Jacques was probably not the best choice of name from the standpoint of the boy's future individuation, but it was certainly better than calling him Raymond, a name the Berr family could easily avoid because Jews do not name after the living.

two significant gaps over these twenty-three months. The first extends for nine months from November 28, 1942 to August 25, 1943. This interruption begins shortly after her boyfriend Jean Morawiecki leaves for the *Zone libre* on November 26. Hélène Berr then traverses a series of what one can only imagine were difficult times, the most devastating being the July 30, 1943 deportation of a close friend, Françoise Bernheim, who was seized in a roundup of all those who worked at the Jewish social services organization UGIF,[9] a roundup that Hélène Berr eluded by the sheer luck of not being at the office that day. Grieving the loss of these two individuals, Jean and Françoise, seems to have blocked any will to write, since before and after it is not her busy life or the gravity of the wartime situation that impede Hélène Berr from taking time to record her thoughts and feelings about important events, the weather, physical ailments, her studies, or about family members, friends, acquaintances, or total strangers.

The second interruption is a two-week gap that starts, as she says in her own words, at the moment the decision has been made to experiment with a nomadic life of hiding from the French and German police:

Tuesday — February 1, 1944
This time, again, a period is over. It will be necessary to adopt a bohemian life, a nomadic life. Here ends my "official life."

Monday — February 14, 1944
Schwab, Marianne, Gilbert.
I stopped writing this diary more than eight days ago while I asked myself if I had come to a turning point in my outward life. Nothing has happened yet. I continue to sleep at Andree's, my parents at the Loiselet's apartment. (288)

---

9   L'Union générale des israélites de France. I return to her involvement in this organization later in this chapter.

We see here that, unlike Martha Dodd for whom a promiscuous, bohemian life of constantly changing partners and places
became second nature, Hélène Berr, who earlier had stated
her aversion to change and her preference for routine and
continuity,[10] finds this nomadic existence to be a sort of living
hell. However, she yields to her father's argument in its favor
knowing that he, Raymond Berr (now a ghost of his former
self also named Raymond Berr), had already experienced the
alternative non-metaphorical hell of Drancy prison. Therefore
she accepts, reluctantly, that in order to eventually stay (alive)
they must leave their home near the Eiffel Tower at 5, avenue
Elisée Reclus 75007 Paris. Why she and her parents returned to
sleep at their apartment five weeks later on March 7 after having
adopted the sensible plan to stay on the move in order to avoid
arrest is the great mystery of Hélène Berr's *Journal*. What is clear
is that for some time — one can date it from various moments,
arguably even from April 7, 1942, the very day she began her
journal — Hélène Berr had been living, as she says months later,
"a posthumous life."[11] But she knew the dying and dead were capable of exerting a certain power over the living and the not
yet alive. This knowledge had been passed on to her first by her
dead sister Jacqueline who lived on spectrally through Hélène
Berr, and then from her acquaintance with classical music and
literature where she knew from first-hand experience how cer-

---

10 November 2, 1943: "[N]ul n'était plus ennemi des changements que moi.
C'était au point que je redoutais les réjouissances, les expériences nouvelles, si prometteuses fussent-elle (comme un voyage, ou un événement
imprévu), à cause du désordre qu'elles mettraient dans mon existence,
parce que aussi elles *m'intimidaient*" [No one was more an enemy of
change than I. It was to the point that I became wary of rejoicings, of new
experiences, no matter how promising they might be (such as a trip or an
unexpected event), on account of the disorder they would bring into my
existence, and because they *intimidated me*] (229).

11 Hélène Berr writes this as she is thinking about how, but for a stroke of
luck, she should have been rounded up with Françoise Bernheim and her
other coworkers at the UGIF on July 30, 1943: *"J'oublie que je mène une vie
posthume, que j'aurais dû mourir avec eux"* [I forget that I'm living a posthumous life and that I ought to have died with them] (243). It's a moment
of "There but for the grace of God, go I."

tain notes or the words of someone like Keats, who died almost exactly one hundred years before she was born, could stimulate all her senses and an array of feelings such that it was hard to tell who was alive and who was dead or had been dead until that moment of playing or reading.[12] She knew that the dead and their experiences could live on and would only live on in the memory of the living and the not yet born, including her own not yet born future self, a 30- or 40- or even 100-year-old Hélène Berr, uncertain if she will be allowed to become that person.

Put another way, with less of the poetic and gothic flair she may have picked up from reading Keats, Shelley, or William Wordsworth, she was leading a double life — that of an exuberant, capable, loving young woman raring to go, and that of an observant and often indignant witness and analyst, wise beyond her years as one says, who used journal-writing to record the gradual darkening and hardening of Paris and many Parisians during the Occupation and her own struggle to remain positive — to not succumb to the self-hatred and self-doubt spread by fascist "thinking" that was corrupting the souls and sapping the energy of so many.

The start of this double life takes place one fine day during a year when everything good and true and beautiful that she believed in seemed to be under assault. It is the spring day Hélène Berr begins her journal. April 7 is her second birthday, the start of her life as a writer, and the most important event on that day, besides beginning her journal at 4 p.m. in order to record it, is her return from the home of Paul Valéry, France's most famous living poet in those days, an elderly man fifty years her senior

---

12 Hélène Berr is an assiduous recorder of the many times she plays classical music with others; the same is true for all her reading, clearly a quasi-religious act for her, a communion or meeting of hearts and minds as is evident in the many pages where she writes out and writes about particular lines and their authors such as Montaigne's thoughts on death, Roger Martin du Gard's *Les Thibault* and *Épilogue,* portions of "Adonais," Shelley's tribute to Keats (253), or Keats's apostrophic eight-line poem "This Living Hand" (207) which she calls, "ces vers saisissants" — grasping verses. This short poem is Hélène Berr's cheerful teacher and guide.

who had not yet fled south as he would later do, ironically outliving Hélène Berr by roughly four months. In a bold move, which, she notes with pleasure, surprised even her mother, Hélène Berr had some time earlier dropped off a copy of a volume of Valéry's poetry for it to be signed, if possible, by the great poet himself. On April 7 she screws up her courage to go and see if it's ready. The little packet is handed back to her by Valéry's concierge. She first sees that her name has been written neatly in black ink on the paper she had wrapped the book in. Once outside she unwraps it and discovers on the first page the following words[13]:

Exemplaire de mademoiselle Hélène Berr
« *Au réveil, si douce la lumière, et si beau ce bleu vivant* »
Paul Valéry

Hélène Berr is overjoyed. She experiences, as she says, "a little feeling of triumph" that she's eager to share with her parents, and a surge of confidence that dreams can come true, or as she says, *"l'impression qu'au fond l'extraordinaire était réel."*[14] This victory brings with it an "I am somebody" realization, a spiritual awakening aided by Valéry's validating inscription addressed uniquely to her, Hélène Berr. It's the all-important moment in the emergence of the individual, described by Fromm multiple times, when one makes the leap from the severed primary ties (*freedom from*) to forge an original relation to the universe. And suddenly the meaning of life becomes crystal clear: I am a free and independent individual put on this earth by an act of love (followed by a lot of hard work by my primary caregivers) and welcomed to freely love and work in my turn through my spontaneous emotional, sensuous, and intellectual pursuits that unite me with the world. Americans of all kinds may hear in this affirmation an echo of the exhortation "trust thyself" that rings out in the writings of transcendentalists from Ralph Waldo Em-

---

13 A copy for Miss Hélène Berr. "Upon waking, the light so soft, and so beautiful this lively blue."

14 "… the impression that in fact the extraordinary was real."

erson to Mary Oliver to Barack Obama, and perhaps most bracingly in "Our Deepest Fear" by Marianne Williamson:

Our deepest fear is not that we are inadequate.
Our deepest fear is that we are powerful beyond measure.
It is our light, not our darkness
That most frightens us.

We ask ourselves
Who am I to be brilliant, gorgeous, talented, fabulous?
Actually, who are you *not* to be?
You are a child of God.

Your playing small
Does not serve the world.
There's nothing enlightened about shrinking
So that other people won't feel insecure around you.

We are all meant to shine,
As children do.
We were born to make manifest
The glory of God that is within us.

It's not just in some of us;
It's in everyone.

And as we let our own light shine,
We unconsciously give other people permission to do the
same.
As we're liberated from our own fear,
Our presence automatically liberates others.[15]

Heftler's Auschwitz testimony strongly suggests that Hélène Berr became just the sort of liberator described in these lines,

---

15 Marianne Williamson, *A Return to Love: Reflections on the Principles of a Course in Miracles* (New York: HarperCollins, 1992), 165.

a young woman who could turn the world on with her smile. How did that happen? What does Hélène Berr *do* on Day 2, 3, and so on now that she has decided to both live the active life of a 21-year-old in Paris during the Occupation and also write about it? If we consider the *Journal* as divided in two parts — before and after the double loss of both Love (Jean Morawiecki) and Friendship (Françoise Bernheim) — it can be said of part one that it is primarily focused on introspection: Hélène Berr's efforts to identify, sort out, and think through her thoughts and feelings as she goes about the daily plans and projects she constructs as well as the events, some pleasurable but many painful, that she undergoes. If in part one the reader is more a witness of "the formation of thoughts while thinking" (Heinrich von Kleist), in part two Hélène Berr's voice changes somewhat as she more self-consciously takes on the role of witness, reporter, and *passeur*.[16] This change is partly understandable as now with her love gone, the journal at times reads like a letter to the absent Jean, who abandoned his law studies, and Hélène Berr herself, to join De Gaulle's army in Africa. But if the journal takes on the character of something intended to be read by a special someone who is being granted access to bits of her private self, Hélène Berr also seems to be writing both still for herself — especially in all the passages where she is trying to figure something out — and now also for a wider readership in addition to the young man with whom she had been able to enjoy a brief union of hearts and minds for three or six months. This open letter gesture is most in evidence when Hélène Berr is being her most declarative and teacherly, even preachy. There's the idea clearly stated in the entry for October 10, 1943 that this is a rough draft sent into the future for her, or someone like her, to polish and expand on later to show people what those times were like: *"Il

---

16 I acknowledge here the pioneering work on witnesses, witnessing, and testimony carried out by my former teacher and dissertation director Shoshana Felman, especially a seminar of hers that I was lucky enough to attend that featured the poetry of Paul Celan, the Hollywood film *Judgment at Nuremberg* (1961), and the documentary *Shoah* (1985) by Claude Lanzmann.

faudrait donc que j'écrive pour pouvoir plus tard montrer aux hommes ce qu'a été cette époque" (187) [Therefore I must write so that later I can show people what this time really was].

If she falls short of having all the insights of the narrator of Williamson's poem, her journal also avoids the transcendentalist's over-wrought boosterism. One could say that the many spontaneous sprinklings of English words throughout the *Journal*, and even more so the many quotations from literary works, some lengthy, that proliferate in the second half, are modest transcendental experiments in trying on another voice, or voices. They are role-playing, like one finds in the serious play of the rapper MF Doom, preludes to what Hélène Berr might have undertaken in a more public, literary vein had her development as a writer and a human being not been arrested by a "fever" more random and incomprehensible to her than the one that had killed her oldest sister Jacqueline.

But there is a distinctive voice of her own that becomes increasingly audible in the second, less girlish half of the *Journal,* a voice that still expresses joy and enjoyment but now, often, also disappointment and especially indignation that she and others just starting out in life should have their beautiful dreams, their potential, cut off violently and arbitrarily. She also notes how many older people (thankfully not her grandmother who gets to die of old age in the same bed in which Hélène Berr and her mother were born) are also robbed of their dignity by an unnatural death ordered by the German administration and carried out by collaborators whom she rejects en masse as *"des fanatiques et des automates"* (281). She did not need to know about gas chambers in order to understand that the goal, especially if one is deporting young children, was extermination:

La monstrueuse incompréhensibilité, l'horrible illogisme de tout cela vous torture l'esprit. Il n'y a sans doute pas à réfléchir, car les Allemands ne cherchent même pas de raison, ou d'utilité. Ils ont un but, exterminer. (292)

The monstrous incomprehensibility, the horrible illogic of it all tortures your spirit. One should probably not even try to come up with an explanation because the Germans are not basing this on reason or utility. They have one goal, to exterminate.

This passage and the whole last seven-page entry for Tuesday, February 15, 1944 — three weeks before her arrest, perhaps written on her new bed *chez Andrée* — displays the mature voice of Hélène Berr that has now reached maximum intensity and incisive clairvoyance. Only to be cut off. Her last three words, presumably written at night on that same day, are *"Horror! Horror! Horror!"* It is a complex fusion of climactic moments in Shakespeare's *Macbeth,* Joseph Conrad's *Heart of Darkness* (1902), and the life of Hélène Berr that punctuates her act of witnessing and relaying as a reader and writer.

***

Hélène Berr's *Journal* is a coming-of-age story, which means one can expect an account of acquiring new powers but also an apprenticeship of loss.[17] The familiar arc, as old as Adam and Eve, from childish things (*"ces choses enfantines,"* 19) to adult matters, from innocence to experience, is in evidence on every page. The details of that arc could be listed chronologically as a series of events that take place after the inaugural literary encounter with "the truly great" Valéry. Among the major events recorded are the day when she has to start wearing the yellow star that forces her to "represent" as JUIVE (51–54)[18]; the arrest of her father, sup-

---

17 In a similar vein, a 16-year-old Jewish teenager in 1940s Paris is the focus of Sandrine Kiberlain's beautiful film, *Une jeune fille qui va bien* (2022). A film adaptation of the *Journal of Hélène Berr* would likely be darker.

18 Hélène Berr's indignation about the "Jewish star" recurs over thirty pages and culminates with her observation that in the street she was constantly forced to represent and that just going outside had become an ordeal. *"Dans la rue, on est sans cesse obligé de représenter, c'est une épreuve de sortir"* [In the street one is constantly obliged to represent, it's a torment

posedly for wearing the star pinned instead of stitched on, and his detention at Drancy starting on June 23, 1942 (72–76)[19]; the arrest of 13,152 Jews on July 16 and 17, 1942, the infamous *Rafle du Vél' d'Hiv* (104–7), the largest mass arrest in France during World War II[20]; her father's release from Drancy on September 22, 1942 (144–45); Jean's departure on November 26, 1942 (165)[21]; the arrest of Françoise and others at the UGIF offices on July 30, 1943 (186)[22]; Denise's wedding on August 12, 1943 (183); the death of her maternal grandmother (249); and her parents' decision that they go into hiding (286–89).

In addition, Hélène Berr records a multitude of other events, reactions, and replies that also cross back and forth between

---

to go out.] (86). Besides dealing with the gaze and reactions of others, Hélène Berr objects to being forced to participate in the Nazi racialization of a religion that she happens to have been born into with all the gradual reductions of one's rights that follow from this "Jewish race" stigmatization, from exclusion and persecution to deportation and extermination.

19 Hélène Berr's relationship with Jean heats up, so to speak, in the summer of her father's three-month absence during which she receives only occasional letters from Drancy and must have wondered if she would ever see him again — a hanging scenario that repeats itself, but for a longer duration, after Jean Morawiecki leaves.

20 The *Journal* states 12,884 were arrested. The figure 13,152 is the number that appears on the commemorative plaque at the location of the former cycling stadium where those arrested were held before their deportation.

21 Impossible to know how much Jean Morawiecki's decision to leave was influenced by the return of Hélène Berr's father.

22 Hélène Berr writes about this roundup across several entries. She was clearly upset that some claimed she and her UGIF co-workers were collaborating with the enemy as a way to win favors or protection from deportation. While crushed by the deportation of Françoise and the others, their arrest, as she notes, is clear evidence that the UGIF gave no one shelter from the storm. Even so, Hélène Berr recognizes the "sinister" dimension of being part of an organization that lures Paris's Jewish population into cooperating with the French authorities and their German supervisors (241–43). Like the segregating ordinances, the UGIF was a tool for *Gleichschaltung* — getting everyone on the same page, falling in line, following orders. The position allowed Hélène Berr to witness and learn more about the management of Jewish affairs than she otherwise could have. In a sense, it's her beat, and therefore serves the cub reporter dimension of her journal-writing activity. See Michel Laffitte, "L'UGIF, collaboration ou résistance?" *Revue d'Histoire de la Shoah* 2, no. 185 (2006): 45–64.

physical states and mental states. These include how she met Jean and their subsequent dates and courtship; her constant crisscrossing of Paris from her home to the Sorbonne, to her library job, to her job at the UGIF offices that expands into taking orphaned kids out for nature walks, to her German lessons, and to her grandmother's house; her day trips to the family's country house at Aubergenville located fifty kilometers northwest of Paris; her playing chamber music with family; various errands by bus, subway, or on foot to the doctor, bookshops, a cobbler, the post office; meals and meet ups with friends, especially with Jean until he's gone, and meetings with authorities, whether professors or the police, and of course her daily rendezvous with her books, pens, and paper.

There is no need to go into the details of all these events; however, it is worth noting the large number and variety of activities that fill her days. She is certainly on the move, and the maps provided in the center of the paperback edition give some idea of the distances involved. They, along with the half dozen photos included, also provide a visual supplement to the less visible inner journeys and crossings Hélène Berr makes or undergoes. One sees that her double life is itself composed of a great number of paired items that are in tension or dialogue and that her body and brain are constantly moving or mediating between these poles. Among them are Paris versus Aubergenville; Occupied Zone versus Free Zone; school versus home versus prison versus park versus street; the stability of home versus the uncertainty of changing addresses; confinement versus freedom; Jews versus non-Jews; French Jews versus foreign Jews; England versus France; French versus Germans; the German language and music versus "the Germans"; family versus friends; casual friends versus special friends; the core Hélène Berr family versus the extended family and in-laws; the pleasure of falling in love versus the pain of lost love and of her father's arrest; university studies versus independent studies — especially "careless people" at the Sorbonne, professors and students, who seem to tune out the human tragedy that's going on versus Hélène Berr who has that reality pressing down on her and shoved in her face practically every day.

Patrick Modiano is right to devote part of his introduction to Hélène Berr's account of a casual exchange at the boat basin in the Luxembourg Garden where she and a non-Jewish classmate are discussing who will win the war. The young man thinks the Germans will win. "But what will become of us if the Germans win?" Hélène Berr asks. "Nothing will change," he says, "there will still be the sun and the water" (30-31). To which Hélène Berr forced herself to say, *"Je me suis forcée à dire: 'Mais ils ne laissent pas tout le monde jouir de la lumière et de l'eau !'"* [But they don't let everyone enjoy the light and the water]." And then in her journal adds, *"Heureusement, cette phrase me sauvait, je ne voulais pas être lâche."* [Luckily, that sentence saved me, I didn't want to be a coward]. The French word *lâche* is both a noun and an adjective, *coward* or *cowardly,* but it also relates to the verb *lâcher,* to release, loosen, or free, the opposite of tight, taut, controlled, strict. For Hélène Berr, being *lâche* means being too loose, too relaxed, free but the bad kind of free that results from blindness, willful ignorance, or excessive egotism. There's a time for being carefree — playing or listening to music, reading, picnicking at Aubergenville, and she loves all that with real gusto. But at the wrong time, carefree turns into the carelessness and casual cruelty she has observed in so many people. At base, the high-strung Hélène Berr is an intensely sensitive moralist. That's why she admires Roger Martin du Gard (208-13) but can't stand André Gide (223). It's why she risks taking a chance on loving and being loved by Jean who, though not Jewish, seems to *get it,* but remains uncertain about his mother whom she suspects may be yet another conforming automaton harboring prejudice against people of Hélène Berr's *"catégorie"* — or *"espèce,"* another sanitizing and dehumanizing euphemism she mocks. And it's certainly why she could not possibly run away with Jean but must instead stay in Paris where she will continue to irritate, bother, and annoy French and Germans alike as she goes about her business, even if that means being frequently upset and, as she often says, *éreintée,* physically and emotionally exhausted.

But there's one thing that exhausts Hélène Berr more than all her physical exertions and more than all the heartache of her own losses and witnessing the losses of others. Starting in November 1943, the 22-year-old is regularly wracking her brain to figure out how nazism has managed to turn so many Germans and French people into automatons, fanatics, zombies who look like normal people but manifestly have lost nearly all capacity for thinking or feeling beyond brute animal instincts. She just doesn't get how fascism works, and this is very unsettling to a smart and sensitive person whose father is a prominent engineer and industrialist who no doubt raised his children to believe in science, logic, rationality, and the idea that there is an answer to every question, a solution to every problem — including the problem of nazism.

For all her interest in literature — especially Shakespeare, the English Romantic poets, and two leading inventors of children's literature, Milne and Lewis Carroll — and despite occasional use of the words *cauchemar* (60) [nightmare] and *rêve* [dream] and even the description of a dream of hers with Jean in it (217), it is somewhat surprising that the *unconscious* figures hardly at all in her journal.[23] Her explanations for nazism's rise and dissemination grasp at the usual physical metaphors of intoxication and infection, but she has no clue that there might actually be a "psychology of Nazism" — even though Freud, Freudians, and post-Freudians had been publishing their ideas for four decades already; and one of them, Fromm, had published a clear account of the "Psychology of Nazism" in 1941 in both English, *Escape from Freedom,* and German, *Die Furcht vor der Freiheit.* I am not faulting Hélène Berr for not reading Fromm, she's in good company there, but it is odd that someone who clearly has plenty of money to spend on books, who works part-time at a humanities library, knows many smart people, and is the child

---

23 In the middle of her commentary of some writings of Roger Martin du Gard, she intriguingly affirms the novel's power to reveal psychological truths: *"Je crois à la révélation psychologique dans le 'roman'"* [I believe in the psychological revelation of novels] (209).

of a prominent scientist forced to work from home after his release from Drancy and of a mother and grandmother who seem
to have been two tireless listeners and comforters would have
taken no notice of arguably the most important shift in Western
thinking since the influential writings of Karl Marx and Charles
Darwin. From this angle, her denunciations of others' blindness
start to sound like the pot calling the kettle black. But she's only
22, right?

Hélène Berr's problem, easier to see for someone more than
twice her age, is that she approaches the Nazi Problem with an
overly compartmentalized division between the Classical doctrine and the Romantic movement instead of seeing that these
two ways of thinking, and the very division that we imagine to
exist between thinking and feeling, are really much more porous
and mutually interdependent, as any poet, novelist, or storyteller
knows. Put another way, Hélène Berr is overthinking it, and my
guess is that it's because up until the war she was mostly insu-
lated from vulnerability by all the advantages that automatically
came with being the fourth child in an established, loving, and
fairly well-off family. The entry for Saturday, July 18, the day following the *Vél d'hiv'* roundup — a time when one would assume
there to be widespread sensitivity about vulnerability across all
of Paris — includes a tell about Hélène Berr's class consciousness:

> *Le peuple est admirable. Il paraît qu'il y avait beaucoup de pe-
> tites ouvrières qui vivaient avec des israélites. Elles viennent
> toutes demander à se marier, pour éviter à leurs maris la dé-
> portation.* (106)

The people are admirable. It seems that there were lots of
working-class women who lived with Israelites. They are all
asking to get married to keep their husbands from getting
deported.

When I read those sentences today, I see a rag-tag bunch of
demonstrators being observed by people looking out from the

windows of apartments that cost over 10,000 euros per square meter; I see a woman sunning herself on the deck of some island or mountain getaway while she reads *The New Yorker* staff writer Rachel Aviv's investigative journalism about a battered women's shelter in Boston or homeless transgender people in New York; I see myself, a white male with tenure raised in a middle class two-parent family. From far away, one is tempted to laugh or cringe when one reads *"Le peuple," "petites,"* and *"israélites"* in this account of a French "Sadie Hawkins Day" carnival atmosphere during wartime. But the July 18 entry also contains more sobering moments such as the dark exchange she records of a chance meeting in the Paris subway with one of her UGIF colleagues, Madame Baur:

> *Dans le métro, j'ai rencontré Mme Baur, toujours superbe. Mais elle était très abattue. Elle ne m'a pas reconnue tout de suite. Elle avait l'air étonné que nous soyons là. J'ai toujours envie d'être fière lorsque je réponds à cela. Elle m'a dit que nous aurions beaucoup à faire rue de Téhéran. Elle ne m'a pas caché non plus que le tour des Françaises allait venir. Lorsqu'elle m'a parlé d'Odile, il m'a semblé que c'était infiniment loin.* (106)

In the subway, I met Madame Baur, so classy looking as usual. But she was really very down. She didn't recognize me right away. She seemed surprised we were there. I'm always inclined to feel proud when I reply to that remark. She told me we would have our hands full at the rue de Teheran [the address of the UGIF]. She also told me she thought that French women would be getting their turn soon. When she spoke to me about Odile, it seemed to me that that was a long way away.

It's not her fault, one could say, she did nothing wrong, she was doing her best, she has nothing to atone for; and yet, in the entry for July 2, 1942 during her father's detention at Drancy and shortly after learning of the ransom deal for his release — in other words at a highly vulnerable moment — Hélène Berr writes,

"I had a desire for expiation, I don't know why" (91). Vulnerability can be a good teacher, the old "school of hard knocks." But too much vulnerability, and for too long, and crazy talk sets in.[24] You can start doubting yourself or losing your mind, or you may become self-destructive or destructive of others.[25]

Hélène Berr was on the winning side of Paris's unequal distribution of socio-economic vulnerability for the first eighteen years of her life — good for her. But Hélène Berr's vulnerability emerges in September 1939 and ramps up between June 1940 and July 1942 when her Jewish father — despite being wealthy, well-connected, French, and a war veteran — is exposed to the very real possibility of being arbitrarily deported along with the thousands of other more vulnerable foreign Jews. There are signs that some vulnerability actually sharpens her eyesight and focuses her pen, so long as it stays at moderate levels. Her analysis of what's wrong about the ransom deal and what the Vichy-German government's motives are for making it are spot on: "But with Papa disappearing into the Free Zone, the whole thing is calmed down, flattened out, that's their wish. They don't want any heroes" (92). Another example comes in the entry for October 30, 1942, a somewhat calmer moment a month after her father's release. Here the words are actually from Roger Martin du Gard, but it doesn't matter because it's Hélène Berr who copies them out, her hand energized, I believe, by the truth that she knows is in these lines:

> Il est tentant de se débarrasser du fardeau exigeant de sa personnalité ! Il est tentant de se laisser englober dans un vaste mouvement d'enthousiasme collectif ! Il est tentant de croire, parce que c'est commode, et parce que c'est suprêmement confortable ! (222)

---

24 See Neil Postman, *Crazy Talk, Stupid Talk: How We Defeat Ourselves by the Way We Talk — And What to Do About It* (New York: Delacorte, 1976).

25 Fromm, *Escape from Freedom*, 177–83.

It's tempting to get rid of the demanding burden of one's personality! It's tempting to allow oneself to be sucked into a vast all-encompassing movement of collective enthusiasm! It's tempting to believe, because it's convenient, and because it's supremely comfortable!

In these three sentences published in 1940, Hélène Berr has zeroed in on what triggers the escape from freedom as identified by Erich Fromm in 1941: feeling insecure at the prospect of having to be an adult individual and believe in oneself. These adult attitudes are particularly challenging to sustain for those who are experiencing acute or chronic vulnerability. Such panicky individuals, as we've said from the start, may be very willing to give up their freedom and their free institutions and submit to authoritarian or fascist leaders, be it a large company, church, state, or a combination of all three. What Hélène Berr does not quite see is how this self-sabotage and surrender can lead to massive numbers of dead people, either by active extermination, as in the Nazi example and other genocides, or, as is more often the case today, through "sadopopulism";[26] in other words, passive neglect by allowing disease, poisoning, or environmental disasters to run rampant among outgroups whose lives are judged meaningless, worthless, or expendable by those in charge.[27]

It's hardly surprising to see Hélène Berr's indignation toward French and German persecution of Jews increase over the last

---

26 This apt term was coined by Timothy Snyder in his important study *The Road to Unfreedom: Russia, Europe, America* (New York: Tim Duggan Books, 2018), 272–75.

27 Stalin's starvation of Ukrainians is a classic case; but the contemporary United States provides many examples such as the opioid epidemic (a record 100,000 overdose deaths in 2021 alone), the water poisoning in Flint, Michigan, the wildfires in Paradise, CA, and of course the Covid-19 catastrophe. The United States currently has the lowest life expectancy among advanced countries. Jared Ortaliza et al., "How Does US Life Expectancy Compare to Other Countries?" *Health System Tracker,* September 28, 2021, https://www.healthsystemtracker.org/chart-collection/u-s-life-expectancy-compare-countries/#item-le_total-life-expectancy-at-birth-in-years-1980-2017_dec-2019-update.

fifty pages as her explanatory power stalls and stutters. This may happen because her mind is so vulnerable now to the prospect of her own arrest, deportation, and death that she is too spent, *éreintée,* to make the connection between the desire to escape from freedom and the willingness to aid in the extermination of millions of people, and in the most sadistic individuals the active desire to do so. And yet she was close to seeing it as she copied out the passages from Martin du Gard's *Thibault.*

Therefore, instead of coming up with an explanation, Hélène Berr repeatedly denounces those she considers blind (226). She denounces fatalistic thinking (226), the *"abrutissement"* [animal stupidity] of people, their "total loss of moral conscience" (232), and "Germans." About Germans, she affirms, "all intelligence is dead among them," before adding, "[b]ut one hoped that among us [the French] things would be different" (233), implying they are not. These blanket statements continue ten pages later: Germans are "intoxicated, they no longer think, they have no critical faculties left, 'The Führer thinks for us,'" she mockingly writes (248). She's not wrong exactly. It's just a bit too easy and exaggerated, and therefore, she's smart enough to know, not satisfying or consoling because the root cause has still not been clearly identified.[28] This flailing around, evidenced by the increasing number of doubting questions, such as about the character of her possible future mother-in-law (260–61), increases after her grandmother dies and again after the dreadful prospect of having to change addresses becomes a reality. Hélène Berr is being forcefully reminded that *l'accomplissement de mon moi* (266) [the fulfilment of her *self*] through the work she wanted to accomplish — her dissertation on Keats and the translation of Shelley, for starters — is being stymied by the "tyrannical call of reality," in other words, the increasing likelihood that the conflict of World War II would very soon enter her home and disrupt and perhaps terminate her natural life.

---

28 Hélène Berr's anger and exasperation remind me of the indignant speeches of the earnest Greta Thunberg.

When she's not denouncing or simply recording, she passes into a mode of lamentation as she imagines herself and those like her being robbed of their youth and all their potential: "exactly like a violin," she writes, "full of still dormant possibilities, capable of awakening the deepest and purest emotions, [...] broken by a brutal, sacrilegious force" (287). This emotivism culminates with the triple repetition of "Horror!" Again, more heat than light.

But in this regard Hélène Berr is not without some prestigious company, namely all those who see the extermination of six million individuals under the direction of the same *"peuple"* that produced Bach and Beethoven as something irreducibly mysterious. One such person is French historian Annette Wieviorka, who, in a handy little book entitled *Auschwitz expliqué à ma fille* [*Auschwitz Explained to My Daughter*] published in 1999, therefore nine years before Hélène Berr's *Journal,* concludes her Introduction with these remarks (my translation):

> Even though it is easy for me as a historian to describe Auschwitz and explain how the genocide of the Jews unfolded, there remains an inherently incomprehensible and therefore unexplainable mystery [il reste un noyau proprement incompréhensible, donc inexplicable]. Why did the Nazis want to eradicate the Jews from the planet? Why did they spend so much energy searching across the four corners of the Europe they occupied from Amsterdam to Bordeaux, from Warsaw to Salonika, rounding up children and the elderly to then simply assassinate them?[29]

Those questions could have been written by Hélène Berr. She asks similar ones that also go unanswered. But must we really give up so easily? Must this remain an unsolved riddle? What good does that do? And for whom? Fromm did not claim absolute certainty, but there is a plausible hypothesis articulated in *Escape from Freedom* and groped at, like in a pin-the-tail-on-

---

29   Annette Wieviorka, *Auschwitz expliqué à ma fille* (Paris: Seuil, 1999), 10–11.

the-donkey game, over many pages of Hélène Berr's smart and sensitive *Journal*. Put crudely and simply, the hypothesis is this:

> I am nobody, therefore you cannot be somebody, therefore I have to kill you and erase all memory that you ever existed.

The passive-aggressive version preferred by those who wish to outsource the killing would be:

> I am nobody, therefore you cannot be somebody, therefore I have to see that you die and that all memory of your existence is erased.

The escape from freedom is always an escape from the burden of being somebody, of being an individual, of having to "get a life," "earn a living," stand on your own two feet, and put up with one's "mortal coil," and let others do the same. Here is Fromm writing in the first person to convey to his reader the odd logic of the destructive personality's leap beyond mere sadism:

> I can escape the feeling of my own powerlessness in comparison with the world outside myself by destroying it. To be sure, if I succeed in removing it, I remain alone and isolated, but mine is a splendid isolation in which I cannot be crushed by the overwhelming power of the objects outside myself. The destruction of the world is the last, almost desperate attempt to save myself from being crushed by it.[30]

The burden is heaviest for those who are most acutely and chronically vulnerable, or at least think they are. Others tend not to see it that way unless a day comes along when they experience some reversal of fortune or landslide of the mind. When that happens, empathy may sprout up, one's circle of concern may widen. Cultivating empathy through an act of imagination, though never quite as good as knowing it in your bones, as

---

30 Fromm, *Escape from Freedom,* 177.

Hélène Berr learned from Keats (228) and from personal experience, is what the poem "First They Came" is all about:

They came first for the Communists,
And I didn't speak up because I wasn't a Communist.

Then they came for the Jews,
And I didn't speak up because I wasn't a Jew.

Then they came for the trade unionists,
And I didn't speak up because I wasn't a trade unionist.

Then they came for the Catholics,
And I didn't speak up because I was a Protestant

Then they came for me
And by that time no one was left to speak up.

There exist several versions of this text which all derive from a
public confession made by the German Lutheran pastor Martin
Niemöller on January 6, 1946 in Frankfurt. This one happens
to be the inscription etched in stone at the New England Holocaust Memorial in Boston, Massachusetts.[31] Besides the empathy-building exercise at work in this poem, there is a modest
proposal, an unspoken suggestion that in the future individuals
or groups could or should advocate more or better for the vulnerable and the persecuted, the mute and the mutilated.

---

31 For an updating, see Timothy Snyder's July 25, 2020 reply to Rachel
Maddow asking about the vital importance of protest on the occasion of
President Trump's deployment of federal troops to Portland, Oregon: "If
first they come for the undocumented, […] then they come for the Blacks,
[…] then they come for the protesters […]. At some point you have to turn
it around and say like those moms in Portland are doing, 'if they're coming
for the protesters, I have to stand up for those people, I have to stand up
for my fellow people.' If you're not protesting now, this would be a good
time to start." @MaddowBlog, Twitter, July 25, 2020, https://twitter.com/
MaddowBlog/status/1286874121968680960.

FASCISM, VULNERABILITY, AND THE ESCAPE FROM FREEDOM

Kibbitzing about whether Hélène Berr ought to have spoken *out* or *up* more, done more, played her cards differently, and so forth is something I leave to others. I prefer to conclude with a few observations about the circumstances surrounding the publication of the *Journal* in 2008, a year I witnessed unfold as I traveled between Lyon, Toulouse, and America. If Hélène Berr's deepest wish was to *gêner* — bother, annoy, irritate — she would be pleased to know that her ex-boyfriend and niece collaborated to have her journal appear smack in the middle of the rancorous debates about the place of Islam in France, about the good or evil of the "veil laws" of 2004 and 2010, and ultimately about who has full personhood and gets to participate in France's post-Vichy democratic *république,* and who doesn't. I am not claiming that this coincidence was intentional, it may have been the furthest thing from their minds; but the *Journal* arrives like the proverbial fly in the ointment (or *comme un cheveu sur la soupe* [like a hair in the soup], as the French say) if one notices the similarity between the infamous Vichy-era ordinances, especially the requirement for Jews to wear the yellow "Jewish star" in public, and the veil laws requiring certain people who shall not be named (psst, Muslims) to *not* wear something that also shall not be named (psst, a hijab or burka). I suspect many did not notice this *téléscopage* of back then and here now, or its wider implications.

By 2008 enlightened France had moved on from bullying Jews, at least in public; in fact, it was made officially illegal through laws against hate speech and negationism (la loi Gayssot, 1990). Two cheers for legislating morality. However, over the 1990s and into the new century, intolerance falling on *"les Arabes,"* especially Muslims, and especially Muslim women (*"toujours sur la femme,"* as Hélène Berr noted) became widely tolerated. The most fervent proponents of the veil laws did not hesitate to claim that they were passed *for their own good*; that is, for the good of the Muslim women.[32] The clothing restric-

---

32 For one American assessment of the early stages of this controversy, see Jane Kramer, "Taking the Veil," *The New Yorker,* November 22, 2004,

tions advanced their emancipation, it was said. It took others to point out the Orwellian ring to this claim as well as the sinister aspects of the piling on that took place, after President Sarkozy had left office, under the Socialist presidency of François Hollande (2012–17). His governing majority passed a law requiring rules for secularism, *La Charte de la Laïcité* (2013), to be posted in all public buildings, especially schools, right next to the *Declaration of the Rights of Man and the Citizen*. This was followed in late 2015, in the wake of two devastating terrorist attacks on January 7–9 and November 13, by the creation of a new French national holiday, Le jour de la Laïcité — December 9, which is the anniversary of the passage of the 1905 law separating church and state. That law, in effect the state's atonement for its culpable role in the Dreyfus Affair, was supposed to require the French Third Republic to be a neutral, tolerant supervisor of all religions without favoritism or stigmatization.

It is within this vexed social and political context that Hélène Berr returns, unforeseen and unbidden, in 2008, one year into the presidency of Nicolas Sarkozy who was so concerned about possible vulnerability on his right flank that he was willing to sometimes get out front and do the work of France's neofascist National Front party with little prompting. Sarkozy was the French "blue lives matter" president *avant la lettre*, eager to dogwhistle that he would be tough on *les Arabes,* against headscarves (unless they were Hermès), and slow walk the colonialism apology talk that had developed under Presidents François Mitterrand and Jacques Chirac. Sarkozy's successor François Hollande faced similar "law and order" temptations in 2015 when public surveys showed majorities favored stripping French nationality

---

https://www.newyorker.com/magazine/2004/11/22/taking-the-veil. For a later comparative study, see Denis Lacorne, *The Limits of Tolerance: Enlightenment Values and Religious Fanaticism,* trans. C. Jon Delogu and Robin Emlein (New York: Columbia University Press, 2019), ch. 8, "Of Veils and Veiling," 157–71, and Robert Zaretsky, "How French Secularism Became Fundamentalist," *Foreign Policy,* April 7, 2016, https://foreignpolicy.com/2016/04/07/the-battle-for-the-french-secular-soul-laicite-charlie-hebdo/.

from *"binationaux"* (read: Black people and Muslims) convicted of terrorism. The idea was criticized and eventually abandoned in March 2016 on the grounds that it would create two categories of French citizens and therefore violate the principle of equality guaranteed by the French constitution.

Where does Hélène Berr fit into all this? I'm ready to believe the publisher's infomercial that states the book was "translated in twenty-six countries" and that within the space of "a few months" the *Journal* became *"un texte mythique"* (3). But I have a hunch that all major political parties and most French people, to the extent that they took any notice of the publication of the *Journal,* were pleased to see it become an instant *Jewish* classic — "represent, represent" — seized on by professors of Holocaust studies and the curators of Holocaust memorials. Consecrating Hélène Berr as "the French Anne Frank" was the surest way to not have her become "the French Malala Yousafzai" — or, horror, horror, horror — just be herself, Hélène Berr.[33] By making her disappear into a mausoleum, Academia. edu, or Goodreads, the whole thing is calmed down, flattened out, borne back into the past. Well, if that's how it is, I make the wish that Hélène Berr be allowed to return, again and again, to continue to bother, *gêner,* with all of her force, just like the poets and other artists she found so inspiring.

---

33 It is worth noticing that the publisher of both the French and US English editions of the *Journal* chose for the cover a young teenage picture of Hélène Berr that makes her resemble Anne Frank in appearance and age. This girlish picture does not correspond to her age or appearance during the years she kept her journal. If the English edition, now out of print, is ever reissued, I hope it will use the picture of Hélène Berr in a dynamic, kneeling pose that appears in the middle of the book. The picture of her with the child on her back would also be a nice choice. On the (mis)use of Anne Frank, see Cynthia Ozick, "Who Owns Anne Frank?" *The New Yorker,* October 6, 1997, https://www.newyorker.com/magazine/1997/10/06/who-owns-anne-frank.

5

Blindness and Insight of an Ivy League Alcoholic

Leslie Jamison, *The Recovering: Intoxication and Its Aftermath* (2018)

> In my younger and more vulnerable years my father gave me some advice that I've been turning over in my mind ever since. "Whenever you feel like criticizing any one," he told me, "just remember that all the people in this world haven't had the advantages that you've had."
>
> — F. Scott Fitzgerald, *The Great Gatsby*[1]

I begin with this literary reminder handed down by the fictional Nick Carraway's fictional father not simply because it contains the word *vulnerable,* but also because it's the sort of advice that I like to imagine Gary Greenberg was mindful of as he set about writing his review of Leslie Jamison's addiction memoir, *The Recovering: Intoxication and Its Aftermath* (2018).[2] It is an excellent

---

1 F. Scott Fitzgerald, *The Great Gatsby* (London: Penguin, 2000), 7.
2 Leslie Jamison, *The Recovering: Intoxication and Its Aftermath* (New York: Little, Brown and Co., 2018). Hereafter cited parenthetically throughout

book review from the April 2, 2018 issue of *The New Yorker,* now free and downloadable and even listenable at the magazine's website.[3] Gary Greenberg (1957–) is a practicing psychotherapist, the author of books on recovery and depression narratives, and a regular contributor to magazines and newspapers where he offers thoughtful pieces on the intersection of science, politics, and ethics.[4] As such, he knows how to be tactful, and he doesn't forget who's buttering his bread.

Greenberg alternates between using material from Jamison's text and making his own points that she either only obliquely suggests or completely ignores. This is a common reviewer's technique that Greenberg may have picked up in any number of places, but perhaps it crystallized for him in graduate school; those coming-of-age years when, for practical reasons if nothing else, one decides whose lessons one is going to follow and which stones are going to be left unturned. Greenberg turned 26 years old and was probably writing his thesis in 1983, the year Leslie Jamison was born. The year 1983 means many things: Ronald Reagan is president; the US Embassy in Beirut is bombed, killing sixty-three people; Andrzej Wajda's film *Danton* is released; the Apple Lisa personal computer is invented, and I go off to Lyon, France, not yet 20, and live with the Angrand family as part of my off-campus program there. One other event: December 21, 1983 marks the death of Paul de Man, a once famous literature professor and specialist of literary theory who, only five years later, would be Nazi-shamed out of academia because in those Cold War years most everyone was sure they knew the difference between good and evil, right and wrong. Few entertained the idea that anyone they knew, let alone themselves, would

---

this chapter.

3   Gary Greenberg, "Leslie Jamison's 'The Recovering' and the Stories We Tell About Drinking," *The New Yorker,* April 2, 2018. https://www.newyorker.com/magazine/2018/04/02/leslie-jamisons-the-recovering-and-the-stories-we-tell-about-drinking.

4   For a recent representative piece, see Gary Greenberg, "In Grief Is How We Live Now," *The New York Times,* May 7, 2022, https://www.nytimes.com/2022/05/07/opinion/grief.html.

ever be tempted in their younger and more vulnerable years by right-wing exclusionary populism. Given his age and profession, I suspect Gary Greenberg is familiar with the Paul de Man story and his postwar writings, essays such as "Autobiography as Defacement," "The Rhetoric of Temporality," and "The Resistance to Theory," for example. Judging from her book and bibliography, I also suspect that Jamison is not, which would also be fairly normal and expected since one can't know everything by age 30, even if one did go to Harvard and Yale, and because the Nazi-shaming seems to have done a good job at "cancelling" both de Man's life and his irritating texts on irony, the trickiness of life writing, and the complex relationship between the political and the personal, among other topics.[5] But Jamison's escape from theory could alter since she is still young, has demonstrated a prodigious appetite for exploring archives and gathering oral testimonies, and, according to her father, has been a keenly curious person from the day she was born (77). The dynamic *-ing* in her title would seem to affirm her Keatsian "negative capability" and acceptance of being a work in progress. She also has a stubborn streak, not unlike Hélène Berr, and seems to be attracted to things that would annoy, bother, or irritate many other people. If she stays healthy and free, she may return to de Man later, on her own schedule, and even teach a new generation to read him differently, perhaps with more empathy for his singular resistance to any escape from freedom.

Presumably she paid close attention to Greenberg's somewhat tetchy review, especially its de Man-like moments where

---

5 Works by Peter Brooks, Frank Kermode, and Ben Yagoda listed in Jamison's eight-page bibliography are the only signs of her appropriation up to this point of the academy's critical conversation on life writing. No de Man; no Genette; no Philippe Lejeune; no MLA "approaches" volume on *Teaching Life Writing Texts*. It would be interesting to know, as part of the history of the humanities curriculum in the US, if Jamison's three PhD co-directors steered her clear of "theory" or if that cancellation had begun earlier in the relationship between her directors and their own thesis directors closer to the time of the polemics surrounding the so-called Yale school of criticism.

he passes from paraphrasing what Jamison claims she is doing to affirming what is actually happening, and from blanket praise to measured reservation:

> Leaping into the A.A. ocean, Jamison finally finds a way of disappearing without destroying herself.
>
> Or so she says. Despite itself, her book tells a different story. Not about her sobriety — about how hard-won it was, how necessary to her survival as both a writer and a woman — but about the value of a story that isn't unique at all. Jamison is concerned from the outset that her book will not escape "the tedious architecture and tawdry self-congratulation of a redemption story" — that it will, in short, be boring. She needn't have worried; such is her command of metaphor and assonance that she could rivet a reader with a treatise on toast. We perhaps have no writer better on the subject of psychic suffering and its consolations.
>
> But the book does flag, tellingly if briefly, when, near the end, she turns the story over to fellow-addicts….[6]

Greenberg's hyperbole — "such is her command…," "she could rivet a reader…," "We perhaps have no better writer…" — is the sort of language one associates with blurb copy for books to be sold in airports and train stations. But those lines follow and precede two sternly sober observations Greenberg is making. First, addiction and life writing about addiction are inherently *political* matters. And second, Jamison's book is at its best when she is being herself and weakest when she is yielding to the soft despotism of clubby lit-crit discourse with its obligatory inventories of themes and tropes; or, alternatively, to the chummy but equally imperious dictates of the Big Book — the "bible" of Alcoholics Anonymous — that cajole and bully one to embrace cliché, the ordinary, and to "get over oneself"; that is, to escape from the freedom to be an individual (writer or reader, for ex-

---

ample) and instead join A.A. group-think as the surest road to physical and spiritual recovery.

Greenberg's review develops the *addiction is political* line of thinking over its first five paragraphs before turning to Jamison and her book. It is here in this prelude that Greenberg takes ownership of this review and plants himself as Jamison's helper and not merely her servant or slave. The idea he develops with the use of Jack London, Thomas De Quincey, and most originally and effectively with a letter of Thomas Jefferson is that starting in the eighteenth century many so-called free thinkers no longer see *addiction* — turning oneself over to another as a servant or slave — as neutral or positive. Greenberg quotes Jefferson expressing his disinclination to join the Federalists or "any party of men":

> Thomas Jefferson, in a letter to a friend, from 1789, explained his refusal to join the Federalist Party thus: "Such an addiction is the last degradation of a free and moral agent." He told his correspondent that he had in mind not only the Federalists but "any party of men whatever in religion, in philosophy, in politics, or in any thing else where I was capable of thinking for myself."

He next uses De Quincey to make a similar point: "addiction […] robs us of self-determination":

> In "Confessions of an English Opium-Eater," he argued that what made his dependency monstrous was not the visions it induced — which were sublime as well as terrifying — but, rather, what he would later call "the tyranny of opium." Pick up any of the thousands of recovery memoirs that have been written since De Quincey kicked off the genre and you are likely to find at its heart this notion of addiction: that it is an evil because it robs us of self-determination.

Greenberg then concludes his prelude with an affirmation that could have been written by Fromm:

Whatever its other depredations, addiction afflicts modern people in a way specific to our time. It renders us unable to dive into our deeps, discover what we want, and fashion out of that desire a unique life story in which we achieve it.[7]

In other words, by the nineteenth century, addiction, whether achieved or thrust upon one, is considered an escape from freedom and a surrender to a tyrannical master. This new slant on addiction reinforces the claim Greenberg had made at the start with his use of Jack London's conversion narrative, *I was blind-and-in-denial, but now I see,* as cautionary tale:

Chemistry may indeed lie behind alcoholism, but its hallmark symptom is not liver failure or hypertension or any other physical debility. It is, as London recognized, a moral problem: the inability to control desire, and thus to direct the course of one's own life. One might even say that the pathology is political: the surrender of the will to a form of tyranny.[8]

Greenberg's "One might even say…" shows all of the psychotherapist's caution about bludgeoning patients with the truth of their neuroses. But since I am not a psychotherapist, I share my surprise that nowhere in Jamison's 500 pages does one find the word *political.* Nor does one find the terms *opioid epidemic* or *opioid crisis,* which, for a book published during that crisis in the Trump era by a recovered/ing alcoholic and smoker who spent years in close contact with addicts of all kinds across the Americas, is, well, surprising.

To be fair, in isolated instances Jamison does use the words *opiates, painkiller, Vicodin, fentanyl,* and *Dilaudid.* In the early chapter three, "Blame," she conducts a brief and interesting discussion of the evolution of policy toward addicts depending on whether they are female or male, white or people of color. Her pages on Harry Anslinger and Joe Arpaio, the Narco Farm, Pres-

---

7   Ibid.
8   Ibid.

ident Nixon's cynical War on Drugs extended by Reagan and Bush, and quotes from Michelle Alexander's *The New Jim Crow* and Margo Jefferson's *Negroland,* which both found their way into her hands sometime after 2010 and 2015, respectively, all point in the direction of what this reader hoped would become a full-fledged discussion of the asymmetrical politics of addiction discourse and addiction policies in Washington but also in state legislatures, at school board and parent-teacher association meetings, among judges, defense attorneys, and prosecutors, in neighborhoods, the family, the media, show business, and so forth — a discussion that might even have asked about the possible connection between addiction and the Trump supporter or about Trump's own addiction to grievance, revenge, and pain.[9] But that discussion never gets off the ground. In an eleventh hour author's note — a four-page supplement that may have been added at the insistence of her publisher relaying criticism of this omission from an outside reviewer — Jamison acknowledges that Alcoholics Anonymous is one addiction treatment method among others and that "any ethically responsible vision of treatment needs to include a much broader array of options" and then names a few (449). The next eight paragraphs read like a hurried effort to not have the reader close the book thinking the author has been irresponsible for the past 448 pages and eighteen years since graduating from high school. The landslide of the mind in these four pages is palpable, as though one were witnessing Jamison's struggle to decide if storytelling and the resulting "vision" can effectively shape politics or if it's more the other way around. This aporia stands out particularly in the last paragraph which breaks off with her giving the last word to a certain Johnny Perez instead of speaking in her own name and

---

9   See Greeley Miklashek, "Trumpism: The Psychology of Trump Supporters," *Academia.edu,* November 8, 2020, https://www.academia.edu/70412114/Trumpism. On containment and compassion for Trump's addictions, see James Kimmel, Jr. "What the Science of Addiction Tells Us About Trump," *Politico,* December 12, 2020, https://www.politico.com/news/magazine/2020/12/12/trump-grievance-addiction-444570.

voice — a type of outsourcing that I always advise my thesis students, especially women, to avoid:

> It's not just a question of policy, but a question of radically restructuring the way we think about addicts as villains — and, for that matter, criminals as villains — worthy only of punishment. It's not just about compassion, but pragmatism: What will help people get better? It's about adjusting our vision. Johnny Perez, a formerly incarcerated man now working as a criminal justice reformer, puts it like this: "If we see people as people, then we'll treat people as people. Period." (452)

What is one to make of these last words? Is it profound speaking from the heart or half-baked, fortune cookie gibberish? Both? Neither? Whatever it is, Jamison has performed a debunking of the A.A. recommendation to *keep it simple* by showing, in extenso, the irreducible complexity of the addiction problem which ultimately is the burden — more difficult for some than for others, and lived differently by the very same person at different life moments — of being a conscious living, breathing adult forced to make one's way on a warming, crowded planet.

This burden is what Greenberg, like his colleague Fromm before him, is nudging each of us to accept as our true responsibility. His formulation of this conviction in the last paragraphs of his review makes use of Jamison's evocation of the case of the former addict Gwen:

> Gwen — Jamison changed the names of the interviewees — was a Seneca House patient who went on to become its director, and who, in the midst of trying to get insurance accreditation for the facility, and organizing her son's wedding, became overwhelmed and broke down in tears at work. It happened only the one time, Gwen tells Jamison, but she came to work shortly afterward to find a group intervention awaiting her. Many years later, it still smarts, this insistence that her tears signified a disease that had among its symp-

toms her inability to know she was sick — and for which the only cure was more rehab. Jamison offers a diagnosis of Gwen's ongoing resentment: "It was clear that there were certain kinds of vulnerability that Gwen had readily admitted into her narrative [...] and other kinds of vulnerability her story hadn't fully metabolized." [387] But maybe what Gwen had failed to metabolize was an injustice meted out by her friends and colleagues, who were convinced that her passion was pathological. Denial may not be a river in Egypt, as the A.A. catchphrase goes, but it can be a way to shut people up when their story ventures outside those formal constraints.

Jamison indulges in a clever metaphor, "metabolized," that may leave the reader hanging; whereas Greenberg, who's more experienced at reading half-articulated emotions, zeros in on what's really at stake: Gwen is angry that her mates at A.A. may never allow her to be a normal healthy person just having a bad day. In other words, denial can flow both ways: an individual can deny that the shoe fits and refuse to wear it; or the society or some subset thereof can deny that the shoe doesn't fit and seek conformity by every means possible, in this case by shoehorning someone into vulnerability whether they like it or not, feel vulnerable, or feel like performing vulnerability, or not.[10]

Greenberg states that Jamison is capable of seeing the rub, but "largely as an aesthetic problem," such as in a passage she picks out (not included by Greenberg who's working under a strict word count) from an even longer addiction text, *Infinite Jest* (1996) by David Foster Wallace who killed himself at age 46.

The book understands [writes Jamison] the discomfort of hearing the program promise, *Let us love you until you learn*

---

10   "For nonconformity the world whips you with its displeasure," declared Emerson in the essay "Self-Reliance" back in 1841 (in *Essays, Vol. 1* [London: Arthur L. Humphreys], 59), exactly a century before Fromm, a time of heavy drinking with temperance movements already well underway. Emerson recommended that the epic poet "drink water out of a wooden bowl."

> *to love yourself,* and the aggressive insistence of being hugged
> by strangers. After a meeting, one character asks a stranger,
> "You gone risk vulnerability and discomfort and hug my ass,
> or do I gone fucking rip your head off and *shit* down your
> neck?" (360)

The vulgarity of this excerpt gets Jamison's point across about
what she first mildly calls the "weirdness of depersonalized
goodwill in recovery" before more pointedly calling it the "aggressive insistence" of A.A.'s "love." However, Wallace's mimicking of Black English, in the tradition of Mark Twain's ventriloquism of Jim's way of talking to Huckleberry Finn — the
whole then quoted by Jamison — is cringey on several levels. Does Wallace's A.A. member have to speak non-standard
"jive talk"? Some might find this condescending and a sign of
the shortcomings of Jamison's, and Wallace's, largely apolitical
belles-lettristic, faux-edgy, upper-class, white literary treatment
of other, more vulnerable, people's addictions.[11] When Jamison
learns of the horrific story of Marcia Powell from 2009, her conclusion is "What luck. What luck not to wake up in a cage, or
a 140-degree tent in the Arizona desert; not to serve time for
the thrall that had already corroded me" (406). She knows full

---

11   For anyone with a political bent, another problematic moment occurs
     when Jamison, who seems unburdened by any Marxist-style hypothesis
     that material conditions shape individual behaviors, describes the alcohol-
     ism of poor Nicaraguans as "just a way of being" as though they were
     naturally alcoholic. She sees her drinking buddy Felipe's radical acceptance
     as liberating: "The way he put it, being alcoholic wasn't anything that made
     him special. It was just true for him and for a lot of the guys he'd grown up
     with. He wasn't packing up his drinking and taking it on an international
     flight or to his job at a Santa Monica inn. He wasn't busy blaming his
     frequent-flier father. He didn't feel particularly sorry for himself — this was
     just a way of being, and it wasn't his alone" (101–2). So because he and the
     guys he had grown up with cannot manage to get angry or get organized
     about the political and economic conditions that result in massive rates of
     alcoholism (or obesity or criminality or other ills), that means she is not
     allowed to get upset at the root causes of her alcoholism? One may wonder
     if Jamison's argument with its ironic tone lets all parties duck accountabil-
     ity and be denied treatment.

well that what separates her addiction story from that of Marcia Powell has *everything and nothing* to do with luck. Elites like her know she's being ironic — but irony is unhelpful here if it is not followed up with a straight affirmation that what separates their two stories is, as noted elsewhere, a variable geometry of vulnerability, "hidden asymmetries in daily life" (Nicholas Taleb), the different rights and "scripts" granted (407); that is, the different policies and politics applied depending on the time, the subject (whether defendant, villain, victim or patient, white or non-white, male or female, straight or gay), and the place (whether hospital, court, campus, or church basement). Passing the empathy exam, as we saw with Paxton, requires paying attention to the socio-economic context and the politics at work, and thereby finding a passage between the reefs of conflation and nominalism.[12]

Greenberg has the merit of filling in Jamison's ellipses. For example, he concludes that the author's note at the end of the book falls short of providing an "ethically responsible vision of treatment":

Jamison is not blind to the ideological implications of the twelve-step logic, the way that it forces everyone to read from the same script. Indeed, she's preoccupied with it, but largely as an aesthetic problem; it's not until an author's note at the end of the book that she explicitly connects that ideology to deeper problems with our understanding of suffering.

---

12 Jamison does usefully call out the addictiveness of resonance. "It's easy to feel good about resonance. It's actually quite addictive, the nodding rhythm of communion — *Yes, I know how you feel.* This presumed empathy tastes righteous and expansive on the tongue. During my early days of sobriety, I started seeing resonance everywhere, like a primary color I'd never noticed" (363–64). She continues, " a stranger had carved in the wood: *I am a virgin.* Then others had written around that: *Me too. So am I. So am I! So am I!* But the flip side of communion's humility, being willing to say *I'm not the only one,* is the danger of assumption or conflation: I've felt what you felt." #MeToo, a legal, political, social, economic movement that broke in October 2017, after Jamison's manuscript had been submitted for publication, one presumes, is everywhere and nowhere in her text.

In the note, she points out that A.A.'s insistence on universal abstinence — not just from the problem drug but from all drugs — has interfered with medication-assisted treatments like buprenorphine for opiate addiction, and serves to justify various cruelties of the drug war: the court-ordered drug testing that often lands illicit-drug users in prison, the obstruction of needle-exchange programs, the unavailability of Narcan for first responders. Even then, Jamison does not confront the way that this inflexibility arises from the foundation of A.A. doctrine: not merely the belief in abstinence but the suspicion of autonomy that is embedded in the idea of turning our lives over to a higher power.

Greenberg is willing to grant that Jamison is aware of the political dimension of certain policy disputes, but he criticizes Jamison for not confronting what he sees as a more fundamental political problem: the contest between autonomy and autocracy. This problem leads him to be suspicious of the motives of A.A.'s "suspicion of autonomy"; in other words, the organization's undermining of the individual self that on certain days Jamison wants to see as an affirmation of a DIY democratic commons, a vision that includes praise for the value of the nonexpert, folksy contribution, a belief in unmediated "single-entendre writing" (349), a love of the f-word and other salty language, and all things ordinary. On those days she thinks singularity is an illusion (307) and feels disgusted by her own infinite need to be *interesting* and *special*.[13] On other days, however, Jamison recoils

---

13 It's worth noting in this regard that Jamison uses the more specific word "intoxication" in her subtitle instead of having it be "Addiction and Its Aftermath." She also refuses to have her kind of addiction be lumped together with all uncontrolled cravings: "I'm wary of attributing addiction so broadly it ceases to mean anything besides compulsively desiring something capable of causing harm" (364). Why? Because all addictions are equal, but some addictions are more equal than others? Jamison also refuses to go along with Gabor Maté's materialist hypothesis that all addiction is the translation of "an aching emptiness" that is related to something lacking in one's social environment (153). Hence her attraction to Charles Jackson's *The Lost Weekend* "for its rejection of the idea that you could

at "A.A.'s larger insistence that we were all the same, which was basically saying *fuck you* to my entire value system" (222). Hers is a high modernist value system inherited from tasteful Renaissance Humanists, the Bloomsbury group, and clever Enlightenment-era believers in reason, and thus attracted to refinement, beauty, complexity, virtuosity, and difficulty as well as repulsed or simply bored by the mediocre, the average, and the clichéd. "Giving up on singularity was like giving up on the edges of my own body. What would I *be,* if I wasn't singular?"[14] Some might feel more repelled than riveted by her frequent swearing or by how she seems to have never met a "like" she didn't like. But Jamison, more in the mode of analysand than analyst, makes her point which in the end coheres with what the analyst Greenberg is saying in different more precise language proper to a theorist who has less trouble being interested in both the general history and in particular stories.

It's telling that in Jamison's memoir there are only passing references to what is going on in the world. Obama and Occupy Wall Street each get a brief mention as do Hurricanes Irene and Sandy, and the Deepwater Horizon oil spill. That's about it. No Tea Party, no opioid epidemic, no Trump. In this regard she offers a version of the not entirely unearned cliché of self-absorbed campus life, perhaps especially among many humanities and MFA students. Greenberg, on the other hand, more explicitly relates the problems raised in Jamison's addiction memoir to

---

easily or automatically turn drinking into meaning. It insisted that you couldn't always trace the self-destruction back to a tidy psychological myth of origins" (119).

14 Jamison continues in this philosophical vein: "What was identity if it wasn't fundamentally a question of difference? What defined a voice if not distinction? I was still a little girl at the dinner table, trying to prove myself by coming up with something better than a few clichés balled up in my throat. Recovery started to rearrange these urges" (313). "Trying to prove myself" — proving to oneself and to others that I am somebody — there is the burden, taken up or thrown aside, there is man's *fate* according to Emerson, what Emmanuel Levinas called *difficile liberté,* the difficulty of being free. See Emmanuel Levinas, *Difficile liberté* (Paris: Albin Michel, 2006).

the political climate of the first two decades of the twenty-first century — the time of Jamison's long apprenticeship in adult-ing — a climate that includes a surge of right-wing populist poli-tics from Putin's Russia to Trump's America, with many non-anonymous bullies in between (Bolsonaro, Rodrigo Duterte, Recep Tayyip Erdoğan, Viktor Orbán, to name just a few). A *New Yorker* reader in 2018 does not need Greenberg to name all of these Führers, who, as de Man and other French theorists from Roland Barthes to Derrida pointed out before Greenberg came along, make ample use of clichéd figurative language to bake in the idea that there is no alternative to their mythical and magical marching orders. Here Greenberg shares some of what he has learned about the history of "manufacturing depression":

> A.A. has ridden to hegemony on some of our strongest cul-tural winds: Protestantism, self-improvement, abstemious-ness, scientism. Its offer of fellowship in a fraternal order of the wounded gains appeal as injury increasingly becomes the polestar of identity. The "tyranny of abstinence," as Jamison calls it, has surely saved many addicts; it beats blackouts and wrecked lives hands down. […] But it's still tyranny, and ty-rants thrive on cliché, on language that declares itself beyond questioning.[15]

Greenberg then brings his review in for a landing, hits a solid line drive, stands up for the "irreducible stories of individuals," including the one he has just told, in a final paragraph that he allows to burst with metaphors as though to show Jamison that two can play at that game:

> It may be instructive that the cure for addiction is to trade in one tyrant for another. Tyrannies seem to be on the march; this may reflect a yearning for something outside ourselves,

---

15 Gary Greenberg, *Manufacturing Depression: The Secret History of a Mod-ern Disease* (New York: Simon & Schuster, 2010). See also Mark Fisher, *Capitalist Realism: Is There No Alternative?* (Hants: Zero Books, 2009).

something to relieve us of the burden of fashioning our own plotlines out of the thin air of our lives, or of sorting out the competing stories that increasingly are falling on us like a poisoned rain. Our narrative engines may not be up to the task of making sense of our yearnings, and we may find ourselves unyoked from them, and leashed to someone else's. In the meantime, the irreducible stories of individuals, such as the one Jamison tells about herself — the great and prickly autobiographies of addicts struggling to understand their thrall and teaching us about ourselves in ways beyond what they intend — may be the best balm against our inadequacy that we have.

Best to resist, like Jefferson, becoming an *addictus* or overly attached to anything that might lead to a "narrative-deficit disorder," says Greenberg. Best to face not flee the burden of fashioning our own plotlines is Greenberg's recommendation — taking inspiration and courage from the "great and prickly," and learning from the "autobiographies of addicts" who can teach all of us what we're up against while talking endlessly and messily about themselves.

Thanks to Greenberg's review with its discreet recycling of past discoveries of literary theory, it almost does not matter when the extent of Jamison's theorization about the challenge of life writing amounts to repeating an off-hand remark: "A friend of mine once observed that writing about yourself is 'like trying to make a bed while you're still in it'" (412). Jamison offers this demotic A.A. nugget while sharing her reaction to reading John Berryman's novel *Recovery* which she calls "a document of maddening repetition rather than progressive redemption." While reading this and other instances of Jamison reading, whether before or after Greenberg's review, one might hear echoes of de Man's marmoreal pronouncement at the end of an essay published in *The Rhetoric of Romanticism* in 1984, the year after he died: "Autobiography veils a defacement of the mind of which it is itself the cause."

***

Before leaving Jamison to continue on her "journey" (448) "with her husband, the novelist Charles Bock [1969–], and their two daughters" (see back dustjacket) — not to mention her prestigious job as director of "the graduate nonfiction program at Columbia University," none of which, I dare say, she achieved by being "anonymous," ordinary, or self-effacing — I would like to share some supplementary observations about this mega-memoir that collages Jamison's own addiction memoir with her 2016 PhD dissertation on addiction memoirs.[16] For example, her carefully curated Wikipedia entry contains a warm, hippy-looking, eyes-forward photo that could not be more different from the icy glamour pic on the memoir's dustjacket. It also contains links to admiring reviews of her work. Perusing all this information, I was struck by the names of her parents, Dean Jamison and Joanne Leslie, who go unnamed in *The Recovering*. She refers to them as "my father" and "my mother." What's odd is that, unless her birth certificate tells a different story, *she has no name of her own* — her parents having made the unusual and I would say unwise decision, from a parenting standpoint, to make their daughter simply carry both family names: *Leslie* from her mother, *Jamison* from her father. But what about the blessed infant babe? Why doesn't she get her own first name?

One wonders if LJ — let that be her name! — was a desired, late arrival, a wished for and welcomed girl in a chapter two of the Leslie-Jamison marriage after a chapter one that had brought into the world two sons who are nine and ten years older at the time of her birth. Or was she the result of an unwanted pregnancy in a marriage that was perhaps going stale due to both parties being more wedded to their careers than to each other? If so, then not giving LJ a name of her own looks awfully like some sort of nasty acting out, a revenge on this innocent child

---

16 It's this collage technique that sets Jamison's memoir apart from straight no-chaser addiction memoirs such as Erica C. Barnett's *Quitter: A Memoir of Drinking, Relapse, and Recovery* (New York: Viking, 2020).

for having the nerve of forcing these two busy people with all their important work in the service of the nutrition and economic prosperity of faraway others to turn their attention back to changing diapers and preparing bottles and baby food.

We are told LJ's parents separate when she is nine (so no chance for yet another late arrival), and her father goes off to live on the other side of the country. They officially divorce when she's eleven. It's decided she will live with her mother who becomes or already always was the dominant figure of order; whereas the father becomes the bounteous gift-giver, jolly holiday-maker, and rule-breaker with whom LJ can eat unhealthy food and be a "wild thing" in a clear two-against-one hurtful undermining of Joanne Leslie and her household that Dean Jamison flies in and out of self-importantly obeying a higher calling of saving the world, which is the mother's calling too.

Indeed, everyone's a flashy superhero at the Jamison table, it sounds like — a living hell of non-stop performance, a battle of five people all acting like bullying eighth graders no matter their actual age, practicing either weaponized silence or verbal jujitsu with a constant barrage of one-upping each other, *bons mots* (preferably in French), put-downs, gotcha moments, and a whirligig of "I'll show you" and "I told you so." One reviewer of *The Recovering* asks, "Where's the train wreck?" implying that Jamison's addiction memoir does not have a sufficiently sensational rock-bottom moment.[17] The book passes with no major breakdown or accident from "Shame" (a chapter about alcohol dependency with Jamison "sitting on this futon with my arms wrapped around my knees" and admitting sadistic pleasure at annoying her boyfriend Dave, 188) to "Surrender," the chapter that kicks off Jamison's long association with A.A. It's pretty obvious that LJ's train wreck happened between the ages of nine and eleven. This is the time when, according to Fromm's devel-

---

17 Ruth Shalit Barrett, no stranger to conflict and crisis herself, asks, "Where's the Train Wreck? Can Leslie Jamison Top 'The Empathy Exams' with Her Mega-memoir of Addiction?" *Vulture,* March 18, 2018, https://www.vulture.com/2018/03/leslie-jamison-the-recovering-addiction-memoir.html, and in print in *New York Magazine,* March 18, 2018.

opmental model, one is becoming self-conscious in both the positive and precarious senses of the word, and a time when one would prefer to have no ambient crises (such as divorce, a move, a death in the family) upset that already challenging transition from *freedom from* one's primary ties to *freedom to* become the free artist of oneself; to "forge in the smithy of one's soul" whatever one feels like forging; to fashion "our own plotlines out of the thin air of our lives," and similar Romantic impulses to build, make, do, and be. That transition, one suspects, did not go well for LJ despite signs of precociousness and high achievement. How could it in such a tyrannical, snarky home where one is always either a contingent ally or an enemy, constantly judged, and never allowed to just be oneself?

LJ gives the reader a glimpse of that "train wreck" in three snapshots related to each of her early caregivers: her father, mother, and two older brothers who, given the age gap between them and the baby sister and the busy lives of the parents, were no doubt enlisted, whether they liked it or not, as paid or unpaid babysitters. First come the brothers:

My brothers were witty and kind but also a tough crowd, smart and reserved — not willing to give up their laughter or praise for just anything. (My oldest brother, Julian, taught me how to solve an equation for x when I was seven. "Great," he said, "but can you solve when x is on *both* sides?") I loved my brothers wildly, extravagantly. Loving them was like flinging myself against something — as I often flung myself at their tall bodies to hug them, demanding their love with the sheer force of my hurtling forty-pound body. I was always loved, but I always wondered, also, what that love depended on. It did not seem unconditional. I wondered what I had to do to keep deserving it. I can't remember a time when I wasn't trying to figure out what to say at the dinner table, especially on French nights — when everyone was practicing a language I didn't speak. (78)

French nights? Anyone who has attended a meal, meeting, or meetup where not everyone speaks the language being used knows how uncomfortable this is for the excluded person. From LJ's telling, however, such destabilization is just part of a normal day *chez les Jamison.* One can also see from this passage the messed-up idea of "love" that develops early on in LJ's head: she's not being loved by these wanton boys, she is being manipulated via affection starvation to press the right lever that then delivers, maybe, some *token* of affection, not real affection which is given freely and not in exchange for good performances or services rendered. LJ says that over time "certain truths" became clear to her: "People would probably leave, it was just a question of when. Attention was something I had to earn, not something I could take for granted. I had to seduce at all moments" (78). But LJ's caregivers get her so turned around that the *child abuse* inflicted on her for no good reason gets covered over, literally recovered, as though with new upholstery or a book cover, and appears as her *privileged childhood* which gets thrown in her face regularly as something she's supposed to feel ashamed of; "the guilt of my privilege, or my survival" (407). She may have more in common with Billy Holiday than she realizes, but serious, published people have convinced her that as the "nice upper-middle-class white girl" (68) she does not get to sing the same blues or complain the same way. There's a queue for the "pity pot," and she takes her place, ever the rule-follower, at the back of it.

Of course, her brothers did not fall far from the tree, and what they were doing to their sister was probably displaced payback for the child abuse they had received from their narcissistic parents whom they were presumably too dependent on to lash out at directly. As Fromm explains in the chapter "Mechanisms of Escape," and so many others have repeated since in various ways, narcissists seek out codependent slave-addicts and then one day the slaves, having escaped to school and jobs and their own leases or mortgages, find others to enslave in their turn. Alice Miller's research on Hitler and other sadists exposed similar cycles of abuse when it came to spanking and other forms of physical and symbolic violence: the bullied, including the affection-starved "spoiled child," often become the bullies if given the opportunity.

LJ's father, according to her testimony, was a man of extremes. Either Mr. Jamison was the impish *Cat in the Hat* playmate with whom LJ would keep secrets and break rules while the law enforcing mother was away: "The few times I stayed alone with him, when my mother went out of town for work, all we ate was ramen and popcorn and milk shakes" (77);[18] or, at the other extreme, and especially after the divorce, LJ figured out that when she stayed with her father, who was now all business, she had to fish scraps out of the fridge on her own and be ready to be interrogated about her grades should they fall below the Jamison family standards.

> Whenever my father praised my intelligence, it was like a bread crumb in the forest. If I could just keep doing that, he'd keep paying attention. [...] I craved his approval like I craved perfect grades, perfect test scores, or I craved these things like I craved his approval. Getting good grades was the natural extension of being a little girl trying to figure out the next right thing to say at the dinner table. I was alternately stone-faced and sarcastic [like father, like daughter] in those days of early adolescence — shy at school, convinced I smelled bad, that I loomed like a giraffe — and quiet with my father. I couldn't ask for what I wanted then because I didn't know I wanted it. Loving him was always like reaching for something luminous. Reaching was what love felt like. (76, 78–79)

Here the Leslie Jamison of some year closer to 2018 than to 2000, I presume, has put all the pieces together to realize that as a child she mistook codependent power relations for love.

---

18   It's likely Dean Jamison did not know how to cook and didn't see any reason to learn so long as Joanne Leslie pulled a second shift as the multi-tasking traditional housewife — the model of today's "tradwife" revival.

This makes it all the more poignant when she falls in, I won't say love, with the poet Dave, a sort of "enchanted [giving] tree" (137).[19] She never uses the term *codependency* to describe their relationship that stumbles on for three years and hundreds of pages. "Dave" is one name for Jamison's other tyrannical addiction to "love" that cohabits alongside her undiscussed need for cigarettes, to be right, to write beautiful grotesqueries ("mugs of black coffee filmed with broken lily pads of grease," 14), and to use the f-word whenever she f***-ing feels like it. Nor does Jamison ever use the word *bargaining* — her preferred term is "contract logic" — which from an early age becomes her default setting for how all relationships work.[20]

Jamison's most vivid memory of anything her father actually said to her is something she repeats twice but neither time in quotation marks, first as reported speech (76) and then in italics after a colon: *Drinking isn't dangerous for everyone, but it's dangerous for us* (80). Had the 49-year-old Dean Jamison elaborated, his remark could have been the start of a helpful discussion with his 9 year old who had come to ask him about drinking. "Why did people drink? Why did some people do it so much" (75)? But Jamison gives no indication that anything more was said on the subject, and by her own account there was something more important to her at that precise moment than the attraction or chemistry of alcohol: "It was thrilling to share any type of *us* with my father, who was a magical figure to me. There was always some part of him that was elsewhere" (76). Starting at age 13 and for the next thirteen years or so — her own magical

---

19 I am alluding to Patrick J. Carnes, *Don't Call It Love: Recovery from Sexual Addiction* (New York: Bantam Books, 1992), and to Shel Silverstein, *The Giving Tree* (New York: Harper & Row, 1964).

20 The word *bargaining* does appear once when the Jamison family has their monthly or bimonthly "calendar sessions," which coordinate who's doing what, when, and where (76). Her parents are both high-achieving social scientists, and Dean Jamison's father was in the military and moved the family about a lot and was also an alcoholic. Bargaining, the inevitable clingy stage in any grieving process, is constantly performed in the memoir but never named. Chapter 8 is called "Return," but a more accurate title would have been "Relapse and Bargaining" because that's what happens.

mystery tour — LJ sets out to prove her father right, and she gets a lot of mileage from that dangerous, vulnerable persona modeled on the allure of her absent alcoholic aunt, Phyllis, including occasionally the succor of bruised and bruising men such as Dean and Dave.

LJ's mother, Joanne Leslie, who, like many woman caught in the double bind of the early women's liberation movement, suffered her share of the slings and arrows of outrageous fortune (including, we learn, being cheated on by Dean), is also the focus of a primal scene of rupture around a stereotypical female art: baking. The story is told in the second paragraph of the chapter "Thirst" which relates the early stages of Leslie Jamison's first attempt at sobriety.

> When I was seven years old, I'd told my mom I was pretty sure I could make an apple crumble topping better than hers: a brown sugar crust baked with cinnamon and nutmeg. She gestured at the kitchen — unfazed, smiling — and said, "Go ahead." I made a disgusting concoction with too much butter and, for whatever reason, raw macaroni, and then, too proud to admit I'd failed, I sat there eating the mixture in front of her, pretending that I loved it. Sobriety felt like that. (231)

This story is supposed to illustrate Leslie Jamison's point that sobriety was not making her feel better. Her needs were not being met by not drinking any more than they had been met by drinking, cutting herself, starving herself, running cross-country, good grades, or by Daniel, Peter, Felipe... or Dave. This childhood memory is told years later after LJ has become an accomplished baker under the tutelage of a substitute mother-figure named Jamie (162, 338). The story exhibits the Jamison family's competitiveness that the reader remembers from 100 pages earlier. But never before has Jamison focused on her nutritionist mom, Joanne Leslie, whom we see here is not above taking sly pleasure in setting up her spunky but inexperienced 7-year-old for failure. What if instead of saying "Go ahead," and then witnessing her daughter fail and harm herself, Joanne had said to her daughter, *Well that's possible, honey, but how about we make three apple crumble toppings together over the next three weekends, and then if you like you can make one all on your own?* In other words, instead of reinforcing the zero-sum thinking that had been drilled into LJ, Joanne Leslie, an adult whose profession is to teach people that there is another better way of nourishing oneself, could have modeled a different, collaborative approach to the task. Doing so would have given LJ a special mother-daughter moment to look forward to each week, taught her some practical skills and wisdom (e.g., recipes exist for a reason), and allowed them to bond further with shared pride as they presented each carefully prepared delicious dessert to "the boys" and Dad. Most importantly, it would have sent the signal, *Yes, you're worth my time. I love you. I care about you. I want to help you grow into a self-confident, capable individual who can succeed at many things.* Besides, did LJ really want to outdo her mom or was she behaving like the Runaway Bunny, testing her mom, and actually hoping they'd bake together? In that case eating the concoction containing too much butter and raw macaroni, which must have been quite painful to chew as well as disgusting, was a precocious example of "mortification of the flesh" to express her rage at the mother, the life-giving creator, for abandoning the daughter (flesh of her flesh): Mother, why have you forsaken me?

Aren't the ramen, popcorn, and milkshake binges as well as her later unhealthy eating and drinking habits all attempts to get her mother's attention? She was asked that very question by a psychologist during the time when she was anorexic, she tells us, and was "so irritated by how obviously *irrelevant* my therapist's question had been" (46). "My mother was not the problem." Jamison refuses to wear that shoe. Interpreting her behavior as a textbook example of acting out would be too boring, so Jamison tells a more richly layered story.

She'd written her doctoral dissertation on infant malnutrition in rural Brazil. She'd spent months weighing underweight babies in a village near Fortaleza. Her career in nutrition didn't have anything to do with the self-indulgent angst of her anorexic daughter. Plus, I added, I already had my mother's attention. My mother wasn't the problem. In fact, I said, my eating disorder had been more like a pathetic betrayal of everything wonderful about my mother, especially her largely untroubled relationship to food and to her body; her selfless devotion to problems that actually merited it [i.e., her attention]. I was so irritated by how obviously *irrelevant* my therapist's question had been. (46)

This passage illustrates what Jacques Derrida, following Freud, nicknamed "the kettle logic" typical of the embarrassment-dream of being naked, "wherein one uses multiple arguments to defend a point, but the arguments are inconsistent with each other."[21] It's embarrassing to be exposed as having needs when one has been trained to believe one can't have any.

With the opaque deictic *that* — "Sobriety felt like that" — Jamison is not spelling out that *Sobriety left me feeling needy just like my mother and all my caregivers left me feeling needy,* but we get the picture. Therefore, telling this story is a gentle but firm way to call out her mom, albeit indirectly to the reader, for failing to parent her the way she would have liked. Jamison, daughter of a nutritionist and an economist, is counting calories and settling accounts. Happens all the time. It's easy for children who have gone off to college or to the University of Life to get indignant that their parents are imperfect "ABC gum" (already been chewed), instead of arriving — like most of us do as newborns — in mint-condition with a piercing gaze that never lets go. "More, more, more," said the (monarchical) baby.

Who's to say where Dean Jamison and Joanne Leslie really fell along the parenting spectrum from wicked to "practically perfect in every way"?[22] And what does it matter? They may even be

---

21 The relevant bibliography can be found at *Wikipedia,* s.v. "Kettle logic," https://en.wikipedia.org/wiki/Kettle_logic.

22 I would like to reserve judgment, as Nick Carraway's father advised, however it is odd that none of LJ's caregivers taught her how to ride a bike,

dead by now or soon will be. According to a wise book by a man on his second marriage, and with input from that second wife, it does matter, or should, *to the living*. The book's thesis is that one is unlikely to be able to form healthy, loving relationships and raise independent, capable children without a keen awareness of the strengths and weaknesses of our primary caregivers and the pleasures and pains they caused us in our early years.[23] Furthermore, says the author, we do not "fall in love" with just anybody, but always with a person that our self-protective, unconscious radar has picked out as someone with whom we are likely to be able to revisit old pleasures and old wounds. The trouble is that unless a person becomes aware of those unconscious motives, one just ends up getting wounded a second, third, or nth time, especially since one's partner has fallen in love for the very same reason but has their own agenda determined by their own hauntings. "What about my needs," says Dave, "We never talk about those" (227). The author has sold over two million copies of this book, but there is no sign he wrote it to show off or to make money. The author's full-time job is helping couples in deep pain go from an unconscious partnership, where each person always has one eye on the door and the other on a hatchet, to a conscious partnership that creates a sacred space of mutual trust and respect worthy of the name love.

Getting the Love You Want (1988) by Dr. Harville Hendrix is the kind of guide that a certain Leslie Jamison, the one stuck in a revolving door with Dave, would probably dismiss as "dime-store psychoanalysis" (155), perhaps because that Jamison views as an existential threat any and every explanatory narrative (Marxist, Freudian, Martian) of her alcoholism. Therefore all such stories must be declared "insufficient." Here she is in one of her Holden Caulfield solo riffs trying to convince the reader and herself of this:

---

and it falls to Dave to try (and fail) to teach her at age 26 while they are on vacation together in Italy (159–60).

23 This is also the claim of Cécile David-Weill in *Parents under the Influence: Words of Wisdom from a Former Bad Mother* (New York: Other Press, 2019).

My drinking had something to do with my family, and something to do with my brain, and something to do with the values I was raised to worship: excellence, enchantment, superlative everything. All these tales of *why* are true and also insufficient. A state of insufficiency is part of being human, and I responded to my particular state of insufficiency by drinking — because I was wired for it and groomed for it, because once I started doing it, it was so eloquent in its delivery of a particular bodily guarantee: *With this, you will feel like enough.* (157)

Yes, but to quote Dave quoting Berryman or any number of other addiction memoirists, "I think this is the alcohol talking" (266). This passage comes from the chapter "Shame" where Jamison is still fired by the alcohol that turbocharges her faculty of rationalization. Later, in a more tranquil look back at her long acquaintance with the wisdom writing of Joan Didion on storytelling as equipment for living, Jamison views the matter in a way that would maybe allow her to be receptive to Hendrix's hypothesis about our lovers being not only themselves but also the ghosts of our early caregivers. First she took Didion's words as gospel, she says, then she read them as an incitement to doubt: "trusting stories was naïve, a refusal to confront actuality in all its senselessness," Jamison writes.

But in recovery, I started to believe again that stories could do all the things Didion had taught me to distrust, that they could lend meaningful arcs of cohesion; that they could save us from our lives by letting us construct ourselves. I'd always had faith in doubt — in questioning and undermining, looking for fissures, splitting the seams of tidy resolution to find the complexity teeming underneath — but I started to wonder if sometimes doubt was just an easy alibi, a way to avoid the more precarious state of affirmation, making yourself vulnerable by standing behind something that could be criticized, disproven, or ridiculed. Maybe it was just as much a crutch to doubt stories as to stand behind them. It was so easy to point out gaps without filling them, to duck into the foxhole of ambivalence. Maybe sometimes you just had to accept that the story of your life was a crafted thing — selected, curated, skewed in service of things you could name and probably other things you couldn't. Maybe you could accept all that, and still believe it might do you, or someone else, some good. (371)

This paragraph, with its Seussian repetition of "maybe" ("Maybe Christmas doesn't come from a store…"), gets my vote for best moment in this mega-meta-memoir. The full weight of the uncertainty and undecidability contained in each "maybe" needs to be appreciated and seen as the starting point for "standing behind something" regardless; that is, *Standing by Words* to recall the title of one of Wendell Berry's wisdom books. Responsibility and accountability begin there out of the grieving that one cannot in fact know for sure *why,* but the simultaneous determination that one must and will forge ahead anyway. "And you don't quit." This paragraph is Jamison's exhortation to herself, following in the footsteps of earnest memoirists who came before her such as Berryman (412), to continue the recovering as best she can. But those earlier stances are not banished so much as they are mourned in a kind of respectful vigil — Jamison's wake.

What is *The Great Gatsby* if not a book of mourning? And isn't that what all addiction memoirs are performing, more or less successfully, depending on one's unreserved judgment? "One man's trash is another man's treasure," to quote more A.A.-style folk wisdom. "One man's waste is another man's soap" (MF Doom). Value is variable, but what is certain is that mourning all kinds of loss is happening over and over in this memoir. But like the missing word *bargaining,* I don't recall coming across the word *mourning* or *grieving* in these pages, nor any explicit discussion of the recovery process, whether through A.A. or some other method, as a multi-step farewell to one's addicted self and the acceptance and determination to move forward un-addicted, confident in one's ability to get stuff done (338), and mindful of one's wider responsibilities to the living and the dead. Maybe to Jamison it was obvious that A.A. is the five-step model of grief stretched out to twelve steps, or in her case to fourteen chapters.

Jamison writes, "Sometimes it hurts to remember how selfish I was" (268). How much must it also hurt to remember how she was taught by her supercilious bullying caregivers to hate herself? How much does it hurt to grieve the confusion and the time spent to untangle her confusion between selfishness, self-love, and self-hatred? And the number of years she mistook power and domination for love and care? Lost weekend? How about lost decade? No, not lost, but spent the way it had to be spent, one must conclude. In any case, time irretrievably gone, no matter how much those years may be remembered and collaged by her or others. "You can't turn a pickle back into a cucumber" (240). Now is she accepting to be (in) that "pickle" — practicing losing farther, losing faster — instead of endless re-cucumbering as the earlier bargaining Jamison spent so much time doing?

The five stages of grieving, sometimes remembered with the acronym DABDA — Denial, Anger, Bargaining, Depression, Acceptance — are indeed a special kind of journey.[24] It took her 500 pages, a lot of hard work, and some good fortune (such as a boutique publisher letting her have a very generous word count and a lot of freedom) but Jamison got herself unstuck and moving forward — "thirty going on thirteen" (424) — secure in the knowledge that giving up magical thinking does not mean one need give up on making magic happen if one believes in oneself and one's powers. Maybe friends like Dave, her starter-partner, taught her that.

It wasn't nice, it's true, for her parents not to give her a name of her own, but she went ahead and made a name for herself. Similarly, although *The Recovering* was a good choice of first title — naming both a process and those engaged in that process — it might have been better to have the subtitle be "Addiction and Its Aftermath," not *Intoxication*. Using the word *Addic-*

---

24 See Elisabeth Kübler-Ross, *On Death and Dying* (New York: Macmillan, 1969).

tion would have been a way to acknowledge and maybe help a larger more diverse public. It would have signaled a wider circle of concern and opened a pathway to more empathy.[25] It would also have been more accurate, truer to the book's story of a thousand-and-one struggles with tyrants of all kinds, and it would have made her book no less special.[26]

However, despite her qualifications (a recovering alcoholic who had the contagion of addiction in her family history and a longtime victim of gaslighting and *Selbstgleichschaltung* in her home life and formal education), Jamison has left to others, or to a future LJ, the task of denouncing late capitalism's harmful privatization of anxiety and addiction, and the job of broadcasting the message that mental health is a political issue with vast public ramifications, for good or ill, depending on how it's handled, and therefore emphatically not simply a private matter.[27] The argument in every chapter of the book you are reading is that fascism is "our malady"; in other words, the consequence and accelerant of widely shared mental health problems that are further complicated by acute and chronic vulnerabilities — some spiritual but most material in nature. A malady made worse by

---

25 Empathy is important to Jamison. See her *Empathy Exams* (Minneapolis: Graywolf, 2014). See also the memoir by Sherry Turkle, an expert on relationships in the internet age, *The Empathy Diaries: A Memoir* (New York: Penguin Books, 2021).

26 The day I finished the rough draft of this chapter, April 13, 2020, my friend Charles Hadley sent me a link to a piece by Leslie Jamison in *The New York Review of Books* dated March 26, 2020, "Since I Became Symptomatic," https://www.nybooks.com/daily/2020/03/26/since-i-became-symptomatic/. The text details her struggle with Covid-19 while trying to be a good mom to her two-year-old daughter. It also mentions her recent divorce from Charles Bock without naming him or their daughter. More mourning. On the first anniversary of the pandemic, Jamison was given an opportunity to do more public mourning and call for more reflection and mutual aid: "This Year Has Taught Me a Lot about Nostalgia," *The New York Times,* March 11, 2021, https://www.nytimes.com/2021/03/11/opinion/covid-isolation-narrative.html.

27 Mark Fisher, "Why Mental Health Is a Political Issue," *The Guardian,* July 16, 2012, https://www.theguardian.com/commentisfree/2012/jul/16/mental-health-political-issue. See also Timothy Snyder, *Our Malady: Lessons in Liberty from a Hospital Diary* (New York: Crown, 2020).

charismatic superspreaders of negative emotions (principally anger, envy, and disgust), who, if left untreated and uncontained, severely compromise the overall health of the infected society. Yet, despite all we know now about the role of the Sackler family and other bad actors who literally manufactured the opioid overdose epidemic,[28] and despite what we have learned since Covid-19 and the riot at the US Capitol, book sales and other data indicate large numbers of Americans are still convinced that vulnerability, however regrettable, is the problem of the vulnerable individual to solve on their own.

It is worth noting that the dominant vulnerability discourse in the United States over the past two decades has not put the focus on the *powerlessness* that characterizes the vulnerability associated with political persecution, social stigmatization, or economic deprivation. Instead, the loudest voice on vulnerability is that of a middle-aged white woman from Texas who has the chutzpah to speak (ad nauseam, say her detractors) about "the power of vulnerability." Casandra Brené Brown (1965–) is a smiling vulnerability harvester who has made a fortune advising men, women, and children to believe in the benefits of embracing the risks and uncertainty of expressing emotions and allowing one's weaknesses and insecurities to be seen or known; in other words, the plus side of being vulnerable. She is one of the latest avatars in America's self-help industry that goes back through Daniel Goleman and Stephen Covey to Emily Post and Benjamin Franklin. It's more of the can-do discourse winners love and that has always operated in partnership with the sharp-elbowed variant of global capitalism denounced through the years by the late Mark Fisher, C. Wright Mills, David Smail, and

---

28 Patrick Radden Keefe, *Empire of Pain: The Secret History of the Sackler Dynasty* (New York: Doubleday, 2021). On a smaller scale, but no less damning, is the exposé of the spate of suicides associated with the toxic work environment during the privatization of France's public utility, France Télécom. See Dominique Decèze, *La Machine à broyer: De France Télécom à Orange, quand les privatisations tuent* (Paris: Jean-Claude Gawsewitch, 2004).

many others besides Fromm.[29] However, Brown's incitement to embrace "uncertainty, risk, and emotional exposure," can sound like a first world problem or luxury good, not to say insulting, to the growing number of people facing food, job, housing, or health insecurity, social ostracization, and other forms of persecution and rough handling. Nor, as Alex McElroy has pointed out, does Brown's feel-good vulnerability offer much to guard against "petulant vulnerability" that "feigns emotional fragility as a means of retaining power."[30]

Having survived Covid-19, divorce, motherhood, and addictions, Jamison is still free to join the open-ended democratic counter-discourse now rumbling through Reddit and other forums.[31] That discourse would turn the primary focus of vulnerability away from the tone-deaf or cynical hucksterism of Brown's "empire of emotion"[32] and back to its first meaning as actual suf-

29 Louis Menand, "What Our Biggest Best-Sellers Tell Us about a Nation's Soul," *The New Yorker,* May 31, 2021, https://www.newyorker.com/magazine/2021/06/07/what-our-biggest-best-sellers-tell-us-about-a-nations-soul; Alexandra Schwartz, "Improving Ourselves to Death," *The New Yorker,* January 8, 2018, https://www.newyorker.com/magazine/2018/01/15/improving-ourselves-to-death; Mark Fisher, *Capitalist Realism and Ghosts of My Life: Writings on Depression, Hauntology, and Lost Futures* (London: Zero Books, 2014); Adam Grant, "The Dark Side of Emotional Intelligence," *The Atlantic,* January 2, 2014, https://www.theatlantic.com/health/archive/2014/01/the-dark-side-of-emotional-intelligence/282720/; David Smail, "Power, Responsibility and Freedom," unpublished manuscript, 2005; and C. Wright Mills, *The Power Elite* (Oxford: Oxford University Press, 1956).

30 Alex McElroy, "'This Isn't Your Old Toxic Masculinity. It Has Taken an Insidious New Form," *The New York Times,* January 13, 2022, https://www.nytimes.com/2022/01/13/opinion/toxic-masculinity.html. Also left out of account are those who have good reasons to fear that "being vulnerable" in the Brené Brown sense of confiding would expose them to even greater vulnerability and insecurity — at work, home, or other settings with known or hidden power asymmetries.

31 See u/Trader_Joe_Mantegna, *r/CriticalTheory, Reddit.com,* https://www.reddit.com/r/CriticalTheory/comments/qmlott/why_do_i_hate_brene_brown/.

32 Sarah Larson, "Brené Brown's Empire of Emotion," *The New Yorker,* October 25, 2021, https://www.newyorker.com/magazine/2021/11/01/brene-browns-empire-of-emotion. Rather than offering some critique or sorting

fering from attack or realistic fear of probable future harm felt by various individuals or groups living in specific uneasy social, economic, and political circumstances. The next six chapters, on three popular novels and three eloquent manifestos, are more contributions to that conversation.

_____

of pros and cons, Larson's piece is a fawning infomercial timed to coincide with the latest product drop in Brown's vulnerability business, *Atlas of the Heart: Mapping Meaningful Connection and the Language of Human Experience* (New York: Random House, 2021).

III

Fictional Narratives

6

Channeling Orwell, Banking on an Antiprediction

Margaret Atwood, *The Handmaid's Tale* (1985)

« Je vous parle d'un temps que les moins de vingt ans ne peuvent pas connaître… »

Above are the first words of one of the most famous songs, "La Bohème," by one of France's most famous singer-songwriters, Charles Aznavour (1924–2018). The lyrics, written by Jacques Plante and set to music by Aznavour, start in on the work that poets and storytellers have done since forever: carrying over from a there then to a here now so that we can "all talk here now and in the future about how what happened there then affects us here." In this way, poets and storytellers have something in common with the task of the translator and with the theorist, in the ancient Greek sense, who performs the important duty of witnessing and passing an event into public discourse.[1]

---

1   For more on the task of the theorist, see Wlad Godzich's essay "The Tiger on the Paper Mat," which serves as the foreword to the Paul de Man essay

"I am speaking to you of a time that those under twenty can-not know," sings Aznavour who is already forty when this song about a paradise lost is released in 1965. *"Arma virumque cano,"* Virgil sings of the arms and the man that built the Roman em-pire. And twenty-one centuries later, the Notorious B.I.G. raps, "And if you don't know, now you know," to let others share in his celebration of overcoming adversity.

In times of real or perceived vulnerability, many turn to fas-cism; but many also turn to poetry and literature in general for solace or guidance or help, and the poets come forth — if they have not all been killed off and all their words banned or for-gotten — as though in answer to a call. Sometimes third par-ties guide the one in need of these "liberating gods" (Emerson).[2] "You must go, Mrs. Frisby, to the rats under the rose bush. They are not, I think, like other rats" (Robert C. O'Brien). The poet, whether rat, mouse, or human, provides nourishment in hard times and is appealed to almost instinctively. "What about your supplies, Frederick?" ask the cold hungry field mice in the clas-sic children's tale *Frederick* (1967) by Leo Lionni.

When the coronavirus pandemic spread worldwide in the spring of 2020, Americans under 20 years old had already lived through two moments that incited massive panic-stricken turns to poets and storytellers: the aftermath of September 11, 2001 with the destruction of the World Trade Center in New York; then the morning after November 8, 2016 and the serious shake-up of democracy in the United States with the election of Donald J. Trump. September 11, or 9/11 as Americans call it, seemed to mark a turning point between a lost world in a "time before" and "the way we live now."[3] 9/11 was responded to in

---

collection T*he Resistance to Theory* (Minneapolis: University of Minnesota Press, 1986), xiii–xv et passim.

2   See Margaret Renkl's praise for Amanda Gorman and other poets one year into Covid-19, "Thank God for the Poets," *The New York Times,* April 5, 2021, https://www.nytimes.com/2021/04/05/opinion/poets-poetry-month. html: "We know now how vulnerable we are."

3   Russia's invasion of Ukraine on February 24, 2022 was called "Europe's 9/11" by European officials, reported Russian-born journalist Julia

countless ways including for many by excavating, sharing, and even reading a poem by W.H. Auden, "September 1, 1939". It begins, "I sit in one of the dives / On Fifty-second Street / Uncertain and afraid / As the clever hopes expire / Of a low dishonest decade," and continues on for almost a hundred lines with many standout moments that made the poem sound like an uncanny open letter sent from the dawn of World War II to a time very out of joint which some may have feared and others perhaps desired to be the start of a World War III.[4] It turned out to be only the start of a new hot and cold regional war, sold as "the war on terror," that would not seriously interrupt regularly scheduled programming or anyone's desire to shop.

The second event, Trump's 2016 election as the forty-fifth president of the United States, despite receiving almost three million fewer votes than his Democratic opponent Hillary Clinton, was also marked by an outpouring of strong emotions[5], marches, earnest analyses, and — right on call — appeals to poets and storytellers. By popular acclaim, *The Handmaid's Tale*,[6] everybody's "feminist" protest novel, was recruited to play the

Ioffe in "Europe's 9/11," *Puck News,* March 3, 2022, https://puck.news/europes-9-11/. About the same time, to a new group of students studying "Tocqueville and Democracy in the Internet Age," I called the war in Ukraine Putin's Afghanistan; that is, a "quagmire" not unlike Vietnam for the Americans, Algeria for the French, or India for the British. For background, see Timothy Snyder, "The War in Ukraine Is a Colonial War," *The New Yorker,* April 28, 2022, https://www.newyorker.com/news/essay/the-war-in-ukraine-is-a-colonial-war.

4   For two takes on this poem, one admiring by Ian Samson, one critical by Dan Schneider, see Harriet Staff, "On Auden's 'September 1, 1939'," *Poetry Foundation,* September 26, 2019, https://www.poetryfoundation.org/harriet/2019/09/on-audens-september-1-1939, and Dan Schneider, "The Twin Towers & W.H. Auden," *cosmoetica.com,* http://www.cosmoetica.com/S14-DES9.htm.

5   *The New Yorker* published many scathing pieces directly after Trump's election, such as this one by the editor-in-chief, David Remnick, who, like many, initially supported the second Iraq war post-9/11: "An American Tragedy," November 8, 2016, https://www.newyorker.com/news/news-desk/an-american-tragedy-2.

6   Margaret Atwood, *The Handmaid's Tale* (Toronto: McClelland & Stewart, 1985). Hereafter cited parenthetically throughout this chapter.

role of witness and passer between the 1980s Reagan era and, less than forty years later, the time of Trump. Unlike with Auden who died in 1973, in this case the poet-storyteller Margaret Atwood (1939–) is still alive and has herself been a willing participant in the enthusiastic rediscovery of her "dystopian fiction" from 1985 by a new generation of readers of all ages and nationalities. And viewers, one must add, since a successful Hulu series has attracted large audiences, larger no doubt than the 1990 Harold Pinter and Volker Schlöndorff movie or the 2000 opera spin-off.[7] Since 2016, *The Handmaid's Tale* has evolved from a 300-page work of canonical literature taught in many college and high school classrooms into franchise status with handmaid's cloaks and bonnets sold on Amazon for private parties or public demonstrations, and in 2019 a prize-winning sequel, *The Testaments,* also written by Atwood, that coordinates with the television series on which the author served as a producer. There is something unseemly about all the profiteering around the fear and loathing and perverse attraction of the novel's lurid authoritarian world.

Everything about this book seems to be in the millions — copies sold, "likes," the author's Twitter followers, and of course profits for Atwood who is perhaps no J.K. Rowling or Stephen King but nevertheless well beyond having to rent the "huge German-keyboard manual typewriter" that she felt the need to mention in her 2017 *New York Times* backward glance. In this short autobiographical text where the author is clearly trying to shape the reception history of her work — why let reviewers and anonymous internet trolls have all the fun? — everything from the typewriter to her closing message of "hope" in the age of Trump is interesting both for itself and as symptom of *The Handmaid's Tale* as incarnation or allegory of a certain zeitgeist.

---

7   The movie got mixed reviews. Owen Gleiberman, who gave the movie a C–, remarked that "visually, it's striking," but he adds, "paranoid poppycock — just like the book." "The Handmaid's Tale," *Entertainment Weekly,* March 9, 1990, https://ew.com/article/1990/03/09/handmaids-tale-2/.

In particular, the essay gives her the opportunity to answer three questions she says come up often. First, is *The Handmaid's Tale* a feminist novel? Her answer is no and yes.

> If you mean an ideological tract in which all women are angels and/or so victimized they are incapable of moral choice, no. If you mean a novel in which women are human beings — with all the variety of character and behavior that implies — and are also interesting and important, and what happens to them is crucial to the theme, structure and plot of the book, then yes. In that sense, many books are "feminist."[8]

In a second follow-up paragraph she lists bad things that do happen to women in books and the real world, in the past and now, and she is opposed to abuse and violence against women but also sees these more broadly as a large recurring category of human rights violations. In this regard, her position is consistent with the declaration that Hillary Rodham Clinton would make ten years later in an underappreciated speech, called by some her finest hour, to the United Nations Fourth World Conference on Women in Beijing, China on September 5, 1995: "human rights are women's rights and women's rights are human rights."[9]

Atwood continues, "The second question that comes up frequently: Is *The Handmaid's Tale* antireligion? Again, it depends what you may mean by that." Atwood develops a longer reply to this question and summarizes it this way: "So the book is not 'antireligion.' It is against the use of religion as a front for tyranny; which is a different thing altogether." Question three:

8   Margaret Atwood, "Margaret Atwood on What 'The Handmaid's Tale' Means in the Age of Trump," *The New York Times,* March 10, 2017, https://www.nytimes.com/2017/03/10/books/review/margaret-atwood-hand-maids-tale-age-of-trump.html.
9   Hillary Rodham Clinton, speech to the United Nations Fourth World Conference, Beijing, China, September 4–15, 1995.

Is *The Handmaid's Tale* a prediction? That is the third question I'm asked — increasingly, as forces within American society seize power and enact decrees that embody what they were saying they wanted to do, even back in 1984, when I was writing the novel. No, it isn't a prediction, because predicting the future isn't really possible: There are too many variables and unforeseen possibilities. Let's say it's an antiprediction: If this future can be described in detail, maybe it won't happen. But such wishful thinking cannot be depended on either.[10]

What these "forces" are, who "they" is, and what "they were saying" recently and "even back in 1984," is all left a bit vague; but by "antiprediction" we are meant to understand a technique by which one attempts to ward off some negative event, similar to throwing salt over one's shoulder or saying "jinx" or other magic words for self-protection.[11] This type of calculated wishful thinking, *I will write down my nightmare so that it doesn't come true,* is just the kind of behavior one can easily imagine from someone raised on Grimm's Fairy Tales and who in the fateful year 1984 was channeling George Orwell who professed to have been doing exactly the same thing when he sat down to write *1984* in 1948; that is, writing about an illiberal future so as to protect liberalism in the present.[12] Orwell's nightmare vision of the future was "a boot stamping on a human face — forever." Atwood's nightmare is a bunch of dicks screwing over women — forever. It is worth noting that Orwell and Atwood, two trochee names, were both in their early forties when they began their dysto-

---

10 Atwood, "Margaret Atwood on What 'The Handmaid's Tale' Means in the Age of Trump."

11 In French this behavior is called *conjurer le sort* (countering the spell). Potter specialists know all about this.

12 For a contemporary example, see Timothy Snyder's (anti)prediction about a possible future breakup of the United States should another minoritarian president take power in 2025. Interview with Chris Davis, "Yale History Professor Timothy Snyder Told 'Insider' He Fears American Democracy May Not Survive Another Trump Campaign," *Business Insider,* January 14, 2022, https://www.businessinsider.com/timothy-snyder-fears-democracy-may-not-survive-another-trump-campaign-2022-1.

pian novels, and both were older parents of young children juggling writing and caregiving. It's my hunch that Orwell, *né* Eric Blair, chose the year 1984 because by that time his adopted son, Richard, would be roughly the age his father was at the moment he was writing. Today Atwood's daughter Eleanor (b. 1976) is roughly the age her mother was when writing *The Handmaid's Tale*. So by making their "antipredictions" about futures they wanted *not* to occur, Orwell and Atwood took toil and trouble to make the world safe for their children.[13] And Atwood (b. 1939) has not stopped fighting on many fronts to prevent her bad dream from coming true.

Except in times of crisis, few pay attention let alone a living wage to most poets, essayists, and novelists, and so by way of compensation — call it symbolic capital — they get the darndest ideas and may pay themselves the compliment of being the unacknowledged legislators of the world or having pens mightier than swords. In another essay published in *The Nation* just before Trump's inauguration, a sobering moment indeed, Atwood demurred.

There's nothing inherently sacred about films and pictures and writers and books. *Mein Kampf* was a book. Plenty of creative people in the past have rolled over for the powerful. In fact, they're especially subject to authoritarian pressures because, as isolated individuals, they're very easy to pick off. [...] The pen is mightier than the sword, but only in retrospect: At the time of combat, those with the swords generally win."[14]

---

13 It would seem that the work of the philosopher Kate Manne is also trying to make the world a better place for her daughter's generation. Besides *Down Girl: The Logic of Misogyny* (Oxford: Oxford University Press, 2017) and *Entitled: How Male Privilege Hurts Women* (New York: Crown, 2020), see "Diet Culture Is Unhealthy. It's Also Immoral," *The New York Times,* January 3, 2022, https://www.nytimes.com/2022/01/03/opinion/diet-resolution.html.

14 Margaret Atwood, "What Art under Trump?" *The Nation,* January 18, 2017, https://www.thenation.com/article/archive/what-art-under-trump/.

Orwell, who saw actual combat during the Spanish Civil War and almost died there, would probably agree. So would, I think, Ahmet Altan, a writer and journalist who spent five years jailed in Erdoğan's Turkey.[15]

Atwood's answers in the FAQ section of the *Times* essay are straightforward and sensible, but she doesn't stop there. With a coercive *But* that reminds me of the opening pages of *Walden* ("But men labor under a mistake") and the start of many paragraphs in Jamison's addiction memoir, Atwood seeks to inscribe her *Handmaid's Tale* within the prestigious and lucrative tradition of confession and witnessing.

> But there's a literary form I haven't mentioned yet: the literature of witness. Offred records her story as best she can; then she hides it, trusting that it may be discovered later, by someone who is free to understand it and share it. This is an act of hope: Every recorded story implies a future reader. Robinson Crusoe keeps a journal. So did Samuel Pepys, in which he chronicled the Great Fire of London. So did many who lived during the Black Death, although their accounts often stop abruptly. So did Roméo Dallaire, who chronicled both the Rwandan genocide and the world's indifference to it. So did Anne Frank, hidden in her secret annex.[16]

Offred, or is it Atwood, the Canadian Anne Frank? Based on this paragraph, someone who had not read the novel could get the false idea that *The Handmaid's Tale* is a fictional diary. But it is certainly not a diary in the conventional sense, since, as this paragraph correctly states, a first-person account cannot narrate the moment of one's arrest or slaughter. It will instead "stop abruptly" as happens at the end of the journal of Hélène Berr.

---

15 Ahmed Altan, *Je ne reverrai plus le monde: Textes de prison* (Arles: Actes Sud, 2019). Altan was released from prison on April 14, 2021 following a decision in his favor by the European Court of Human Rights.

16 Atwood, "Margaret Atwood on What 'The Handmaid's Tale' Means in the Age of Trump."

"The French Anne Frank," as she has been called, recorded her story with pen and paper as best she could over a two-year period, then she gave it to her family's cook, a non-Jew, trusting and hoping the cook would not destroy it and that it would be read again later by her special friend Jean, her family, and perhaps even herself, were she to survive the war. But the "I" speaking in *The Handmaid's Tale* seems to narrate her own abduction on the last page:

> The van waits in the driveway, its double doors stand open. The two of them, one on either side now, take me by the elbows to help me in. Whether this is my end or a new beginning I have no way of knowing: I have given myself over into the hands of strangers, because it can't be helped.
>
> And so I step up, into the darkness within; or else the light. (295)

The logical problem of who can be speaking or writing this abduction scene — a feat as clever as making one's bed while lying in it — is not resolved by the contrivance of the supplementary "Historical Notes" that follow the above quotation. Those thirteen dense pages are presented as the "partial transcript" of a university symposium on the "soi-disant manuscript," to quote the pompous Professor Pieixoto — a figure of fun, I presume, for the then 46-year-old Atwood who never completed her PhD and who here allows herself a potshot at phallogocentric academia. It's her party. However, the provenance of the "document" — when it was supposedly written, by whom, and how — cannot be explained easily within the terms of the fictional universe posited, since the society in which the narrator lived strictly prohibited all writing and recording and sought to squash all language that could vehicle consciousness and self-consciousness of handmaids such as Offred. The amount of detail and the frequent use of the present tense are dissonant if the reader is supposed to believe that the document was created later, *post facto,* by the protagonist once she has escaped Gilead and managed to acquire the requisite recording instruments.

Perhaps somewhere in the once favored land of academia, amid the vast quantities of published literary criticism and all the student papers this novel has generated, someone has come up with a convincing answer to the professor's question; but one notices that his own reply first pivots to the question of identifying the narrator, and then after confessing his failure to identity "the narrator herself directly," the professor pivots again in favor of open-ended speculation about the society the narrator belonged to. The book ends with Atwood priming the pump for the lit crit and royalty checks to follow: *Applause*. "Are there any questions?"

Are we supposed to let the whole matter of "Who's speaking?" slide by on the non-stick surface of poetic license and willing suspension of disbelief? Maybe. I suspect many readers never even read these historical notes, unless their teacher says they'll be on the test; and many probably don't care about these details of narratological precision one bit. But if that's the case, then I propose we not think of it as a fictional diary, and instead stick to the idea that this text is really the transcription of Margaret Atwood's mid-1980s nightmare — a text composed and published as an act of hope that the illiberal, authoritarian state it envisions would not come true... and that it might make her some money. The latter goal has been achieved, probably beyond Atwood's wildest dreams, and the former political ambition is of course open-ended, but so far there is no place in the world that has created a society that resembles Gilead though aspects of it existed before 1985 and still do. Similarly, although *Orwellian* has entered the vernacular to describe various cruel and ironic institutions and practices past and present, there is no place in the world quite like the nightmare society described in *1984*, a novel that also concludes with an erudite and implicitly optimistic postface that Thomas Pynchon helpfully discusses in his introduction to a common paperback edition.[17]

---

17 I discuss Pynchon's Introduction within a reading of *1984* in my book *Tocqueville and Democracy in the Internet Age* (Ann Arbor: Open Humanities Press, 2014), specifically in the chapter "Restore Previous Session."

My point is that it is incorrect and potentially harmful, especially in the age of Trump, to classify either of these two canonical examples of dystopian fiction within "the literature of witness." To do so is to debase the word WITNESS, which then comes to mean *Anything I've seen, imagine I've seen, or claim to have seen.* This would be to play into the hands of Trump and his assault on truth and reality-based discourse and behavior.[18] Therefore, neither Offred nor Margaret Atwood, who has written many essays and granted countless interviews but so far not published her autobiography or memoirs as such, should be compared to people who have written true diaries, journals, and memoirs, such as Leslie Jamison, Hélène Berr, Samuel Pepys, Roméo Dallaire, Anita Hill, Anne Frank, and so many others.

All language is testimony in a broad sense; therefore all witnessing is testimony, but not all testimony is witnessing. There is false or fake or invented testimony, either deliberate or accidental. There is also nonsense ("Twas brillig and the slithy toves…"; "Colorless green ideas sleep furiously"). Whether *The Handmaid's Tale* is "paranoid poppycock" is for the reader to decide, but it is not nonsense. Best to stick with the self-description written at the top of the copyright page: "This is a work of fiction. Any resemblance to persons living or dead is purely coincidental." If we want a clever label that borrows from Orwell, who called *Animal Farm* (1945) a "fairy story," and from Saturday morning TV that Margaret Atwood may have watched in her younger years, we could say *The Handmaid's Tale* is a "fractured fairy tale."[19] A more traditional label would be *conte philosophique* — a philosophical fable, story, or tale — a genre

---

18 See Michiko Kakutani, *The Death of Truth: Notes on Falsehood in the Age of Trump* (New York: Tim Duggan Books, 2018). See also Sheldon S. Wolin on lying as "a crime against reality" in "Democracy's Prospects," in *Democracy Inc.: Managed Democracy and the Specter of Inverted Totalitarianism* (Princeton: Princeton University Press, 2010): ch. 13: "The problem today is that lying is not an isolated phenomenon but characteristic of a culture where exaggeration and inflated claims are commonplace occurrences" (262).

19 The cartoon series *Fractured Fairy Tales* ran from 1959 to 1964 and then in reruns all through the 1970s and '80s.

associated with the slippery French polymath Voltaire. *Candide* (1759) and other texts of this genre belong to a larger category of cerebral fiction that includes much science fiction, fantasy, romance such as the gothic novel and tale, and the fantastic. Philosophical tale is a good fit for Atwood who, biographers tell us, turned from philosophy to literature in her college years and studied under the great Canadian theorist of archetypes, Northrop Frye — a commander of a certain faith in criticism that was popular "in the time before."

***

So what is *The Handmaid's Tale* (hereafter *HMT*) all about? For all the curious Rip Van Winkles who ignored this novel for the past thirty-five years, whether deliberately or accidentally, and who are only just now having its significance in the Western cultural landscape come into view, I recommend getting your bearings via testimonies by four astute witnesses: two older, Michiko Kakutani and Rebecca Mead; and two younger, Emily Nussbaum and Jia Tolentino. Some of my observations in what follows build on information and claims made in these review-essays.[20] Kakutani's piece appeared in the *New York Times* on September 3, 2019 on the occasion of the publication of the supplementary *Testaments*. She claims the most chilling lines of *HMT* come early when Offred and therefore the reader is invited by Aunt Lydia to accept that a fascist setup can become ordinary,

---

20 Michiko Kakutani, "The Handmaid's Thriller: In 'The Testaments' There's a Spy in Gilead," *The New York Times,* September 3, 2019, https://www.nytimes.com/2019/09/03/books/review/testaments-margaret-atwood-handmaids-tale.html; Rebecca Mead, "Margaret Atwood, The Prophet of Dystopia," *The New Yorker,* April 10, 2017, https://www.newyorker.com/magazine/2017/04/17/margaret-atwood-the-prophet-of-dystopia; Emily Nussbaum, "A Cunning Adaptation of 'The Handmaid's Tale,'" *The New Yorker,* May 15, 2017, https://www.newyorker.com/magazine/2017/05/22/a-cunning-adaptation-of-the-handmaids-tale; and Jia Tolentino, "Margaret Atwood Expands the World of 'The Handmaid's Tale,'" *The New Yorker,* September 5, 2019, https://www.newyorker.com/magazine/2019/09/16/margaret-atwood-expands-the-world-of-the-handmaids-tale.

just as, since Hannah Arendt, we speak of "the banality of evil." The piece sets Atwood's latest creation within the tradition of testimony literature, recalling at the end that Gilead means "hill of testimony." Mead's *New Yorker* profile from April 2017 reprises Atwood's entire career in the aftermath of the consecration of sorts that came with the Hulu series being promoted a few months earlier in Superbowl half-time advertising. Mead does precisely what Atwood, using Br'er Rabbit-style reverse psychology, claims she doesn't want, namely, to be called a "prophet," while she, Atwood, laughs all the way to the bank.[21] The piece by Emily Nussbaum, a Pulitzer Prize-winning TV critic at the *New Yorker,* was published after the broadcast of the first episodes of season one of the Hulu series in May 2017. Among its strengths are Nussbaum's summary of the whipsaw 1980s environment, her naming of the Gilead regime "Biblical fascism" (non-identical twin of so-called Islamo-fascism), and her observation that a TV show's basic need to keep viewers viewing in order to survive leads inevitably and predictably to steering the new Offred away from the geeky, hang back witness of the novel toward a badass telegenic heroine who "persisted."[22] The fourth piece by Jia Tolentino, also a *New Yorker* staff writer and, usefully for this assignment, a survivor of twelve years at a Baptist school in Texas who has intimate knowledge of indoctrination techniques, also appeared in September 2019. Her piece makes use of the original novel, the sequel, and many more episodes of the Hulu series to comment on the complicity and compromises required for constructing such a frightening future, as art and in life. Yet besides a sketch of a military coup, she notes that both the novels

---

21 See Atwood's *Guardian* interview with Lisa Allardice, "I am not a prophet. Science fiction is really about now," January 20, 2018, https://www.the-guardian.com/books/2018/jan/20/margaret-atwood-i-am-not-a-prophet-science-fiction-is-about-now.

22 Nussbaum's allusion is to the hashtag-friendly spat in the US Senate between Elizabeth Warren and Mitch McConnell. The larger point is that Offred's Sufi-like mysticism may be fine, but it does not fit the Christian mega-church-size audiences the show's investors want it to reach. See Nancy Workman, "Sufi Mysticism in Margaret Atwood's 'The Handmaid's Tale,'" *Studies in Canadian Literature* 14, no. 2 (1989).

and TV series lack detail about how Gilead was established and later destabilized: "a landscape obscured by fog," she calls it. She also notes how Aunt Lydia's testimony in Atwood's sequel adds moral complexity that some may have overlooked in *HMT*.

Any or all of these pieces offer a great way into thinking about the *HMT* franchise, if one is so inclined. There is also of course the always useful square one of the Wikipedia entry for the novel. It contains many references to scholarly and general public articles, and the search engines of JSTOR and the MLA bibliography provide many more. *HMT* was so popular so quickly that criticism anthologies, such as the MLA's *Approaches to Teaching* series, started appearing less than twelve years later.[23] The academic success of a dystopian fiction whose action is set in and around Cambridge, Massachusetts and America's most famous institution of higher education, Harvard University — now turned into the capital of a totalitarian state with fascist décor — is remarkable to say the least. The novel's recent escape in the last three years from the "love" bestowed on it in college and high school classrooms has turned it back into a free-floating wildcard, or, put another way, into still unplayed Scrabble tiles, whose future use and value is anyone's guess.

***

I will return to the scenes of Scrabble playing in the novel, however it's important to first say more about the 1980s even if we do not have any clear dating of the Gilead fascism taking root, getting power, and exercising that power. We do know it's the decade that empowered Margaret Atwood and "riveted" many of her readers. This look back will argue that many of the problems in the world of Gilead that younger or forgetful people might see as evocative of the Bush–Obama–Trump era were actually

---

23 Sharon B. Wilson, Thomas B. Friedman, and Shannon Hengen, eds., *Approaches to Teaching Atwood's "The Handmaid's Tale" and Other Works* (New York: Modern Language Association, 1996). See also Coral Ann Howells, ed., *The Cambridge Companion to Margaret Atwood* (Cambridge: Cambridge University Press, 2006).

already problems in the 1980s, only now with 2020 hindsight we see they were then size M and have ballooned into size XL.

Emily Nussbaum's piece contains a longish paragraph about the 1980s. Here is the beginning, an important remark from the middle, and the end. It comes just after she has noted how the TV series resonates strongly with recent trends and events, including the January 21, 2017 Women's March that took place only three months before the season one kick-off:

> But, for many readers of my generation, *The Handmaid's Tale* is also a time machine back to the Reagan era, a mightily perverse period for sexual politics […].
>
> On the right, there was the anti-abortion New Christian Right — led by figures like Phyllis Schlafly and the televangelist Tammy Faye Bakker — intent on restoring traditional marriage. On the left, there was the anti-porn movement — spearheaded by the feminist philosopher Catharine MacKinnon and the gonzo polemicist Andrea Dworkin — which argued that consensual sex was often an illusion and gender a cruel hierarchy […]
>
> My strongest memory of reading Atwood's book is the rude jolt of a joke between college students like me. "You're so trendy," the narrator, Offred, recalls teasing her friend Moira, about the subject of a term paper. "It sounds like some kind of dessert. *Date rapé*." (*HMT*, 38)[24]

Rapé in French means grated, as in grated carrots: *carottes rapées* (*-ées* because carottes is feminine plural); and it also rhymes with *frappé* — beaten. The French word for rape is *viol*. Here Offred outsources her edgy side to her lesbian sidekick, but not without an *ad hominem* deflation of Moira's decision to write on a politically charged topic with the cutting adjective *trendy*. This microaggression is consistent with a 1980s pattern developed by

---

24 Page references will be to an Anchor Books edition of 1998. The Wikipedia entry includes alternate wording for some passages. Is there an official MLA edition as there is, say, for *Walden* and some other classics? I don't know.

conservative culture warriors to constantly belittle liberal consciousness-raising initiatives as hollow "political correctness," a
clever containment strategy that contributed to keeping calls for
political change to repair large-scale systemic harm from getting
a hearing or even formulated.

The late twentieth century "culture wars" planted the seeds
for twenty-first century polarization and neofascist *us* versus
them discourse. In relation to *HMT*, the 1980s could be said to
begin in 1979, long before anyone was talking about "controlling
the narrative," with the publication of Paul de Man's *Allegories of
Reading* and, in the same year but another mode, Susan Gubar
and Sandra Gilbert's *The Madwoman in the Attic,* an influential text in the world of feminist literary criticism that borrowed
from Virginia Woolf to argue that women and especially female
authors had to be agile to circumvent the strictures of patriar-
chy and that it would often come at great cost to themselves.[25]
Outside of academia, an important event in 1979 was the Iran
hostage crisis which along with an inflationary economic cycle would hobble the presidency of Jimmy Carter, a humble
Christian-farmer-businessman and Navy war veteran. The hostage crisis arguably tipped the 1980 election in favor of Reagan,
a former vaudeville-style movie actor, corporate ad-man, and
governor of California associated with the state's "tax revolt"
and by some with the "unmaking" of the state's public university
system.[26] Reagan, the son of an alcoholic who inoculated himself against gloom with a stack of 3 × 5 cards filled with jokes, became a polarizing figure in the United States. He was idolized by
the religious Right, the National Rifle Association, the military,
and the pro-business, anti-tax, "small government" lobby. He

---

25 Sandra Gilbert and Susan Gubar, *The Madwoman in the Attic: The Woman
Writer and the Nineteenth-Century Literary Imagination* (New Haven: Yale
University Press, 1979). Published by the same press was de Man's *Allego-
ries of Reading: Figural Language in Rousseau, Nietzsche, Rilke, and Proust*
(New Haven: Yale University Press, 1979).

26 Christopher Newfield, *The Unmaking of the Public University: The Forty-
Year Assault on the Middle Class* (Cambridge: Harvard University Press,
2008).

was widely seen as both jovial and a stern law-and-order man who could stand up to Russia. For the Left he was an unfunny puppet of special interests that sought to advance financialized capitalism and the military-industrial complex and to dismantle fifty years of hard-won increments of social-democratic progress from Roosevelt to Johnson.[27]

I witnessed the rightward shift of the country while a student at Dartmouth College, when my arrival in 1981 coincided with David T. McLaughlin's first year as the school's president. McLaughlin, the former CEO of Toro Corporation, a maker of lawnmowers, replaced a professor-president, the Hungarian American mathematician and co-inventor of the BASIC computer language, John G. Kemeny, who then returned to teaching. (He was my professor in a class on probability.) McLaughlin's seven-year tenure as president also coincided with the rise of the infamous *Dartmouth Review,* a mischievous campus newspaper which launched the careers of right-wing ideologues Dinesh D'Souza and Laura Ingraham — the former an author, filmmaker, and convicted felon pardoned by Trump; the latter a Fox TV news host, Trump supporter, and former Reagan speechwriter among other conservative postings.[28]

The 1980s was the decade of Madonna and Michael Jackson, but also of Dead Kennedys, Talking Heads, Sonic Youth, Van Halen, and Christian rock. It was a decade of backlash against the advances of feminism, notably the sometimes violent pushback against the legalization of abortion and against the Equal Rights Amendment which failed to be ratified by enough states

---

27 For a critical look at Reagan that breaks through the hagiography on the right, see the documentary by Matt Tyrnauer, "The Reagans," reviewed by Adam Nagourney, "Was Reagan a Precursor to Trump? A New Documentary Says Yes," *The New York Times,* November 11, 2020, https://www. nytimes.com/2020/11/11/arts/television/the-reagans.html, and, one year later, Claire Bond Potter, "The Shadow of Ronald Reagan Is Costing Us Dearly," *The New York Times,* November 11, 2021, https://www.nytimes. com/2021/11/11/opinion/reagan-social-welfare.html.

28 For a sketch of Ingraham's authoritarian personality, see Anne Applebaum's *Twilight of Democracy: The Seductive Lure of Authoritarianism* (New York: Doubleday, 2020), 164–71.

before the appointed deadline of June 30, 1982.[29] In addition, there was still the Cold War, the space shuttle *Challenger* disaster that killed the teacher-astronaut Christa McAuliffe, the AIDS epidemic, the savings and loan crisis, the rise of Rush Limbaugh on radio, of Oprah Winfrey on television remaking an old platform as a Black female talk-show host, and of Bill Gates, a smart, privileged white man, launching a new platform with Microsoft Windows; and there was the Chernobyl nuclear disaster, the fall of the Berlin Wall, and the Tiananmen Square massacre all reminding Americans about life on other continents thanks to CNN. The 1980s ended triumphantly in 1991 for Reagan fans with the collapse of the Soviet Union. For feminists and other democracy sympathizers, however, 1991 is remembered with bitterness as the year of the bipartisan US Senate denigration of Professor Anita Hill's sexual harassment charges against US Supreme Court nominee Clarence Thomas — the epitome of a decade of dreams deferred and a milestone in the conservative movement's capture of the courts.[30] Just as an upper-middle-class white woman, Phyllis Schlafly, became the weapon of choice to defeat the Equal Rights Amendment, conservatives got a Black man and woman to help halt feminism and the civil rights movement in one blow with the 52 to 48 vote that placed Clarence Thomas on the US Supreme Court.[31] Irony — as noun, adjective, or adverb — was on everyone's lips in the 1980s.

---

29 The woman who led the fight against the Equal Rights Amendment, Phyllis Schlafly, is featured in a 2020 television mini-series *Mrs. America* starring Cate Blanchett.
30 See Jane Mayer and Jill Abramson, *Strange Justice: The Selling of Clarence Thomas* (Los Angeles: Graymalkin Media, 1994); Corey Robin, *The Enigma of Clarence Thomas* (New York: Henry Holt, 2019); and Anita Hill, *Speaking Truth to Power* (New York: Penguin Books, 1997).
31 Beyond the non-explanation of "How ironic!" one could use Nancy Leong's *Identity Capitalists: The Powerful Insiders Who Exploit Diversity to Maintain Inequality* (Stanford: Stanford University Press, 2021) to see Schlafly and Thomas as "identity entrepreneurs" working an ingroup and outgroup identity marketplace that grows as the US moves from King's Dream and Johnson's Great Society toward Atwood's caste-bound Gilead.

The 1980s is the start of the shrinking of the middle class and increased economic vulnerability reported in Barbara Ehrenreich's 1989 bestseller *Fear of Falling: The Inner Life of the Middle Class.*[32] Status anxiety then was not about being surpassed by China but by Japan, symbolized at the time by Sony Corporation with its successful Walkman, stylish new Sony Tower, and the bold Japanese purchase of Rockefeller Center in midtown Manhattan. Atwood, a Canadian who had no dog in that race, crafts a hilarious, for an outsider, scene of comic reversal when Offred and Ofglen are asked by the interpreter for a delegation of Japanese visitors to Gilead if they wouldn't mind being photographed (think gawkers passing through Pennsylvania Amish country). And then if the handmaids are happy:

> "Excuse me," says the interpreter again, to catch our attention. I nod, to show I've heard him.
> "He asks, are you happy," says the interpreter. I can imagine it, their curiosity: *Are they happy? How can they be happy?* I can feel their bright black eyes on us, the way they lean a little forward to catch our answers, the women especially, but the men too: we are secret, forbidden, we excite them.
> Ofglen says nothing. There is silence. But sometimes it's as dangerous not to speak.
> "Yes, we are very happy," I murmur. I have to say something. What else can I say? (28)

There is intense fulfillment competition and ambient pressure to be *very happy* in 1980s America. But as with Fromm's description of the fallout from increasing stratification and segmentation that takes place in Europe during the late Middle Ages and early Renaissance, happiness was *very* unevenly experienced in the 1980s, in part because freedom was *very* unevenly distributed, in part because economic inequality was widening

---

32 The effects of a second decade of extreme income inequality became the focus of another Ehrenreich bestseller about the working class: *Nickel and Dimed: On (Not) Getting By in America* (New York: Metropolitan, 1996).

and social and political equality (i.e., a fair shot at the American dream) was either still missing, stalled, or receding. It was a great decade for the powerful like Donald Trump who were "free to choose" (the revamped, 1980s *laissez-faire* dogma promulgated by economist Milton Friedman) and who could easily ignore the mosquito bite of a fey writer like Thomas Wolfe and his *Bonfire of the Vanities* (1987).[33] It was not such a great decade, however, for a lot of women whose hardscrabble situation was captured by the 1991 road movie *Thelma and Louise.* It's the story of the personal liberation movement of two working-class, white women that ends with them "free to choose" to drive their car off a cliff. The 1980s sow the seeds of a future politics of resentment and rage that was then still on the margins, expressed indirectly and in sign language, so to speak, because of the "morning again in America" pressure to be *very happy.* It was a *grotesque* decade by which I mean there was the frequent and abrupt juxtaposition of heterogeneous categories — animal, vegetable, mineral; high/low, sacred/vulgar, nutritious/poisonous, haves/have-nots, Western/non-Western, straight/gay, straight/ironic, straight/crooked, and so on. But aren't all decades like that, you ask? Maybe, but to many of us the grotesque seemed to ramp up in the 1980s. We were "amusing ourselves to death," warned Neil Postman, angling off Marshall McLuhan and Huxley more than Orwell, in his 1985 study of public discourse in the age of television. And lo, in the middle of that provocative decade comes *The Handmaid's Tale,* published in 1985 but written in 1984, the year of the patriotic Olympic Games in Los Angeles (one cycle after the 1980 Moscow Olympics) and the year the Americans doubled down on Reagan, who, as luck would have it, survived an assassination attempt in 1981, thus adding to his amiable, tough-guy persona. Reagan was chosen for a second term in a landslide victory over his Democratic challenger Walter Mondale (Carter's vice-president) and his female run-

---

33 On Trump and Wolfe, see Paul Wells, "Donald Trump Is Stuck in the 80s," *Maclean's,* April 9, 2017, https://www.macleans.ca/culture/books/donald-trump-is-stuck-in-the-1980s/.

ning mate Geraldine Ferraro.[34] At the end of 1984, the United States was divided between those who thought Reagan was a smiling version, and therefore all the more sinister, of Orwell's Big Brother, and those who thought he was the best protection against the US sliding toward *1984*-like statism.[35]

HMT, like the Aznavour song mentioned above, performs an elegiac carrying over of this "time before" with sympathetic descriptions of physical objects and allusions to landmarks of the 1980s. Offred says, "I am a refugee from the past, and like other refugees I go over the customs and habits of being I've left or been forced to leave behind me. […] I sit in this chair and ooze like a sponge" (227). One oozing from earlier in the same chapter 5, which ends with the Japanese scene, concerns the theme of freedom, in particular the freedom experienced at a former movie theater — an artistic venue — now converted into a commercial space where handmaids order their dresses. "Lilies of the Field, it's called."

> Lilies used to be a movie theater, before. Students went there a lot; every spring they had a Humphrey Bogart festival, with Lauren Bacall or Katharine Hepburn, women on their own, making up their minds. They wore blouses with buttons down the front that suggested the possibilities of the word *undone*. These women could be undone; or not. They seemed to be able to choose. We seemed to be able to choose, then. We were a society dying, said Aunt Lydia, of too much choice.

34 About Mondale, Jane Mayer says he "told voters the hard and politically costly truths they didn't want to hear. […] Mondale refused to peddle the magical thinking." Jane Mayer, "Remembering Walter Mondale," *The New Yorker,* April 19, 2021, https://www.newyorker.com/news/postscript/remembering-walter-mondale.

35 Dennis O'Brien, then president of the University of Rochester, first jokes he's not related to the character in Orwell's novel with the same surname and then offers a year-end meditation that would seem to invite all parties to the table for civilized discussion in a conciliatory tone appropriate to the holiday season. Dennis O'Brien, "Orwell, '1984' and the Elections," *The Christian Science Monitor,* December 31, 1984, https://www.csmonitor.com/1984/1231/123148.html.

> I don't know when they stopped having the festival. I must have been grown up. So I didn't notice. (25)

Atwood studied at the University of Toronto but also at Harvard, so it can be assumed that she knew the Cambridge area well.[36] Besides containing an example of the recurring marker of the imperfect tense, "used to," and commas that add weight to *before* and *then,* the passage features an example of the many instances of double take, second thought, and revision. Here it's the quick reversal achieved by Aunt Lydia's haunting words: Choosing was good, wasn't it? No, it was bad! It should be noted that Offred is often carrying over not one but two worlds in her testimony: 1) the pre-Gilead world of her childhood and young adulthood in the Cambridge area; and 2) the world of pain and indoctrination she endured at the Rachel and Leah Center that trained her to think and act truly *as,* not merely *like,* a handmaid. As Emily Nussbaum states, "the regime's goal is to get women not merely to accept their roles but to embrace them."

If the roommate Moira is the Offred foil that represents *freedom to,* the resident advisor Aunt Lydia, the official voice and enforcer of Gilead ideology, argues for the superior value of *freedom from,* as here in another passage from chapter 5:

> I think about laundromats. What I wore to them: shorts, jeans, jogging pants. What I put into them: my own clothes, my own soap, my own money, money I had earned myself. I think about having such control.
>
> Now we walk along the same street, in red pairs, and no man shouts obscenities at us, speaks to us, touches us. No one whistles.
>
> There is more than one kind of freedom, said Aunt Lydia. Freedom to and freedom from. In the days of anarchy, it was

---

36 For a walking tour of the novel's Cambridge settings, obviously popular since the start of the TV series, see Greg Cook, "'The Handmaid's Tale': A Walking Tour of the Novel's Cambridge Settings," *Wonderland,* May 10, 2019, https://gregcookland.com/wonderland/2019/05/10/handmaids-tale-walking-tour/.

freedom to. Now you are being given freedom from. Don't underrate it. (24)

Here the absence of quotation marks around what Aunt Lydia said is a nice way to emphasize Offred's internalization of this lesson. Note also the possibilities of the sentence "I think about having such control." Does that mean, I recall once having such control but with no regrets, with some regrets, or with a desire to have such control again one day? As for Aunt Lydia's lesson, it does not really matter whether Atwood learned it from reading Fromm or from Isaiah Berlin's "Two Concepts of Liberty" essay from 1958, or thought it up on her own. The point is Aunt Lydia is extolling the benefits of *escaping from freedom,* which she associates with the libertinage of the old "days of anarchy," and embracing the safety and protection guaranteed by the strict law and order of Gilead. It's the standard fascist sales pitch, and one that worms its way particularly well into the ears of the vulnerable, especially those weakened by a recent loss of status, income, or a loved one as is the case with Offred.

Thus, it is not surprising that the news of Moira's escape from the indoctrination center provokes mixed feelings in Offred, ranging from dread to giggles.

The story [of Moira's escape] passed among us that night, in the semidarkness, under our breath, from bed to bed.

Moira was out there somewhere. She was at large, or dead. What would she do? The thought of what she would do expanded till it filled the room. At any moment there might be a shattering explosion, the glass of the windows would fall inward, the doors would swing open…. Moira had power now, she'd been set loose, she'd set herself loose. She was now a loose woman.

I think we found this frightening.

Moira was like an elevator with open sides. She made us dizzy. Already we were losing the taste for freedom, already we were finding these walls secure. In the upper reaches of the atmosphere you'd come apart, you'd vaporize, there would be no pressure holding you together.

Nevertheless Moira was our fantasy. We hugged her to us, she was with us in secret, a giggle; she was lava beneath the crust of daily life. In the light of Moira, the Aunts were less fearsome and more absurd. Their power had a flaw to it. They could be shanghaied in toilets [a reference to Moira's seques-tration of Aunt Elizabeth in the washroom]. The audacity was what we liked. (133)

This passage, especially "we were losing the taste for freedom, already we were finding these walls secure," convinced me to in-clude *HMT* in this book because it lays out the crux of the moral dilemma Offred must confront — and by extension the reader and any conscious human being tasked with making their way in the world: shall I risk pursuing self-mastery and self-deter-mination? Are those goals possible for me? A delusion? Is free-dom a human birthright? A luxury of rich people? An acquired taste that can also be lost? Just another word for nothing left to lose? Something else? Depending on one's own background, present circumstances, and near prospects, a range of thoughts and feelings, perhaps similar to the range enumerated by Of-fred, is possible. I imagine this passage is a favorite of professors wishing to "teach the conflicts" in their classroom discussions of this novel.[37] *HMT* meditates on this question of freedom, and understandably so since the main character is a novel category of sex worker under contract (a serially raped surrogate mother) under contract, and its author likely had a deadline to meet and was getting by with an old, rented German-keyboard typewriter in West Berlin at the time. These constraints and others make the passages treating the questions of freedom, choice, escape, and their opposites and gradations particularly stimulating.

We have already quoted and briefly discussed three such mo-ments. Several more deserve an honorable mention. Without

---

37 See Gerald Graff, *Beyond the Culture Wars: How Teaching the Conflicts Can Revitalize American Education* (New York: W.W. Norton & Co., 1992).

ranking but simply from the beginning, we can note the first occurrence of the word *escape,* actually in the plural, "escapes" (8), within a discussion of fleeing, suicide, and also, more subtly, the escape of writing and contemplation: "those other escapes, the ones you can open in yourself, given a cutting edge." The opening here can be a physical one as with a knife or razor, or a metaphysical, spiritual opening that might be initiated with a writing instrument — the metaphor does not work so well in the age of typewriters and computers, but in fact Atwood first wrote *HMT* mostly in longhand on legal notepads, she says.

Offred remembers happy conversations about making big plans with Luke, her lover-then-husband from the time before: "We used to talk about buying a house… We… We… we… we… it was something to talk about, a game for Sundays. Such freedom now seems almost weightless" (24). In contrast is this earlier remark from the time she first arrived at her new posting: "I envy the Commander's Wife her knitting. It's good to have small goals that can be easily attained" (13). The wonderfully named character Serena Joy, the wife in question and a smoker, speaks plainly to Offred: "I've read your file. As far as I'm concerned, this is like a business transaction. But if I get trouble, I'll give trouble back. You understand" (15)? Offred, in turn, describes plainly her relation to her shopping partner Ofglen: "The truth is that she is my spy, as I am hers. If either of us slips through the net because of something that happens on one of our daily walks, the other will be accountable" (19).[38]

Choice and chance encounters on these walks offer a constant tension between freedom and constraint, taking liberties and renunciation, giving and withholding. Note her remark describing the Western dress of the Japanese visitors: "I used to dress like that. That was freedom." The formulation leaves undecidable whether this is affirmation or distance-taking by the old-

---

38 About spies, one should remember that *HMT* is a Cold War-era book written before the time of internet trolls but attuned to the world of double agents, secret services, and the like, written by a Canadian woman living at the time on one side of a physically and politically divided Berlin, a time when accountability was taken seriously.

er, un-duped Offred ("thirty-three years old… five seven without shoes," 143).[39] There's the constraint of their white bonnets ironically first called wings, but there's no flying nun in Gilead: "Given our wings, our blinkers, it's hard to look up, hard to get the full view, of the sky, of anything. But we can do it, a little at a time… We have learned to see the world in gasps" (30). Night offers more freedom than daytime partly because surveillance is more difficult in the dark: "The night is mine, my own time, to do with as I will, as long as I am quiet" (37).

Reminiscence and meditation fill the sections entitled "Night" and one called "Nap," alternating with the daytime sections that also contain daydreaming and observations on the side of the action. In chapter 9 within the section "Waiting Room," Offred first affirms her own room in Woolfian fashion, before recalling the hotel rooms where she used to rendezvous with Luke, who was cheating on his wife, in the days before they were married: "My room, then. There has to be some space, finally, that I claim as mine, even in this time… Will I ever be in a hotel room again? How I wasted them, those rooms, that freedom from being seen. Rented license" (50).

Near the start of chapter 10, Atwood-Offred (two trochee names) offer well-known words from the hymn "Amazing Grace," the standout lines being, "Who once was lost, but now am found / Was bound, but now am free" (54). Tocqueville had read Blaise Pascal and Jean-Jacques Rousseau and had traveled through America's Bible Belt. Thus he understood how this submission to a religious order could be viewed as swapping a bad

---

39 Being 33 obviously links Offred to the first Christian martyr, Jesus of Naza-
    reth. If we imagine the action taking place in 1984, that would mean she
    was born in 1951, very much a Cold War baby boomer with all the bonuses
    and baggage of that generation. We learn her mother had her at age 37, so
    that would mean she was born in 1914, a Depression-era child who would
    have been 19 in 1933, the year Hitler takes power and Professor Dodd
    moves to Berlin. We can also keep in mind that Offred's daughter was
    born in the 1970s and is around 8 years old at the time of Offred's posting
    to Fred's house where the main action picks up in springtime ("daffodils
    are now fading and tulips are opening their cups, spilling out color," 12),
    roughly five weeks after her arrival.

yoke for a good "salutary yoke" (*joug salutaire*) and therefore experienced as freedom. Offred, channeling her inner Emily Dickinson or Stevie Wonder, attuned to the freedom that comes with being nobody, recalls her ordinary, marginal life in the time before: "We were the people who were not in the papers. We lived in the blank white spaces at the edges of print. It gave us more freedom. We lived in the gaps between the stories" (57).[40] There is regular use of caesura in *HMT* — blank space, unused, open, free — perhaps a carryover from Atwood's poetry habits.

Offred visits her ob-gyn who offers his "help": "I hesitate. He's offering himself to me, his services, at some risk to himself… I put on my clothes again, behind the screen. My hands are shaking. Why am I frightened? I've crossed no boundaries, I've given no trust, taken no risk, all is safe. It's the choice that terrifies me. A way out, a salvation" (61). "In a bathroom, a bathtub, you are vulnerable, said Aunt Lydia. She didn't say to what" (62). "I've learned to do without a lot of things. If you have a lot of things, said Aunt Lydia, you get too attached to this material world and you forget about spiritual values. You must cultivate poverty of spirit. Blessed are the meek. She didn't go on to say anything about inheriting the earth" (64). Whether embracing this poverty mentality, a certain asceticism, is wise or stupid — for whom? when? why? — is a conflict that Gerald Graff or others might teach when discussing *HMT*.

Note the variable perception of time depending on how much one has and one's duties and resources: "There's time to spare. This is one of the things I wasn't prepared for — the amount of unfilled time, the long parentheses of nothing" (69). There is the ritual slut-shaming of Janine (72), a scene Atwood says she found "horribly upsetting" in its TV representation. There is a recurring giving up to forms, rituals, and ceremonies invented and imposed by others — even bashing someone's head and tearing him limb from limb: "we are permitted anything

---

40 In the Stevie Wonder song "Big Brother" from the album *Talking Book* (1972), the prophetic voice sings, "Your name is big brother. […] My name is nobody."

and this is freedom" (279). But freedom within a framework, like school recess inside a playground: "A rat in a maze is free to go anywhere, as long as it stays inside the maze" (165).

For many, it seems, the most striking example of ritual is a scene some readers find obscene and gratuitous; namely, the monthly ceremonial "nothing"; that is, the annihilation (*Vernichtung*) of the handmaiden. If repopulating Gilead were the sole objective, artificial insemination of surrogate mothers by the techniques practiced routinely on cows since the 1930s would have sufficed, but there is a double purpose of creation and destruction at work in this scene.[41] Critics often call what Offred undergoes rape, but her own account of her experience rules out this appellation as well as "making love" and "copulating." The Commander's penetration of "the lower part of my body" with his erect penis is described using the f-word twice, and then Offred says, "nothing is going on here," which I think it is permissible to read as something (*etwas*) and not nothing (*nichts*); namely, her dehumanization and annihilation is going on, reducing her to nothing, an action captured well by the German noun *Vernichtung*. Nothing is going on here, she says, "that I haven't signed up for. There wasn't a lot of choice, but there was some, and this is what I chose" (94). Here "chose" is similar to the "choice" of Thelma and Louise, or the choice of low-wage textile workers in Bangladesh, for example, who, *The Economist* tells us, are "willing" to work for next to nothing — accent on *next to* nothing, but not nothing if they hope to stay alive. Early on Offred displays keen awareness of the local economy — from the Greek *oikonomia,* household management — she lives within: "Like other things now, thought must be rationed. There's

---

41 It is possible that in her preferred storytelling mode Atwood is weighing in on the debate that followed the publication of Susan Brownmiller's paradigm-shifting book *Against Our Will: Men, Women, and Rape* (New York: Simon & Schuster, 1975) in which the author argued that rape was about power not sex. For a short review of this debate, see Noam Shpancer, "Rape Is Not (Only) about Power: It's (Also) about Sex," *Psychology Today,* February 1, 2016, https://www.psychologytoday.com/us/blog/insight-thera-py/201602/rape-is-not-only-about-power-it-s-also-about-sex.

a lot that doesn't bear thinking about. Thinking can hurt your chances, and I intend to last" (8). And she knows, like any sex worker, that the contract binds on both sides: "This is not recreation, even for the Commander. This is serious business. The Commander, too, is doing his duty" (95). It's precisely to escape this seriously sadistic business that the Commander, being the master of the house with the power to stiffen or soften the rules, chooses to send Nick the chauffeur with a message: "He wants to see you. In his office… Tomorrow" (99).

Thus begin Offred's graduate studies, so to speak, marked by new relationships with two additional teachers besides Moira and Aunt Lydia who influenced her in her younger years. One teacher is a previous handmaiden of Fred, Offred-before-Offred, who, before committing suicide, left behind a short, one-sentence diary entry scratched in an obscure corner of Offred's dorm room: *Nolite te bastardes carborundorum,* "Don't let the bastards grind you down" (186). Is this a reminder to oneself, like tying a string on one's finger, or is it addressed to another like the proverbial message in a bottle? To Offred it sounds sometimes like a prayer, other times more like a command (147). It must be in Latin, or some approximation thereof, since this is the history-rich hallowed ground of Harvard, or what once was Harvard, where even tattoos must be in Latin to show off one's high fidelity, lineage, and exclusivity.

That Offred, who knows the words *obverse, sylph, larynx, susurration,* and *cornucopia,* for example, is stumped by the *Nolite* sentence strains credulity. But one should not forget that *HMT* is, among other things, a campus novel, and therefore given the teacher–student dynamic Atwood posits, it's important to have the one who unlocks this "useless hieroglyph" (147) for her be the Commander, "rapist"-annihilator, Scrabble partner, and teacher Fred. He's never addressed by that familiar diminutive, however, nor do we learn his surname or Offred's real name. Only the chauffeur Nick, Saint Nick, so lively and quick with his lean, whimsical "French face" — I imagine him looking like Charles Aznavour — learns her real name. A classmate from the 1980s might have called the Commander's behavior *icky*. Today's preferred term might be *cringey*. But Offred does not see it that way, or not only that way — her meetings with him are also an opportunity, a chance for larger rations of thinking, freedom, and skincare products.

"I'd like you to play a game of Scrabble with me," says the Commander (138). She wants to laugh, and for good reason. Offred, or whatever her name is, has had to *scrabble*; that is, "scrape, scratch, struggle to grab or collect something in a disorderly, frantic way" for years. But it hasn't been a game, it's been hard work. In comparison, being invited now to play a *game* of Scrabble — a calm and orderly turn-taking process of first scrambling then assembling letters into words — is a holiday. How so? Because for the duration of the game Offred and the Commander will operate within a Rawlsian paradise of justice and fairness. They will have the same rights (freedoms) and responsibilities (to respect the other's rights, to not cheat) dictated by mutually agreed on rules, with the impersonal arbiter of a dictionary if necessary. Neither cheats in the sense of taking unfair advantage, there's only an occasional relaxation of effort, on both sides, to let the other win as a gesture of flattery (184). For once they constitute a We, she notices ("He said *we*," 156). They are taking a holiday from Gilead's fascist-authoritarian hierarchy and living democratically as coequals.[42] Not equality of outcomes, but equality of chances, a level playing field. Such relations were unimaginable to Offred before the invitation, and then strike her as absurd and dangerous.

The significance of the absurdity[43] of the Commander's request unfolds gradually: "Now of course it's something different.

---

42 See Erich Fromm, *Escape from Freedom* (New York: Henry Holt, 1969), 171: "In authoritarian philosophy the concept of equality does not exist."

43 By absurdity, I don't mean nonsensical but a process or state of inversion of customs, habits, and precedence, including a reversal of the normal hierarchy of signifieds over signifiers, sense over signifying. Literature of and on the absurd is vast, but one treatment of the topic that I have found helpful is Sartre's essay on the 1942 novel *Aminadab* by Maurice Blanchot, reprinted in the collection *Situations I* (1947). In the same volume is Sartre's essay on Camus's *L'Étranger* (1942). Both are exercises in French Hegelianism.

Now it's forbidden, for us. Now it's dangerous. Now it's indecent. Now it's something he can't do with his Wife. Now it's desirable. Now he's compromised himself. It's as if he's offered me drugs" (138–39). Then as she's actually touching the tiles and placing her words, she says "The feeling is voluptuous. This is freedom." There's the freedom of all that open space on the board, the freedom to use the tiles she freely chooses to spell the words she freely creates; but there's also a more volcanic freedom, like the giggles that erupt when she's thinking of Moira's escape. It comes with the realization that all this Gilead stuff is a bit of a charade, a con that disguises the one-sided imposition of different rules for different categories of people that always shore up the powerful and shaft the weak.

Offred's discovery and the accompanying volcanic feelings (146) are similar to what Dorothy Gale and her persistent friends experience when they discover a wizened little old man with a microphone pulling levers behind the curtain next to The Great and Powerful Oz. Offred's jubilation is also similar to what dawns on Mr. Trexler in E.B. White's short story, "The Second Tree from the Corner," when he realizes the pettiness of his psychiatrist's desires: "So he wants a new wing! There's a fine piece of theatrical gauze for you! A new wing," on his house in Westport, he says. In both stories and in *The Wizard of Oz* one has this conversion moment. It's the amazing grace. Atwood's heroine is born again: no longer just Offred but also *off-red,* like off-white, no longer pure red precisely because she's now read her situation differently — pun intended. Atwood orchestrates this decisive event of consciousness-raising, a turning point in the power relations of the novel, roughly halfway through the book's 300 pages which is consistent with the timing of the 33-year-old Offred's apprenticeship that begins in earnest, "Nel mezzo del cammin di nostra vita" (Dante Alighieri).

But Offred, like Trexler, knows that this new perspective, this new outlook in *her head,* doesn't suffice to change real asymmetrical power relations, *the facts on the ground*: "Better not go too far, he mused. Better not lose possession of the ball." But it does allow Offred, or her reader, to listen from here on out with

Sufi-like concentration and detachment when, for example, the Commander makes arrogant and condescending remarks of self-congratulation about what the enlightened Gilead regime has done for women:

> We've given them more than we've taken away, said the Commander. Think of the trouble they had before. Don't you remember the singles' bars, the indignity of high school blind dates? The meat market. Don't you remember the terrible gap between the ones who could get a man easily and the ones who couldn't? Some of them were desperate, they starved themselves thin or pumped their breasts full of silicone, had their noses cut off. Think of the human misery. (219)

Atwood has the Commander continue his preening plaidoirie for another paragraph. One can imagine Offred listening politely like the student in the presence of the star professor during office hours. "Now, tell me," says the Commander at the end of his soliloquy, "You're an intelligent person, I like to hear what you think. What did we overlook?"

> Love, I said.
>> Love? Said the Commander. What kind of Love?
>> Falling in love, I said. The Commander looked at me with his candid boy's eyes. Oh yes, he said. I've read the magazines, that's what they were pushing, wasn't it? But look at the stats, my dear. Was it really worth it, *falling in love?* Arranged marriages have always worked out just as well, if not better. (220)

This passage is pure gold and may be why, according to Rebecca Mead, a friend of Atwood's told her that *HMT* was going to make her rich. One rarely sells a million of anything if one is not appealing to all kinds of customers. In this passage, the preceding page, and for the whole second half of the book, one has the send-up of Gilead's dirigiste "Nanny state" which will please liberty defenders and conservatives, just as they were attracted to Tocqueville and Orwell throughout the Cold War; and of course hippies and other Lefties are going to dig Offred's defense of romantic love, a vision that conveniently sweeps under the rug the psychopathology of everyday life summarized in those "stats" the Commander is referring to, such as the 149 *fémini-cides* — women killed by their partner — in France in 2019, 121 in 2018, 109 in 2017.[44]

But Atwood does not stop there. After a caesura, comes this third voice: "*Love,* said Aunt Lydia with distaste. Don't let me catch you at it. No mooning and June-ing around here, girls. Wagging her finger at us. *Love* is not the point" (220). Atwood's Aunt Lydia uses her stern, scoffing voice to, one could say, squash or swat away the possibility of girl-on-girl or boy-girl sexual activity, the kind of activity associated in the South, in the summer with the mating rituals of what are called June bugs. Readers have wondered if Offred's real name is June. The question is similar to wondering "How many children hath Lady Macbeth?" Is June her real name or another nickname — June, June bug, Jezebel — who knows? What matters is that with the word *June-ing,* Atwood — an entomologist's daughter who wrote her book at least partly in the homeland of the Volkswagen Beetle — is associating Offred and the other "girls" with large, leaf-eating scarab beetles noted for being attracted to light, a certain clumsiness and crashing into things, sexually explicit mating rituals, and said to be an excellent source of protein and calcium; that is, they are edible. *The Edible Woman* was the novel from 1969 that established Atwood's reputation.[45] But that is not all.

---

44 For a fact check of these alarming figures that vary somewhat among different sources, see Cédric Mathiot, "Le nombre de féminicides augmente-t-il vraiment?" *Libération,* November 20, 2019, https://www.liberation.fr/checknews/2019/11/20/le-nombre-de-feminicides-augmente-t-il-vraiment_1763789.

45 I agree with Jia Tolentino's assessment of Atwood's "tonal range": "As a novelist, she has a wide tonal range, moving from sarcasm to solemnity, austerity to playfulness; she can toggle between extremes of subtlety and

Atwood's Aunt Lydia (the tattooed lady[46] and she could also very well be Black[47]), has the wagging finger and some of the

---

unsubtlety from book to book." "Margaret Atwood Expands the World of 'The Handmaid's Tale.'"

46 This earlier Lydia (a Harlequin heroine's name) was immortalized in the 1939 song "Lydia the Tattooed Lady," sung by Groucho Marx in the movie *At the Circus* and, later, Kermit the Frog on "The Muppet Show." It includes the line "You can learn a lot from Lydia / She can give you a view of the world." Courbet's controversial painting from 1866, "The Origin of the World," is a close-up of the lower part of a nude female body showing the genitals in a way that some associate with the back of a female June bug. Google it, and then go to YouTube to see for yourself. For colloquial uses of "June bug," connoting a sexually available woman, a vagina, and so forth, see the entries in *Urban Dictionary* and the commentary of the lyrics to the danceable song "Junebug" [1989] by the B-52's.

47 Some people claim that Atwood's Gilead world is very white. But to those who ask, "Where are all the Black people?" one should reply, "How do you know there aren't any?" Isn't it possible that Lydia is, as one says, a "mixed race" person of color who is "passing"? Maybe Rita too, as she is in the Hulu series. And besides, what's Black got to do with it? Well, everything, if you are in the danger zone of some political regime's color wheel, and nothing, if you have the privilege to safely articulate the position that Black rights are human rights and human rights are Black rights once and for all in a gesture of solidarity and empathy talk that could be hollow or sincere. (Looking at you Hillary "Stronger Together" Clinton.) Offred and her "sisters" know that, like the song says, you can learn a lot from Lydia, and one of her lessons concerns the stereotypically female art of playing the double game. Aunt Lydia teaches her girls the necessity and power of metaphor: "'Men are sex machines,' said Aunt Lydia, 'and not much more. They only want one thing. You must learn to manipulate them, for your own good. Lead them around by the nose; that is a metaphor. It's nature's way, It's God's device. It's the way things are'" (144). "Sex Machine" (1970) was a hit song by James Brown. As a Black man, James Brown could sing "Say It Loud, I'm Black and I'm Proud," the title of his 1968 hit, but the Aunt Lydias of the world know they have to express their pride differently because they do not have the same *freedom to* that men have. Finally, it should be remembered that according to history, Lydia was the first female convert to Christianity, so it would be normal that she have the convert's zeal on the outside but the newcomer's caution as a stranger in a strange land. In fact, Atwood includes an allusion to that ancient Lydia directly after the passage just cited. "Aunt Lydia did not actually say this, but it was implicit in everything she did say. It hovered over her head, like the golden mottoes over the saints, of the darker ages. Like them too, she was angular and without flesh" (144). This is probably a reference to the Giotto

swagger of Tina Turner in the song "What's love got to do with it." They are making essentially the same point: men are sex machines, as Lydia says elsewhere (144) echoing James Brown, and women forget that at their peril.[48] Referencing hit songs[49] is not just whimsical since there's plenty of evidence that Offred's mind is often invaded by spontaneous, involuntary memories in the way made famous by Marcel Proust and featured in many pop songs including the Beatles cover of "Young Blood" ("I can't get you out of my mind"). Beatlemania was taking place when Atwood was in her 20s and writing more poetry than stories; and Tina Turner (another trochee name) was very much in the air while Atwood was writing *HMT*.

After another caesura, the next lines revert to the male authority: "Those years were just an anomaly, historically speaking, the Commander said. Just a fluke. All we've done is return things to Nature's norm" (220). Here again Atwood's Offred leaves off the quotation marks to suggest the words are playing in her mind's ear. Perhaps she wonders why he calls arranged marriages "Nature's norm," an idea so different from Lydia's

---

frescoes of the thirteenth century and could be a point of overlap between Atwood's study of symbol and allegory and the work of de Man who also paid attention to Giotto in his reading of Proust in *Allegories of Reading*.

48 Tina Turner became famous in the 1980s for surviving domestic violence inflicted by her partner Ike Turner, leaving him, and relaunching her singing career with the spectacularly successful Private Dancer Tour in 1985 that promoted the album of the same name released the previous year. Tina Turner won three Grammy Awards in 1985 for Best Female Pop Vocal Performance, Record of the Year, and Song of the Year for "What's Love Got To Do with It." The song's lyrics allow for two opposed or complementary interpretations: either the singing "I" is rejecting love as pure illusion or, as one anonymous internet comment puts it, "the singer is desperately trying to suppress and deny growing feelings of love towards someone and trying to pass it off as lust only." Maybe, but what if the "pass off" is not being pursued desperately but daringly? Afterall, Tina Turner and Aunt Lydia graduated from the same school of life.

49 Tina Turner's "What's Love Got To Do with It" was the second biggest single of 1984 after Prince's "When Doves Cry," which includes the memorable line "Animals strike curious poses." A reading would be possible of this song and Turner's using the imago approach of Harville Hendrix as presented in his guide, *Getting the Love You Want*.

thinking, or what he means by "those years." The 1980s? The '60s counterculture and its spillover into the '70s? The roaring '20s and their spillover into the fascist '30s? Or does he have in mind the entire history of courtly love since the Middle Ages? A 1,000-year anomaly? Is all of modernity, then, a mistake that Gilead would be correcting in a latter-day "counter-reformation"? It makes no sense to ask if Offred might be pondering these questions while thinking about what to spell next with the Scrabble tiles she's holding, since obviously she's just a character in a book — but we can.

For many readers it's hard to resist the idea of Offred thinking deep thoughts, especially since the character called Offred is said to be "an intelligent *person*." But in her vulnerable situation, and not born with a silver spoon in her mouth, *intelligent* means being mindful of the delicate balance of unequal power in the Commander's household, aware that she doesn't have the luxury to not see color, for example, and must exercise forethought when asking questions.[50] She can be persistent and daring in her own way though, as in this passage:

> "You want my life to be bearable to me," I say. It comes out not as a question but as a flat statement; flat and without dimension. If my life is bearable, maybe what they're doing is all right after all.
>
> "Yes," he says, "I do. I would prefer it."
>
> "Well then," I say. Things have changed. I have something on him, now. What I have on him is the possibility of my own death. What I have on him is his guilt. At last.
>
> "What would you like?" he says, still with that lightness, as if it's a money transaction merely, and a minor one at that: candy, cigarettes.
>
> "Besides hand lotion, you mean," I say.

---

50 On "I don't see color" and other stressors and microaggressions, see Sam Louie, "I Don't See Color — Then You Don't See Me," *Psychology Today*, February 22, 2016, https://www.psychologytoday.com/us/blog/minority-report/201602/i-dont-see-color.

"Besides hand lotion," he agrees.

"I would like…" I say. "I would like to know." It sounds indecisive, stupid even, I say it without thinking.

"Know what?" he says.

"Whatever there is to know," I say; but that's too flippant. "What's going on." (188)[51]

The final echo of Marvin Gaye's popular anti-war song "What's going on" from 1971 (also without the question mark, just as with the Tina Turner hit) is a nice way to conclude this additional small important victory that Offred has pulled off as she realizes how needy and therefore vulnerable the Commander is despite his superior rank. One does not need to be familiar with Hegel's master–slave dialectic to see that this is an empowering moment for Offred, the sex worker, as she realizes that the Commander needs her alive.[52] A death of despair, such as the suicide of her predecessor, who did not follow her own advice perhaps and *did* let the bastards grind her down, and the death of Ofglen, a politically motivated suicide it's suggested, would have the potential of pulling the whole curtain down on the Commander, all the Commanders, and the whole sham Gilead setup. The possibility that she might kill herself or simply expire from a too unbearable situation is her weapon, she realizes, since it would be his undoing. This is the triumph behind the "At last," which also contains the echo of the early affirmation of her intention to *last*; in other words, endure and maybe *outlast*. Back then she was

---

51 A similar exchange continues in chapter 32 within the "Jezebel's" section. The relevant portion begins with this memory: "The Commander, last night, fingers together, looking at me as I sat rubbing oily lotion into my hands." These two pages would merit a textual commentary of their own. The exchange ends with this back and forth: "We thought we could do better. Better? I say, in a small voice. How can he think this is better? Better never means better for everyone, he says. It always means worse, for some" (209–11).

52 G.W.F. Hegel presents the master–slave dialectic in *The Phenomenology of Spirit* (1807), summarized here: "Hegel on Master-Slave Dialectic – Summary," *Cultural Reader,* http://culturalstudiesnow.blogspot.com/2017/03/hegel-on-master-slave-dialectic-summary.html.

inclined to believe that one ought not think too much because it hurt your chances of survival (8). Ofglen's replacement would seem to share this position, since she recommends that Offred clear her mind and eliminate "echoes" (284). But Offred, being who and what she has now become, namely *off-red,* is ready to revise her earlier thinking and exercise her negative capability.[53] She glimpses the payoff, for example, of thinking beyond "a money transaction merely," while the Commander insists on measuring what *falling in love* is worth in "stats."

The decisive victory is not getting some *thing* from the Commander. She had that experience already with Serena Joy who gave her a cigarette in a furtive moment of sister bonding over shared adversity. Her victory comes from getting him, without even trying, to ask the question "What would you like?" The very question constitutes her as a subject (who must exist since there is a verb) and places him in the position of needy servant (*touché,* because now revealed as less than all-knowing). That's why she cannot immediately think of anything to ask for, because she's already got what she wanted without even actively desiring it at the precise moment when it suddenly arrived; namely "knowledge" of what she calls "his guilt." Guilt? What does she know of his guilt? Nothing. But seizing the power of positing (a guilty story) allows for the retrieval of her consciousness of herself as somebody, who is wronged every time she is annihilated during the Ceremony. Viewed at that moment and in that light, which brings self-affirmation if not yet much self-mastery (you've got to learn to walk before you can bring the house down), her new situation, though not yet very enviable,

---

53 This is the famous term coined by Keats in a late December letter to his brothers while under quarantine in Naples in 1817: "[S]everal things dovetailed in my mind, and at once it struck me what quality went to form a Man of Achievement, especially in Literature, and which Shakespeare possessed so enormously — I mean Negative Capability, that is, when a man is capable of being in uncertainties, mysteries, doubts, without any irritable reaching after fact and reason." John Keats, *Letters of John Keats,* ed. Robert Gittings (London: Oxford University Press, 1970), 43. The Commander, so often seen reaching and rationalizing, would seem to have less of this capability than his female counterpart.

reveals unexpected potential; in other words, power. For example, the letters that spell G I L E A D, are capable of being scrambled and reassembled differently by an A G I L E person into new meaningful constructions, just as Aunt Lydia has scrambled the words "penis envy" and reconstructed their letters as "Pen is envy": "And they were right, it is envy. Just holding it is envy. I envy the Commander his pen. It's one more thing I would like to steal" (186).

Given this newfound power, it may no longer be so important or urgent for Offred to flee the house and Gilead. Perhaps there are good enough reasons to stay, and who knows, maybe more things will come her way, turn in her favor, if she plays her cards or Scrabble tiles well. She is already exempt from cooking and cleaning; she does light shopping that isn't burdensome, especially given the frequent shortages, plus it gives her a chance to get exercise and explore. And now, bonus, she's getting some action with Nick and maybe will get to continue to play Scrabble with the Commander, have a pen of her own, bum cigarettes off his withdrawn Wife and imitate "her version of freedom" (163), or get to see her daughter or attain "greater freedom."[54] Things are looking up, she can think, "finding these walls secure" (133), when she's not feeling "erased" (228) or "abject" (286). If Gilead is within her and knows no bounds (23), then there's no limit to what she can achieve, to becoming an agile Woman of Achievement, maybe just not yet or all at once, but she can start organizing, take some risks, put herself out there. OK Boomer, but what about Moira and the other girls? What does she owe that other "*we*" (169)? Does she have a wider social responsibility, or does she stick her neck out for nobody?

Like Hélène Berr, Offred is more a homebody than a heroine, so why "leave, escape, cross the border to freedom" (271) if she likes it well enough where she is? Also, like Hélène Berr, Offred

---

54 In chapter 41 within the section "Salvaging," Offred replies to the Ofglen-Moira voices in her head: "The fact is that I no longer want to leave, escape, cross the border to freedom. I want to be here, with Nick, where I can get at him. [...] I have made a life for myself, here, of a sort" (271). This passage exhibits the balancing act of negative capability.

has mood swings, but who wouldn't, given their compromising working conditions? "Nothing is going on here that I haven't signed up for. There wasn't much choice, but there was some, and this is what I chose."⁵⁵ This is an act of accepting personal responsibility — instead of looking to blame it on the sun, circumstances, forces, or a mad villain — that could have been spoken by Hélène Berr about her work at the UGIF, although their respective situations are quite different.

∗∗∗

Offred, off-road like Thelma and Louise, grows into being more responsible and accountable, just as, outside of the fictional Gilead, Americans have the opportunity, still for now, to take some responsibility, one by one, each time they elect or reelect a Commander-in-Chief. Being chosen once can always have been a lucky day, a fluke, also called a one-off, but going through that ceremony of choosing a second time means there is no excuse for not knowing what you're signing up for. What's wrong with Gilead? It is stuck inside what the historian Timothy Snyder has named and denounced as the twin ahistorical mistakes of a politics of eternity and a politics of inevitability.⁵⁶ Thinking *it was ever thus* and *it can't be helped*: "It is what it is." That herd fatalism and inertia — "It stinks in the crowd, but it's warm"⁵⁷ — is part of the "small town philosophy" described

---

55 An extended discussion of this passage could examine the different tenses employed in this report about signing up for something. For this, all Derrida's texts about signing and signatures would be helpful; for example, the essays in *Limited Inc* (1988). Jacques Derrida (1930–2004), a Man of Achievement if ever there was one, was at the height of his powers in the 1980s, but now sleeps with the fishes.

56 Timothy Snyder, *On Tyranny: Twenty Lessons from the Twentieth Century* (New York: Tim Duggan Books, 2017), 117–26. For a longer exposition of this argument, see Timothy Snyder, *The Road to Unfreedom: Russia, Europe, America* (New York: Tim Duggan Books, 2018), 257–58.

57 Miroslav Krleza (1893–1981), a prominent Croatian-language intellectual. The translation is by Sladjana Jeremic and appears in her "Serbian Fascism in Online Comments: A Case Study of 'Small Town Philosophy' of Ra-

by Serbian thinker Radomir Konstantinović who was familiar with Eastern European "bloodlands" but knew less about the industrious New England towns where Tocqueville and Atwood sojourned. It takes thinking historically to grasp the twin mistakes that Snyder sees being made today from Mar-a-Lago to Moscow; and thinking historically entails more than telling or retelling the story of past moments, but also seeing the possibility of being "the cocreator of another."[58]

Margaret Atwood may realize that performing historical thinking in storytelling mode runs the risk of having her work be mistaken as antihistorical which in one sense it is since *HMT* is a work of fiction (*une œuvre*). But *the work* of fiction (*le travail*) — in so far as 1) it takes work to produce; 2) gets produced which is its own event; and 3) may generate other events in the aftermath of its publication — is historical. But the event or advent of literature is not self-evident to many people who want to simply cut to the "lurid figures" (Neil Hertz).[59] The possibility of being "riveted"[60] (i.e., rendered unfree) and the resulting confusion between a work of fiction and *the work* of fiction may explain why Atwood so readily steps out from behind the curtain lately — to escape from Gilead and her attic, live off campus, do interviews, and call for and participate in collective protests; for example, signing an open letter opposing the caging of children at the US–Mexican border ordered by the Trump administra-

---

domir Konstantinović" (unpublished MA thesis, Université Jean Moulin-Lyon 3, 2015), 20.

58 Timothy Snyder, *On Tyranny: Twenty Lessons from the Twentieth Century* (New York: Tim Duggan Books, 2017), 125.

59 See Francine Prose's objections to the TV series, "Selling Suffering," *The New York Review of Books*, May 4, 2017. The adjective *prurient* is used by Prose, *lurid* by Mary McCarthy in a negative *The New York Times* review from February 9, 1986. Offred uses *lurid* to describe herself at the end of chapter 36 in the "Jezebel" section.

60 *To rivet*, a verb associated with women's work since World War II, occurs in Tolentino's testimony about rereading Atwood's novel *Cat's Eye* (1988): "I reread it recently, and felt a sensation I associate with reading Atwood: nothing was really happening, but I was riveted, and fearful, as if someone were showing me footage of a car crash one frame at a time." Tolentino, "Margaret Atwood Expands the World of 'The Handmaid's Tale.'"

tion.[61] For a fuller explanation, we can return to her statements in the press.

Sometimes Atwood seems to be forgetting the drug dealer's first rule: don't get high on your own supply. In her *New York Times* piece from 2017 when she affirms that *HMT* is an anti-prediction, she follows that up with classic magical thinking.[62] "Let's say it's an antiprediction: If this future can be described in detail, maybe it won't happen. But such wishful thinking cannot be depended on either," she says.[63] It's true, wishful thinking cannot be depended on to alleviate pain. But not only will a description of suffering not eliminate or prevent suffering, there's a chance it will lead to more suffering. The idea that description, explanation, comparison, or translation actually does something, let alone something good, is the mass delusion of those who spend too much time with their noses in books or in front of screens. It's the quack remedy that Freud denounced in his essay on "Wild Psychoanalysis" (1910), and the nutty idea that de Man, he who (pro)claimed "metaphors are much more tenacious than facts," tried (and failed) to mock out of the room with his tart comment about the efforts of those who seem to think

---

61 Margaret Atwood is the co-signer of an open letter, Alberto Manguel et al., "Concentration Camps for Kids: An Open Letter," *The New York Review of Books,* November 6, 2018, https://www.nybooks.com/daily/2018/11/06/concentration-camps-for-kids-an-open-letter/. For a condemnation of the "banal complicity" when it comes to the enablers of Trump's anti-immigrant policy of child-parent separation, see Jennifer Senior, "Rod Rosenstein Was Just Doing His Job," *The New York Times,* October 15, 2020, https://www.nytimes.com/2020/10/15/opinion/rod-rosenstein-family-separation.html. See also, Ezra Klein's interview with Margaret Atwood, "Transcript: Ezra Klein Interviews Margaret Atwood," *The New York Times,* March 25, 2022, https://www.nytimes.com/2022/03/25/podcasts/transcript-ezra-klein-interviews-margaret-atwood.html.

62 Wishful thinking and magical thinking are often used interchangeably. I prefer magical thinking here because I think it captures better the conjuring trick of *Let's say* — the sheer power of positing that makes stuff appear out of thin air — the gesture of God's *Fiat lux*. See de Man on positing in *Allegories of Reading* and Joan Didion's *The Year of Magical Thinking* (New York: Alfred A. Knopf, 2005).

63 Atwood, "Margaret Atwood on What 'The Handmaid's Tale' Means in the Age of Trump."

they can grow grapes by the light of the word *day*. "But men labor under a mistake," said Thoreau — women and nonbinary people too! — for we see every day that wishful thinking *can* and *is* depended on, and there's nothing wrong with that per se, so long as no one gets hurt. The mischief comes in believing that such thinking *alone* can get anything done outside your head to change the facts on the ground. It's great to give people hope, but at least point them in the right direction for a possible achievement of their stated goals. Doing anything less is peddling false hope, taking your and their eyes off the ball, ducking responsibility, and you, the adult, have set the hopeful and vulnerable younger generation up for failure.

Sometimes I worry there's not much daylight between Atwood, daughter of a dietician, and the nutritionist mother of Leslie Jamison. The sinking feeling comes, for example, in her piece in *The Nation* published days before the Women's March in January 2017: "There will, of course, be protest movements, and artists and writers will be urged to join them," she writes.[64] Is this prophecy or antiprediction? What we know is that during the three years after that piece was published, there were no large sustained nationwide protests in America's streets to defend the rights and livelihoods of artists, teachers, and other vulnerable people that would constitute the kind of pro-democracy politics that I believe Atwood wants to see advance. There was no mass protest about the US Senate's unconstitutional blockade of President Obama and his Supreme Court nominee Merrick Garland before Trump got elected, and nothing but small scattered actions after his election. There was the "Women's March" on January 21, 2017. (The Right must have relished the Left's self-inflicted wound with that marginalizing label.) Then came its pale annual copies. But tokenism is not activism. Yet between January 2017 and January 2021 there was no shortage of violations of American values, democratic institutions, norms, laws, and human rights on Trump's watch, many of his own doing, to get worked up about. What were people waiting for?

---

64 Margaret Atwood, "What Art under Trump?"

In truth, there is nothing "of course" about protests, and voting with your feet is as important as voting with your hands — something Democrats, who tend to think they're pretty smart, haughtily ignore, to the delight of Republicans. No one in the French government or anywhere on the planet could have predicted the Yellow Vest protests or that they would go on for sixty straight Saturday afternoons starting on November 17, 2018. No one could predict Trump's election or Macron's or Brexit or Covid-19 a year or even six or three months before they happened. Why? — because events are different from discourses. Freud was not a Freudian. A virus doesn't "go viral." Events make history that then get talked about and written up in histories, stories, reports, diaries, and so on. The latter can also make history, but when and if that happens is not something they can dictate or predict.[65]

Earlier in the same *Nation* piece Atwood declares, "Nothing is predictable except unpredictability." Maybe, but that means the "of course" five paragraphs later is a zombie-like return of wishful thinking.[66] Protests are *off course* not *of course,* guaranteed, or a logical consequence — that's the Kool-Aid we drink later in history class or sitting in front of The History Channel or Hulu. When a celebrity author, journalist, or anyone says "of course," you can be fairly sure they're speaking bullshit to power[67] and giving Leftist creatives — who generally are down with OPP, short-cuts, outsourcing, and prostheses of all kinds — an

---

65 That said, it is worth noting that at the beginning of episode 3 of season 1 that first aired in 2017, Atwood's leading Handmaid, Offred, recalls, "When they slaughtered Congress, we didn't wake up," a line that gained resonance after the riot at the US Capitol on January 6, 2021.

66 Today those who indulge in wishful thinking, but who also half-realize they are not supposed to, sometimes use the term "aspiration" or "aspirational goal" — perhaps to put a better face on what they're doing.

67 Credit for that expression goes to Avishai Green, "Speaking Bullshit to Power: Populism and the Rhetoric of Bullshit — A Conceptual Investigation," talk given at the Department of Social Science, Hebrew University Conference, 2019. See also Harry G. Frankfurt, *On Bullshit* (Princeton: Princeton University Press, 2005).

excuse to stay home and tune out: either ignoring or genuinely forgetful that "Freedom isn't free."

In April 2020 I was writing the first draft of this chapter, by which time there were over 500,000 cases and 50,000 deaths in the US linked to the Covid-19 epidemic that few Americans saw coming and plenty denied even as it was happening. That month members of Trump's famous base, who may not be big readers of Atwood and likely have strong herd immunity that protects them from the dangers of too much thinking, demonstrated in public by the hundreds, some say thousands, against social distancing and stay-at-home orders and in favor of their Constitutional right to a haircut and golf, and above all to defend their idea of Liberty.[68] They held up signs such as "Social Distancing = Communism" and "Stop Government Over-Reach"; they marched here and there in streets and parks; they honked in their cars; they yelled into megaphones or spoke to journalists to amplify their grievances. Ironically, as we word people like to say, these events accidently, by ricochet, made staying home and doing nothing, or watching *The Handmaid's Tale,* or doing some other indoor activity into a noteworthy political act. Suddenly members of America's do-nothing party became activists in a pitched battle against members of today's know-nothing party. It was only after the death of George Floyd on May 25, 2020 that the Left got off their couches and the internet and began protesting in the streets even more vigorously than the know-nothings who by that time were coming down with Covid-19 in large numbers and suddenly feeling more vulnerable than in April.

Maybe Atwood went from philosophy to literature so that she could do politics by other means. Along the way she learned of the Promethean power of *Let's say* and why that first fire-stealer had to be chained to a rock and tortured daily; and why poets,

---

68 The Right in the United States often prefers to defend Liberty, while the Left generally prefers to defend Freedom. See Paul Krugman's claim that liberty and freedom among conservatives is code for "defense of privilege." "'Freedom,' Florida and the Delta Variant Disaster," *The New York Times,* August 2, 2021, https://www.nytimes.com/2021/08/02/opinion/Covid-Florida-vaccines.html.

essayists, and novelists ever since can find themselves thrown in jail. Descendants of Juno and the Greek convert Lydia taught Margaret Atwood how to escape that fate and remain free.

7

Allegories of Fascism

Philip Roth, *The Plot Against America* (2004)

"What is now proved was once only imagin'd"
— William Blake, *The Marriage of Heaven and Hell*

If adaptation as a TV miniseries (in March 2020, during the early Covid-19 chaos) and focus of a cathartic group reading by famous actors (in October 2018, after the Pittsburgh synagogue mass shooting) are accepted as evidence, then it can be said with confidence that Philip Roth's novel *The Plot Against America* is a close runner-up to *The Handmaid's Tale* when it comes to the spontaneous turning to poets and storytellers in times of disorientation and vulnerability.[1] As though when people could never

---

1   For a review of the miniseries see A.O. Scott, "Once Upon a Timeline in America," *The New York Times,* April 20, 2020, https://www.nytimes.com/2020/04/20/arts/television/plot-against-america-alternate-history.html. See also Richard Brody's anticipation of the series focused on the novel, "The Frightening Lessons of Philip Roth's 'The Plot Against America'," *The New Yorker,* February 1, 2017, https://www.newyorker.com/culture/cultural-comment/the-frightening-lessons-of-philip-roths-the-plot-against-america. Scott's piece reviews several recent TV and movie

have imagined what is in fact happening to them, they needed to turn to imagination specialists to help them get a grip on their new reality. On a first encounter, many are astonished to discover that *The Plot Against America* was published in 2004 and not closer to the 2016 US presidential election.[2]

The turn or return to *The Plot Against America* (hereafter *PAA*) in the Trump era is noteworthy since the plot of the novel centers on the turn of a majority of America's electorate in 1940 away from the hard-working, prosaic Roosevelt, a Democrat who had guided the United States out of the worst years of the Great Depression, to embrace a dashing, poetic figure — the 38-year-old aviator Charles A. Lindbergh. With little forcing of the historical record, Roth depicts Lindbergh as an isolationist anti-war candidate who wins first the Republican nomination in June 1940 and then the presidency on November 5, 1940 by skillfully mimicking George Washington's recommendation

experiments in alternative history, including *Watchmen* and the British series *Years and Years*. On the group reading of Roth's novel in New York that coincidentally took place shortly after the Pittsburgh synagogue massacre of October 27, 2018, see Paige Williams, "Reading Philip Roth after the Pittsburgh Massacre," *The New Yorker,* November 12, 2018, https://www.newyorker.com/magazine/2018/11/12/reading-philip-roth-after-the-pittsburgh-massacre; Judith Thurman, "Philip Roth E-Mails on Trump," *The New Yorker,* January 30, 2017, https://www.newyorker.com/magazine/2017/01/30/philip-roth-e-mails-on-trump; and Charles McGrath's e-mail interview with Roth, "No Longer Writing, Philip Roth Still Has Plenty to Say," *The New York Times,* January 16, 2018, https://www.nytimes.com/2018/01/16/books/review/philip-roth-interview.html. Roth died on May 22, 2018.

2   Philip Roth, *The Plot Against America* (New York: Houghton Mifflin, 2004). Hereafter cited parenthetically throughout this chapter. It would not surprise Spencer Ackerman, however. See his *Reign of Terror: How the 9/11 Era Destabilized America and Produced Trump* (New York: Viking, 2021). Ackerman summarizes his twenty-year argument in "How Sept. 11 Gave Us Jan. 6," *The New York Times,* September 9, 2021, https://www.nytimes.com/2021/09/09/opinion/how-sept-11-gave-us-jan-6.html. See also Michelle Goldberg, "How 9/11 Turned America into a Half-Crazed, Fading Power," *The New York Times,* September 9, 2021, https://www.nytimes.com/2021/09/09/opinion/how-9-11-turned-america-into-a-half-crazed-fading-power.html.

that the United States avoid foreign entanglements, such as World War II, which had been going on for just over a year by that time, and by echoing another father-of-his-country recommendation that drawing the line at two terms as president was a guarantee against dynasty and tyranny—thereby allowing Lindbergh to pose as the true democrat and cast Roosevelt as a power-mad warmonger.

Thus, instead of winning his third presidential election against the Republican Wendell Wilkie (55 percent to 45 percent in the popular vote, and 449 to 82 in the electoral college) as Roosevelt really did, Roth uses the known facts of Lindbergh's nationalism, isolationism, anti-Semitism, and Aryan sympathies to craft an alternative or counter-factual history of fascism in the United States that goes on for two unsettling years (June 1940 to October 1942). This fascist derailment of American democracy ends as abruptly as it started following the mysterious disappearance of Lindbergh, and the novel then rejoins the historical record as we know it after Roosevelt first regains the upper hand over Lindbergh's vice-president in a power struggle in mid-October 1942 and then returns to the White House after a special election in November 1942. The United States then enters World War II against Germany and Japan in late 1942 instead of 1941, and so Roth is required to have Pearl Harbor occur in December 1942 instead of December '41, a modification that many readers probably do not even notice. Opening up this two-year wrinkle in time between a presidential election and the following mid-term election gives Roth the opportunity to pick up where Sinclair Lewis's 1935 semi-satirical novel, *It Can't Happen Here,* left off; that is, imagining a fascist takeover and the establishment of totalitarian rule in the United States based on patriotism and traditional (read: white, Christian) family values.[3] Roth even has the real mayor of New York at the time, Fiorello H. La Guardia, allude to that earlier novel in an

---

3   For a profile of Sinclair Lewis, also the author of *Babbitt* (1922) and a
     Nobel Prize winner, see Robert Gottlieb, "The Novelist Who Saw Middle
     America as It Really Was," *The New York Times,* January 2, 2022, https://

anti-Lindbergh eulogy to honor the gadfly reporter and radio personality Walter Winchell. The fictional Winchell, based on a real person who lived from 1897 all the way to 1972, is assassinated in Kentucky on Monday, October 5, 1942 (all the dates in the novel match up with the real calendar) while campaigning for president against Lindbergh and the Republicans, an incident that begins the rapid unraveling of America's fascist experiment.[4] La Guardia gives a eulogy in New York the next day.

> For speaking his mind in the state of Kentucky, W.W. was assassinated by the Nazis of America, who, thanks to the silence of our strong, silent, selfless president, today run rampant throughout this great land. It can't happen here? My friends, it is happening here — and where is Lindbergh? *Where is Lindbergh?* (365)

Before discussing that question and other matters related to the story and plot of *PAA*, it's worth asking why Roth is thinking about Sinclair Lewis and the 1930s during the presidency, not of Trump, but of George W. Bush back in the early years of the twenty-first century. Perhaps it's for the same reasons that led Robert O. Paxton late in his career to write and eventually publish his *Anatomy of Fascism* the same year as Roth's novel. Paxton's *Anatomy,* as we've said, is both a history book and a warning written by a defender of liberalism who believes the pain fascism caused in the twentieth century should be avoided in the twenty-first century. It's hardly a stretch to imagine that Roth looked out at the same social, political, and economic landscape

---

www.nytimes.com/2021/12/31/books/review/sinclair-lewis-babbitt-main-street.html.

4   Roth may have taken inspiration from the real-life rapid unraveling of enthusiasm for Senator Joe McCarthy's anti-communist "witch hunts" starting on June 9, 1954 when, in Louis Menand's retelling, "the bamboozler was bamboozled." See "Joseph McCarthy and the Force of Political Falsehoods," *The New Yorker,* August 3 and 10, 2020, https://www.newyorker.com/magazine/2020/08/03/joseph-mccarthy-and-the-force-of-political-falsehoods.

as Paxton at the turn of the century — a troubled time marked first by a "stolen election" made possible by the anti-democratic electoral college and a dubious 5-to-4 Supreme Court vote that halted a recount of ballots in Florida; and less than a year later by a turn toward hyper-nationalism, warmongering, and reduced civil liberties following the terrorist attacks of 9/11 — and he decided to write his own more indirect antifascist warning with the tools of the novelist instead of the historian.

As we said of Paxton, in 2004 Roth is a world-famous writer with nothing to prove and no financial worries. Born in 1933, the year Hitler comes to power, he is 71 in 2004 (Paxton was 72), an age when many people are retiring from full-time work and turning to other activities if they're lucky enough to not already have serious health problems. If he had wanted, Roth could also have produced his thought experiment during the McCarthy era or during the years of Kennedy, Nixon, or Reagan — all periods he lived through and all offering an atmosphere of intrigue and conspiracy theories suitable for accommodating his alternative history. Whether an outline for this book or notes or typed pages existed years earlier matters less than that it actually gets published one year into the second Gulf War in Iraq, the same year when Americans are being asked to accept or reject George W. Bush's bid for a second term as president. It's not hard to imagine that both Paxton and Roth would have been pleased if their books had played some role to help defeat Bush in 2004, chasten the 58-year-old president and his cronies, principally Dick Cheney and Donald Rumsfeld, or could at the very least perform a consciousness-raising service directed at book-reading Americans. Bush's reelection in 2004, beating out a more honorable, articulate, and experienced public servant, Senator John Kerry of Massachusetts, by roughly three million votes and 286 to 251 in the electoral college, was another disaster for Democrats who were outmaneuvered again, just as in 1984 when Reagan scored a decisive victory playing the smiling yet firm anti-communist containing Soviet aggression.

Bush's campaign managers — especially his lead media strategist and no-nonsense storyteller Mark McKinnon — proved

more effective in crafting and controlling a narrative that cast
George W. Bush as the hero who was successfully slaying the
dragon of Al Qaeda and needed to be reelected to finish the job.[5]
Looking back on his tactics in the 2004 campaign, McKinnon
openly states his aim was to exploit people's fears:

> People respond to fear because it plays on people's emotions
> and the things that they worry about most. So, the threat now
> [in 2004] is international terrorism, the victims are 9/11, the
> villain is Al Qaeda, the resolution is a very aggressive policy
> against the foreign threats, and the hero is George W. Bush.
> That's what all campaigns are all about. They're about one or
> two things: fear or hope.

Roth was no doubt aware of the power of fear, especially in the
wake of 9/11, which may be why the novel begins this way:

> Fear presides over these memories, a perpetual fear. Of
> course no childhood is without its terrors, yet I wonder if
> I would have been a less frightened boy if Lindbergh hadn't
> been president or if I hadn't been the offspring of Jews.

Of particular note is the choice of verb, "Fear *presides*" — fear is
exerting a dominant force, says the narrator, over the very narrative that is to follow, a force, we're told, that may have been intensified by the Lindbergh presidency and by experiencing that
chapter in United States history as a child of Jews.[6] If the electoral results are any indication, clearly not enough people were
worried that Bush was taking the country in a Lindbergh-like
fascist direction; or if they did worry, maybe they considered

---

5   See the op-doc, "How to Win an Election," narrated by Mark McKinnon
    and introduced by Sarah Klein and Tom Mason, *The New York Times,* Feb-
    ruary 18, 2016, 4'38"–5'05", https://www.nytimes.com/2016/02/18/opinion/
    how-to-win-an-election.html.
6   For a different but analogous situation, see Amy Waldman, *The Submis-
    sion* (New York: Farrar, Straus & Giroux, 2011), which depicts experiencing
    New York as a Muslim before and after 9/11.

his presidency of fear to be the lesser of two evils weighed in the balance alongside the threat of international terrorism. It could also be that Roth's novel did not attract wide attention in 2004 beyond the circle of his admirers among the declining number of Americans who still read texts longer than *The Very Hungry Caterpillar*.

However, what goes around comes around, and so between 2016 and 2018, that is around the time of Trump's election and Roth's death at age 85, *The Plot Against America* gets a second look and its allegorical dimension, just as with Atwood's dystopian fiction, comes to be considered "eerily prescient,"[7] uncanny, a foreshadowing of the United States under Trump[8] and no longer a satirical warning of of a political situation closer to the time of its composition[9] or a sentimental backward glance by a 70-year-old at the Newark of his childhood. Allusion to a "climate of hate emanating from the White House" (319) is just one Trumpian echo.[10] Same novel, different times, different per-

---

7   See Charles McGrath's e-mail interview with Roth, "No Longer Writing, Philip Roth Still Has Plenty to Say."

8   The two *New Yorker* pieces by Judith Thurman and Paige Williams both review notorious parallels. Here is Thurman's: "The historical Lindbergh was an isolationist who espoused a catchphrase that Donald Trump borrowed for his Presidential campaign, and for his Inaugural Address: 'America First'. The fictional Lindbergh, like the actual Trump, expressed admiration for a murderous European dictator, and his election emboldened xenophobes. In Roth's novel, a foreign power — Nazi Germany — meddles in an American election, leading to a theory that the President is being blackmailed. In real life, US intelligence agencies are investigating Trump's ties to Vladimir Putin and the possibility that a dossier of secret information — kompromat — gives Russia leverage with his regime" ("Philip Roth E-Mails on Trump"). The Williams piece adds to those parallels in the wake of the Pittsburgh synagogue massacre ("Reading Philip Roth after the Pittsburgh Massacre").

9   For a study of *PAA* and a review of the critical conversation around the novel shortly after its publication, see chapter 8, "Heil to the Chief: Sinclair Lewis, Philip Roth, and Fascism," in Richard Ned Lebow, *Forbidden Fruit: Counterfactuals and International Relations* (Princeton: Princeton University Press, 2010), 222–58.

10 After Herman is called a "loudmouth Jew" by another tourist as the Roth family is visiting the Lincoln Memorial, he blames it on the climate of

spectives. These are the normal cycles of re-reading and reinter-
pretation that give literary works with universal human themes
their simultaneous timely and timeless quality. The upshot is
another acclaimed TV miniseries for non-readers to enjoy and
more praise for Roth's "dark, humane masterpiece."[11]

Another similarity between Atwood's dystopian fiction and
Roth's political novel is that both received early negative reviews
by influential senior critics in major media outlets and for the
same reason: the plot is too unbelievable, each claimed, following T.S. Eliot's panning of *Hamlet* for lacking an objective cor-
relative. In other words, they do not see fascism happening in
the United States. At age 74, Mary McCarthy looked out at 1980s
America and could not see what Margaret Atwood was getting
all spooked about.

Surely the essential element of a cautionary tale is recognition. Surprised recognition, even, enough to administer
a shock. We are warned, by seeing our present selves in a
distorting mirror, of what we may be turning into if current
trends are allowed to continue. […] Yet I can admit to a general failure to extrapolate sufficiently from the 1986 scene.
Still, even when I try, in the light of these palely lurid pages,
to take the Moral Majority seriously, no shiver of recognition
ensues. […] Liberality toward pornography in the courts, the
media, on the newsstands may make an anxious parent feel
disgusted with liberalism, but can it really move a nation to

---

hate emanating from the White House: "You think you'd hear that here if
Roosevelt was president? People wouldn't dare, they wouldn't dream, in
Roosevelt's day […] now they think they can get away with anything. It's
disgraceful. It starts with the White House…" (78).

11 See Paul Berman, "'The Plot Against America' by Philip Roth," *The New
York Times,* October 3, 2004, https://www.nytimes.com/2004/10/03/
books/review/the-plot-against-america.html. Berman calls the plot of
PAA "creepily plausible" and offers Paxton-like insights into a functional
equivalent of fascism possibly developing out of Bush's post-9/11 America.
For another insightful review from 2004, see Joan Acocella, "Counterlives:
Philip Roth's 'The Plot Against America,'" *The New Yorker,* September 20,
200, https://www.newyorker.com/magazine/2004/09/20/counterlives 4.

install a theocracy strictly based on the Book of Genesis? Where are the signs of it? A backlash is only a backlash, that is, a reaction. Fear of a backlash, in politics, ought not to deter anybody from adhering to principle; that would be only another form of cowardice.[12]

McCarthy says she is not afraid of a theocracy establishing itself in the United States so no one else should be either and if they are, well, they're cowards. Atwood's defenders see this critic's "general failure to extrapolate sufficiently" as having more to do with McCarthy's blinkered insularity than anything else. In a follow-up letter to the editor from March 1986, Virginia Low wonders if McCarthy has gotten off campus or left Manhattan lately:

> As for Miss McCarthy's not taking the Moral Majority seriously, I wonder where she has been. Has she been informed of the gradual conservative takeover in the courts by appointment of the "right" judges? Has she traveled much in this country lately and checked out the number of private fundamentalist schools, totally segregated and totally oriented toward their religious beliefs?

In a similar vein, online admirers of the Hulu series, such as Lara Zarum, shoot back, "Mary McCarthy was Wrong: 'The Handmaid's Tale' is Scary Because It's True"; or consider this headline from Elena Nicolaou, "The Original Review of 'The Handmaid's Tale' Got it SO Crazy Wrong."[13]

---

12 Mary McCarthy, "'The Handmaid's Tale' by Margaret Atwood," *The New York Times,* February 9, 1986.

13 Lara Zarum, "Mary McCarthy Was Wrong: 'The Handmaid's Tale' is Scary Because It's True," *Flavorwire,* April 13, 2017, https://www.flavorwire.com/603492/mary-mccarthy-was-dead-wrong-the-handmaids-tale-is-scary-because-its-true, and Elena Nicolaou, "The Original Book Review of 'The Handmaid's Tale' Got it So Crazy Wrong," *Refinery29,* May 17, 2017, https://www.refinery29.com/en-us/2017/05/154866/handmaids-tale-hulu-timing-review-mary-mccarthy.

Perhaps because he's a man, Clive James has not received the same drubbing, but there's still time.[14] In 2004, James, then 65, was allowed nearly 3,000 words to say that *The Plot Against America* has an "insuperable problem" because according to his inspection of American history there has been "no case of a minority's being permanently threatened with violence backed by federal law"; so therefore *PAA* is just Jewish paranoia. To convince the reader or himself of this, he repeats this claim in his last paragraph:

> There was never a hotel that Roth couldn't get into, but he can be excused for inventing an alternative and worse American past in which his father would be told that the room he had been given was unavailable after all. It's an understandable bad dream. But it hasn't led to a good book, and couldn't have. The United States will never be free of racial prejudice for the same reason that it will never enshrine racial prejudice in anything like the Nuremberg Laws: it's a free country. Being that, it is bound to be full of things we don't like, but the federally sanctioned destruction of a racial minority isn't among them, and hasn't been since Wounded Knee. As Roth must have realized long before he finished writing it, the insuperable problem with *The Plot Against America* is that America is against the plot.

For James — a white Australian who, he tells us, enjoyed the funny bits of *Portnoy's Complaint* in his youth — the United States in the early twenty-first century is a tolerant liberal democracy and Americans simply won't buy the novel's premise that the country could go fascist. Jamelle Bouie, Jelani Cobb, George Packer or any number of other writers more familiar with twentieth- and twenty-first-century America than James, especially its structural racism and not only in the authoritarian South, could have taken James by the hand and showed him things

---

14 Clive James, "Fatherland," *The Atlantic,* November 2004, https://www.theatlantic.com/magazine/archive/2004/11/fatherland/303564/.

to make him change his mind.[15] James died in 2019, however, so that won't be happening and I do not know if Trump's election led him to revise his judgment of Roth's novel or America. But it is clear that in 2004 James would have preferred if Roth had stuck to Jewish minstrelsy to entertain the goyim instead of bothering the world with a political novel that challenged his preferred vision of the United States as a free country where persecution of selected out-groups is impossible.[16] "You had to be there to see what it looked like," says a horrified Herman Roth to his friends after getting back from Lindbergh's Washington, "They live in a dream, and we live in a nightmare" (91).[17]

The problem may be that neither McCarthy nor James was vulnerable enough, or knew enough people who were, to see what Atwood and Roth were getting at. This is particularly interesting in the case of Roth since the whole book can be viewed as a 400-page treatise on how vulnerability — high, low, medium, chronic, acute, and so forth — shapes one's entire view of the world along with one's sympathies, hatreds, explanations, theories, thoughts, and feelings about others and oneself. But it is not a treatise, it's an allegory, and more precisely the story

---

15 On the federal government's long record of direct and indirect harm to Black people, see Charles Blow, "States Keep Failing Black People," *The New York Times,* May 13, 2020, https://www.nytimes.com/2020/05/13/opinion/black-people-states.html. See also this unsigned editorial of *The New York Times* concerning the federal government's endorsement of white supremacy by naming military bases after Confederate generals, "Why Does the U.S. Military Celebrate White Supremacy?" May 23, 2020, https://www.nytimes.com/2020/05/23/opinion/sunday/army-base-names-confederacy-racism.html.

16 On the political dimension of Roth's oeuvre, see Claudia Franziska Brühwiler and Lee Trepanier, eds., *A Political Companion to Philip Roth* (Lexington: University of Kentucky Press, 2017).

17 Contrary to Clive James for whom the novel is exaggeratedly dark, for James Poniewozik it is "too feel-good"; he prefers the TV miniseries adaptation which offers a cliffhanger ending with the outcome of the 1942 special election uncertain and the specter of meddling "reimagined in ways that get more unsettling and relevant as our own election season goes on." See "When Democracy Dies in Daylight," *The New York Times,* September 1, 2020, https://www.nytimes.com/2020/09/01/arts/television/plot-against-america-election.html.

of two years of memories narrated in alternating fashion by an acorn and an oak: a 7-year-old basically healthy but obviously dependent boy named Philip Roth growing up in Newark, New Jersey in 1940 (thus an exact contemporary of the author Philip Roth, who was born in 1933 in Newark, New Jersey) and the grown-up 70-year-old Philip Roth (the narrator not the person) telling the story of how that Jewish boy and his 12-year-old brother Sandy and parents, Herman and Bess, experienced the two years of the Lindbergh presidency. In the following pages I call the author of the book Philip Roth or just Roth; and I refer to the two characters, the older narrating "I" and the younger narrated "I," as Philip.

It's clear from the opening sentence that the thoughts and feelings expressed in the novel are too crafted and wise to be those of a 7-year-old; but having the story told as though from the perspective of a child gives the novel that "out of the mouths of babes" quality of unadorned truth and wisdom that one gets in Hans Christian Andersen's tale *The Emperor's New Clothes* and J.D. Salinger's novel *The Catcher in the Rye.* Also, if one recalls Fromm's discussion of the crucial stage of child-hood development when one is severing one's first ties with primary caregivers, Roth's novel offers a wonderful time-lapse double birth of consciousness with the two boys, Philip 7 and Sandy 12, emerging individually but within the same household from an almost unmediated age of enchantment and blind trust (stamp collecting and drawing are their hobbies) into an age of reasoning and complex often contradictory emotions. Growing up means coming into new powers (*savoir faire*) and a growing awareness of good and evil, man's inhumanity to man, as well as his capacity for kindness and bravery. It also means mourning the loss of one's childhood and accepting the responsibilities and mental attitude that go with adulting. In short, *PAA* is a classic coming-of-age story that can be appreciated on its own terms without any reference to Bush or Trump; simply an instructive and entertaining tale about a boy's journey from innocence to experience through the transition time of fear, hope, and vul-nerability typical of any young person, but perhaps intensified beyond ordinary levels, he wonders, by the fact of being Jewish in an anti-Semitic America teetering between democracy and fascism.

Coming of age in times of high anxiety over vulnerability, such as in a country starting a new decade and barely recovered from the Great Depression and worrying over the prospect of another debilitating world war, presents extra challenges because adults themselves can regress and think and act like insecure children: desiring simplicity and continuity, believing in magic, seeking out protectors, placing blame, throwing tantrums, being mean — the usual stuff. Adults not acting their age makes it more difficult for actual children to make their choices about who to trust, who to follow, and who to emulate when it comes to choosing models for one's future thinking and behavior. These are the daily challenges that Philip faces, or runs away from, and witnessing his predicament constitutes a large part of the reading experience of the novel. It soon becomes clear to Philip and the reader-witness that just about everything is in flux and open to multiple interpretations in Newark in 1940, beginning with America as both idea and substance, which is why the very title of the book deserves some attention.

The first meaning of *plot* in this context is "secret plan or scheme to accomplish some purpose, especially a hostile, unlawful, or evil purpose." The Roth family shares the belief that Lindbergh's presidency is a plot to overthrow the core values of America's liberal democracy ("a plot being hatched by antidemocratic forces," 212), especially the values of tolerance and fairness that allow all citizens a right to life, liberty, and the pursuit of happiness. In contrast, Lindbergh and his supporters believe that Jews are plotting against America through what they consider to be self-serving Jewish clannishness ("the Jewish conspiratorial plot against America," 378) — what some French people suspicious of Muslims today condemn as *communautarisme*.[18] Jews counter that this is pure anti-Jewish prejudice and

---

18   The "obsession with a plot" was singled out by Umberto Eco as one of
     the fourteen characteristics of what he termed "Ur-Fascism," *The New*

group defamation since other groups, whether based on religion or country of origin, such as Italian or Irish Americans, are not looked on as threats simply because of their voluntary or obligatory associative behavior. Herman Roth's idea of America, which is that of the framers and Abraham Lincoln, and relayed every Sunday evening by his radio show idol Walter Winchell, contrasts sharply with the Aryan America supported by Lindbergh, the Bund, and other right-wing populists.[19] Philip Roth wants this basic difference in outlook to be clear to the reader, which is why I think he includes in chapter 1, though leaving off the date, an excerpt from Lindbergh's actual Des Moines speech from September 11, 1941, that is, the year of Fromm's *Escape from Freedom* and Pearl Harbor. The entire speech with date appears in a postscript along with extensive bibliography for further historical reading about the Roosevelt era, a "true chronology of the major [historical] figures" in the novel, as well as short biographical notices of "other historical figures in the work." Roth even gives his website source for the Lindbergh speech entitled "Who Are the War Agitators?"

The Lindbergh speech does at least three things that Herman Roth finds offensive: first, it performs an "othering" of Jews by speaking in terms of a "We... them... they... their," thus creating an in-group of true Americans and an out-group of suspect Americans who are denied equal stakeholder status and co-

---

York Review of Books, June 22, 1995, https://www.nybooks.com/articles/1995/06/22/ur-fascism/. See also Toni Morrison's list of ten steps to fascism in her 1995 address to Howard University, published as "Racism and Fascism," *The Journal of Negro Education* 64, no. 3 (Summer 1995): 384–85. On communautarisme, see Nadia Kiwan, "A Disorienting Sense of Déjà-vu? Islamophobia and Secularism in French Public Life," *Berkeley Center for Religion, Peace and World Affairs, Georgetown University, Washington, DC*, May 18, 2021, https://berkleycenter.georgetown.edu/responses/a-disorienting-sense-of-deja-vu-islamophobia-and-secularism-in-french-public-life.

19 For an inventory of twentieth-century, fascist-leaning groups in the US, see Sarah Churchwell, "American Fascism: It Has Happened Here," *The New York Review of Books*, June 22, 2020, https://www.nybooks.com/daily/2020/06/22/american-fascism-it-has-happened-here/.

ownership of "our country" and are barred as co-participants in defining and directing the national interest; second, it then further divides that stigmatized group into the "few far-sighted Jewish people" and the mass of non-farsighted Jews who can be taxed with any number of faults including, and this is the third source of irritation for Herman, being accused of favoring war "for reasons which are not American"; in other words to advance "their own [Jewish] interests."[20] The main portion of the speech that Roth reproduces, with "the politics of us and them" (Jason Stanley) on full display, is this:

A few far-sighted Jewish people realize this and stand opposed to intervention. But the majority still do not. […]
   We cannot blame them for looking out for what they believe to be their own interests, but we must also look out for ours. We cannot allow the natural passions and prejudices of other peoples to lead our country to destruction. (15–16)

What is America, who is American, who gets to decide who is American and who is a traitor or un-American — including the possibility that Canadians in 1940 are the true Americans — these are some of the emotionally charged questions that fuel the drama of this novel.
   Another way of understanding the high drama named in the title is to consider another meaning of the word "plot"; the one proposed by E.M. Forster in his instructive guide to prose fiction, *Aspects of the Novel* (1927). Forster clearly distinguishes between *plot* and *story*:

We have defined a story as a narrative of events arranged in their time-sequence. A plot is also a narrative of events, the emphasis falling on causality. "The king died and then the

---

20 The text of this speech is available here: "Des Moines Speech: Delivered in Des Moines, Iowa, on September 11, 1941, This Speech Was Met with Outrage in Many Quarters," *Charles Lindberg: An American Aviator,* http://www.charleslindbergh.com/americanfirst/speech.asp.

queen died," is a story. "The king died, and then the queen died of grief" is a plot.[21]

Forster then goes on to underscore the higher faculties of intelligence and memory that are required to appreciate plots; whereas basic curiosity ("Then what happened?") is enough for understanding stories:

A plot cannot be told to a gaping audience of cave men or to a tyrannical sultan or to their modern descendant the movie-public. They can only be kept awake by "and then — and then — ." They can only supply curiosity. But a plot demands intelligence and memory also.

Curiosity is one of the lowest of the human faculties. You will have noticed in daily life that when people are inquisitive they nearly always have bad memories and are usually stupid at bottom.[22]

One way of thinking about what it means for Philip and Sandy and their cousin Alvin to grow up is that they must go from hearing stories (i.e., mere sequences of events) to understanding and choosing plots. But this is no simple matter because there are so many competing narratives; in other words, competing causal chains that may be marshalled to describe, explain, interpret, or translate even the simplest event and most certainly to "figure out," as Philip says, any complex event such as Lindbergh's election (or Bush's or Trump's, we can add). What's more, competing interests seek to control those narratives which means transmitting them in such a way that they become the official story and accepted as truth to the point where the step of having made a choice about causality is forgotten and the story is presented from the start as plotted, that is, with the causal

<hr />

21 E.M. Forster, *Aspects of the Novel* (New York: Harcourt, 1985), 86.
22 Ibid.

chain built in.[23] And *chain* offers a good metaphor, because in the plot-story pair, the intelligent plot often seems to overmaster and enslave the raw, cave man-like story. But other events can come along and, as it were, liberate the story from a given plot which is rejected for some new reason, after which the events can remain "unexplainable" — such as the odd disappearance of Philip's stamp album and later of Lindbergh — or they can be inscribed in a new interpretation, such as when Herman and Bess's decision to not emigrate to Canada can go from seeming foolhardy at one moment to being a wise and courageous choice at another moment. Or when Lindbergh, like Philippe Pétain in France, can flip from being viewed as a Nazi collaborator and be seen instead as a shield protecting the country from a worse fate.[24] Explaining and interpreting different events, plotting them, is what the young hero of this book is constantly engaged in. It's obviously basic to the very act of reading, which will include chance encounters with the unforeseeable, the unexplainable, and the undecidable. If we accept America as not just a geographic location but as a set of events that take place, then *The Plot Against America* on the most general level is an example of the endless interaction of figure and ground, plot against story, and story against plot. Foregrounding this struggle over meaning and over who gets to make meanings and whose meaning-making will stick is another similarity between *PAA* and *The Handmaid's Tale* — two examples of "postmodern," cerebral fiction.

In some cases, who is telling the story, or put more accurately plotting the story, and to whom is as or more important than

23 According to Google Books Ngram viewer, the expression "control the narrative" became increasingly popular starting in the 1970s — the time of Nixon and his famous tape recordings and the beginning of narratology in modern language departments — and hit a peak right around 2004. Recent spikes of internet use of this term coincide with the Trump–Ukraine affair in 2019 and the Covid-19 crisis in 2020.

24 Paxton first became famous for debunking the myth or narrative of Vichy as the "shield against the total Nazi diktat" in his paradigm-changing study, *Vichy France: Old Guard and New Order, 1940–1944* (New York: Columbia University Press, 1972).

what is being said. An instructive example of this comes when Rabbi Bengelsdorf, one of Roth's finely drawn fictional characters in this novel, speaks at the Republican National Convention (thanks to bribery, according to Alvin) to explain away Lindbergh's unsavory visits to Germany and the aviator's acceptance of a medal from the Nazi government, "But all the while, my friends, all the while secretly exploiting their admiration in order better to protect and preserve our democracy and to preserve our neutrality through strength" (46). Herman Roth, enraged, cannot believe that any Jew is going to fall for Bengelsdorf's explanation, and he asks, rhetorically, "Has he completely lost his mind? What does this man think he is doing?" To which Alvin replies, "Koshering Lindbergh […] Koshering Lindbergh for the goyim." Herman, a very decent fellow but who did not even graduate from high school, still doesn't get it, so Alvin spells it out:

> "They didn't get him up there to talk to Jews. They didn't buy him off for that. Don't you understand?" Alvin asked, fiery now with what he took to be the underlying truth. "He's up there talking to the goyim — he's giving the goyim all over the country his personal rabbi's permission to vote for Lindy on Election Day. Don't you see, Uncle Herman, what they got the great Bengelsdorf to do? He just guaranteed Roosevelt's defeat!" (48)

This is wonderfully theatrical, straight out of Arthur Miller, and was no doubt easy to adapt to the TV series. I confess that with all my higher education I did not see that coming, but once Alvin says "Koshering Lindbergh for the goyim," it makes perfect sense. It's so persuasive in fact that it got me wondering whether Robert Paxton's piece "American Duce: Is Donald Trump a Fascist or a Plutocrat?" that appeared in *Harper's Magazine* less than six months after his inauguration in the May 2017 issue was perhaps "koshering Trump for the goyim."[25] In this case the officiating personage is a secular cleric, the dean of "fascism studies," and so if Paxton says Trump is not a fascist but only a plutocrat, then the normalization of the Trump presidency can proceed because, after all, wasn't George W. Bush a plutocrat and his father before him, and Roosevelt, and Washington?

Maybe I'm overreacting, inflamed by Alvin's "fiery" conviction, and I'm certainly not suggesting that Paxton accepted a bribe to not label Trump a fascist, but the explanatory power of Alvin's declaration to Herman did make me reread the Paxton piece and consider the possibility that this was not just academic hairsplitting but an exercise in whitewashing for the country club set and other Trump supporters so they could sleep better.[26] And maybe Paxton was technically right, but it may have been the wrong time and place to make that intervention — and counterproductive since Paxton's whole career has been devoted to defending liberal democracy against fascism. It's ironic to say the least that he of all people would do Trump a favor. These are the sorts of moral messes that *PAA* dramatizes and that readers may find interesting if one is willing to go along with Roth's "memories" and keep an open mind.

In *PAA* the term *fascist* — a two-syllable word much easier to say than *totalitarian* or *authoritarian* or *plutocrat* — comes up quite often and means exactly what the users intend it to mean: someone in favor of exclusionary right-wing populism (and hostile to democracy's core-principles of inclusiveness, equal rights, and a level playing field) where a victimized group is scapegoated to the benefit of unifying the plutocrats and a chosen subset of "the people" (invariably white and Christian)

---

25 Robert O. Paxton, "American Duce: Is Donald Trump a Fascist or a Plutocrat," *Harper's Magazine*, May 2017, https://harpers.org/archive/2017/05/american-duce/.

26 On Trump's country club constituency, see Evan Osnos, "How Greenwich Republicans Learned to Love Trump," *The New Yorker*, May 3, 2020, https://www.newyorker.com/magazine/2020/05/11/how-greenwich-republicans-learned-to-love-trump: "In Greenwich, Trump's rise was less a hostile takeover than a joint venture."

who are promised patronage from the managers, financiers, and owners who run things. "The fix is in," says Alvin, another snarky zinger that comes easily to the bitter tongue of a 21-year-old Jew smart enough to have figured out how the first world works and that he may be excluded from joining it. The words *fascist* and *fascism* come easily to Herman Roth and to the Jewish reporter, Winchell, who have also figured this out. Here are all the times the words are used by these two characters and others:

> Fascist bastards!… Fascism in America… America's going to go fascist… condemned Lindbergh for dealing with a murderous fascist tyrant… America wasn't a fascist country and wasn't going to be… All you little fascists are in the saddle now!… an English fascist government… Where is the fascist statism? Where is the fascist thuggery? Where are the Nazi Brown Shirts and the secret police? When have you observed a single manifestation of fascist anti-Semitism emanating from our government?… This fascist dog is still their hero… the fascist dog had by now become the hero of virtually every paper in the country… Alvin had volunteered to fight the fascists… first to sign on with the fascists… the fight against fascism… You know what a fascist is, don't you, Phil?… since the fascists had come to power nearly ten years before… the deep fascist fellowship uniting the Bund… a Quisling blueprint for a fascist America… the fascist fifth column of the Republican right… fascist strategy to isolate Jews and exclude them from the national life… 'The Lindbergh fascists'… the fascist plot to destroy American democracy… Winchell was canned for crying 'Fire!' in a crowded theater. Mr. and Mrs. New York City, the word wasn't 'fire.' It was 'fascism'[,] Winchell cried — and it still is. Fascism! Fascism! And I will continue crying 'fascism' to every crowd of Americans I can find until Herr Lindbergh's pro-Hitler party of treason is driven from the Congress on Election Day… And when, God forbid, America goes fascist… fascist barbarism… 'the fascist in the White House'… They elect a fascist

instead. Not just an idiot like Coolidge, not just a fool like Hoover, but an out-and-out fascist with a medal to prove it. They put in a fascist and a fascist rabble-rouser... 'It's the beginning of the end of fascism in America! No Mussolini here, Cucuzza—no more Mussolini here!'... Our president is a fascist sympathizer, more likely an outright fascist—and Walter Winchell was the enemy of the fascist.[27]

It's not necessary to comment on each example; it's obvious that the term is playing an energizing and organizing role in the novel, structuring these oppositions: fascism versus freedom; low fascists (dogs, barbarism) versus high human/humane freedom fighters; movement and change ("to *go* fascist") versus stasis and continuity; fascism's subterfuge versus freedom's openness; disorder and division ("fascist rabble-rouser") versus freedom's peace-loving inclusiveness and toleration. In most instances one is not surprised, given the context and who's speaking, to see the word come up. Its occurrence is more striking in an early exchange between Philip and his brother Sandy who has done some drawings of Lindbergh. Sandy is relaying to Philip the views of their cousin Alvin who lives with them, and one doesn't know if he shares or rejects those views.

"He's going to be president," Sandy told me. "Alvin says Lindbergh's going to win."

He so confused and frightened me that I pretended he was making a joke and laughed.

"Alvin's going to go to Canada and join the Canadian army," he said. "He's going to fight for the British against Hitler."

"But nobody can beat Roosevelt," I said.

"Lindberg's going to. America's going to go fascist."

27 Page numbers vary in different editions of the novel, but in my Vintage paperback edition, London, 2005, these passages occur on the following pages: 12, 20, 31, 65, 67 (the trip to DC), 82, 121, 132 (Bengelsdorf's lecture to Herman), 150, 160, 174, 187, 197–98 (the FBI agent), 207, 209, 212, 274, 288–89, 310, 311, 315–16, 341, 342, 364.

> Then we just stood there together under the intimidating spell of the three portraits. Never before had being seven felt like such a serious deficiency. (30–31)

This passage is a good example of the spare, direct way of speaking that Roth gives the children, and also of the way the 70-year-old narrator comments on the inner life of a 7-year-old who is incapable of putting all this into words (for one reason because if he's living it, he cannot also be reporting it), but we are meant to believe that "Phillie," as he's sometimes called, is feeling the "intimidating spell" and the "serious deficiency" wordlessly.

Philip naturally looks up to his older brother, literally and figuratively, just as Sandy looks up to Alvin. But after Alvin goes away to Canada and then to Europe, there's a hole which comes to be filled by his aunt Evelyn and her boyfriend the Rabbi Bengelsdorf who together make it possible for Sandy to participate in Lindbergh's "Just Folks" program run by "the newly created Office of American Absorption as 'a volunteer work program introducing city youth to the traditional ways of heartland life'" (101). Sandy leaves for his "apprenticeship" with a Kentucky tobacco farmer on the last day of June 1941 and has the time of his life. So good that when he returns to New Jersey, he enthusiastically accepts the invitation to help recruit others into the program. In effect, he is koshering the Office of American Absorption for the Jews, lest they think, as his father and mother certainly do, that it's part of the fascist plot against America akin to the Hitler Youth or, a better analogy in relation to *PAA*, to Pétain's rural work and fitness summer camps, the *Chantiers de la jeunesse,* that began in the Unoccupied Zone in 1941 also. Sandy's parents do not forbid him from giving the recruitment talks, but when he gets invited to the White House, they put their foot down which causes a huge rift. His parents claim that Sandy is being manipulated ("They are only making you their tool," says his mother); Sandy swears at his parents ("Bullshit!"), asserting that there is no fascist plot, that his parents are "frightened, paranoid ghetto Jews" (270) and that his father's interdiction makes him "a dictator worse than Hitler" (229).

Earlier Sandy had been blindsided along with his brother and parents by the anti-Semitism directed at them during the vacation trip to Washington, DC — a trip meant to reassure everyone in the Roth family that "America wasn't a fascist country and wasn't going to be, regardless of what Alvin had predicted" (67). After Lindbergh's election, young Philip takes to reading his father's newspaper, *PM*, "to have in my hands documentary proof that, despite the incredible speed with which our status as Americans appeared to be altering, we were still living in a free country" (67). When they get ejected from their Washington hotel, Sandy has to explain what's happening to Philip who at first doesn't get why his family is being mistreated ("'Anti-Semitism,' he whispered," 83). But the summer work vacation in Kentucky and then all the praise from his aunt and the rabbi turn Sandy's head, and so he becomes the "first to sign on with the fascists" (174). Alvin, on the other hand, "had volunteered to fight the fascists" (160), and therefore gets a lot of free dental work later from Dr. Lieberfarb: "unlike 'the rich Jews' who astonished my father by imagining themselves secure in Lindbergh's America, Lieberfarb remained undeluded about what 'the many Hitlers of this world' might yet have in store for us" (160). Here and elsewhere one sees the gradual progression of the us versus them division often organized around the question of whether someone is *plotting,* who it is, what they're plotting, for whom, against whom, should one be worried, and so forth. It's a cram course in hermeneutics, or as the 70- or 7-year-old Philip remarks, "The pressure of what was happening was accelerating everyone's education, my own included" (121). And since Philip is inevitably confronted with the moral question of where he stands — "Which side are you on?" — when facing "the terror of the unforeseen" (135), it's understandable that he is often either seeking to escape (by running away or indulging in fantasy) or lamenting that he cannot escape or turn back now:

A new life began for me. I'd watched my father fall apart, and I would never return to the same childhood. [… He was] crying like both a baby abandoned and a man being tortured — because he was powerless to stop the unforeseen. And as Lindbergh's election couldn't have made clearer to me, the unfolding of the unforeseen was everything. Turned wrong way round, the relentless unforeseen was what we schoolchildren studied as "History," harmless history, where everything unexpected in its own time is chronicled on the page as inevitable. The terror of the unforeseen is what the science of history hides, turning a disaster into an epic. [...] I'd never before had to grow up at a pace like this. Never before — the great refrain of 1942. (135, 204)

Just as the investigative reporter Evan Osnos witnesses and historicizes what he calls "the long battle between the self and service" in his ultra-rich and Christian childhood community of Greenwich, Connecticut over the forty years from Reagan to Trump, Philip Roth in novelistic mode allows the reader to witness through young Philip's eyes a similar battle going on in lower-middle-class Newark, New Jersey in the early 1940s.[28] Asymmetries in daily life when it comes to vulnerabilities and advantages are likely to influence one's explanation of individu-

---

28 The final two paragraphs of the long piece by Osnos, published exactly three years after Paxton's magazine article, give the gist of his argument: "As Americans have reckoned with the origins of our political moment — the Trump years, the fury on all sides, the fraying of a common purpose — we have tended to focus on the effects of despair among members of the working class who felt besieged by technology, globalization, immigration, and trade. But that ignores the effects of seclusion among members of the governing class, who helped disfigure our political character by demonizing moderation and enfeebling the basic functions of the state. We — or they, depending on where you stand — receded behind gracious walls. On the ground where I grew up, some of America's powerful people have championed a version of capitalism that liberates wealth from responsibility. They embraced a fable of self-reliance (except when the fable is untenable), a philosophy of business that leaches more wealth from the real economy than it creates, and a vision of politics that forgives cruelty as the price of profit. In the long battle between the self and service, we have, for the moment, settled firmly on the self. To borrow a phrase from a neighbor in disgrace, we stopped worrying about 'the moral issue here.'" Osnos, "How Greenwich Republicans Learned to Love Trump."

al choices, in other words, the plotting or assignment of causal chains to the events in someone's life. Does Sandy just make the most of his talents and an opportunity "to be somebody" that comes his way or is he an "opportunist" (221, a notion Alvin teaches Philip)? Is Evelyn's gold-digging power-marriage to Lionel Bengelsdorf, a man twice her age, just a case of taking what she had coming to her, her fair share, after so many years of sacrifice and service to others? What about Bengelsdorf — an optimist-realist and "identity entrepreneur" (Nancy Leong) or a deluded stooge and conceited scammer? What about Alvin — a selfless war hero or a reckless, self-pitying, "professional misfit" acting out? Selfish and sellouts (217) or people doing what they have to do (to get by)? For 400 pages it's a "battle royal" (350) of competing narratives fought with dueling words, passive aggression, or active deeds: ignoring, hiring, firing, or transferring someone, slapping or spitting, punching and wrestling, or murder. Newark is no playground for young Philip. He does not get a lot of downtime to just be a kid, and when it's offered to him, such as playing chess with his neighbor Seldon, he gets annoyed. His mother calls him "the strangest child" (281). In a late moment of self-reflection at age 9 (or 70, depending on whose voice you hear), he says, "I was still too much of a fledgling with people to understand that, in the long run, nobody is a picnic and that I was no picnic myself" (413). True. Philip says, "I wanted nothing to do with history" (277) and yet he is constantly trying to figure out the crazy shit the adults are doing while also making time for his own, such as random bus rides to follow Christian strangers, plans to run away, become an orphan, or work in a pretzel factory, and schemes to save his family from ruin ("There was nobody left to protect us except me," 249). And if Philip is no picnic, it's probably (note the plotting!) because his parents are complex people — "round characters," as Forster famously said — capable of contradiction, surprise, change, and a range of behaviors and emotions including anger.

The two people who choose service over self in *PAA* are Herman Roth and Bess Roth (phonemically close to Betsy Ross, an iconic patriot). The passages where they appear on stage, so to speak, are among the most beautiful pages in the novel because they exemplify America's highest ideals, display anguish and anger when those ideals are ignored or trampled on, and have touching, vulnerable moments when one or the other loses it because events overwhelm their ability to reason, explain, convince, plan or plot; and in those moments they are reduced to a childish state, sobbing or weeping uncontrollably. Had the TV miniseries elected to go for a retro, black-and-white look, they could have used a couple similar to George and Mary Bailey in Frank Capra's Christmas classic *It's a Wonderful Life* (1946). The Jewish insurance salesman Herman Roth is cut from the same cloth as the savings and loan director George Bailey played by Jimmy Stewart, a patriotic everyman role he had already perfected in *Mr. Smith Goes to Washington* (1939). Bailey's idealism conveyed in his speech to Mr. Potter and the loan board about the whole noble purpose of a savings and loan as offering a chance at home ownership to working class people and Mr. Smith's "Love thy neighbor" speech to Congress are each consistent with the decency, passion for goodness, and aversion to bullying that Herman Roth displays in plain words and actions to his family, coworkers, and neighbors. Bess Roth's service to her family and neighbors is equally exemplary. A lot of cracks, bruises, and loss happen to the Roth family over the novel, but Herman and Bess are shown as ever united like two boats lashed together with bow and stern lines of trust and respect to survive a hurricane: They each use the power of positing like an anchor. First Bess: "There's nothing to be afraid of. Everybody will be home, everybody is coming home, we'll have our dinner," she said reassuringly, "and everything is going to be fine" (202). Then Herman: "This is a home. We are a family," affirms the puny patriarch during the same stormy moment when nothing was any longer "fine" (203).

Philip's appreciation of the sterling character of his parents is a gradual revelation punctuated by moments of doubt as he sees them, the adults, as disarmed and disoriented as he is by certain events. When young Philip sees them with no more clue, maturity, or self-assurance than a 7-year-old, it is deeply unsettling until it dawns on him that children can know stuff that adults don't, and adults don't always act their age or have it all figured out; for example, they too can contract "that not uncommon childhood ailment called why-can't-it-be-the-way-it-was" (205). Philip also sees how easy it is to trick his childish Aunt Evelyn when he sneaks off to her office, and he sees his mother, usually so gentle and welcoming, angrily turn away her *collabo* sister who has shown up at their door, as Philip says, "made as ugly and vulnerable-looking by disaster as by her own theatricality" (404). The all-important normalcy that Bess Roth relies on and strives to maintain has fallen apart at this point in the story, with her former neighbor Mrs. Wishnow killed, Roosevelt arrested, and her husband and Sandy driving south on a desperate rescue mission to bring back the orphaned Seldon Wishnow from Kentucky. Philip watches his mother break down, and then as she stops crying he suddenly sees her differently:

> "Where is your brother? Where is your father?" Where too, she seemed to be asking, is that orderly existence once so full of purpose, where is the great, great enterprise of our being the four of us? "We don't even know where they are," she said, but sounding as though it were she who was lost. "To send them off like that… What was I thinking? To let them go when the entire country… when…"
>
> Deliberately she stopped herself there, but the trend of her thought was clear enough: when the goyim are killing Jews in the street.
>
> There was nothing for me to do except watch until the weeping had drained her to the dregs, whereupon my whole idea of her underwent a startling change: my mother was a fellow creature. I was shocked by the revelation, and too young to comprehend that there was the strongest attachment of all. (406)

What follows is a paragraph in which Philip tries to make sense of his mother's emotions and behavior toward Aunt Evelyn, and he recognizes that "even for the mother who performed each day in methodical opposition to life's unruly flux, there was no system for managing so sinister a mess" (407).

No *full-proof* system, but there were systems, habits, institutions to manage messes and face the terror of the unforeseen, and Philip has watched his father practice several of them: reading a newspaper, conversing with family and neighbors, listening to news on the radio, taking himself and his sons to the Newsreel Theater, investing in a set of encyclopedias, being involved in the local schools, and being in the insurance business — the purpose of which is not to make millions for shareholders but to help ordinary people face "life's unruly flux" and the "unknowable future" (305).[29] Although Herman's decision to turn down a promotion that would have meant moving to a less hospitable neighborhood and then his decision to quit his job outright rather than accept the quasi-deportation to Kentucky are both important events in the novel, Roth does not draw much attention to the day-to-day particulars of Herman's job as an insurance salesman. However, he does sketch Philip's last memory of his father which centers on the relation between Herman and a man with no legs stationed outside his office building whom he greets in a civil manner each day.

> [My memory] of my father was of him greeting the stump of a man who begged every day outside his office building. "How you doin', Little Robert?" my father said, and the stump of a man replied, "How you, Herman?" (201)

Roth leaves this memory as is, pure event, without explanation, comment, or plot, and I will too; unlike this other memory that flows into praise for Herman's prudence and his resistance to being bullied or othered. It occurs after they have waved goodbye to other insurance agent families who agreed to the relocation measures.

---

29 My math professor in college who taught me probability, John G. Kemeny, said one day out of the blue, "You know what insurance is? Insurance is a bet that you're happy to lose." Vulnerable people get that.

[T]he most harrowing moments so far, when our defense-lessness became real to me and I sensed the beginning of the destruction of our world. And when I realized that my father, of all these men, was the most obstinate, helplessly bonded to his better instincts and their excessive demands. I only then understood that he had quit his job not merely because he was fearful of what awaited us down the line should we agree like the others to be relocated but because, for better or worse, when he was bullied by superior forces that he deemed corrupt it was his nature not to yield — in this instance, to resist either running away to Canada, as my mother urged our doing, or bowing to a government directive that was patently unjust. There were two types of strong men: those like Uncle Monty and Abe Steinheim, remorseless about their making money, and those, like my father, ruthlessly obedient to their idea of fair play. (304–5)

Other passages could be aligned that demonstrate this same mixed vision about the efficacy of arguments and reason given the bonds of *instincts* and one's *nature,* what William James called *temperament,* something he believed was partly unknowable and yet as or more determinate than abstract first principles in deciding conduct. Herman was raised in the same household as his slave-driving brother Monty and yet they operate from different playbooks; though Monty too has a heart even toward his layabout nephew Alvin whom he tries to help by getting him to verbalize his war story and by offering him a job to get him back on his feet, prosthesis and all.

The takeaway in the world according to Philip is that you do not get far without decent caregivers and some rules, and that it also helps to be lucky.

No one should be motherless and fatherless. Motherless and fatherless you are vulnerable to manipulation, to influences — you are rootless and you are vulnerable to everything. (427)

285

In the end, what we learn is nothing very earth-shattering but more a reminder of old truths such as one never steps into the same river twice, the future's not ours to see, shit happens, history large and small sometimes turns on chance events that could have gone another way, maybe, but didn't. By chance Seldon saves Philip's life; by chance Lindbergh's wife or was it the sniper that kills Walter Winchell or something else (?) sets in motion a chain of events that allows Roosevelt to be re-elected president. Another lesson is that it's important to use your words to increase your chances of having your needs met. At the end of the novel young Philip Roth, as though to pay off a debt, agrees to be the prosthesis, the caregiver, for the traumatized orphan and nag Seldon Wishnow. For traumatized, stumped-but-not-yet-Trumped America, an older Philip Roth, unbidden and unforeseen, offered *The Plot Against America*.

8

The Talking Cure for Fascism and Exploitive Relationships

Sally Rooney, *Conversations with Friends* (2017)

"In times of crisis, we must all decide again and again whom we love, / And give credit where it's due"

— Frank O'Hara

I first read *Conversations with Friends* backwards starting at chapter 31 and then backtracking, 30, 29, 28, and so forth until I got to the beginning.[1] I had first planned on reading it the usual way, and I had started the novel twice, but teaching duties or something else, I can't remember, got in the way and I had to interrupt my reading. When I was finally ready to give it my full attention in May 2020, I couldn't bear rereading the scenes of the encounter between the four main characters for the third time, and so I decided to read backwards. Backwards reading or jumping in here and there and reading a bit and then moving on

---

1   Sally Rooney, *Conversations with Friends* (London: Faber & Faber, 2017). Hereafter cited parenthetically throughout this chapter.

is a technique that I advise all my students to practice as a way to catch typos in their writing that their eyes simply slide over when they only proofread their work from beginning to end. In a similar way, this deliberate disruption of the usual linear reading experience can focus one's attention on aspects of the novel that the tyranny of the story's advancing plot makes more difficult to see. It's liberating to notice things more for themselves instead of in relation to chronological causal chains. It can sharpen one's ear for the significance of bits of dialogue, for example, or lead one to ponder why these particular inter-texts (allusions to certain books, music, films, and historical events) were deployed instead of others or nothing at all. In the case of *Conversations with Friends* (hereafter *CWF*), this alter-native way of reading happens to be consistent with the way the characters themselves are depicted revisiting in non-linear fashion bits of text message or email; or indulging in reminis-cences of past conversation. This shared approach to text and time is not something I could have planned, but it's a happy accident that maybe put me more in tune with the emotional world and modus operandi of this novel which could have been entitled *Conversations with Friends Revisited* or *Remembrances of Conversations with Friends Past.* There are no time indicators in *CWF* that specify when the narrator, Frances, is telling this story of conversations with friends. Is she a 70-year-old woman, middle-aged, or only slightly older than the 21-year-old Frances whose interactions with Bobbi, Melissa, Nick, and a few others are being retold? Readers are free to imagine the storyteller to be whatever age they like, just as they can imagine whatever they like happening to Frances after the novel's last sentence: "Come and get me, I said." Rooney has primed the pump for sequels and prequels and fan fiction galore from and to anyone who wants to cathect and join her conversations.[2]

---

2   There's more authorial control in Sally Rooney's *Normal People* (London: Faber & Faber, 2018), which features an omniscient third-person narrator, date stamps at the beginning of each chapter to situate the action in time, and frequent but orderly flashbacks.

Based on my backwards reading, I believe a more accurate title for this novel would have been *Competitive Conversations with Frenemies,* because the main characters are not nice people — some even mock the word and notion of "nice" — and their conversations are often "competitive and thrilling, like a game of table tennis" (43), not the relaxed colloquy that peace-loving readers might have expected to find beyond the cover of a book called *Conversations with Friends.* One is not surprised to learn (thank you, Wikipedia) that the book's Irish author was a champion debater at Ireland's top university, Trinity College in Dublin. And not surprisingly the action is set in Ireland — home to Swift, Wilde, and Beckett, all former Trinity students — where thinking on one's feet and witty repartee are practically the national sport alongside the aptly named Hurling and Gaelic Football. In a country known for a certain toughness and "terrible beauty," sassy vulnerable females can be sexy — the Mary Tyler Moore vibe updated to "no future" Millennial times when youth are more snarky than smiling.

CWF is a dialogue-driven illustration of the nastiness of highly competitive people, especially in vulnerable circumstances of scarcity and uncertainty. The action is set, one may or may not notice, during the economic recession post-Celtic Tiger days, so there are layers of spoken and unspoken rivalry between the haves and the have less, the posh and the poorer, owners and renters, the made it and the on-the-make. It's also about that age-old challenge of growing up and making one's way, and the special challenge of doing so in history heavy, ethically tangled, and language-rich Ireland, a country known for heavy drinking and for grinding up or spitting across the sea its own people. Francisco de Goya's painting *Saturn Devouring His Son* captures the intergenerational Irish problem. How much more challenging then for Ireland's women?

Celtic Tiger was the nickname given to the Republic of Ireland during the years 1993 to 2007, approximately, when it benefitted from an economic boom comparable to the rapid growth in some Asian countries.[3] A more accurate name would have been Celtic Tax Haven, since Ireland did not get rich from exporting peat, poetry, or bottled rainwater.[4] Ireland then experienced a severe recessionary period from 2008 to 2014, which corresponds to the secondary school and university years of Sally Rooney (1991–), and of the narrator Frances and her classmate Bobbi, if we imagine that they are all three roughly the same age. References to the war in Syria and to refugees suggest that the time of the novel's action is not long after the 2011 Arab Spring, perhaps between 2012 and 2015, the latter being the year that Ireland began another period of strong economic growth that was brought to a halt along with the entire global economy by Covid-19 in 2020. One can keep in mind, then, that the book's action takes place during a morose economic period — the long Irish recession that followed the bursting of the housing bubble in 2008 and the international banking crisis that ensued. *CWF* received lots of attention just before and after its publication in 2017, perhaps in part because other hard times have hit more broadly: first, the rise of neofascist rightwing populism across Europe and "Tea Party" America starting in 2010, a revolt fanned by the Greek debt crisis and the refugee crisis from Afghanistan and the Middle East that came to a head with German chancellor Angela Merkel's controversial "Wir schaffen das" ("We'll manage this") declaration in 2015; second, the divisive Brexit and Trump victories in 2016; and third, the unforeseen coronavirus pandemic starting in 2020.[5] Therefore, as with Atwood and Roth, it would seem Rooney's writings have

---

3 The four Asian Tigers are the high-growth economies of Hong Kong, Singapore, South Korea, and Taiwan.
4 See Gabriel Zucman, *The Hidden Wealth of Nations: The Scourge of Tax Havens,* trans. Teresa Lavender Fagan (Chicago: University of Chicago Press, 2015). Estimates vary, but it's claimed that Ireland shelters, hides, and launders (pick your metaphor) more money than the entire Caribbean tax haven archipelago, notably for Apple and other major international companies. See also Fintan O'Toole, *Ship of Fools: How Stupidity and Corruption Sank the Celtic Tiger* (New York: PublicAffairs, 2010).
5 In the early months, many smaller, vulnerable countries, sensing it was literally do or die, responded rapidly and well as the pandemic was spread-

been turned to (and turned into a TV miniseries) as a source of comfort and counsel for vulnerable times. The Irish, one could say, with plenty of historical evidence from penal laws to famines to "The Troubles," are specialists of suffering, so no wonder thousands are turning to some of them for consoling wisdom about the painful mess we're in now.[6]

The book begins with an epigraph, a line of poetry by a once famous Irish American poet, Frank O'Hara (1926–66), that would seem to promise sage advice: "In times of crisis, we must all decide again and again whom we love."[7] Rooney's selection here is a subtle repurposing, for the line is not from a somber poem about war or famine, but from O'Hara's exuberant ode "To the Film Industry in Crisis." But it's hardly the film industry that's in crisis in 1957 when this poem is published in the volume *Meditations in an Emergency*; or if it was threatened by television and McCarthyism, those setbacks were short-lived. Alternatively, one can think it is the poet who, when down and troubled and needing a helping hand, finds consolation and courage in the company of the "glorious Silver Screen" to which the poet sings his love, concluding with high praise for the film industry as the modern-day continuation of all instances of greatness in the universe: "It is a divine precedent / you perpetuate! Roll on, reels of celluloid, as the great earth rolls on!"[8] Thus, along with all of Ireland in, let's say, 2012, Rooney at age 21 is in crisis, which is always also a chance, and so, screwing up

---

ing, among them El Salvador, Estonia, Greece, Portugal, New Zealand… and Ireland.

6   For some admiring reviews of *CWF*, see Alexandra Schwartz, "A New Kind of Adultery Novel," *The New Yorker*, July 31, 2017, https://www.newyorker.com/magazine/2017/07/31/a-new-kind-of-adultery-novel; Lauren Collins, "Sally Rooney Gets in Your Head," *The New Yorker*, January 7, 2019, https://www.newyorker.com/magazine/2019/01/07/sally-rooney-gets-in-your-head; and Madeleine Schwartz, "How Should a Millennial Be?" *The New York Review of Books*, April 18, 2019, https://www.nybooks.com/articles/2019/04/18/sally-rooney-how-should-millennial-be/.

7   Frank O'Hara, "To the Film Industry in Crisis," in *Meditations in an Emergency* (New York: Grove Press, 1957), 5.

8   Ibid.

her courage, she takes inspiration from O'Hara's Keatsian ode to cinema to write her own ode "To the Novel in Crisis." In other words, Rooney will (re)turn to the novel in her and Ireland's time of need — an original repetition of a very Irish response to troubles: write about them. If it's helpful, one can also understand Rooney's encounter with O'Hara, however it occurred, as analogous to Hélène Berr's Valéry moment — just as her narrator Frances will unwind and commune with Van Morrison's rapturous *Astral Weeks* album (from the iconic year of crisis and chance, 1968). Frances does this after getting home from the theater after seeing Nick play the role of Brick in *Cat on a Hot Tin Roof,* an experience after which she reports feeling "pure and tiny like a newborn baby" (29).[9] Does this mean the play performed its consciousness-raising magic on her and Philip in the audience just as it does for Brick, Maggie, Big Daddy, and the others on stage; or is she giving expression to her vulnerability because "out of the theatre it was raining again" and they only have one umbrella? It's a bit odd that Frances later says to Bobbi that "the play was bad" (31). Either she meant to say that some of the *acting* was bad, though "Nick was really good," or this is an example of Frances's defensive sophomoric judgments about something that she is either unwilling or unable to under-

---

9   Just as Rooney found a source of inspiration in the American poet O'Hara, the Irish musician Van Morrison (1945–) looked to American blues and folk music instead of pursuing traditional Irish music in the style of the Chieftains or the Bothy Band. For an account of the making of *Astral Weeks,* see Jon Michaud's review of Ryan H. Walsh's book, *Astral Weeks: A Secret History of 1968,* "The Miracle of Van Morrison's 'Astral Weeks,'" *The New Yorker,* March 7, 2018, https://www.newyorker.com/culture/culture-desk/the-miracle-of-van-morrisons-astral-weeks. The album, especially the opening lines of the title song — "If I ventured in the slipstream / Between the viaducts of your dream" — may be the musical analog of the novel's quest for transcendence via intensity of feeling, experimentation, and role-playing. See also by a classmate and close friend of Van Morrison, Gerald Dawe, I*n Another World: Van Morrison and Belfast* (Newbridge: Merrion Press, 2017).

stand at that time.[10] "You live through certain things before you understand them," she'll write later (321).

When the novel begins in late May, Frances and her classmate Bobbi have just completed their third year at university, majoring in English and history respectively, thus very much mid-stream, far from the starting line but still far from the finish line and the so-called real world. Therefore, the crisis they face, like for many second- and third-year students, is that they know they should have their shit together, but they don't. However, at their age, putting up a good front — fake it 'til you make it — is more common than admitting that they're "clueless in academe" and seeking help. They certainly won't ask for help from their elders whom they mostly resent and distrust like any cohort of 20-somethings but more so around 2011, '12, and '13 — the time of the Arab Spring, Occupy Wall Street, and new social media — all movements marked by ageism sharpened recently by Greta Thunberg's Generation Z and "OK Boomer" hostility.[11]

Frances and Bobbi are in the "no future" quandary faced by many "indignant"[12] young adults across Europe between 2010 and '20, disillusioned with global capitalism's shady and predatory habits, suspicious of democracy as fake, toothless, and on the take, aware that their parents' road to middle class stability (home ownership, vacations, food security, cars) will not

---

10   One wonders what might have gone through the mind of Frances, Philip, or Nick when Big Daddy hurls at his son Brick these lines: "You, Skipper, and lots like you, living in a kid's world, playing games, touchdowns, no worries, no responsibilities. Life ain't no damn football game. Life ain't just a bunch of high spots. You're a 30-year-old kid. Soon you'll be a 50-year-old kid... pretending you hear cheers when there aren't any. Dreaming and drinking your life away. Heroes in the real world live 24 hours a day, not just two hours in a game."

11   See Taylor Lorenz, "'OK Boomer' Marks the End of Friendly Generational Relations," *The New York Times,* October 29, 2019, https://www.nytimes.com/2019/10/29/style/ok-boomer.html, and the viral French OK Boomer song, Mcfly et Carlito, "OK Boomer (clip officiel)," *YouTube,* February 27, 2020, https://www.youtube.com/watch?v=1-ac8jxb66U.

12   In 2010, 93-year-old concentration camp survivor and résistant, Stéphane Hessel, published *Indignez-vous!* (translated as *Time for Outrage!* though, literally, *Get Indignant!*) — a pamphlet intensely admired and criticized.

be available to many of them, and wondering where to turn. In their case the Irish recession has been a central reality for the entire time they've been politically aware; therefore, one can easily imagine they don't feel a lot of agency or *freedom to* because they've not experienced reliable amounts of *freedom from* — principally from the fear of economic insecurity. Thanks to her father's government job, Bobbi has more money than Frances whose father spends more time drinking than working it seems. Neither of their mothers had a career of their own. Because the novel is set in Catholic-dominated Ireland and because prior to 2018 abortion was not yet legal except for certain categories of pregnancy, one must keep in mind that Frances and Bobbi, like all Irish women then, would have to be on their guard and do not have the freedom to live their sexuality in the same way as many other middle class white women in and outside the English-speaking world — in the UK, the rest of Europe, and North America notably.[13] On top of that, their parents are divorced: Frances's when she was 12, Bobbi's during the summer of the novel's action, though it is suggested that the marriage of Bobbi's father Jerry, "a high-ranking civil servant in the Department of Health," and "hysterical" Eleanor had been only limping along for some time.

Were they growing up in Hungary, Turkey, Poland, Germany, or France, with all of their vulnerability, underemployment, resentment, and unavowable guilty feelings, these young women would have been ripe to join some right-wing nationalist group such as France's Jeunesses identitaires. Right-wing populism, however, requires having some out-group to hate on (Jews, Muslims, immigrants, people of color, multiculturalists,

---

13 My friend Joan Boyle who attended Trinity College from 1967 to 1972 shared with me in an email that there were always Family Planning clinics in Ireland with "often a small clique of holy women saying the Rosary outside! They were from the Legion of Mary! [...] Even in the late '60s in Dublin it was possible to get the pill in pharmacies, but you had to get a prescription from the Doctor saying that it was for regulating irregular periods. All the female students in Trinity at the time had irregular periods!!!"

experts, scientists, "libtards," queers, quiche-eaters). But being from a Catholic background and female, they belong to the British Isles' most hated on group since the Reformation; therefore, their insecurity, fear, and anger has been channeled in other ways, at least in this novel.[14] Like the real-life Leslie Jamison and Martha Dodd, these fictional, middle-class white women turn to a menu of leftist redoubts (the humanities, performance art, sexual experimentation, bookish communism, theory), socially acceptable addictions ("bowl-sized glasses" of wine, cigarettes, coffee, tea), nonlethal sadistic and masochistic behaviors, and plenty of witty, cutting remarks.

In a fitful moment of restlessness, Frances enrolls in a dating app in the second half of the novel and later agrees to meet up with "somebody called Rossa." It turns out he's a hard-working medical student. As a good-natured gesture to establish rapport with his slacker English major date, he says he once won a school prize for composition and that he loves poetry. "I love Yeats" — a remark Frances feels obliged to shoot down with the f-word when she says, "Yeah, I said. If there's one thing you can say for fascism, it had some good poets" (208). Maybe, but the comment seems a bit sophomoric and mean to both Rossa and Yeats since the poet's politics, especially late in life, defy easy labels; nor is it certain that fascism produced any great art, though some good artists and other adventurers may have been tempted by the emotional lava of nature, nation, family, blood, soil and toil that fascism spouted.[15] At age 21, sitting in a bar on a first

---

14 Beyond this fictional world some are choosing right-wing populism. See Conor Gallagher, "The Far Right Rises: Its Growth as a Political Force in Ireland," *The Irish Times,* September 19, 2020, https://www.irishtimes.com/news/ireland/irish-news/the-far-right-rises-its-growth-as-a-political-force-in-ireland-1.4358321.

15 For a look back at the complexity of Yeats (1865–1939) on the occasion of the 150th anniversary of his birth, see "Philosophy and a Little Passion: Roy Foster on W.B. Yeats and Politics," *The Irish Times,* June 10, 2015, https://www.irishtimes.com/culture/books/philosophy-and-a-little-passion-roy-foster-on-wb-yeats-and-politics-1.2241504. My friend Luis González informs me that at least as regards Spain, Falangists like Luis Rosales, Dionisio Ridruejo, José María Pemán, and Agustín de Foxá were

FASCISM, VULNERABILITY, AND THE ESCAPE FROM FREEDOM

date, it's easy to pillory a pillar of the Irish literary establishment, just as in the company of her tender pianist friend Schroeder, Lucy van Pelt can mock Beethoven for not having his picture on a bubblegum card. Not surprisingly, Frances adds, "He didn't have anything else to say about poetry after that." As though to prove Frances "right" however, Rooney has the sex be both "bad" and "rough": "He asked me if I liked it rough and I told him I didn't think so, but he pulled my hair anyway. I wanted to laugh, and after that I hated myself for feeling superior" (209).[16] There's a scene for "teaching the conflicts" when Rooney's book joins *The Handmaid's Tale* on some future high school or college syllabus, assuming literature's priests don't allow leopards to destroy all the temples.

When the curtain rises, so to speak, we discover Frances and Bobbi Connolly (we never learn the surname of Frances nor the birth name of Bobbi) are performers of spoken word poetry and perhaps "doing some radical lesbian thing or whatever," as their friend Philip calls their on-again, off-again relationship. Their poetry performances — never scenically described nor is a poem ever shared with the reader — have come to the attention of a certain Melissa who is a smart, attractive freelance photographer and published author in her early thirties. The age gap is important because Melissa and her husband Nick had the good fortune to be in their early twenties during the Celtic Tiger boom years; therefore, getting established as "creatives" may have been easier for them, when more money was floating around, than it promises to be for Frances and Bobbi. A dynamic of jealousy and envy is seething in both directions;

---

pretty good poets and novelists, and that Dalí was close to Francoist politics too. To what extent fascism was central or incidental to the artistic merit of these or other artists is a question Frances may not have wished to debate, but one that Rooney may discuss elsewhere. On the Spanish case, see Nil Santiáñez, *Topographies of Fascism: Habitus, Space, and Writing in Twentieth-Century Spain* (Toronto: University of Toronto Press, 2013). On Ireland, see Elizabeth Cullingford, *Yeats, Ireland and Fascism* (London: Palgrave Macmillan, 1981).

16 Rooney also explores the complexities of sadomasochistic behavior in her second novel, *Normal People* (2018).

from Frances and Bobbi who can feel both desirous and bitter as they witness the comfortable lives of two successful artist types and from Melissa and Nick because they may doubt their talent, wondering perhaps, as awards and work opportunities level off, if their success was the result of lucky circumstances and because they're on the far side of 30 and therefore may be uneasily mourning "on the pavements grey" their lost twenties, lost illusions, roads not taken, or happier days.[17]

Consciously or not, Rooney's game of substitutions in *CWF* is recycling a template for romantic comedies that goes back to Goethe's *Elective Affinities* (1809) and to Shakespeare and the wisdom literature of fable and fairy tale. The central concern — what is love, what is it not, and "Who even gets married?" — is summed up well by Bobbi in the second to last chapter, so near the beginning for me, as Frances and Bobbi are "half-watching a Greta Gerwig film":

> We didn't know how codependent they were, Bobbi said. I mean, they were only ever in it for each other. It's probably good for their relationship to have these dramatic affairs sometimes, it keeps things interesting for them.
>
> Maybe.
>
> I'm not saying Nick was intentionally trying to mess with you. Nick I actually like. But ultimately they were always going to go back to this fucked-up relationship they have because that's what they're used to. You know? I just feel so mad at them. They treated us like a resource.
>
> You're disappointed we didn't get to break up their marriage, I said.
>
> She laughed with a mouth full of noodles. On the television screen, Greta Gerwig was shoving her friend into some shrubbery as a game.

---

17 Just to be clear, envy is the emotion of coveting what someone else has, while jealousy is the emotion related to fear that something you have will be taken away by someone else.

> Who even gets married? said Bobbi. It's sinister. Who
> wants state apparatuses sustaining their relationship?
> I don't know. What is ours sustained by? (305)

Instead of showing Bobbi and Frances performing on stage, Rooney gives the reader this glimpse of the offstage Bobbi-Frances duo as they watch two other women in their twenties acting.[18] Note the self-assured plotting of the causal chain by the history major Bobbi. Note the interrogative mode of the poet English major Frances who has more negative capability and therefore can hold in her mind multiple competing narratives for a single series of events and even think up an alternative history that didn't happen, or not yet, the end of Nick and Melissa's marriage. Bobbi is not wrong, but her sense of grievance is probably sharpened by her one-sided telling. A master of projection, she does not consider, or at least bother to mention, that she and Frances also benefitted from their relationship with Melissa and Nick: plenty of free food and drink served at parties in their cozy home in Monkstown, professional contacts, a free week of beach vacation in Brittany, and an ego boost in the form of an admiring magazine profile complete with flattering, interest-creating photos. Plus, it's not true that Bobbi always liked Nick as this passage suggests. Early on, Nick was considered weak and became the butt of jokes as the "trophy husband," a role he accepted too willingly for his own good. But it was a familiar role he had played countless times since childhood when his parents forced him to be a freakish child savant on some ironic TV show, the long shadow of the grotesque 1980s.

Bobbi's claim about Nick and Melissa's codependency is a good example of the expression "It takes one to know one." She's

---

18 The film in question is *Frances Ha*, dir. Noah Baumbach (New York: ICF Films, 2012). For a discussion of the movie and novel, see Konstantinos Pappis, "Conversations with 'Frances Ha': The Intersection between Sally Rooney's Millennial Fiction and Greta Gerwig's Mumblecore Classic," *ourculture*, October 26, 2019, https://ourculturemag.com/2019/10/26/conversations-with-frances-ha-the-intersection-between-sally-rooneys-millennial-fiction-and-greta-gerwigs-mumblecore-classic/.

too smart not to have noticed that she and Frances are also a codependent pair, with Bobbi playing the sadistic bully and narcissist, and brainy Frances her masochistic, reflecting echo, and narcissist-in-training, a "mean girl" persona she can spring on some unsuspecting victim when a displaced payback opportunity arises. Just to drive home the point, so to speak, Rooney has Frances cut, scratch, pinch, press, and puncture her own skin — more mortification of the flesh.[19] Bobbi, very much the frenemy, would seem to have a sixth sense for dosing her controlling techniques to the right level so that the potion keeps Frances enthralled instead of making her leery of its possible toxicity and rebellious against her chains. Frenemies, like all bullies, are at bottom insecure and self-hating, and therefore need to have exclusive control over their vulnerable prey lest the news and views of others break the spell that the narcissist has cast over the codependent sidekick.[20] Hence Bobbi's early tendency to be dismissive of Nick and to break up larger gatherings into smaller units, such as when Bobbi suggests she and Frances leave a tense conversation with friends expressing various thoughts and feelings and go outside to bond one-on-one around the private campfire of their cigarettes and Bobbi's logos (252–57). Bobbi is Prospero to Frances's Miranda, the Belle Dame sans Merci to Frances's knight-at-arms, alone and palely loitering on the cold hillside. Or is Frances or could she become someone else, maybe "someone worthy of praise, worthy of love"? (41)

The encounter with Melissa and Nick presents Frances with an opportunity to play dress-up and imagine herself in differ-

---

19 After bizarrely calling Rooney's novels "cruelty-free," Madeleine Schwartz's review "How Should a Millennial Be?" zeros in on the self-harm.

20 For ten warning signs of a frenemy, see this unsigned list: a frenemy wants instant attention, over-shares, intentionally sabotages, elicits that nagging feeling, frequently insults others, likes to dig up dirt, disguises complaints as humor, makes us feel as if we're wrong, overreacts when challenged, and is insensitive: "10 Warning Signs of a Frenemy," *Power of Positivity*, September 6, 2015, https://www.powerofpositivity.com/10-warning-signs-frenemy/.

ent future adult roles. She certainly does not want to become someone's doormat (the mistake her mother made) or a trophy spouse mistaking power for love like Nick. But does that mean her only other option is to become a pushy "autocrat" (142) like Melissa if she's ever going to write her way out of poverty and her other insecurities? Wouldn't that be a betrayal of her anti-capitalist convictions? Using Nick's "grey cashmere coat with blue silk lining" (197) that Frances "loved," Rooney has her hero-ine face the contradictions of the "limousine liberal" and "caviar communist." Like the young Barry Obama, she doesn't want to topple the bourgeoisie, she wants to join it. How then will she fly by those nets, make a living, and be able to live with herself?

This problem becomes her summer research project which stretches into the fall semester — call it her "Astral Months" album — and part of it involves giving the relationship with Bobbi a second chance, which is why she asks her after sum-mer vacation is over and reality is back in focus, symbolized by the endometriosis diagnosis she has received: "Is it possible we could develop an alternative model of loving each other?" (299). The codependent, largely transactional basis of their high school, uni, and stage relationships, built on Falstaffian riffing, ribbing, and rogue behavior, is no longer meeting Frances's needs, namely for more self-worth and security, transcendence, and transformation. It's unclear though that Bobbi is willing or able to give her what she wants. Bobbi has her own troubles to work through with her parents divorcing. She may actually be wounded underneath her armor and would be understandably negative about marriage at that moment.[21] This comes through loud and clear in her cold answer to Frances's question about what sustains their relationship:

---

21 In a rare unguarded moment while they are having their private smoke, Bobbi says to Frances, "I feel like shit lately… All this stuff at home, I don't know. You think you're the kind of person who can deal with something and then it happens and you realise you can't" (255).

THE TALKING CURE FOR FASCISM AND EXPLOITIVE RELATIONSHIPS

Who even gets married? said Bobbi. It's sinister. Who wants state apparatuses sustaining their relationship?

I don't know. What is ours sustained by?

That's it! That's exactly what I mean. Nothing. Do I call myself your girlfriend? No. Calling myself your girlfriend would be imposing some prefabricated cultural dynamic on us that's outside our control. You know?

I thought about this until the film was over. Then I said: wait, so does that mean you're not my girlfriend? She laughed. Are you serious? she said. No. I'm not your girlfriend. (306)

Here again, Bobbi is not exactly wrong. She may have good reasons to reject what she calls the "prefabricated cultural dynamic" and to be cautious about letting anything escape "our control," by which she means "my control, me Bobbi." But Frances the poet may be wondering if there still couldn't be a *fabricated* dynamic between two individuals that might develop freely below the radar of culture's institutions and codes. In any case she does not seem happy with Bobbi's answer to her initial question which probably explains the second withdrawal symbolized by her not sharing with Bobbi the news about her medical diagnosis, just as earlier she withheld from Bobbi the edgy short story she wrote about a fictionalized, edgy Bobbi, the news of its publication for money, and "all kinds of weird things" (307, again Philip's way with words) that she was doing with Nick.

Unable to attain liftoff with Bobbi nor with Philip who may actually be fond of Frances but is hopelessly "wussy and effeminate" (*dixit* Bobbi), at the end of chapter 30 Frances at least manages a tender patch-up with her mom after they've bonded around the trip to the hospital and the feelings each has, despite all, for Frances's ailing father ("She laughed then, and I felt better. She reached for my hand across the table and I let her hold it," 310). It's with this love in her heart, and likely hungry for more, that Frances is surprised out of the blue by an accidental telephone call from Nick that takes up all of the last chapter of the book. From one perspective Rooney offers a feel-good ending suited to the Christmas holidays. Frances is out shopping for

Bobbi and Nick for Melissa — same as it ever was — but instead of a formulaic "Merry Christmas" wish and awkwardly hanging up, they both drop what they're doing and offer themselves to each other: "You know, I still have that impulse to be available to you. You'll notice I didn't buy anything in the supermarket… I closed my eyes… Come and get me, I said" (321). The End. Roll the acknowledgements page and the promotional copy for Rooney's second novel, *Normal People.*

I laughed to myself when I realized that Frances's beau has the same name as Offred's — one more Saint Nick! Ho, Ho, Ho! Rooney's last chapter reads like the transposition to real life (within the fictional world of a novel, it's true) of the song "Baby, It's Cold Outside" that Frances heard Melissa and Nick performing in their home (in the Sadie Hawkins version with the woman importuning the man — all this before #metoo and the brouhaha surrounding that 1949 film song) thanks to an old video posted to Melissa's Facebook wall (292).[22] And just to make sure the reader makes the connection, Rooney has Frances spell it out: "I thought of Nick and Melissa singing 'Baby It's Cold Outside' in their warm kitchen with all their friends around them" (320). Now it's late December in Dublin, it really is cold outside — "My feet were getting cold in their boots then" (318) — and here's this hunky guy I knew or know or thought I knew calling me again, he *says* by accident. Rooney's last page gives the reader a Choose

---

22 See the English text of Catherine Deneuve's letter defending "une liberté d'importuner." The last paragraph reads: "I am a free woman, and will remain so. Let me acknowledge those of my fellow women who have been the victims of abhorrent acts and felt offended by the article in *Le Monde.* I apologize to them, and to them alone." "#MeToo Controversy: Read Catherine Deneuve's Letter Published in 'Libération,'" *Libération,* January 15, 2018, https://www.liberation.fr/debats/2018/01/15/metoo-controversy-read-catherine-deneuve-s-letter-published-in-liberation_1622561. See the text of the petition Deneuve co-signed in *Le Monde* (January 9, 2018) here: "Nous défendons une liberté d'importuner, indispensable à la liberté sexuelle," *Le Monde,* January 9, 2018, https://www.lemonde.fr/idees/article/2018/01/09/nous-defendons-une-liberte-d-importuner-indispensable-a-la-liberte-sexuelle_5239134_3232.html.

Your Own Adventure ending that one can complete a thousand ways. A very shrewd marketing tool and sop to romantics?

Hard to say. If it's not possible for Frances and Bobbi, though maybe it still is, is it possible for Frances and Nick to develop an alternative model of loving each other? Lubricated by holiday drinks and mistletoe, sure; but an alternative model that would free Frances and Nick from destructive patterns, with each other or anybody, over the long-haul would require not closing but opening their eyes to those patterns, something Frances got help with in the four-page email from Melissa back in chapter 24 to which she replies, "Lots to think about" (239). Or are Frances and Nick addicted to destructive patterns "that would make everything else complicated" (320) and unwilling or unable to break them? Melissa's email, written in the firm and lean, declarative mode characteristic of Bobbi, sheds some light on that question. A short quotation is enough to get the gist of her message and tone.

> I think it's important that we're on the same page with this. Nick doesn't want to leave me & I don't want to leave him. We are going to keep living together & being married. I'm putting this in an email because I don't trust Nick to be straight with you about it. He has a weak personality & compulsively tells people what they want to hear. […] You will not be able to draw a sustainable sense of self-respect from this relationship you're in. I'm sure you find his total acquiescence charming now, but over the course of a marriage it actually becomes exhausting…. (234–35)

This long email, set in a smaller different font like the other email snippets and text messages that come up here and there, is one of the most impressive pieces of writing in the whole book. Is Melissa right? Who knows, but she is speaking her truth and, like a midwife or older sister, her message gives Frances (an only child, unlike Bobbi who has a younger sister, Lydia) much to think about, especially concerning the existence of the unconscious and mental illness such as compulsive behavior that she seems to have underestimated as she says herself in one of the most important paragraphs of the entire novel if we understand it to be essentially the story of Frances's emancipation and self-invention, with a little help from her friends.

> The only part of the email I really wanted to know about was the information relating to Nick. He had been in psychiatric hospital, which was news to me. I wasn't repelled as such; I had read books, I was familiar with the idea that capitalism was the really crazy thing. But I had thought people who were hospitalized for psychiatric problems were different from the people I knew. I could see I had entered a new social setting now, where severe mental illness no longer had unfashion-able connotations. I was going through a second upbringing: learning a new set of assumptions, and feigning a greater lev-el of understanding than I really possessed. By this logic Nick and Melissa were like my parents bringing me into the world, probably hating and loving me even more than my original parents did. This also meant I was Bobbi's evil twin, which didn't seem at the time like taking the metaphor too far. (238)

The wisdom of this passage, which goes beyond what one would expect most 21-year-olds to be capable of articulating, leads one to ponder again how old the narrator of this story must be and from what vantage point she is looking back "at the time" of the events she relates. I am struck, for example, by how she has hit on the truth that it took Harville Hendrix much longer to for-mulate[23] and for me to understand; namely that we do not fall in love with just anybody. We fall in love with those who resemble our primary caregivers in very specific ways, and those stand-ins for our parents or other primary caregivers are seized on by us with the idea that we will be able to recreate what was good and repair what was harmful about those past relationships. "To be born again," as Van Morrison sings it in "Astral Weeks." Ten

---

23 Harville Hendrix, *Getting the Love You Want: A Guide for Couples* (New York: St. Martin's Press, 2008).

years apart, Melissa and Frances happen to have fallen in love with the same man. Why is that? Melissa has an explanation that is at least worth considering:

> You love him, don't you? He tells me your father is an alcoholic, so was mine. I wonder if we gravitate toward Nick because he gives us a sense of control that was lacking in childhood. (235)

Melissa's "I wonder" is nicely undogmatic, an inviting verb choice that extends the open opportunity for Frances to join her in thinking about the secret logic of unconscious drives if she wishes. Inversely, it stands to reason that no conscious partnership between Frances and Nick, or Nick with Melissa, is likely unless he too were to question why he gravitates toward women like Melissa and Frances. Maybe that insight is something he could achieve in conversations with friends or perhaps it's something that would require crossing the doorstep of a trained listener, a therapist of some sort, and not just relying on an amateur good listener at a gym, bar, beach, or dinner party. The same goes for Bobbi, and it's interesting that she's the one who suggests counselling to Frances:

> You could go to counselling, she said.
> Do you think I should?
> You're not above it. It might be good for you. It's not necessarily normal to go around collapsing in churches. (302)

Bobbi is referring to when Frances fainted from nervous exhaustion while resting in a church; not the first time she has responded to painful circumstances by inflicting further harm on herself. I also take Bobbi's remark as another example of "it takes one to know one…," who could benefit from counselling. One hopes the Bobbies of the world shall one day overcome

their own resistance and seek help rather than venting to accomplices or aggressing bystanders.[24]

Belatedly, Ireland legalized abortion. Perhaps the country
will lead the de-stigmatization of mental health services, maybe
even teaming up with the British royal family. Finally putting
physical and mental health on an equal footing would be a good
personal supplement, twenty years on, to the political Good
Friday Agreement of 1998.[25] Perhaps it's already underway.[26] If
there's a moral to Sally Rooney's *Conversations with Friends* and
Normal People, it is that one is never too young or too old to get
closer to getting the love you want and breaking free of exploitive
relationships, but it can be hard to do on one's own. This is what
Timothy Snyder calls "the paradox of freedom": "no one is free
without help. Freedom might be solitary, but freedom requires
solidarity […] we cannot be ourselves without help."[27] Therefore
it's best to have some "prefabricated cultural dynamic," such as

---

24 In *Normal People* the male protagonist Connell pursues therapy on the
    suggestion of a friend and sticks with it. His improved mental health, it is
    suggested, is what gives him the strength to rescue his close friend Mari-
    anne from self-destruction at the hands of her abusive brother and mother.
    Perhaps a future Rooney novel or essay will feature more normalization of
    seeking and benefitting from mental health services.

25 On the role of Kevin Boyle and Tom Hadden in drafting the conversa-
    tion (starting in 1992, a year of nearly 100 political killings on the island
    of Ireland) that would culminate in the 1998 Good Friday Agreement, see
    Mike Chinoy, *Are You With Me? Kevin Boyle and the Rise of the Human
    Rights Movement* (Dublin: The Lilliput Press, 2020), ch. 22. On advancing
    mental health services in the UK, see the website of Heads Together, a non-
    profit organization sponsored by the Duke and Duchess of Cambridge and
    Prince Harry: "We have seen time and time again that shattering stigma
    on mental health starts with simple conversations." "Heads Together: The
    Duke and Duchess of Cambridge and Prince Harry's Campaign to End
    Stigma around Mental Health," *royal.uk,* https://www.royal.uk/heads-
    together-duke-and-duchess-cambridge-and-prince-harrys-campaign-end-
    stigma-around-mental-health.

26 See Mark Fisher, "Why Mental Health Is a Political Issue," *The Guardian,*
    July 16, 2012, https://www.theguardian.com/commentisfree/2012/jul/16/
    mental-health-political-issue.

27 Timothy Snyder, *Our Malady: Lessons in Liberty from a Hospital Diary*
    (New York: Crown, 2020), 79, 109.

the British National Health Service or the Irish Department of Health where Bobbi's father works, to defend the rights of those seeking help and to offer affordable health insurance so that cost is not a barrier for anyone who wants to improve their mental or physical health. In contrast to Atwood and Roth's dark worlds, Rooney imagines a brighter alternative where worst case scenarios, such as debilitating mental illness and burnout or the violence and destruction of stage-five fascism or other extremism can actually be prevented — before deprogramming and deradicalization are necessary — with dialogue, pragmatism, and love under principles of universal human dignity and full personhood. *CWF* would seem to support the view that only a functioning national democracy operating in the interest of the general public good is capable of implementing and managing non-profit public health services over the long-term and protecting them against predatory, for-profit ventures that make money for the Few by exploiting the poor health and defenselessness of the young, the old, and other vulnerable populations. Covid-19 has boosted Sally Rooney's efforts to advance that conversation.[28]

---

28 It is no exaggeration to say this is a global conversation. For example, Covid-19 has spurred a desire to remove the stigma associated with talking about mental health in Japan, and elsewhere. See Motoko Rich and Hikari Hida, "As Pandemic Took Hold, Suicide Rose Among Japanese Women," *The New York Times,* February 22, 2021, https://www.nytimes.com/2021/02/23/world/as-the-pandemic-took-hold-suicide-rose-among-japanese-women.html.

IV

Manifestos

9

Lessons from a Philosopher of Vulnerability

Martha C. Nussbaum, *The Monarchy of Fear: A Philosopher Looks at Our Political Crisis* (2018)

The fourth and last part of this book will consider three examples of what the French call *essai,* a genre that used to mean, and still does, a roughly twenty-page piece of argument-driven prose coming from a somewhat personal angle — the stuff of Michel de Montaigne, William Hazlitt, Ralph Waldo Emerson, and longish *New Yorker* pieces. In French today, *essai* commonly refers to a roughly 220-page, argument-driven piece that takes up some painful topic of general public interest such as global warming, war, poverty, prisons, education, healthcare, and the like. This long-form French *essai* or manifesto is usually light on footnotes and the implied reader may be a news junkie who is already familiar with the topic and reading to get the author's "takeaway" and "the upshot" on whatever XYZ affair happens to be the focus. One example is Emmanuel Todd's *Après l'empire* (2002) which I translated into English as *After the Empire: The Breakdown of the American Order* in 2003. In that

book, a leading French demographer and public intellectual offers his thoughts on America's growing inequality, retreat from
universalism, and waning hegemony. His *essai* reported on and
contributed to foreign resistance to the "war on terror" on the
eve of the second Gulf War.[1]

In English, books of similar length are often written by university professors who are trained to document sources with
footnotes and bibliographies. These medium-sized books are
the novella of academic prose, longer than a scholarly article
(the short story) but shorter and less fleshed out than the scholarly monograph (the novel). One might come across them at
an airport terminal convenience store or in Europe at a train
station news agent. These texts explore a controversial topic in
more depth than a simple editorial or magazine piece can do, all
the while giving suggestions for further reading to those who
want to know more and perhaps learn from the professor's own
teachers. They often include personal asides that allow the reader to glimpse the author's emotional stake in the problem being studied. They also contain programmatic signposts toward
solutions that are more sketched than specific. One could say
the reader is getting a condensed version of an undergraduate
seminar at a fraction of the cost of tuition at the fancy schools
these authors generally hail from; and the professor-author has
the satisfaction of getting out of the ivory tower, reaching wider
audiences (two-thirds of Americans don't have a college degree), and appearing alongside the work of an Atwood, Roth, or
Rooney, while at the same time remaining peacefully far from
the madding crowd and the messiness of the rooms where policy directions are hammered out and voted on.

The three examples featured here were all spurred by the unstable social, economic, and political situation that persisted in
America roughly ten years after the Great Recession of 2008–9
— a decade of uneven economic recovery across the two terms
of the first African American president, Barack Obama, (who

---

1 At the time, the book was said to have influenced France's foreign policy
   decision to not take part in that war.

may never have been elected were it not for the economic disaster that unfolded during the previous Republican presidency
of George W. Bush), and the first two years of his replacement,
Donald J. Trump, America's first president with zero government or military experience (who eked out a slim victory in the
electoral college thanks to doses of resentment, racism, misogyny, Russian meddling, FBI meddling, billionaire meddling, voter
suppression tactics, longstanding voter apathy, and a refusal of
the states' electors to vote in favor of the national winner of the
popular vote, Hillary Clinton). In other words, the background
of all three books is American democracy in crisis, weakened
by extreme wealth and income inequality, polarized on nearly
every topic imaginable, and paralyzed by political gridlock and
by personal debt, despair, and distrust. In short, the context is
a barely contained civil war on the day-to-day surface, like in
the 1850s and 1930s, with hot emotional lava underneath and
regular violent outbursts in public: the perfect conditions for
fascism to take root and take power.

Martha Nussbaum (1947–), a tenured professor at the University of Chicago who holds an endowed double appointment
in the department of philosophy and the law school, is the
author or editor of over twenty books, and her recent Trump-
era study, *The Monarchy of Fear: A Philosopher Looks at Our
Political Crisis,* is a model of teacherly clarity and good sense.[2]
That said, Nussbaum's *description* of the mess America is in — a
situation worsened by choosing as president someone from the
vertically organized corporate world who is openly hostile to
democracy's horizontal ground rules of transparency, accountability, due process, and equal rights — is more convincing than
her prescription, the rough sketch of "capabilities" and the cul-
tivation of hope, faith, trust, and love that she considers to be
components of any strategy of repairing mistakes and reducing
the pain caused by that mess. Her book offers a "look at our

---

2   Martha Nussbaum, *The Monarchy of Fear: A Philosopher Looks at Our
    Political Crisis* (New York: Simon & Schuster, 2018). Hereafter cited paren-
    thetically throughout this chapter

political crisis" that rings true and extends beyond US borders since democracy in America often sets the example, positive or negative, in many parts of the world; but it is short on specific policy recommendations. Perhaps this is because she does not sufficiently loop back to her early insight to underscore the fact that intense fear — and the toxic anger-blame, disgust-blame, and envy-blame that it engineers — has its origin in "life-inse-curity" (9) which registers as unavowable intimations of vulner-ability, exposure to loss and lack, wounding and mortality.

Nussbaum's talent derives in part from her acceptance, in-deed her embrace of vulnerability as central to the philosopher's craft:

[F]or me philosophy is not about authoritative pronounce-ments. It is not about one person claiming to be deeper than others or making allegedly wise assertions. It is about leading the "examined life," with humility about how little we really understand, with a commitment to arguments that are rigor-ous, reciprocal, and sincere, and with a willingness to listen to others as equal participants and to respond to what they offer. Philosophy in this Socratic conception does not com-pel, or threaten, or mock. It doesn't make bare assertions, but, instead, sets up a structure of thought in which a conclusion follows from premises the listener is free to dispute. [...] the philosophical speaker is humble and exposed: his or her po-sition is transparent and thus vulnerable to criticism. (10–11)

Nussbaum is very much a philosopher of vulnerability. It is both her subject matter and her method, an approach very much in tune, as she says, "to the goals of democratic self-government, in which each person's thought matters" (11). Socrates, who is Nussbaum's favorite "guiding spirit," along with Lucretius and Kant it would seem, "said he was like a gadfly on the back of the democracy, which he compared to a 'noble but sluggish horse': the sting of philosophical questioning was supposed to wake democracy up so that it could conduct its business better" (11);

and, we could add, remain aware that a society is *not* a business.[3] *Vulnerability* comes from the Latin for wound, *vulnus* and *vulnerare*. The sting of the gadfly is therefore a wounding designed to prevent greater harm, a type of *pharmakon* or as the French say, *un mal pour un bien,* a cousin of the English "tough love," which must be dosed carefully.

Of all the autobiographical details Nussbaum shares in her ten-page preface, the most interesting for our purposes is that her racist lawyer father, who seems to have sprung from the same mold as Goldwater, Reagan, Charles Murray, and Fred Trump, inadvertently opened her eyes — by endorsing his daughter's foreign study experience in the home of a working class Welsh family — to the fallacy of the standard, conservative "bootstrap" claim that the poor and the vulnerable are responsible for their own misery due to weakness of the will or flawed characters that leave them addicted to government "coddling." Her trip to Wales, the Appalachia of the United Kingdom, at the tender age of sixteen woke up the privileged Martha Nussbaum, née Craven, to the stinging reality that "obstacles imposed by poverty often lie deep in the human spirit, and many deprived people can't follow my father's path [from the working class in Macon, Georgia to a partnership in a Philadelphia law firm].… He didn't notice how being white gave him huge advantages. […] So, I saw myself in a new perspective, as not just a very smart kid but as the product of social forces that are unequally distributed" (xiv).[4] In other words, the American dream of up-

---

3   I would argue that the crisis described in *The Monarchy of Fear* has resulted from ignoring the alarm bell that Nussbaum was ringing in her earlier manifesto, *Not for Profit: Why Democracy Needs the Humanities* (Princeton: Princeton University Press, 2010). Nussbaum alludes to that connection in *Monarchy of Fear*'s last chapter "Hope, Love, Vision." This is also the argument made by Steven M. DeLue in *How the Liberal Arts Can Save Liberal Democracy* (Lanham: Lexington Books, 2018).

4   One could link this consciousness-raising moment in the life of Nussbaum to similar "looking glass" moments discussed in earlier chapters on Fromm, Martha Dodd and her ambassador father, Hélène Berr, Leslie Jamison, and the three novels. In each case, primary ties and first impressions are revised, and the subject grows into an adult relation to the world,

ward mobility by the steady application of one's abilities through hard work is not nor was it ever available to all: "A just and inclusive America never was and is not yet a fully achieved reality" (3).

But this assessment spurs hope, not angry lamentation, from Nussbaum. This hope is inspired by her love of that particularly but not exclusively American dream (a love widely shared, by Martin Luther King Jr. and many others). That dream is as much or more valuable and vulnerable due to its spiritual dimension (call it *Liberté, Égalité, Fraternité*) than for its promise of material prosperity. King, and before him Franklin Roosevelt, never forgot that spiritual and material wealth are inextricably linked; in other words, that there can be no life-security and therefore no peace and therefore no justice — in short, no "facilitating environment" (38–62) — without an "economic bill of rights" (162–63). This "Second Bill of Rights," meant to stand alongside the political Bill of Rights of 1791, was set forth by Roosevelt in his State of the Union address on January 11, 1944.

"Necessitous men are not free men. People who are hungry, people who are out of a job are the stuff of which dictatorships are made," Roosevelt insisted.[5] At that moment during World War II, he was confident that the Allies would soon defeat the German, Italian, and Japanese fascisms. But he knew that winning the peace, in other words a durable victory, would require addressing the root causes of fascism; namely (fear of) economic insecurity which inevitably translated into violent and often

---

accepts suffering and vulnerability as the price of love, and abandons the impulse to remain a child and escape from freedom. For more background information about Nussbaum, see the profile by Rachel Aviv, "The Philosopher of Feelings," *The New Yorker,* July 18, 2016 https://longform.org/posts/the-philosopher-of-feelings, and letters to the editor in reply to that profile here: "The Mail," *The New Yorker,* September 5, 2016.

5 Franklin D. Roosevelt, "State of the Union Message to Congress, January 11, 1944," *Franklin D. Roosevelt Library and Museum,* https://www.fdrlibrary.org/address-text.

irrational lashing out toward those deemed responsible, and therefore to be blamed and held accountable for that insecurity.[6]

Nussbaum does not present it quite like that because her quotation from Roosevelt's speech occurs within her chapter on the toxic effect of exaggerated envy, but the underlying point is the same.

> Roosevelt saw that rights protect democracy from envy. What every single person has by right, people can't envy in their fellows. Moving some key economic goods into the rights category undercuts envy, to at least some degree. One reason we see so much envy is that people are not secure in their economic lives. (163)

This quotation comes near the end of the chapter "Envy's Empire," a title that works well with the overall theme of *The Monarchy of Fear* because Nussbaum's main claim in this book is that *fear* (of life-insecurity, vulnerability, wounding, death) engenders the three negative emotions of anger, disgust, and envy that tend to drive out the positive emotions of hope, trust, and love which are necessary for life, liberty, and the pursuit of happiness.

Nussbaum's discussion of envy as an aggravating factor in the political crisis she describes first attracted my attention because my own "favorite guiding spirit," Tocqueville, had also identified envy as one of the four reasons why in normal times citizens living in democracies tend to choose mediocre leaders over mani-

---

6   Recent publications have made it more widely known that the New Deal was a raw deal for people of color who were largely kept away from home ownership and from participating in social security. The shot heard 'round the internet by Ta-Nehisi Coates ("The Case for Reparations," *The Atlantic,* June 2014, https://www.theatlantic.com/magazine/archive/2014/06/the-case-for-reparations/361631/) was followed by the extensive research of Richard Rothstein in *The Color of Law: A Forgotten History of How Our Government Segregated America* (New York: Liveright, 2017). In effect, America's victory over European fascism would leave its own racialized authoritarianism and persecution of minorities unaddressed for another twenty to eighty years.

festly more qualified and promising candidates. Nussbaum does not make use of Tocqueville, but both of them were students of the Enlightenment thinkers and Humanists who in turn were indebted to classical Greek and Roman sources. Tocqueville observes the power of envy to derange the faculty of judgment:

> Moreover, it is not always the ability to choose men of merit which democracy lacks but the desire and inclination to do so.
>
> One must not blind oneself to the fact that democratic institutions promote to a very high degree the feeling of envy in the human heart, not so much because they offer each citizen ways of being equal to each other but because these ways continuously prove inadequate for those who use them. Democratic institutions awaken and flatter the passion of equality without ever being able to satisfy it entirely. This complete equality every day slips through the people's fingers at the moment when they think they have a hold on it; it flees, as Pascal says, in an eternal flight. The people become excited by the pursuit of this blessing, all the more priceless because it is near enough to be recognized but too far away to be tasted. The chance of success enthuses them; the uncertainty of success frustrates them. Their excitement is followed by weariness and bitterness. So anything which exceeds their limitations in any way appears to them as an obstacle to their desires and all superiority, however legitimate, is irksome to their eyes.[7]

Until a better argument comes along, I take this as a pretty good explanation of how a Trump can beat a Hillary Clinton, a Bush can beat a John Kerry, or a Reagan can beat a Jimmy Carter: when times are generally better compared to a recent past, but the recovery is uneven or felt to be uneven, one can expect a cohort of the envious will go along with scapegoating

---

7   Alexis de Tocqueville, *Democracy in America; and, Two Essays on America*, trans. Gerald Bevan (London: Penguin Books, 2003), 230–31.

some more fortunate individual or group as responsible for this "unfairness."[8] Only in times of widely acknowledged danger, says Tocqueville, do citizens in democratic lands set aside their passive-aggressive hissy fit of envy and resentment and accept to be guided by "great characters":

> When great dangers threaten the state, the people often make a happy choice of those citizens best suited to save them.
>
> It has been noticed that, in the face of imminent danger, a man rarely remains at his normal level; he either rises well above himself or dips well below. The same happens to nations. Extreme dangers, instead of lifting a nation, sometimes end by bringing it low; they arouse its passions without giving them direction and confuse its perceptions without clarification. [...] But more commonly, with nations as with men, extraordinary courage arises from the very imminence of the dangers. Then great characters stand out like those monuments hidden by the darkness of the night and seen suddenly in the glare of a conflagration. Genius no longer disdains to appear on the stage and the people, alarmed by the dangers facing them, momentarily forget their envious passions.[9]

Five years later in 1840 when Tocqueville publishes a second more psychological and philosophical study of democracy in America, he will return to envy as a partial explanation of the vainglorious, restless, agitated, and quarrelsome tendencies among citizens of democracies. The key in all these observations is the tension that arises out of the gap between the promise of

---

8   In his other famous book on *The Ancien Régime and the Revolution,* Tocqueville made a similar claim that revolution is most likely not when things are at their worst but when they are starting to be marginally better than they had been: "Going from bad to worse does not always mean a slide into revolution. More often than not, it occurs when a nation which has endured without complaint — almost without feeling them — the most burdensome laws, rejects them with violence the moment the weight of them lightens." Alexis de Tocqueville, *The Ancien Régime and the Revolution,* trans. Gerald Bevan (London: Penguin Books, 2008), 175.
9   Tocqueville, *Democracy in America,* 232.

equality and the daily lived reality of inequality which, rightly or wrongly, is felt as insulting and unjust. The paradox underlined by Tocqueville is that prosperity exacerbates anxiety and public disquiet if there is a strong feeling that it's unfairly distributed and of uncertain duration. Injustice can exist (school budget disparities, for example) and should be combatted, preferably nonviolently; but there is also the fallacy of the "just world" which Nussbaum joins Melvin J. Lerner in labeling "a fundamental delusion" that causes mischief when one forgets that life is not fair and goes looking for scapegoats to blame, or beat up, for one's troubles (82–83).[10]

Skillful use was also made of Lerner's 1980 classic by John Marsh in a book that fell on deaf ears among the promoters of both Barack Obama's Race to the Top initiative and George W. Bush's No Child Left Behind education reforms. The book has a catchy title, *Class Dismissed: Why We Cannot Teach or Learn Our Way Out of Inequality* (2011). The short answer is that both major political parties indulge in what Marsh calls the narcissism of meritocracy (166); in other words, the delusion, not to say con, that everyone gets what they deserve and deserves what they get. Neither party can stand to hear much less accept that income and wealth inequality is not primarily about a skills gap or character flaws, but rather a lack of will in government and the private sector to pay all workers a living wage.[11] A meatpacker or home health aide with a PhD or MFA is only paid the going rate for that job — with no *magna cum laude* bonus — and a forty-hour week at that rate is not enough to cover rent, groceries, day care, medical insurance and bills, clothes, and gas for a used commuter car.[12] Paying workers as little as

---

10 Melvin J. Lerner, *The Belief in a Just World: A Fundamental Delusion* (New York: Springer, 1980).

11 On Amy Glasmeier's calculator to define a living wage, see Nick Romeo, "The M.I.T. Professor Defining What It Means to Live," *The New York Times,* December 28, 2021, https://www.nytimes.com/2021/12/28/opinion/living-wage-calculator.html.

12 The federal minimum wage has not budged since 2009 when it was set at a measly $7.25 per hour. Besides Barbara Ehrenreich's classic on not

the employer can get away with is considered by many to be one of the fundamental moral failings of modern global capitalism, but for two generations, both political parties[13] have preferred to blame the vulnerable rather than hold capitalists accountable to other stakeholders besides shareholders.[14]

This material world, and the attendant fear, shame, despair, and anger felt by those who "have not" basic control over their lives, is underemphasized in Nussbaum's otherwise excellent chapters devoted to the provenance of *fear* and its destructive side-effects as anger, disgust, and envy which impede the sustainability of hope, trust, and love. After her discussion of those three negative emotions, Nussbaum conducts an equally persuasive analysis of the workings of misogyny, usefully distinguished from mere sexism, as a particularly nasty form of hatred that acts as an "enforcement mechanism" of lower status (165–96). Nussbaum praises Kate Manne's *Down Girl: The Logic of Misogyny* (2017) for its analysis of male, and sometimes female, anger-blame directed at uppity women who have "gotten out of hand," with attendant anxiety about "down-ranking" or dis-

---

getting by, *Nickel and Dimed: On (Not) Getting by in America* (New York: Metropolitan, 2010), see *The New York Times*, "Why These Disneyland Employees Can't Afford Rent | NYT Opinion," *YouTube*, September 5, 2018, https://www.youtube.com/watch?v=3P8fsrWg6No.

13 "Whether voters cast their ballots for Clinton, Bush, Obama, or Trump, they somehow get Goldman Sachs," Robert Kuttner, *Can Democracy Survive Global Capitalism?* (New York: W.W. Norton & Co., 2018), 19.

14 See Thomas B. Edsall, "Why Do We Pay So Many People So Little Money?" *The New York Times*, June 24, 2020, https://www.nytimes.com/2020/06/24/opinion/wages-coronavirus.html. See also Anne Case and Angus Deaton, *Deaths of Despair and The Future of Capitalism* (Princeton: Princeton University Press, 2020), reviewed by Atul Gawande, "Why Americans Are Dying from Despair," *The New Yorker,* March 16, 2020, https://www.newyorker.com/magazine/2020/03/23/why-americans-are-dying-from-despair. Stakeholder capitalism has become a new buzzword — talk is cheap — but has not improved the lives of the 99%. Occupy Wall Street, it should be recalled, was inspired by the Arab Spring, not a homegrown conversation about class and inequality. It barely lasted four months in the fall of 2011 and received no serious backing from President Obama and the Democratic Party. Angry, disgusted, and afraid, it's no wonder working people either stayed home or voted against the establishment candidate in 2016.

ruption of a supposed natural, male-dominated hierarchy. But she politely criticizes Manne for not taking sufficient account of fear-driven *disgust-misogyny* ("anxiety about bodily fluids, birth, and corporeality in general," and the destructiveness of *projective disgust*) and *envy-misogyny* ("anxiety about competitive success" and status loss). Nussbaum considers disgust and envy to be equally important drivers of hatred toward women, but also at work in anti-Semitism and in anti-Black, anti-queer, and anti-immigrant sentiments and actions.[15]

Readers who like clear, concise definitions will enjoy reading Nussbaum. What is fear? "Fear is not only the earliest emotion in human life, it is also the most broadly shared within the animal kingdom. […] Aristotle defined fear as pain at the seeming presence of some impending bad thing, combined with a feeling that you are powerless to ward it off" (24). Nussbaum points out that Aristotle's discussion of fear occurs within his manual *Rhetoric*. The monarch and all authoritarian rulers know that fear can and must be weaponized to dominate and control — just as the newborn baby, itself fearful of dying or being dethroned, will wail and cry to strike fear into the heart of the panicky parent to make them feel guilty about possibly not doing one's caregiver duties properly or totally. Whence the French democratic revolt against the *enfant roi,* the child-king, more commonly referred to in English as the spoiled child.

In chapter 3, "Anger, Child of Fear," Nussbaum again borrows from Aristotle to distinguish between anger proper, "a response to a significant damage to something or someone one cares about, and a damage that the angry person believes to have been wrongly inflicted" (72), and *indignation,* which is anger devoid of the "pleasant hope for payback," in other words retaliation or retribution. The latter is the poisonous element in much anger which leads some to believe all anger is bad and needs to be

---

15 Projective disgust can fall on anyone labeled weak or simply different. In William Golding's *Lord of the Flies* (1954), two vulnerable truth-tellers, Simon (called "batty") and the myopic, overweight boy called Piggy, will be first mocked then brutally killed. Labeling writers and journalists "enemies of the people" also seeks subordination enforcement.

overcome by strategies of neutral detachment and low expectations. But Nussbaum cautions against that blanket rejection because then we would also be rejecting love:

> Anger is a distinct emotion with distinctive thoughts. It looks manly and important, not at all timorous. Nonetheless, it is the offspring of fear. How so?
>
> First, if we were not plagued by great vulnerability, we would probably never get angry…
>
> If anger is a response to a significant damage inflicted by someone else on you or someone or something you care about, then a person who is complete, who cannot be damaged, has no room for anger…
>
> The Greek Stoics thought that we should learn not to care at all about the "goods of fortune," that is, anything that can be damaged by anything outside our own control. Then we would lose fear, and in the bargain, we'd lose anger…
>
> The problem, however, is that in losing fear we also lose love. The basis of both is a strong attachment to someone or something outside our control. There is nothing that makes us more vulnerable than loving other people, or loving a country. So much can go wrong. Fear is often rational, and grief an omnipresent reality. (84–85)

In the following pages, Nussbaum concentrates on the crazy-making aspects of fear (of death, loss, and loss of control), which are also of central importance in Keith Payne's study, *The Broken Ladder*. These include fear's tendency to make us jump to conclusions and lash out; to become obsessed with relative status (Thorstein Veblen's "race for reputability"); to focus on payback as a misguided "way of reestablishing lost control and dignity"; or to assign blame to some devil, Fate, or "the stars" as a way of ducking responsibility and allaying feelings of helplessness. The end of the chapter is devoted to indignation, a potentially healthy anger that allows for "protest without payback." It includes Nussbaum's insightful reading of Martin Luther King Jr.'s famous "I Have a Dream" speech delivered on August 28, 1963 as part of the March on Washington.

The following chapter, "Fear-Driven Disgust: The Politics of Exclusion," also contains a crucial distinction. There is "primary disgust," which is "anxiety about animality and mortality, and triggered, therefore, by bodily characteristics, real or imputed, that bear a close relationship to our anxieties about mortality and the vulnerable animal body" (100). This includes anything suspected of being a contaminant or dangerous or that recalls the base, the animal, or the decaying. One of Nussbaum's examples is the Witches' icky potion in *Macbeth*. Then there is *projective disgust,* also called *disgust subordination,* which is a form of scapegoating performed by those fearing their own death, "as if stigmatization were a veritable elixir of life" (113). In other words, to ward off fear of death and feel instead invincible and immortal, the one experiencing unavowable vulnerability will select a vulnerable "disgust-group" (often called an out-group) toward whom the in-group can "punch down" to enforce that out-group's subordination through "disgust-stigma." In typical bully fashion elucidated by Fromm already back in 1941, the one practicing projective disgust never picks on anyone their own size. Nussbaum concludes with a discussion of hate crimes. This chapter lays the ground for her direct negative assessments of Trump's own projective disgust which occur in the misogyny chapter. She claims that his failure to condemn the projective disgust of others, such as the alt-right demonstrators in Charlottesville, Virginia in August 2017, is in effect radicalizing these groups via "signs of permission and approval" (131). This "rot starts at the top"[16] view is similar to what Herman Roth was getting at when he calls out the "climate of hate" emanating from the "dirty dogs" in Lindbergh's White House, in effect countering projective disgust with projective disgust of his own. Simi-

---

16   Also captured by the expression "a fish rots from the head down," a view
     shared by Michelle Goldberg in her lamentation, "America Is Too Broken
     to Fight the Coronavirus," *The New York Times,* June 22, 2020, https://
     www.nytimes.com/2020/06/22/opinion/us-coronavirus-trump.html.

larly, in 2017 "fascism" is countered with "antifa" in an escalating spiral of provocation that culminates with, no surprise, a vulnerable woman — *toujours sur la femme* — Heather Heyer, killed on the street in Charlottesville.

In her last chapter, "Hope, Love, Vision," Nussbaum sketches her response to anger's desire for payback, disgust's desire for subordination, and envy's desire for exclusion of the fortunate rival. Nussbaum's insistence on the value of *practical hope* with a commitment to action over mere *idle hope* sounds good, but it may leave some wondering where she stands in relation to the ancient philosophers who define hope as "the cousin, or flip side, of fear" (203). One may also want to ponder her later declaration, "It appears that the difference is one of focus. It's like the glass half empty, the glass half full. The same glass, a different focus of vision. In fear, you focus on the bad outcome that may occur. In hope, you focus on the good":

> Hope, [Adrienne] Martin argues, is more like a "syndrome" than just an attitude or emotion: it includes thoughts, imaginings, preparations for action, even actions. I don't see this as peculiar to hope; fear also has strong connections to imagination and action. But what are the actions and thoughts characteristic of hope? I'd say that hope involves a vision of the good world that might ensue, and often at least, actions related to getting there. Some of these might be similar to the actions promoted by fear, since warding off a bad possibility can be very similar to promoting a good one. (205)

Fine, but what should be the content of the "vision of the good world that might ensue" and the "actions related to getting there"? Up to this point Nussbaum has been a helpful guide, but after her philosopher's inspection of "our political crisis," she declines to provide much detail about actual measures to resolve or repair that crisis. As she says, "The focus is on capabilities rather than actual functioning because the theory gives great importance to choice" (239). Her list of ten "central capabilities" reads a bit like the *Universal Declaration of Human Rights*

(1948), co-authored by President Roosevelt's wife Eleanor, and there's nothing wrong with that. In her defense, one could say Nussbaum, a professional philosopher, is staying in her lane and leaving policy development, implementation, and enforcement to others whose job description corresponds to those tasks. Critics, however, might see this as an evasion by an invulnerable senior professor whose honor and income are completely secure.[17]

Is there not a touch of the elderly Mary McCarthy in some of Nussbaum's "glass half full" pronouncements that might grate on more vulnerable and less sanguine readers? For example, her belief (in June 2017 at least, when her book went to press) that American academia is basically "healthy" and that "the basic institutions of our government are reasonably healthy. Courts are not ideal deliberative bodies, but they aren't corrupt tools of power either, as in some countries, and the separation of powers works well on the whole" (199). In her 2010 manifesto *Not for Profit: Why Democracy Needs the Humanities,* Nussbaum's closing chapter, entitled "Democratic Education on the Ropes," is a list of what is either breaking, broken, or never got built in the first place in the US and around the world when it comes to the humanities component of the liberal arts model of education that is so indispensable for nurturing the life of the mind and the empathy necessary to sustain tolerant, open democratic societies.[18] What reasons or evidence does Nussbaum have in mind that make her believe the situation has improved and not

---

17 In her profile, "The Philosopher of Feelings," Aviv wonders about Nussbaum's relation to vulnerability: "What I am calling for," Aviv quotes her as saying, "is a society of citizens who admit that they are needy and vulnerable." Aviv then wonders "if she approaches her theme of vulnerability with so much success because she peers at it from afar, as if it were unfamiliar and exotic." Surely aging and then death is the great leveler, even for the mightiest Ozymandias; but one could also call for a society that reduces some vulnerabilities, such as those caused by extreme inequality.

18 Martha C. Nussbaum, *Not for Profit: Why Democracy Needs the Humanities* (Princeton: Princeton University Press, 2010), ch. 7, "Democratic Education on the Ropes," 121–43.

gotten worse since the publication of that earlier manifesto?[19]
Likewise, even though her book was published before the police
killing of George Floyd and glaring recent examples of executive, legislative, and judicial malpractice and dereliction of duty,
she can hardly have forgotten the Rodney King beating (1991),
the Clarence Thomas–Anita Hill confrontation (1991), Colin
Powell's bald lies to the United Nations (2003), the Trayvon
Martin case (2012), or more recently Senator Mitch McConnell's
unconstitutional blockade of President Obama's nomination of
Merrick Garland to the Supreme Court followed by the Republican ramrodding of Trump's pick, preapproved by the conservative Federalist Society, Justice Neil Gorsuch (2017).[20]

---

19 The business model of US higher education was already teetering before
Covid-19. It is now in full-blown crisis according to this editorial by history professor Claire Bond Potter, "The Only Way to Save Higher Education is to Make It Free," *The New York Times,* June 5, 2020, https://www.
nytimes.com/2020/06/05/opinion/sunday/free-college-tuition-coronavi-
rus.html. Other unhealthy symptoms include $1.5 trillion in student debt,
the out-sourcing of teaching to adjuncts without benefits, administration
bloat, the elevation of rankings over learning, and the questionable tilting
of schools toward athletics and wellness centers while remaining clusters
for depression, bullying, sexual assault, and underage and excessive
alcohol consumption. And there's Nussbaum's main concern, even if not
directly addressed in *Monarchy of Fear*: the down-ranking of the humanities in funding and prestige and the corresponding worship of STEM and
business majors. For one account, see Christopher Newfield, *Unmaking the
Public University: The Forty-Year Assault on the Middle Class* (Cambridge:
Harvard University Press, 2008) and his more recent recipe for repairs,
*The Great Mistake: How We Wrecked Public Universities and How We Can
Fix Them* (Baltimore: Johns Hopkins University Press, 2016). For a group
review of new books on the "gloomy," unhealthy condition of American
higher education, see Jonathan Zimmerman, "What Is College Worth?"
The New York Review of Books, July 2, 2020, https://www.nybooks.com/
articles/2020/07/02/what-is-college-worth/.
20 To understand the recent conservative capture of the courts as part of a
long-term strategy, see Herman Schwartz, *Right Wing Justice: The Conservative Campaign to Take Over the Courts* (New York: Nation Books, 2004),
published the same year as Robert O. Paxton's *Anatomy of Fascism* (New
York: Alfred A. Knopf, 2004) and Philip Roth's *The Plot Against America*
(New York: Houghton Mifflin, 2004).

Some pages later, Nussbaum writes, "It always surprises me that I get around thirty people at a book talk in the United States, and regularly get four hundred or five hundred in the [Monarchy of the] Netherlands — and those people are buying tickets" (230). How could that possibly be surprising to her? Has she never cracked open Richard Hofstadter's *Anti-Intellectualism in American Life* (1963)?[21] Or watched *Talladega Nights* (2006)? Or attended a Trump rally or watched a retransmission? If elections have consequences, so do long hours on the internet[22] that took over from the "boob tube," the collapse of hundreds of local newspapers[23] in the last twenty years, and inadequate and unequal school budgets[24] across many states, to name just three factors that might help explain the disparate crowd sizes.

---

21 It's important to note that Hofstadter's argument sees anti-intellectualism as partly a good thing because it's democracy's counterweight to the potential for experts and other educated elites to become dogmatic and arrogant — in a word, to be "anti-intellectual." For a look back at Hofstadter's Pulitzer Prize-winning study, see Nicholas Lemann, "The Tea Party is Timeless," *Columbia Journalism Review,* September/October 2014, https://archives.cjr.org/second_read/richard_hofstadter_tea_party.php.

22 See Nicholas Carr, *The Shallows: What the Internet Is Doing to Our Brains* (New York: W.W. Norton & Co., 2010). For an update on the damage surveyed ten years later, see Charlie Warzel, "I Talked to the Cassandra of the Internet Age," *The New York Times,* February 4, 2021, https://www.nytimes.com/2021/02/04/opinion/michael-goldhaber-internet.html.

23 See Margaret Sullivan, *Ghosting the News: Local Journalism and the Crisis of American Democracy* (New York: Columbia Global Reports, 2020), and Jacob S. Hacker and Paul Pierson, *Let Them Eat Tweets: How the Right Rules in an Age of Extreme Inequality* (New York: Liveright, 2020).

24 On the revolt against cuts in "red state" Oklahoma, see Rivka Galchen, "The Teachers' Strike and the Democratic Revival in Oklahoma," *The New Yorker,* May 28, 2018, https://www.newyorker.com/magazine/2018/06/04/the-teachers-strike-and-the-democratic-revival-in-oklahoma. Covid-19 spotlighted how America pretends to care about education and teachers, "essential workers," with starting average annual salaries of less than $40,000. See Colette Coleman, "The Case for Paying All Teachers Six Figures," *The New York Times,* May 28, 2021, https://www.nytimes.com/2021/05/28/opinion/teacher-pay-covid.html. In 2022 teachers went on strike to complain about grossly inadequate school funding in deep red Ohio.

If those two examples seem like nitpicky attacks on isolated moments of carelessness or wishful thinking, one might consider instead Nussbaum's two-page argument in favor of mandatory national service which she calls an "imperative" to solve a double problem: "because people don't meet one another across major divisions, they have a hard time thinking outside their economic or racial group toward a sense of common purpose" (241). American polarization and the self-sorting by zip code affordability and school district reduce the likelihood of mutual understanding, empathy building, or a sense that "we're all in this together"—which is why, near the end of my Tocqueville book, I too called for implementing "a flexible two-year mandatory national service requirement for men and women with military and nonmilitary options" (306). But former New York Congressman Charles Rangel introduced similar proposals in 2003, 2006, 2007, and 2010 and never gained serious amounts of support. Maybe someone should try again, but at the time 70 percent of Americans opposed the idea.[25] Undeterred, Nussbaum recommends three years not just two or one. But she offers no details about what these young people would be paid if anything, nor who would train and supervise them, or how it would be funded. Would this be an extension of the scam of low and unpaid internships—in effect slavery—now to be sold as one's patriotic duty? And how would she prevent a new generation of draft dodgers? Also, if she thinks it's such a good idea, why doesn't she say why Germany, a country she praises as "one of the more fear-resistant and balanced nations in Europe," abandoned obligatory service in 2011?[26] Nussbaum has not worked out the details, but she's convinced the idea is sound and that people will come around:

---

25 Recently, columnist David Brooks and Delaware Senator Chris Coons have also supported national service.
26 France abandoned its obligatory military or civil service by young men in 1997 during the presidency of Jacques Chirac.

I don't have a detailed plan. Some suitable entrepreneur [Elon Musk?] needs to do it, and since it is now politically unpopular, the first thing must be to sell it to people. The idea that we owe our country some of our work and our time is a very compelling idea if expressed well. The idea has roots in all the major religions and in secular ethics. In an era of shrinking government, we simply lack manpower to perform many essential services. (242)

If you say so, Professor Nussbaum, but something sounds fishy here, especially that last sentence where "an era of shrinking government" is evoked as though it were a natural disaster, like drought or locusts, instead of the result of hundreds of votes by lawmakers at the national, state, and local levels who have made the conscious decision to go along with anti-tax and anti-government propaganda that inevitably leads to budget short-falls and cuts in "essential services" and layoffs or pay-cuts for "essential workers" who fall ever further from earning a living wage and society overall becomes less healthy. Nussbaum herself underlined this in her 2010 manifesto: "Under pressure to cut costs, we prune away just those parts of the educational endeavor that are crucial to preserving a healthy society."[27]

That said, I still believe obligatory national service — military or nonmilitary by all Americans — could be part of a larger scheme (including automatic voter registration when you obtain a driver's license, for example, that likewise would be valid in all fifty states) to shore up the "rational patriotism" (the overlap between personal interest and general interest) that Tocqueville considered essential to guaranteeing high levels of participation in democratic institutions.[28] However, I believe it would need to be *phased in gradually* with realistic expectations

27 Nussbaum, *Not for Profit,* 142.
28 The refusal of many Americans to wear a mask during the Covid-19 pandemic is a reminder, along with perennial low voter-turnout, that solidarity in America is at an all-time low. Rational thinking and other basics Tocqueville took for granted — belief in Truth, Reality, and Common Sense — also seem to have declined in recent years.

(to start out, maybe just twelve flexible months of *decently paid* service performed between the ages of 18 and 38), *properly funded* through public–private partnerships (why not a partial real-location of police and military budgets and personnel working in collaboration with AmeriCorps, the Obama Foundation and the Carter Center perhaps, and other nonprofits or corporate sponsors), and *supervised* by qualified, passionate individuals with imagination and vision who could also serve as mentors to help participants integrate their service within a bigger picture of personal and professional development.

While waiting for the "suitable entrepreneur" who's going to take up the Rangel-Delogu-Nussbaum proposal and "sell it to people," other ways to combat America's extreme inequality and its *de facto* segregation by race and class might also be pursued: establishing affordable health insurance and health care as a universal human right (including for Black bodies!) and not a privilege; expanding to pre-kindergarten and postsecondary schooling the same longstanding belief that says K-12 public education is a collective, tuition-free, taxpayer-funded social responsibility toward every "citizen," and discarding the arbitrary, illogical, and mean-spirited view that considers pre-K and higher education to be optional pursuits paid for by the individual "customer"; pooling property taxes that fund public education at the state level, not at the municipal or county level, and then redistributing that money equitably so as to reduce grossly unfair budget disparities across school districts, and thereby hopefully dial down the anger, disgust, and envy that such disparities (especially harmful to minorities) perpetuate year after year in large and small cities throughout the country[29]; public marching on the first Saturday after tax day, April 15, to remind ourselves that we need to pay taxes for the public good and that tax eva-

---

29 See Nicholas Kristof's lament one year after the killing of George Floyd: "If Only There Were a Viral Video of Our Jim Crow Education System," *The New York Times,* May 21, 2021, https://www.nytimes.com/2021/05/21/opinion/sunday/education-racism-segregation.html.

sion is wrong.[30] These marches would celebrate the year's advances in social justice, criticize declines, and renew advocacy for a more perfect union and fairer tax code in the year to come. It's important to literally walk the walk shoulder to shoulder, and not simply talk the talk about walking the walk. American "slacktivism," particularly among Democrats, often forgets that. These and similar dignity and decency enhancing measures would all be working to make Roosevelt's visionary plan for a "Second Bill of Rights" — in effect, preventive medicine against the return of fascism — a reality.

I conclude by noting a harmonic convergence between the end of Nussbaum's post-Obama diagnosis of the American political crisis and the end of President Obama's pre-Trump manifesto, *The Audacity of Hope: Thoughts on Reclaiming the American Dream* (2006). Making use of her classical sources again, this time Cicero, Nussbaum puts the accent where it should be: on justice and on love. She notes, "we ought to serve the public good, so we had better become people who can stand to do that, not shrinking violets or the delicate unworldly philosopher" (244). Hear, hear! No justice, no peace. No accountability, no unity.[31] No unity, no love, no peace. Nussbaum continues:

> Throughout his all-too-short life, we see Cicero wrestling with his own fear, with fatigue, with stomach trouble, with the temptation to despair — and always coming out with renewed hope for committed service.
>
> It's partly about justice, but, as we understand when we read what he has to say about Rome, it's mostly about love. (245)

---

30 Noam Chomsky makes the case for tax day as a day of celebration in his video and book *Requiem for the American Dream: The 10 Principles of Concentration of Wealth and Power,* eds. Peter Hutchison, Kelly Nyks, and Jared P. Scott (New York: Seven Stories Press, 2017).

31 On the corrosiveness of low or no accountability in the US from the Civil War to the Capitol riot, see Jamelle Bouie, "America Punishes Only a Certain Kind of Rebel," *The New York Times,* July 13, 2021, https://www.nytimes.com/2021/07/13/opinion/jan-6-trump-impunity.html.

The end of Obama's second book, really an extension of where he left off in *Dreams from My Father* (1995), blends Rocky Balboa, Herman Roth, Abraham Lincoln, and Obama himself in a stirring lyrical moment at the stairs of the Lincoln Memorial that concludes with this sentence: "My heart is filled with love for this country."[32]

But for Obama, who grew up in faraway Hawaii and Indonesia, "this country" remains a somewhat abstract idea or set of symbols, as is clear from the preceding paragraph: it is "This nation's founders… And those like Lincoln and King… And all the faceless, nameless men and women, slaves and soldiers and tailors and butchers, constructing lives for themselves and their children and grandchildren, brick by brick, rail by rail, calloused hand by calloused hand."[33] Although one may wonder what he knows about calloused hands outside playing basketball, Obama's love feels genuine, despite also the dissonant adjectives "faceless" and "nameless," which makes it all the more disheartening that the country remained largely captive to "male, white, corporate oppression"[34] on his watch — and that upset a lot of people. The angry, disgusted, and fearful who voted for Trump in 2016 got one thing right, they chose a builder; but they chose a builder whose materials are fear, anger, disgust, envy, and hate. No building with such dark materials can last because as Lincoln said shortly before the Civil War erupted, "A house divided against itself cannot stand."

Those who love the United States and believe in democracy must hope that in future elections at all levels American voters will repair their mistakes and elect leaders who build in a spirit of universal love, dignity, and full personhood that can reverse the fifty-year trend of widening income and wealth inequality

---

32 Barack Obama, *The Audacity of Hope: Thoughts on Reclaiming the American Dream* (New York: Crown, 2006), 362.

33 For more on Obama's idea of hope, see Jelani Cobb, *The Substance of Hope: Barack Obama and the Paradox of Progress* (London: Walker Books, 2010). See also Steven Sarson, *Barack Obama: American Historian* (London: Bloomsbury Academic, 2018).

34 Sonic Youth, "Kool Thing," on *Goo* (DGC Records, 1990).

and renew the country's commitment to liberty and opportunity, justice and accountability for all. And do so in a way that is also more respectful of other species and the environment in general. But since racial and economic injustice were not built in a day, renovations and repairs will also take time. How much time exactly and in what spirit change takes place will depend on the courage and mobilization of those who recognize that repairs are needed, and on how they respond when confronted with the inertia or active resistance of others who see things differently or even prefer the status quo. Nussbaum's manifesto usefully reminds us that no blueprint for "reinventing American democracy for the twenty-first century"[35] will get far without taking into account the depth of fear among the vulnerable, and inviting those wounded or skittish individuals back into the collaborative, interdependent work of shaping their communities and their own lives. If the invitation is genuine and delivered without hypocrisy or condescension, there's reason to hope that a majority will prefer a democracy of trust and confidence over a monarchy of fear.

---

35 American Academy of Arts and Sciences, "Our Common Purpose: Reinventing American Democracy for the 21st Century" (Cambridge: American Academy of Arts and Sciences, 2020), https://www.amacad.org/ourcommonpurpose/report. Among democracy advocates, see Jan-Werner Müller, *Democracy Rules* (New York: Farrar, Straus & Giroux, 2021).

10

How Extreme Inequality Poisons Everything

Keith Payne, *The Broken Ladder: How Inequality Affects the Way We Think, Live, and Die* (2017)

I first read about Keith Payne's *The Broken Ladder* (2017) in an editorial by Nicholas Kristof from June 3, 2017 entitled "What Monkeys Can Teach Us About Fairness."[1] Impressed by Payne's book, I later added it to the syllabus of my seminar on social classes, and I see from some reader reviews on Amazon that I'm not the only professor to have done so. It has 81 percent five-star ratings, including praise from President Obama: "A persuasive and highly readable account." Payne's book is as good or bet-

---

1   Keith Payne, *The Broken Ladder: How Inequality Affects the Way We Think, Live, and Die* (New York: Viking, 2017). Hereafter cited parenthetically throughout chapter. The opinion pages are today's way station between academia and "the street." I always tell my students to read editorials and comments threads from different points of view to become familiar with the arguments and rhetoric around any current problem. I am grateful to Nicholas Kristof and all the journalists and professors whose writings are quoted and referenced in this book.

ter than a similar manifesto from five years earlier, *The Price of Inequality* (2012) by Nobel Prize-winning economist Joseph Stiglitz. There is no shortage of books that all explain "How Today's Divided Society Endangers Our Future," the subtitle of the Stiglitz book.[2] But in half as many pages, Payne zeros in on what is most relevant for understanding the current political crisis in the US, especially its flirtation with fascism, its sixty years of lip service to Martin Luther King Jr.'s dream to reduce racial inequality, and its ever-worsening income and wealth inequality. The focus of Payne's study is "How Inequality Affects the Way We Think, Live, and Die." He examines the pain caused when extreme inequality, which he shows most Americans disapprove of and underestimate by wide margins, scrambles the decision-making faculty of vulnerable people especially but also of the middle and upper classes. Extreme inequality increases arrogance, erodes empathy, and provokes higher levels of polarization, talking at cross purposes, and political gridlock. Among the especially vulnerable, it causes higher levels of reckless risk-taking and self-destructive behavior — a "live fast, die young" mentality and a lawless, "fuck it," "screw you" attitude.

Payne is a professor of psychology looking at the US political crisis, and as such he is comfortable with math like the economist Stiglitz, but he also considers emotional states and their translation into actions to be indispensable for a rich understanding of the problem at hand. This brings him close to Nussbaum's psychology-informed philosophy and to the interdisciplinary approach of Fromm, David Hume, and the Adam Smith of *The Theory of Moral Sentiments* (1759).[3] *The Broken Ladder* is the first effort of a hungry, young professor, perhaps his tenure

---

2   Chapters 5 and 6, "A Democracy in Peril" and "1984 Is upon Us" support my argument. Stiglitz's account of fairness is close to Payne's argument but lacks the discussion of worker sabotage as payback for unfairness.

3   For an introduction to this work which is unjustly overshadowed by his more famous *An Inquiry into the Nature and Causes of the Wealth of Nations* (1776), see *Stanford Encyclopedia of Philosophy*, s.v. "Adam Smith's Moral and Political Philosophy," https://plato.stanford.edu/entries/smith-moral-political/.

book and not the sunset thoughts of a senior professor. Payne is eager to have his points be clear and catchy, argued, and backed up by lots of experiments by colleagues who are all duly named and referenced in footnotes strategically placed at the end so as not to break up Payne's narrative flow. He's a good storyteller with a lean light touch — so much so that the enjoyment one takes in reading his summaries of experiments and his takeaway from each could outshine the grave implications of what his book is exposing; namely that extreme inequality is largely responsible for breaking the American Dream and endangering the health, physical and mental, of all Americans, some more severely and permanently than others.

The broken ladder metaphor refers first to the breakdown of social mobility between quintiles from the wealthiest 20 percent to the lowest and is graphically represented early on page 8 where one sees that income for the lower four quintiles has stagnated for fifty years, and even the top 20 percent have only experienced modest gains. It is only the top 5 percent, 1 percent, 0.1 percent, and 0.01 percent that have experienced significant increases; and income inequality, which exacerbates wealth inequality, is largely to blame.[4] Today there is more chance of moving between quintiles over the course of one's working years in a low-inequality country such as Denmark than in the United

4   Payne's information repeats what has been widely reported by Stiglitz, Paul Krugman, Eduardo Porter, Robert Reich, and others for more than a decade now. Kristof relays one of Payne's illuminating findings; namely that when asked to design income distribution between quintiles, roughly 90 percent of Americans come up with something that resembles the present-day reality of low inequality social-democratic Sweden. Payne also reports that Americans of all backgrounds and affiliations generally believe that top executives should earn no more than four to five times as much as basic workers in a given company, while also admitting that they believe that the true figure is regrettably something like thirty times more — not realizing that their estimate of the disproportion is off by a factor of ten because American CEOs earn on average 350 times what the entry-level employee earns. Payne, *The Broken Ladder,* 194. Payne's goal is to get the news out about the size of income inequality and about the extent of the societal harm, and not just at the bottom, caused by extreme inequality.

States or other high-inequality countries where the rung you are born on is probably going to be the rung you stay on — if you're lucky enough to avoid falling down a rung or two. Payne also shows that income and wealth inequality imperils the spiritual side of the American Dream as well; in other words, the aspirational values of fairness, a level playing field, due process, transparency, and trust in "the arc of the moral universe" that is supposed to be bending toward justice. All those (democratic) values — sometimes unrealistically inflated and therefore a setup for failure as Payne, also a fan of Melvin Lerner's debunking of the just universe fallacy, notes — have eroded in the last forty years. Those values have often been replaced by feelings of resentment and distrust as the vulnerable come to feel that everything is "rigged" and that "I'm never gonna have nothing, so I gotta do what I'm gonna do now" (81), as Keith's older brother Jason, a "live fast, die young" risk-taker, says one day while lighting himself a pot pipe and careening down small roads to avoid a traffic jam on the highway.

Payne, like Nussbaum and Jason Stanley too, skillfully uses a few personal stories to make his points more vivid. But Payne didn't need to go abroad to experience vulnerability. He grew up in a high-inequality state, Kentucky, in a family that one senses was teetering between lower-middle-class and poor (Payne received subsidized school lunches, he tells us). Nearly every chapter contains something he has lived personally, not just read about in books and lab reports. He deftly balances personal anecdote with abundant empirical evidence and thereby avoids having his argument carried solely by his "street cred" while still having his family history be a persuasive supplement to his rigorous scientific method.

One example, especially relevant to the summer of 2020 and the surge of interest in white privilege and anti-Black implicit bias after the killing of George Floyd, comes in his chapter 7 entitled, "Inequality in Black and White: The Dangerous Dance of Racial and Economic Inequality." What Payne means by the dance metaphor is that racial and economic inequality are "intertwined" (174). He openly states what many have suspected in the ten years since a watered down version of President Obama's signature piece of legislation, the Affordable Care Act, finally made it through Congress in 2010, followed by repeated Republican efforts to discredit, wreck, and repeal it: "Many people simply don't feel very motivated to support fighting poverty when they imagine that minorities will be the beneficiaries" (174).[5] This is the conclusion to several argued pages that present the persistence of anti-Black implicit bias, including his own. Payne, who is white, was and probably still is upset by white-on-Black police violence, and he relates how after an incident similar to the shooting of Philando Castile in 2016 (Payne uses instead the Levar Jones incident of 2014, but also mentions Michael Brown, Amadou Diallo, Eric Garner, and Tamir Rice), he set out to design an experiment to test "whether the average person was more likely to believe that a harmless object was a dangerous weapon when it was paired with a black person" (164). The answer is "Yes!" and he's mortified that he himself, the designer of the experiment, tested positive for implicit anti-Black bias too. Payne then relates how he received opposing reactions to his published research: an email from a retired police officer concerned that Payne's findings could be used to categorically condemn officers who may be "forced to make life-or-death decisions in a fraction of a second under complex and uncertain conditions"; and an email from a civil rights activist concerned that defense

---

5   This was a bold declaration in 2017 but has become more common. See Erin Aubry Kaplan's post-George Floyd editorial, "Everyone's an Antiracist, Now What?" *The New York Times,* July 6, 2020, https://www.nytimes.com/2020/07/06/opinion/antiracism-what-comes-next.html: "The last large-scale effort aimed at improving Black lives was the war on poverty back in the 1960s, and the backlash to that was swift and relentless. In some ways, we're still living it. Critics of the war on poverty didn't object just to money being spent, they objected to the notion of helping Black folks specifically because they were not worth helping, at least not to that degree. The idea of Black well-being being worth only so much became so embedded in our political life, we stopped seeing it." Kaplan calls recognizing Black humanity as Step 1 in a 12-step program to recover from a national addiction to injustice and to convenience — the idea that everything must be cheap, easy, and painless.

lawyers will use Payne's research in ways that "might exonerate police officers rather than holding them responsible for biased actions" (166–67). Payne wants his reader to see the dilemma his experiment reveals, and he concludes: "This is the paradox of implicit bias, where actions are uncoupled from intentions, and we don't know where to aim our moral outrage." For the next six pages Payne initiates his reader into a "more nuanced approach" to the problem than is commonly pursued by those who rush to either condemn or exonerate "blue lives." At the end of those pages comes the "Many people simply don't feel very motivated" comment cited above which is consistent with the sharply worded *New York Times* editorial by kihana miraya ross from June 4, 2020 following the police killing of George Floyd: "Call It What It is: Anti-Blackness."[6] The editorial's main claim is that the humanity or personhood of Black individuals has not yet been fully achieved in the United States, and Payne's book about the unreasonable behavior of reasonable people in

---

6   kihana miraya ross, "Call It What It is: Anti-Blackness," *The New York Times*, June 4, 2020, https://www.nytimes.com/2020/06/04/opinion/george-floyd-anti-blackness.html. The definition offered by ross joins up with Nussbaum's discussion of projective disgust: "The word 'racism' is everywhere. It's used to explain all the things that cause African Americans' suffering and death: inadequate access to health care, food, housing and jobs, or a police bullet, baton, or knee. But 'racism' fails to fully capture what black people in this country are facing. The right term is 'anti-blackness.' To be clear, 'racism' isn't a meaningless term. But it's a catch-all that can encapsulate anything from black people being denied fair access to mortgage loans, to Asian students being burdened with a 'model minority' label. It's not specific. Many Americans, awakened by watching footage of Derek Chauvin killing George Floyd by kneeling on his neck, are grappling with why we live in a world in which black death loops in a tragic screenplay, scored with the wails of childless mothers and the entitled indifference of our murderers. And an understanding of anti-blackness is the only place to start. Anti-blackness is one way some black scholars have articulated what it means to be marked as black in an anti-black world. It's more than just 'racism against black people.' That oversimplifies and defangs it. It's a theoretical framework that illuminates society's inability to recognize our humanity — the disdain, disregard and disgust for our existence." We will return to this editorial's argument in the Jason Stanley chapter and our Conclusion.

stressful, vulnerable circumstances backs up that claim. Put another way, Payne's findings lead one to ask, is it realistic to expect Black personhood to have been achieved by 2020 when one recalls that slavery existed in America for 250 years, was only terminated about 150 years ago, and the civil rights movement's reassertion of the 1863 Emancipation Proclamation occurred only a little over fifty years ago? And yet, he concludes, one can and ought to "look forward" to the possibility of truly equal personhood:

> We have seen in previous chapters how the social comparisons we make can alter how we see the world. That also holds true for how we understand racial inequality. The gulf between the view of white and black citizens about current levels of prejudice reflects not only different daily experiences, but also different kinds of comparisons, according to research led by psychologist Richard Eibach. If you ask white respondents how well the country is doing in overcoming racism, they look to the past as a frame of reference. Compared with the bad old days of slavery and Jim Crow, we seem to be making good progress, they will assert. But if you ask black respondents the same question, they look to the future: Compared with what life would be like in a country with true equality, the current situation looks fairly bleak.
>
> White and black people don't inhabit completely different worlds, however. The researchers found that if you invite black and white participants to make the kinds of comparisons the other group tends to make, they end up agreeing. If you urge blacks to think about how bad their status was in the past, then their assessments of the present become more optimistic. And if you encourage whites to imagine what a future with true equality would look like, they become less satisfied and more motivated to change the status quo. Consider this chapter an invitation to look forward. (175)

I bet Barack Obama, whose mother was white it should be remembered, nodded in agreement at the end of those two paragraphs since Payne is repeating here the same hopeful invitation Obama articulated many times from his "More Perfect Union" Philadelphia campaign trail speech from March 18, 2008 to his June 3, 2020 video remarks during the Covid-19 confinement following the killing of George Floyd. The message is the same: there is more common ground than those who benefit from rancor and division would have us believe; and while there's lots of room for improvement, progress toward true equality has happened and, it is reasonable to believe, will continue to happen.

Payne's mediating, peacemaker stance is one of the most valuable aspects of his book, especially because it is data-driven and not idle hope. Pointing out that the American Dream is now broken and unattainable for many people is hardly news.[7] He is also not the first to relay the findings of "spirit level" authors Richard Wilkinson and Kate Pickett who argued back in 2009 that income and wealth inequality was more responsible than poverty for a range of health and social problems.[8] Just as Nussbaum exposes many destructive side-effects of fear, Payne exposes negative mental habits — not just the health and social problems — that develop out of extreme inequality and overly tall hierarchies, and how they lead to regrettable decisions by rich and poor alike. His book's opening anecdote about the airplane rage of first-class passenger Ivana Trump (the only Trump mentioned in the entire book) and coach passenger Joseph Sharkey pointedly illustrates Payne's main claim. Following

---

7   See Johanna Perraudin, "What Is Left of the American Dream? — Taking Stock of America's 'Broken' Society" (unpublished MA thesis, Université Jean Moulin-Lyon 3, 2021).

8   The Wilkinson and Pickett charts were reproduced in many publications at the time, such as Tony Judt's deathbed manifesto *Ill Fares the Land: Essays on Food, Hunger, and Power* (New York: Penguin Books, 2010), but it's understandable that Payne would use them too since they advance his argument. See Richard Wilkinson and Kate Pickett, *The Spirit Level: Why More Equal Societies Almost Always Do Better* (London: Allen Lane, 2009). The book was also published with different subtitles: "Why Greater Equality Makes Societies Stronger" (Bloomsbury Academic) and "Why Equality Is Better for Everyone" (Penguin Books).

the epidemiologists Wilkinson and Pickett, Payne shows how inequality messes with the brains of the wealthy (by encouraging dubious feelings of entitlement and superiority) and of the poor/er (by encouraging dubious feelings of resentment and rage).[9] This brain scrambling tips both groups toward believing righteously in their invincibility or their victimhood and seeking payment or payback accordingly. Payne concludes the story with this thesis statement:

> [W]hen the level of inequality becomes too large to ignore, everyone starts acting strange. But they do not act strange in just any old way. Inequality affects our actions and our feelings in the same systematic, predictable fashion again and again. It makes us [1] short-sighted [2] prone to risky behavior, [3] willing to sacrifice a secure future for immediate gratification. [4] It makes us more inclined to make self-defeating decisions. [5] It makes us believe weird things, superstitiously clinging to the world as we want it to be rather than as it is. [6] Inequality divides us, cleaving us into camps not only of income but also of ideology and race, [7] eroding our trust in one another. [8] It generates stress and makes us all [9] less healthy and [10] less happy. (4)

Payne will fill in his canvas with many examples later, but at this stage the reader can free associate when hearing "self-defeating decisions" and the nine other strange ways on Payne's list. For example, some might think in Thomas Frank "What's the Matter with Kansas?" fashion that it is completely irrational and self-defeating for angry Midwesterners, who are said to distrust coastal elites, to throw a Hail Mary pass by voting for Donald Trump, a coastal elite — as though a narcissistic New Yorker and

---

9   This problem is sometimes analyzed as the meritocracy myth (Robert Frank, Stephen McNamee), meritocracy trap (Daniel Markovits), or the tyranny of merit (Michael Sandel). On destructive rage since Covid-19 and the Capitol riot, see Sarah Lyall, "A Nation on Hold Wants to Speak with a Manager," *The New York Times,* January 1, 2022, https://www.nytimes.com/2022/01/01/business/customer-service-pandemic-rage.html.

silver-spoon heir to papa's millions would be capable of know-ing or caring about their lives let alone advancing their true in-terests back in Washington. But wealthy, powerful, highly edu-cated people can also shoot themselves in the foot. Just ask Yale Law School graduate Hillary Clinton, whose 1992 gaffe about not staying home to bake cookies handicapped her husband's presidency (though her Rhodes Scholar husband did plenty of dumb things all on his own). Later, Hillary Clinton's 2016 "de-plorables" snub, along with totally ignoring the swing state of Wisconsin, harmed her presidential campaign; as did Harvard Law School graduate Barack Obama's ill-judged revival of his "cling to guns or religion" analysis of what's the matter with the "bitter" Trump supporter.[10] Payne argues that extreme inequali-ty provokes a derangement syndrome across all socio-economic categories, it's just that the wealthy and powerful can buy and spin their way out of their mistakes while the bad choices of lower income people can do lasting damage or even be fatal.[11]

Payne expands on all ten items in the above list of symp-toms in nonpartisan ways and without the least mention of Donald Trump, populism, or fascism. The example of spiteful

10 Journalist Janell Ross saw early on that this was an example of putting the same foot back in your mouth: "Obama Revives His 'Cling to Guns or Religion' Analysis — For Donald Trump Supporters," *The Washing-ton Post,* December 21, 2015, https://www.washingtonpost.com/news/the-fix/wp/2015/12/21/obama-dusts-off-his-cling-to-guns-or-religion-idea-for-donald-trump/. Clinton and Obama's comments are examples of a larger problem called "virtue signaling." See Jane Coaston (and the comments thread), "'Virtue Signaling' Isn't the Problem. Not Believing One Another Is," *The New York Times,* April 8, 2017, https://www.nytimes.com/2017/08/08/magazine/virtue-signaling-isnt-the-problem-not-believ-ing-one-another-is.html, and Geoffrey Miller, *Virtue Signaling: Essays on Darwinian Politics and Free Speech* (n.p.: Cambrian Moon, 2019). On a related topic, see Nancy Leong, *Identity Capitalists: The Powerful Insiders Who Exploit Diversity to Maintain Inequality* (Stanford: Stanford Univer-sity Press, 2021).

11 During the Covid-19 pandemic, Trump could repeat as often as he liked that the virus would "sort of just disappear," while also being tested every day or week and receiving the best care when sick; ordinary people who shared his belief and scorned social distancing and masks got sick too and many died.

short-sightedness ("cutting off your nose to spite your face") that caught Kristof's attention, and mine, is the case of monkeys who'd risen to trading stones for grapes and then became resentful when they were downgraded to again receiving measly cucumber slices and would throw them back at the experimenter's face in protest (at the risk of going hungry, 21). Without exactly spelling out the connection, Payne loops back to the monkeys in his penultimate chapter on "The Corporate Ladder: Why Fair Pay Signals Fair Play" with more than one story about how some higher primates, who feel slighted by a company's imposition of "belt-tightening" on low-level workers instead of calling for across-the-board sacrifices by everyone, will use various retaliatory techniques — even ones that harm themselves such as stealing or sabotage — to establish a rough justice of their own making (190). We can extrapolate from Payne's example and observe that in the fall of 2016, a less vulnerable person sees a good reason to vote for the candidate of the Democratic Party that engineered the recovery from the 2008 Great Recession; but a more vulnerable individual who resents that most of the recovery benefitted the wealthy, as was widely reported,[12] might be willing to take a chance on the person least involved in the "fake news" of that so-called recovery, even if it means voting for a morally suspect and mentally unstable candidate with zero governing experience.[13] Take your pick why: racism, mi-

---

12 Robert Kuttner relays studies that show "Just twenty counties, with only 2 percent of the US population, accounted for half of all the new business growth in the recovery," *Can Democracy Survive Global Capitalism?* (New York: W.W. Norton & Co., 2018), 5.

13 Jamelle Bouie essentially expresses the Tocqueville paradox when he observes that in 2016 the relatively improved economic situation for many if not all households gave those who still felt aggrieved an opportunity to act out: "good times may bring some voters to feel that they can afford to vote their resentments." "Maybe This Isn't Such a Good Time to Prosecute a Culture War," *The New York Times,* July 7, 2020, https://www.nytimes.com/2020/07/07/opinion/trump-mount-rushmore-culture-war.html. In this editorial published four months before the 2020 election, Bouie believed that with the deepening economic crisis, voters only want good governance and cannot afford a second round of Trump performing their fantasies of unrestrained id.

sogyny, score-settling, feelings of dignity loss and humiliation[14], or because as Michael Caine, playing the wise butler, says dryly to Bruce Wayne in *The Dark Knight* (2008), "Some men aren't looking for anything logical, like money. They can't be bought, bullied, reasoned, or negotiated with. Some men just want to watch the world burn."[15] It would seem there are a sizeable number of such vulnerable pyromaniacs in the Midwest (and other high-inequality places) going back at least to the journalist William Allen White and his original tirade "What's the Matter with Kansas?" from 1896. But that angry editorial — O cursed fate! — is said to have helped elect President William McKinley whose political views were the opposite of White's progressive preferences. This would be no surprise to Payne whose readings and experiments have given him an appreciation of irony as sharp as that of any historian or post-structuralist literary critic.

Rather than speak of irony, however, Payne prefers the term "mismatch" (27) to characterize how human behaviors that evolved over thousands of years — such as cravings for status, attention, sugar, salt, and fat — are often ill-adapted to contemporary circumstances in many parts of the world. Making endless upward comparisons ("keeping up with the Joneses") can get in our way by distracting us from values (such as love, faith, loyalty, honesty, integrity) that surveys show we care about more than mere status or attention. Similarly, too much sugar and fat make us obese now that calories are plentiful and most of us are more sedentary than fulltime hunters or farmers, and therefore we don't need to stock up to prepare for times of scarcity and prolonged physical exertion like our ancestors did. Payne also uses "mismatch" to describe how stress used to be the body's

---

14 Thomas Friedman, "Who Can Win America's Politics of Humiliation?" *The New York Times,* September 8, 2020, https://eu.registerguard.com/story/opinion/columns/2020/09/11/friedman-who-can-win-americas-politics-humiliation/5765607002/.

15 Anne Frank made a similar observation on May 3, 1944: "There's a destructive urge in people, the urge to rage, murder, and kill." Quoted in Cynthia Ozick, "Who Owns Anne Frank?" *The New Yorker,* October 6, 1997, https://www.newyorker.com/magazine/1997/10/06/who-owns-anne-frank.

own medicine cabinet that would help one get through scrapes such as a surprise attack by a wild animal, but now the same molecules cause serious complications, an example he gives is "stress dwarfism":

> Our ancestors could lie awake in their caves worrying about tomorrow just as we do. But for them, the downsides of stress were massively outweighed by its benefits. Unlike our ancestors, we are now fortunate to live long enough to succumb more often to the diseases of old age, rather than to predators in the grass. The downside of that trade is that the side effects of stress can be more harmful in the contemporary environment than the threats it evolved to protect us from. Today in economically developed countries, some of the most common causes of death are heart disease, stroke, and diabetes, all of which can be caused or worsened by stress. Now that fewer organisms are able to kill us, we are left with a cure that may be worse than the disease. (126–28)

In a further turn of the screw, Payne, who knows about Case and Deaton's work on so-called "deaths of despair" (120–21), offers a less melodramatic description of today's stressors than those relayed in bestselling diagnoses of the plight of today's down and out white man such as *Hillbilly Elegy* (2016) or *Strangers in Their Own Land* (2016):

> The wounds in this group [especially middle-aged white men without a college degree] seem to be largely self-inflicted. They are not dying from higher rates of heart disease or cancer. They are dying of cirrhosis of the liver, suicide, and a cycle of chronic pain and overdoses of opiates and painkillers.
> The trend itself is striking because it speaks to the power of subjective social comparisons. This demographic group is dying of violated expectations. Although high school-educated whites make more money on average than similarly educated blacks, the whites expect more because of their history of privilege. Widening income inequality and stagnant

social mobility, Case and Deaton suggest, mean that this generation is likely to be the first in American history that is not more affluent than its parents. [...] Just as our decisions and actions prioritize short-term gains over longer-term interests when in a crisis, the body has a sophisticated mechanism that adopts the same strategy. This crisis management system [the stress response] is specifically designed to save you now, even if it has to shorten your life to do so. (121)

Notice how Payne gets his point across without the misleading pathos of the word "despair": *This demographic group is dying of violated expectations,* Payne states plainly and then discreetly leaves the reader to decide if this is a legitimate complaint about those "cutting in line" and "getting out of hand," or instead another inappropriate "mismatch" if one believes — contrary to white supremacy thinking and reflexes — that women and minorities, including the gender nonconforming and the disabled, do deserve full personhood and therefore the same right to life, liberty, and the pursuit of happiness as anyone else.[16]

Payne's account is so engrossing one wants to repeat all his stories like so many enthusiastic retweets. I will relay just three more and then conclude with Payne's pragmatic recommendations about how to escape from the crazy-making consequences of extreme inequality and excessive upward comparison. First is his explanation of where the "live fast, die young" mentality comes from. The answer is that it evolved over many generations, and not just in humans, as an alternate "strategy" in times of scarcity. If certain behaviors make it more likely you will pass on your genes to a next generation, even if that's not your conscious goal, more people who lean toward those behaviors will be born and in turn have a greater chance to produce heirs, and so on. Two successful types of conduct have evolved, says Payne: the conservative strategy is to play by the rules over the

---

16 On the high cost of dehumanization and not extending full personhood to all, see Eduardo Porter, *American Poison: How Racial Hostility Destroyed Our Promise* (New York: Alfred A. Knopf, 2020).

long-term, amass wealth, and eventually give one's heirs a leg up (think Big Daddy in *Cat on a Hot Tin Roof*); the second "Hail Mary longshot strategy," let's call it, occurs when the chances of amassing significant wealth are low or zero.[17] Then it pays to be status-obsessed, attention-getting, and sexually promiscuous at a young age even if that means running up debts, excessive gambling, making enemies, committing crimes, getting abused, or betraying friends, family, or coworkers (think of dead, young rap artists, or of Jennifer Lopez's character in the movie *Hustlers* [2019] based on a true story). Payne avoids cultural references, however, and instead relates how bees who are food insecure tend to seek out flowers with a more random — very high or very low — amount of nectar instead of going to the flowers with a reliable, medium-amount of nectar which are the preferred food source for less stressed-out bees who are eating normally. It turns out bees and other species, notably humans, have evolved to be incautious and gamble on longshots when faced with long-term, erratic vulnerability. This and other "birds and bees" stories appear in Payne's chapter "Poor Logic," which flows well into his next chapter about how high inequality exacerbates polarization and may even be contributing to sectarianism.[18]

The polarization chapter contains a better answer, because devoid of condescension, to the recurring "What's the matter with Kansas?" inquiry into why it seems low-income people vote against their own self-interest. First Payne uses studies conducted in Sweden to claim that "choice blindness" is a real thing; and then shifts to the American context where he concludes, "people have almost no idea whether government programs are in their economic interest" (104). What seems often uppermost in people's minds, studies show, is that when people feel rela-

---

17   Also known as "gambling for resurrection," which is discussed along with two other desperate ideas by Peter Coy in an editorial on Vladimir Putin's 2022 invasion of Ukraine, "Here Are Three Reasons Putin Might Fight On," *The New York Times,* March 14, 2022, https://www.nytimes.com/2022/03/14/opinion/putin-rational-irrational.html.

18   Eli J. Finkel et al., "Political Sectarianism in America," *Science* 370, no. 6516 (October 30, 2020): 533–36.

tively rich (let's say earning $100,000 per year in high-inequality Mississippi) they will be less supportive of progressive taxation and redistribution than if they feel relatively poor (let's say with the same $100,000 annual income but in a high cost-of-living area such as Manhattan), in which case they are more likely to favor progressive taxation and government transfers via food stamps, subsidized housing, and the like. One's perceptions regarding extreme income and wealth gaps exacerbate political polarization, Payne argues:

> We've seen so far that people tend to vote for policies that they feel are in their self-interest whether they actually are or not. And we've seen that what feels to be in their self-interest depends on how they compare with other people. As the haves and the have-nots grow further apart, we can expect the effects of social comparisons to weigh more and more heavily. Taken together, these observations suggest that the rise in inequality that has occurred over the past few decades might be contributing to increasingly intense partisanship and political conflict.

Not only is Payne's analysis refreshingly free of condescension, it also avoids essentialist thinking, as though the problem were something debilitating in the genes, water, or diet of Kansans. Instead, Payne focuses on the detrimental fact that Kansas is a relatively high-inequality state, and this matters more than whether it's a rich or poor state. However, being roughly in the middle (eighteenth out of fifty), Kansas has a better chance of avoiding self-inflicted wounds than the crazy-making tendencies in the higher income inequality states that stretch across the entire south from Florida (the forty-sixth) to Texas (the thirty-nineth) to Arizona (the thirty-first).[19] Payne's chapter also gives a better answer to the provenance of what Jonathan Haidt has called the "righteous mind," a mindset whose vehemence, like

---

19 The rankings correspond to the Gini index of inequality of the states: 1 = least unequal; 50 = most unequal.

political polarization, also tracks consistently with income inequality and results in the tendency to think in terms of a superior "us" and an inferior "them."[20] Why? Because, writes Payne, experiments show that "something about feeling superior in profits made people feel superior to other players about their opinions, too" (109).

Payne follows up that observation with a mix of humor and sober testimony that goes far to explain, and not just evoke as Paxton did, that extreme inequality is what heats up the "emotional lava" that can give rise to fascism:

We have a tendency to think that people who agree with us are brilliant and insightful, and that those who disagree with us could use a little help in seeing reality for what it is. As George Carlin put it, "Have you ever noticed that anybody driving slower than you is an idiot, and anyone going faster than you is a maniac?" This propensity to believe that we see the world accurately, while anyone who has a different opinion is benighted, fuels conflicts. As psychologist Lee Ross has argued, if I see the world as it is and you disagree with me, then I have only a few possible interpretations of your behavior: You might be incompetent, you might be irrational, or you might be evil. Whatever the case, I can't reason with you. (109)

What Payne goes on to demonstrate in the chapter devoted to "God, Conspiracies, and the Language of Angels" is that when faced with incomprehensible words, deeds, or phenomena, the powerless are more likely to *manufacture* meaningful (to them) explanatory patterns to account for what they are hearing or seeing. As income equality worsens, by definition that means more people are feeling less powerful and in control, and therefore are becoming more susceptible to inventing and believing "useful delusions" (Shankar Vedantam), relaying conspiracy

---

20 Jonathan Haidt, *The Righteous Mind: Why Good People Are Divided by Politics and Religion* (New York: Random House, 2012).

theories, magical thinking, and supernatural explanations, as well as doubting experts (now dubbed "so-called experts"), denigrating scientific methods, and showing a willingness to select or go along with the selection of scapegoats for dehumanization, victimization, and exclusion. But as we've said before, and Payne underscores, these tendencies can crop up in the thinking of the upper classes too, whether it's Trump's seemingly sincere belief that Covid-19 will "sort of just disappear" or the neoliberal blind faith in the magical efficiency of the "invisible hand" of so-called "free markets."[21] There is the additional problem that the wealthy have powerful tools to be superspreaders of whatever unproven theories cross their minds or newsfeeds, which is why there has been heated debate about whether all posts on social media should be treated equally, or if a certain category of high influencer needs to have their content held to a higher standard of verification and flagging.[22]

Payne's book was published at an earlier stage of the US political and social crisis (pre-Brett Kavanaugh theatrics, pre-Trump impeachments, pre-Covid-19), but his concluding argument in favor of building "flatter ladders" — by reducing income and wealth inequality and "comparing with care" with more mindful and less destructive comparisons between oneself and others — is worth remembering and acting on. In 1835, Tocqueville observed that expanding *equality* of social conditions was the *fait mère* (the "mother fact") that made democracy possible, since it's only with a sizeable middle class that one can build a rough consensus and a common project around shared aspirations. A *consensus* and a *common purpose* may sound quaint today given the mutual hostility in red versus blue America and the eye-popping representations of just how extreme economic inequality has become, such as Payne's Figure 1 on page 6 show-

---

21 See Mehrsa Baradaran, "The Neoliberal Looting of America," *The New York Times*, July 2, 2020, https://www.nytimes.com/2020/07/02/opinion/private-equity-inequality.html.

22 See Shira Ovide, "Bogus Ideas Have Superspreaders, Too," *The New York Times*, July 1, 2020, https://www.nytimes.com/2020/07/01/technology/social-media-superspreaders.html.

ing US income distribution scaled to the height of a human. But does anyone doubt that those two notions, consensus and the common, along with two other c-words, *compromise* and *compassion* are necessary if the United States, or any society experiencing authoritarianization and fascist impulses, is ever to regain its footing as a functioning and basically healthy and happy democratic republic?

With or without the authority of Tocqueville, there is a general consensus that expanding *inequality* of social conditions is the single greatest factor contributing to the breakdown of democracy in the United States and around the world. And that breakdown is cheered on by democracy skeptics and leaders of anti-democratic regimes who are spared the trouble of having to argue in favor of authoritarianism if all it takes is pointing to the allegedly self-inflicted breakdown of democracy to persuade people that they are incapable of self-governance and need a Big Brother.[23] Autocrats and those fond of empire mock or ignore calls for equality, a concept which is entirely foreign to their vertical, domination-obsessed way of thinking. But it should be noted that nobody who criticizes extreme inequality is calling for perfect equality, a state which has never existed nor could it or should it since everyone is a unique individual from the cradle to the grave. Nevertheless, recognizing extreme inequality as a public health problem, as Payne recommends, and work-

---

23 The best summary of how authoritarians win when democracy fails is Timothy Snyder's description of Russia's foreign policy tactic of "strategic relativism": "Russia cannot become stronger, so it must make others weaker. The simplest way to make others weaker is to make them more like Russia. Rather than addressing its problems, Russia exports them; and one of its basic problems is the absence of a succession principle. Russia opposes European and American democracy to ensure that Russians do not see that democracy might work as a succession principle in their own country. Russians are meant to distrust other systems as much as they distrust their own. If Russia's succession crisis can in fact be exported — if the United States could become authoritarian — then Russia's own problems, although unresolved, would at least seem normal." *The Road to Unfreedom: Russia, Europe, and America* (New York: Tim Duggan Books, 2018), 249.

ing to reduce current levels of extreme economic inequality to a level that Americans, when asked, overwhelmingly consider to be normal and acceptable — ironically a setup similar to what exists in "socialist" Sweden — would be a realistic and salutary goal achievable in the near-term.

Payne's second recommendation is predicated on the idea that even if we have evolved in such a way that we generally "crave status," we can learn to avoid comparing ourselves to others in ways that are likely to harm us and instead compare wisely in ways that will help us negotiate "living vertically" in an unequal world that inevitably includes wins and losses, acceptance and rejection, and an unequal distribution of beauty (or what passes for beauty), connections, attention, love, inherited wealth, physical and mental abilities and disabilities, drive, and luck. Payne recommends a pragmatic mix of downward and upward comparisons depending on one's mood and circumstances. Downward comparisons, including those of the "There but for the grace of God go I" type, allow one to cultivate gratitude without falling into negative complacency. Upward comparisons can incite the desire to emulate and the ambition to seek out role models and shoot for the performance level of some higher up individual whom one admires, but with more constructive realism and less destructive envy. Payne says that this mindful style of comparing — what Martin Luther King Jr. called harnessing the "drum major instinct" for good rather than yielding to its negative "exclusivism" — can help one acknowledge the unequal amounts of work, merit, and sheer luck related to different personal circumstances and outcomes. It may also return one to meditating on what's truly meaningful, about which surveys show there is not polarization but in fact broad agreement, despite what newsfeeds and advertisers who profit off endless adolescent bickering and competition would have us think: "Making the conscious effort to consider what genuinely matters interrupts the unconscious default pattern of looking to others to gauge how much we value ourselves" (219). Payne's ultimate message, like democracy's and King's, is a hopeful one: the ladder may be broken; but we broke it — "our bad" — so we can just as well also repair it and have it work again for the Many instead of just for the Few who happened to be at the top when it broke.[24]

---

24 For more on "taking the world in for repairs" (Richard Selzer), see Paul Farmer, *To Repair the World: Paul Farmer Speaks to the Next Generation,* ed. Jonathan Weigel (Oakland: University of California Press, 2020).

11

A Rhetoric of Fascism

Jason Stanley, *How Fascism Works: The Politics of Us and Them* (2018)

In her 2017 *New Yorker* profile of Margaret Atwood, Rebecca Mead recounts that the Canadian novelist took part in the Women's March in Toronto and was intrigued by a sign held by an older woman:

> She attended the Toronto iteration of the Women's March, wearing a wide-brimmed floppy hat the color of Pepto-Bismol: not so much a pussy hat as the chapeau of a lioness. Among the signs she saw that day, her favorite was one held by a woman close to her own age; it said, *"I can't believe I'm still holding this fucking sign."* Atwood remarked, "After sixty years, why are we doing this again? But, as you know, in any area of life, it's push and pushback. We have had the pushback, and now we are going to have the push again."[1]

---

1   Rebecca Mead, "Margaret Atwood, The Prophet of Dystopia," *The New Yorker,* April 10, 2017, https://www.newyorker.com/magazine/2017/04/17/margaret-atwood-the-prophet-of-dystopia.

The mordant humor of the sign comes from the knowledge At-wood and the sign-holder probably share which is that just as there is "ambiguous loss" (Pauline Boss), so too there are ambiguous wins — victories that one can never be sure are definitive, "Won and done." Instead they must be refought over and over against those leading a backlash or some form of counter-reformation to reverse a state of affairs that the backlashers believe to be unjust, unwise, or just plain wrong. Feminists are familiar with this when it comes to the ongoing debate, in the us at least, over a woman's legal right to abortion. Another area that has attracted a recent burst of attention is equal civil rights for people of color. At a Black Lives Matter rally following multiple brutal acts of white-on-black violence in the first half of 2020, there was a sign that read, "If all lives mattered, we wouldn't have to be here." A third familiar case is the declaration "Never again" which is often associated with speeches and memorials about the Holocaust, although those who first used that phrase probably knew that the extermination of six million Jews during World War II was an original repetition of genocide, and that there had been other examples earlier in the very same century — the genocide in German South West Africa (now Namibia, 1904–8), the Turkish genocide of Armenians (1915–23) and Stalin's calculated starvation of Ukrainians (1932–33).[2] Moreover, those invoking that phrase today are likely aware that there have been several more instances of mass killing, ethnic cleansing, or genocide — one needn't quibble over terminology — since 1945 in Cambodia (1975–79), Rwanda (1994), ex-Yugoslavia (1992–95), and Myanmar (2016–17). Perhaps the declaration ought to be amended to "Never again, please" or "Hopefully never again,"

---

2   An estimated four million Ukrainians died during this period known as the Holodomor. See Anne Applebaum, *Red Famine: Stalin's War on Ukraine* (New York: Doubleday, 2017), and Timothy Snyder, *Bloodlands: Europe Between Hitler and Stalin* (New York: Basic Books, 2010). On the Armenian genocide, see Peter Balakian, *The Burning Tigris: The Armenian Genocide and America's Response* (New York: HarperCollinsPerennial, 2003). The mass killing in Namibia was formally acknowledged as genocide by the German government in 2021.

or, given the history of the last hundred years, "Hopefully never again, but maybe right around the corner."

Reading Jason Stanley's *How Fascism Works: The Politics of Us and Them*,[3] one gets the feeling that he is aware of this endlessly revolving door that we could also call the parenting or professor's dilemma. Both parents and professors would like their children and students to "get it," preferably sooner rather than later, once and for all, but they usually don't. This might be taking out the garbage without having to be asked, solving quadratic equations, understanding the Gulf of Tonkin Resolution, saying Please and Thank you, or any number of tasks, facts, and behaviors. In my language classes I joke with my students that thank goodness *they have been making* the same mistakes for years (about the use of the English present perfect, for example) otherwise I'd be out of a job. In Stanley's case, there is nothing funny about his pointed observation that "right now," "at the time of this writing," fascist politics is very possibly "ascendant" and liberal democratic norms are increasingly doubted and flouted (137). In a way similar to Nussbaum and Payne's fusion of the professional and the personal, Stanley combines his training and experience at understanding arguments with a compelling family history to craft an X-ray of the rhetoric of what he calls "the logic of fascist politics" (102). The explicit goal is to rescue liberal democracy from a fascist takeover. The approach is similar to Cécile Alduy and Stéphane Wahnich's timely analysis of the manipulative rhetoric of the current leader of France's far-right party: *Marine Le Pen prise aux mots* (2015).[4] Both

---

3   Jason Stanley, *How Fascism Works: The Politics of Us and Them* (New York: Random House, 2018). Hereafter cited parenthetically throughout this chapter.

4   Cécile Alduy and Stéphane Wahnich, *Marine Le Pen prise aux mots: décryptage du nouveau discours frontiste* (Paris: Seuil, 2015). To my knowledge, this book has not been translated into English. A possible title would be *Marine Le Pen Taken at Her Word: Decrypting France's New Far-right Discourse.* On Trump's rhetoric, see Jennifer Mercieca, *Demagogue for President: The Rhetorical Genius of Donald Trump* (College Station: Texas A&M University Press, 2020). See also the writings of Patricia Roberts-

books are extensions of the template offered by Victor Klemperer's *The Language of the Third Reich* (1947) and of the tools honed by Anglo-Saxon rhetoricians such as Kenneth Burke and the Orwell of "Politics and the English Language," and by so-called French theory from Ferdinand de Saussure and Barthes to Derrida and de Man.

Stanley's sign might read, "I can't believe I too have to battle fascism just like my grandmother did." (He recounts that his grandmother rescued hundreds of Jews from the Sachsenhausen concentration camp, 189.) That would be the parent and professor in him speaking, the one who shares the Enlightenment faith in the liberating power of knowledge, the idea that retellings and rational explanations (i.e., stories with plots) free one from ignorance and error. It's a version of the *Arbeit Macht Frei* — work is liberating — ideology that the leaders of the Auschwitz extermination camp would cynically repurpose. Professor Stanley might indignantly cry "Good grief" at the prospect of having to repeat the work of his grandmother and so many others, including the distinguished senior professors Robert O. Paxton and Sheldon S. Wolin, who each sounded the alarm bell about contemporary functional equivalents of fascism in 2004 and 2008, respectively.[5] It's *Professor* Stanley who writes, "I have written this book in the hope of providing citizens with the critical tools to recognize the difference between legitimate tactics in liberal democratic politics on the one hand, and invidious tactics in fascist politics on the other" (xviii). But this act of recognition is easier said than done, especially since one person's terrorist is another person's freedom fighter, for example, and because the *legitimate* is not merely something that is discovered or encountered — like a student who *recognizes* his teacher on the bus — but instead something that's decided by judges,

---

Miller, notably *Demagoguery and Democracy* (New York: The Experiment, 2017).

5   Robert O. Paxton, *The Anatomy of Fascism* (New York: Alfred A. Knopf, 2004), and Sheldon S. Wolin, *Democracy Inc.: Managed Democracy and the Specter of Inverted Totalitarianism* (Princeton: Princeton University Press, 2008).

armies, elections, legislators, monarchs, and others vested with that positing power.

However, channeling his younger grandson self, or remembering the youth of his own father who escaped Nazi Germany at age 6 in 1939 (xii), a more vulnerable Stanley — Flat Stanley, if you like — knows that shit happens, whether it's a bulletin board squashing you or someone bullying you or persecuting your family; and that these bad things are more likely to happen in times of extreme inequality and generally difficult life conditions (such as in Weimar Germany or in the post-9/11, post-Iraq War, post-Great Recession, debt-ridden, overweight, addiction-addled United States). What's more, as we learned from Keith Payne, this bad shit or crazy shit may happen even though it goes against the better judgment of large numbers of people — or even, spitefully, *because* it does.[6] In such a state of emergency and derangement, aggravated by post-empire status loss anxiety, there is no time to dally over why the work of Arendt, Burke, Paxton, Wolin, and others has not been enough to definitively block a return of fascism because the signs of its return — including large amounts of pain and suffering that one would have to be blind or very cold-hearted to ignore — are plain to see. *Citizen* Stanley, alarmed, he writes, by the normalization of 1) racialized mass incarceration and mass shootings in the US; 2) the mistreatment or elimination of judges, journalists, and professors in many countries; and 3) the brutal treatment of refugees and the undocumented (190), refuses to be a quiet bystander or conference organizer in and for the ivory tower. Perhaps he shares the belief of the psychologist and Holocaust survivor Ervin Staub that the intervention of bystanders can slow or stop the progress of violence and persecution.[7] Perhaps

---

6 On the arsonist-fireman in politics, see Julian E. Zelizer, *Burning Down the House: Newt Gingrich, the Fall of the Speaker, and the Rise of the New Republican Party* (New York: Penguin Books, 2020).

7 I learned about Ervin Staub thanks to an episode of the radio show *Hidden Brain*, "Romeo and Juliet in Kigali: How a Soap Opera Sought to Change Behavior in Rwanda," hosted by Shankar Vedantam, NPR, April 16, 2018, https://www.npr.org/transcripts/602872309. The topic: "Could a radio soap

he feels indebted and grateful to his family and others and acts out of a sense of duty to "pay it forward."[8] Whatever the reason, Stanley's speaking out takes the form of a manifesto of roughly 200 pages that may remind one of the early public intellectual Émile Zola and his *"J'accuse"* intervention (1898) in the Dreyfus Affair (1894–1906). The concluding paragraph to his introduction expresses both alarm and a measure of wishful thinking reminiscent of what we saw in Nussbaum and Atwood: the idea that one can "trigger empathy" (xix). This is a belief in the power of revelation that the very necessity of his intervention would seem to put in doubt.

> Fascism today might not look exactly as it did in the 1930s, but refugees are once again on the road everywhere. In multiple countries, their plight reinforces fascist propaganda that the nation is under siege, that aliens are a threat and danger both within and outside their borders. The suffering of strangers can solidify the structure of fascism. But it can also trigger empathy once another lens is clicked into place. (xix)

One sees with the "lens" metaphor a repetition of Stanley's Enlightenment faith, the idea that empathy is the result of a rational, right-thinking cognition or first principle "All human beings are born free and equal in dignity and rights," one reads in the *Universal Declaration of Human Rights* — rather than being built up over time through experiences of strong shared emotions that weave feelings of love, care, and commonality. Surely empathy involves the desire to see others, whether loved ones or total strangers, experience pleasure and personal growth in a safe

---

opera foster healing, reconciliation, and more cooperative attitudes and behaviors in the aftermath of the Rwandan genocide?"

8   Another warning with a personal indebted "survivor" dimension as motivating factor is Madeleine Albright's *Fascism: A Warning* (New York: HarperCollins, 2018). See Robin Wright's review, "Madeleine Albright Warns of a New Fascism — and Trump," *The New Yorker,* April 24, 2018, https://www.newyorker.com/news/news-desk/madeleine-albright-warns-of-a-new-fascism-and-trump.

environment, not persecution and pain. But Stanley must know that empathy-building, like democracy (or language learning), is a slow, endless process with no guaranteed outcome. On the contrary, as he notes, "the suffering of strangers can solidify the structure of fascism" (xix) when heat-treated with fascist propaganda. Therefore, empathy is quite unlike a light switch, trigger, or lens. Besides, if it were any of those things there'd be no need for his book which is a securely tenured, Ivy-League (Yale, male, pale) original repetition (after Arendt, Burke, Chomsky, Paxton, Wolin…) of his grandmother's gritty rescues carried out in an earlier era of Western civilization.[9]

That said, Stanley has written the best practical guide to fascism since the publication of Paxton's *Anatomy of Fascism.*[10] And just as that earlier study was motivated in part by worrisome fascist elements that developed after 9/11 in the George W. Bush era, Stanley's account of fascist politics updates and completes Paxton's inventory of the fascist décor for the Trump era. Mercifully for those with Trump fatigue, the forty-fifth US president is only mentioned about thirty times, which out of 200 pages represents less than 20 percent. This makes sense since fascist politics existed in the United States and elsewhere long before Trump. Despite all the damage he will have done to the United States and Americans, Trump is unlikely to have a lasting effect on the expansion or decline of fascism and democracy in other places since, as Paxton argues and Stanley confirms, roughly 40 percent of any successful fascist operation depends on a favorable local context, 30 percent is the work of passive and active enablers — both large (today, social media CEOs, and

---

9 And there'd be no need for him to be still sounding the alarm years later on Twitter and in print media. For example, Jason Stanley, "America Is Now in Fascism's Legal Phase," *The Guardian,* December 22, 2021., https://www.theguardian.com/world/2021/dec/22/america-fascism-legal-phase. Stanley opens that piece by recalling Toni Morrison's prescient warning in her 1995 address to Howard University, "Racism and Fascism," *The Journal of Negro Education* 64, no. 3 (Summer 1995): 384–85.

10 There is worthy competition from C. Boggs, F. Finchelstein, J. Goldberg, T. Horesh, M. MacWilliams, and E. Traverso. See also Ruth Ben-Ghiat, *Strongmen: Mussolini to the Present* (New York: W.W. Norton & Co., 2020).

global capitalists) and small (individual citizens and campaign managers) — and 30 percent can be attributed to the words, deeds, and body language of the fascist leader who becomes the movement's public face. This is the epidemiological triangle of environment, host, and agent that can be used to explain social phenomena as diverse as gang violence or video game crazes. Fascist politics undermining democratic norms can also be advanced anonymously by "little people" with no one performing a starring role at the top. Richard Nixon's name is associated with the fascistic "Southern Strategy," but it was actually carried out and continues today thanks to millions of people who probably never heard the term and know next to nothing about Nixon's views, helpers, or his troubled presidency.[11]

Following Paxton's comprehensive "Other Times, Other Places" chapter, Stanley provides evidence of ten fascist strategies he wants to explain and illustrate, drawing on events, including speech acts, of the past 150 years in many places around the globe including Algeria, France, Germany, Great Britain, Hungary, India, Israel, Italy, Kenya, Kosovo, Myanmar, Poland, Russia, Rwanda, Serbia, Slovakia, Switzerland, Turkey, and the United States. Since Stanley is a philosopher of language and politics trained at MIT, we can note that ten is also the round number of strategies to concentrate wealth and power presented by that university's famous senior linguist and gadfly Noam Chomsky in his video and book *Requiem for the American Dream* (2017), which could have been called *Requiem for De-*

---

11 The Southern Strategy "assumes there is little Republicans can do to attract Black Americans and details a two-pronged strategy: Utilize Black support of Democrats to alienate white voters while trying to decrease that support by sowing dissension within the Democratic Party," writes Stuart Stevens, a Republican political consultant, in "I Hope This Is Not Another Lie about the Republican Party," *The New York Times,* July 29, 2020, https://www.nytimes.com/2020/07/29/opinion/trump-republican-party-racism.html. Stevens, the author of *It Was All a Lie: How the Republican Party Became Donald Trump* (New York: Penguin Books, 2020), claims the GOP has become authoritarian and the Southern Strategy was copied by Russia in 2016 to help elect a democracy wrecking ball, Donald J. Trump.

mocracy in America or more bluntly *How to Kill Democracy.* The ten strategies are:

1. Reduce Democracy
2. Shape Ideology
3. Redesign the Economy
4. Shift the Burden
5. Attack Solidarity
6. Run the Regulators
7. Engineer Elections
8. Keep the Rabble in Line
9. Manufacture Consent
10. Marginalize the Population

Taking his cue from Paxton's *Anatomy* and Chomsky's "How To" (kill democracy and lock in plutocracy) book, Stanley identifies ten fascist strategies that he sees as interconnected and mutually reinforcing — an idea that he gets across by having the last paragraph of each of his ten chapters evoke the strategy to be presented in the next one, as though it were a chain or train. Alternatively, one can think of them as ten ingredients of a nearly irresistible secret sauce:

1. mythic past
2. propaganda
3. anti-intellectualism
4. unreality
5. hierarchy
6. victimhood
7. law and order
8. sexual anxiety
9. appeals to the heartland
10. dismantling of public welfare and unity.

In three lean paragraphs that efficiently fulfill the promise announced in the title — [*I, Jason Stanley, will explain*] *How Fascism Works* — Stanley demonstrates how all ten flow from one to the next to form a coordinated fascist playbook to subvert democratic values and habits:

Fascist politicians justify their ideas by breaking down a common sense of history in creating a **mythic past** to support their vision of the present. They rewrite the population's shared understanding of reality by twisting the language of ideals through **propaganda** and promoting **anti-intellectualism**, attacking universities and educational systems that might challenge their ideas. Eventually, with these techniques, fascist politics creates a state of **unreality**, in which conspiracy theories and fake news replace reasoned debate.

As the common understanding of reality crumbles, fascist politics makes room for dangerous and false beliefs to take root. First, fascist ideology seeks to naturalize group difference, thereby giving the appearance of natural, scientific support for a **hierarchy** of human worth. When social rankings and divisions solidify, fear fills in for understanding between groups. Any progress for a minority group stokes feelings of **victimhood** among the dominant population. **Law and order** politics has mass appeal, casting "us" as lawful citizens and "them," by contrast, as lawless criminals whose behavior poses an existential threat to the manhood of the nation. **Sexual anxiety** is also typical of fascist politics as the patriarchal hierarchy is threatened by growing gender equity.

As the fear of "them" grows, "we" come to represent everything virtuous. "We" live in the rural heartland, where the pure values and traditions of the nation still miraculously exist despite the threat of cosmopolitanism from the nation's cities, alongside the hordes of minorities who live there, emboldened by liberal tolerance. "We" are hardworking, and have earned our pride of place by struggle and merit. "They" are lazy, surviving off the goods we produce by exploiting the generosity of our welfare systems, or employing corrupt institutions, such as labor unions, meant to separate honest, hardworking citizens from their pay. "We" are makers; "they" are takers. (xvi–xvii)

These paragraphs encapsulate the book's argument, and the attention-getting device of boldface type along with Stanley's ventriloquism — throwing his voice that he sounds like he belongs to the "We" — makes them a particularly vivid and compelling checklist. The attentive reader will notice that there are only eight terms in boldface; that's because strategies 9) **Appeal to the heartland** and 10) **Dismantle public welfare and unity** are woven into Stanley's retelling of the (manufactured) struggle between "We," the virtuous defenders of the one true nation, and the dehumanized and undeserving "them" — who will be called and treated as "scum," "cockroaches," and "enemies of the people."

The obvious next question is, *Why?* What's the point of fascism? Fascism's proximate goal is clear enough: it's to divide and dehumanize, limit, stop, or reverse any empathy for the pain and suffering of others, and to use cooptation to create vocal or silent accomplices who will play along and endorse and enforce the ten strategies. But what's the point of that? What is the ultimate goal? The best answer Stanley can come up with is *To consolidate political gains and power.* As Fromm noted in 1941, the end in sight seems to be just power for the sake of domination (and to avoid being dominated or held accountable), not *power to* purposefully accomplish anything. But if we recall Fromm's insistence on the importance of sadism and masochism to the psychology of nazism, and for the mechanisms of escape from freedom more generally, we can affirm along with Adam Serwer that *the power to be cruel* to others *is* the point.[12] "A boot stamping on a human face — forever," as Orwell memorably put it in

---

12 Adam Server, "The Cruelty Is the Point," *The Atlantic,* October 3, 2018, https://www.theatlantic.com/ideas/archive/2018/10/the-cruelty-is-the-point/572104/. This argument has also been made by Julianne Hing, "For Trump, Cruelty Is the Point," *The Nation,* March 15, 2018, https://www.thenation.com/article/archive/for-trump-cruelty-is-the-point/; Greg Sargent, "For Trump, the Cruelty Is the Point. But It's Actually Worse Than That," *The Washington Post,* April 9, 2019, https://www.washingtonpost.com/opinions/2019/04/09/trump-cruelty-is-point-its-actually-worse-than-that/; and Masha Gessen who discusses gratuitous cruelty in her book *Surviving Autocracy* (New York: Riverhead Books, 2020).

1984.[13] It is perhaps only in this brutal sense that fascism can be said to have an "ideology," since the power it wins for its leader and his loyalists is not used for any constructive purpose or project that would make some vision or dream come true (such as Fromm's "expression of [one's] intellectual, emotional, and sensuous potentialities"[14]). And since there is no life-affirming vision, no plan, there is arguably no true fascist politics in the sense of a set of policy preferences that would have to compete in argued debate against another set of preferences.[15] If there is such a thing as fascist politics or ideology — and Stanley thinks there is and lists the "central tenets of fascist ideology" as "authoritarianism, hierarchy, purity, and struggle" (5) — it is only insofar as those ideas or principles serve as *the means,* the tools, that allow me and my friends and family to dominate.[16] Fascist or autocratic politics, as Masha Gessen has noted, is really an anti-politics, since the fascist does not want to enter into and win an argument-driven debate about policy A, B, or C. The whole idea of debate, let alone a level playing field or following *Robert's Rules of Order* or other mediation tools, is abhorrent and barely conceivable to the fascist. He wants to dominate and rule, period.[17] Gessen might take issue, therefore, with Stanley's

---

13 Updated to January 6, 2021, that would be a hockey stick whacking Capitol police over the head — forever.

14 Erich Fromm, *Escape from Freedom* (New York: Henry Holt, 1969), x.

15 It's noteworthy that, at the Republican National Convention in August 2020, the party put forward no policy platform whatsoever — a clear sign that the Republican party had devolved into a Trump-centered personality cult.

16 "Fascism talks ideology, but it is really just marketing — marketing for power." Morrison, "Racism and Fascism."

17 And rule immediately and unmediated. See Gessen's chapter, "The Antipolitics of Fear," in *Surviving Autocracy,* 98, and this pertinent observation from the end of the chapter "Words Have Meaning, or They Ought To": "The word 'politics' or 'political' […] ought to refer to the vital project of negotiating how we live together as a city, a state, or a country; of working across difference; of acting collectively. Instead, it is used to denote emptiness: hollow procedure, inflated rhetoric, tactical positioning are dismissed as 'just politics.'" True; however, the term politics is also used properly, such as when someone asks, "What are his politics?" to mean

use of the word "politics" when what he announces as his goal and carries out is really an inventory of fascist *rhetoric,* or as Stanley also says "the invidious tactics" of us versus them. We can go along with Stanley's choice of the word *politics,* so long as one understands it as an anti-politics that seeks to eradicate political debate and a contest of ideas altogether through sheer, unmediated imposition of the leader's will. Traditional and modern tyrants have often faced this problem of having more power than they know what to do with, hence the multiplication of fake projects and real acts of pure cruelty.[18]

The problem on the Right when it comes to "the vision thing" had already reared its head in the United States at the start of the presidency of George H.W. Bush and became all the more apparent during the eight erring years of Bush II, and then in spades with Trump whose vision or circle of concern seemed to extend only as far as avoiding jail and keeping as much power as he could in the hands of his friends and family for as long as possible.[19]

"What are his positions on, say, abortion, the flat tax, labor unions," and so forth. Also, during holidays or other family gatherings when people are wary of "talking politics" lest it spoil the convivial atmosphere, they don't mean discussions of rhetoric or procedure, I don't think, but rather arguments over political principles and policy preferences.

18   See Judith N. Shklar, "Putting Cruelty First," *Deadalus* 111, no. 3 (Summer 1982): 17–27. See also Adam Serwer's follow-up editorial "The Cruel Logic of the Republican Party, before and after Trump," *The New York Times,* June 26, 2021, https://www.nytimes.com/2021/06/26/opinion/trump-republican-party.html, timed with the publication of his book *The Cruelty Is the Point: The Past, Present, and Future of Trump's America* (New York: Random House, 2021).

19   See David Remnick, "Is Donald Trump an Anti-Semite?" *The New Yorker,* December 21, 2021, https://www.newyorker.com/news/daily-comment/is-donald-trump-an-anti-semite. He concludes, "The fact that Trump's hateful stratagems of bigotry and conspiracy are consistent with authoritarian movements all over the world will never cause him a moment of hesitation. Why would they? What matters to Donald Trump is Donald Trump." Yes, but what matters to the rest of us is whether the hate, bigotry, and conspiracy talk will prevent enough eligible voters from ever voting for him or his kind again.

The vacuity of fascist politics, a blindness to the purpose of power,[20] was noticed by Paxton, which is why his chapter "The Long Term: Radicalization or Entropy?" begins with the observation: "Fascist regimes could not settle down into a comfortable enjoyment of power." *Dynasty,* the title of a popular TV soap opera from the 1980s, would seem to be the extent of the vision that dominates right-wing politicians' thinking. But such an exclusive and excluding goal, in the unavowable name of protestant white purity and supremacy, is a hard sell to a nation of over 300 million ambitious immigrants or "mutts" as Bill Murray calls Americans in the 1981 pro-democracy comedy *Stripes.* Many of those millions are "yearning to breathe free" for starters, and when that has been achieved, their "mongrel" children move on to countless other dreams and schemes. And yet unless enough liberals like Stanley and Murray call out and unmask the fascist anti-political tactics (including, number 11, the formulation of abstractly worded vague goals such as purification, combating "race defilement," restoring honor, greatness), *fascism works,* at least for the Few, while it dupes the Many (with flags, rally caps, and incendiary language) into thinking that it works for them too (while really it's killing them softly with its song).[21]

The challenge for liberals who are fortunate to live in societies that still have meaningful elections is shoring up respect for politics as a contest of opposing policy ideas, not personal attacks, and convincing a majority of voters that their long-term interests are better served by the inclusive values of debate-driven, dignity-based liberal democracy — namely equality, liberty, justice, and opportunity for all — than by the divisive opportunistic "politics" of *us* versus *them* which always discredits and disqualifies liberation and equality movements by portraying

20 Alicia Garza, *The Purpose of Power: How We Come Together When We Fall Apart* (New York: Penguin Random House, 2020).

21 See the Lauryn Hill cover of "Killing Me Softly with His Song," the 1973 hit by Roberta Flack. For a review of research on the seductiveness of cults and cult leaders, see Zoë Heller, "Beyond Belief: What Makes a Cult a Cult?" *The New Yorker,* July 5, 2021, https://www.newyorker.com/magazine/2021/07/12/what-makes-a-cult-a-cult.

groups advancing those goals as deviant, devious, dangerous, and undeserving. In authoritarian societies and shallow-rooted democracies that have undergone extensive authoritarianization (such as Hungary since 2010), countering fascist politics or simply antidemocratic backsliding may be more difficult, since citizens in these places, being used to one-party rule, have little practical experience with how liberalism works and how it feels (with its respectful pluralism, a loyal opposition, and good faith efforts at bipartisanship on basic issues such as democracy's ground rules), and therefore no basis for comparing different regimes. Indeed comparison itself is forbidden, or decried as "woke," since the act of comparison acknowledges the existence of other narratives, means, and ends; and it would therefore validate debate with an opposition party capable of one day winning and ruling.

And yet even in established liberal democracies, such as Great Britain and the United States, backsliding happens and there occurs among many a scrambling of one's faculty of judgment — caused by today's extreme economic inequality and the anxiety over status loss ("after the empire," Emmanuel Todd) — and that scrambling provides an opening to the allure of fascism, says Stanley:

> The pull of fascist politics is powerful. It simplifies human existence, gives us an object, a "them" whose supposed laziness highlights our virtue and discipline, encourages us to identify with a forceful leader who helps us make sense of the [new, scary] world, whose bluntness regarding the "undeserving" people in the world is refreshing. If democracy looks like a successful business, if the CEO is tough-talking and cares little for democratic institutions, even denigrates them, so much the better. Fascist politics preys on the human frailty that makes our own suffering seem bearable if we know that those we look down upon are being made to suffer more. (183)

This late paragraph from chapter 10 is a good example of Stanley's demonstration of the interconnectedness, including the projection, behind the fascist strategies: a simple story of good (us) versus evil (them) provides easy and "refreshing" relief to those who may just not like or tolerate complexity and change, as Karen Stenner has claimed,[22] or who are feeling or fearing loss of income, status, security, or potency, whether individually or collectively, as Payne argues.[23]

In the post-Cold War era, without the routines of collective narcissism among the superpowers, the twenty-seven-country European Union — by virtue of being a populous and dynamic transnational economic bloc that governs itself more or less democratically — troubles the self-esteem of Great Britain, post-Soviet Russia, and the United States which have all bristled at their reduced hegemony and the waning of privileges that came with empire.[24] Fascist movements with their domination-driven nationalist campaigns are all attempts to halt or reverse this perceived status loss.[25] The success of such efforts depends on

---

22 Karen Stenner, *The Authoritarian Dynamic* (Cambridge: Cambridge University Press, 2010).

23 Some see the us versus them divide somewhat differently as an opposition between moral universes: the "moral freedom" universe versus the "you are not your own" ethos. See David Brooks, taking inspiration from philosopher Charles Taylor as well as from psychologist Jonathan Haidt, "How Democrats Can Win the Morality Wars," *The New York Times,* May 19, 2022, https://www.nytimes.com/2022/05/19/opinion/democrats-morality-wars.html. This book has argued that bridging that gap starts with reducing social, economic, and political inequality and vulnerability, and continues with lowering chances for the other to be an existential threat.

24 One could add France to this list, a country split between its pro-democracy EU sympathizers and its empire nostalgics who gravitate toward the far-right populist party of Marine Le Pen that seeks to reproduce the colonialist order of white domination over people of color like in the good old days of Napoleon III. Spain's Vox party has similar, elegiac empire yearnings.

25 Stanley makes a helpful distinction between domination-driven nationalisms and "equality-driven nationalist movements" that attempt to see a formerly excluded or disadvantaged out-group attain the same personhood and rights as the dominant in-group: "The point of the slogan Black Lives Matter," writes Stanley, "is to call attention to a failure of equal re-

the people not getting wise to the masquerade or mask stitched from a mythic past, the unreal "fable of the wise nation,"[26] and questionable narratives of aggrieved victimhood. Hence the strict attention to messaging and optics, and the need to maintain tight control over journalists, professors, judges, or anyone else who might notice and denounce the sham. Stanley quotes the widely read *Nation* piece by Greg Grandin from June 2016, "Why Trump Now? It's the Empire, Stupid," as part of his argument that both Brexit and Trump's election (and we can add the desperate "Russian meddling" led by an aggrieved, limp and aging ex-KGB officer[27]) are all of a piece: the vulnerable, especially the newly vulnerable who were long accustomed to dominate,

---

spect. In its context, it means Black lives matter too." Stanley, *How Fascism Works,* 97. Since hierarchy not equality is uppermost in fascist politics, it invariably interprets demands for equality as a disguised (revenge) plot to dominate ("the plot against [white] America"), but that anxiety remains unavowable so as to avoid appearing weak.

26 Timothy Snyder, *The Road to Unfreedom: Russia, Europe, America* (New York: Tim Duggan Books, 2018), 75–78. 101, 106–7, 119, and "Europe's Dangerous Creation Myth," *Politico,* May 1, 2019, https://www.politico.eu/article/europe-creation-project-myth-history-nation-state/.

27 There are dozens of books on Vladimir Putin. For a short profile, written during the 2022 invasion of Ukraine, by the author of *All the Kremlin's Men: Inside the Court of Vladimir Putin* (New York: PublicAffairs, 2016), see Mikhail Zygar, "How Vladimir Putin Lost Interest in the Present," *The New York Times,* March 10, 2022, https://www.nytimes.com/2022/03/10/opinion/putin-russia-ukraine.html. On Putin as a wounded narcissist and vengeful "identity entrepreneur" helping Russians recover from the psychic trauma caused by the collapse of the Soviet Union, see David Brooks, "This Is Why Putin Can't Back Down," *The New York Times,* March 10, 2022, https://www.nytimes.com/2022/03/10/opinion/putin-ukraine-russia-identity.html. On the misguided admiration for Putin inside the Trumpist Republican party, see Paul Krugman, "America's Right Has a Putin Problem," *The New York Times,* March 10, 2022, https://www.nytimes.com/2022/03/10/opinion/putin-ukraine-russia-usa.html. On Putin's underestimation of Ukraine's pro-democracy and anti-authoritarian predisposition, see Yaroslav Hrytsak, "Putin Made a Profound Miscalculation on Ukraine," *The New York Times,* March 19, 2022, https://www.nytimes.com/2022/03/19/opinion/ukraine-russia-putin-history.html. The Russian invasion of Ukraine is a good example of Tocqueville's observation that democracies make repairable mistakes; autocracies, on the other hand, having no braking mechanism, tend to dig the hole deeper.

are particularly susceptible to the Viagra cure promised by fascist politics.[28] This is in line with Erich Fromm's claim that the timing of Hitler's rise to power in Weimar Germany had everything to do with the triple humiliation of the lost Kaiser, the lost war of 1914–18, and the loss of economic security. Rewind sixty years and witness the emergence of the Ku Klux Klan in the anxious aftermath of the South's "lost cause"; and its revival in the early twentieth century to undermine glimmers of a democratic "progressive era" led by two class traitors, as they saw it, from the same elite WASP family, Teddy Roosevelt and Franklin Delano Roosevelt. Then fast forward a century later to Stanley's summary of Grandin's argument:

> With its demise, the citizens of a once powerful empire must confront the fact that their exceptionalism was a myth. Grandin writes that beginning in 2008 — about when Barack Obama won the presidential election — "the safety valve of empire closed, gummed up by the catastrophic war in Iraq combined with the 2008 financial crisis. […] Because Obama came to power in the ruins of neoliberalism and neoconservatism, empire [was] no longer able to dilute the passions, satisfy the interests, and unify the divisions."
>
> When imperial hierarchy collapses and social reality is laid bare, hierarchical sentiment in the home country tends to arise as a mechanism to preserve the familiar and comforting illusion of superiority. (91–92)

When *real superiority* evaporates (especially if it happens, embarrassingly, during the tenure of a "house negro"[29] in the White

---

28 Grandin's analysis, elaborated in his book *The End of the Myth: From the Frontier to the Border Wall in the Mind of America* (New York: Metropolitan Books, 2020), could be extended to explain the rise of the far-right in France after losses in Indochina and Algeria and then the ignominy, for French royalists and fascists, of joining the European Union and the Eurozone as one country alongside, not above, other member-nations.

29 The epithet, common on the internet often with a stronger n-word, was part of a smear campaign to depict Barack Obama as a usurper with

House) — and when, as Paxton noted, the people's trust in traditional politics has been undermined — fascism can provide
the "hierarchical sentiment" and *illusion of superiority,* and it
will ruthlessly police the public square to silence or denounce
as purveyors of "fake news" anyone who might point out the
discrepancy between truth and lie. The word "mask," as verb or
noun, comes up frequently in Stanley's book, especially in the
chapter on propaganda.[30] This is not surprising since his project,
an extension of an earlier and much longer book *How Propaganda Works* (2015), consists in giving his reader practice recognizing the disguises of fascism which are integral to its con or
confidence game.[31]

As I was rereading *How Fascism Works* during the 2020 summer of the pandemic, Stanley's critical tools got me thinking
that the deep reason Trump refused to support wearing a mask
for so long was not only sexual anxiety — fear of seeming weak
and unmanly — but also the intuition that wearing a true cloth
mask would tip people off that he had been wearing a mask and
playacting from day one of his presidency, indeed for his entire
adult life.[32] But why is propaganda's subterfuge so necessary?
Stanley offers a clear answer:

---

questionable loyalties, either serving white elites or "his people"; hence the
sly nicknaming of the Affordable Care Act as "Obamacare," a clever way to
cast doubt on its goal of making healthcare affordable to all Americans.

30 And in a later chapter devoted to the fascist's hatred of labor unions,
precisely because they unify: "Concern for economic independence and
business efficiency was only a mask for Hitler's real antipathy toward labor
unions." Stanley, *How Fascism Works,* 172. As history shows, and Veblen's
theory of leisure class honor explains, fascist politics favors waste over efficiency, division and hierarchy over union and equality, and enslavement
(of vulnerable groups) over freedom and independence.

31 In his rhetoric of propaganda Stanley inventories many examples of its
power to conceal, including the consciousness-raising experiment Payne
designed to investigate whether "stereotypes affect perceptual judgment."
Keith Payne, *The Broken Ladder: How Inequality Affects the Way We Think,
Live, and Die* (New York: Viking, 2017), quoted in Stanley, *How Propaganda Works* (Princeton: Princeton University Press, 2015), 212.

32 Michael Cohen summed it up in his testimony under oath to Congress
on February 27, 2019: "I am ashamed that I chose to take part in conceal-

It's hard to advance a policy that will harm a large group of people in straightforward terms. The role of political propaganda is to conceal politicians' or political movements' clearly problematic goals by masking them with ideals that are widely accepted. A dangerous, destabilizing war for power becomes a war whose aim is stability, or a war whose aim is freedom. Political propaganda uses the language of virtuous ideals to unite people behind otherwise objectionable ends. (24, emphasis added)

"To unite people behind otherwise objectionable ends" is key. Stanley reviews many types and examples; we can stick to the ones that speak of masks or masking: "Masking corruption under the guise of anticorruption is a hallmark strategy of fascist propaganda" (27). In other words, a fascist's promise to "drain the swamp"[33] turns out to be the prologue to removing traitors and troublemakers and restocking the swamp with cooperative loyalists.

In the Confederacy's use of the concept of liberty to defend the practice of slavery, the Southern states' call for "states' rights" to defend slavery, and Hitler's presentation of dictatorial rule as democracy, liberal democratic ideals are used as a mask to undermine themselves. In each we can find specious arguments that the antiliberal goal is in fact a realization of the liberal ideal. (31)

---

ing Mr. Trump's illicit acts rather than listening to my own conscience. I am ashamed because I know what Mr. Trump is. He is a racist, he is a con man, and he is a cheat." See Michael Cohen's full story in *Disloyal: A Memoir* (New York: Skyhorse, 2020). See also Alisha Haridasani Gupta, interview with Anand Giridharadas, "How an Aversion to Masks Stems From 'Toxic Masculinity,'" *The New York Times,* October 22, 2020, https://www.nytimes.com/2020/10/22/us/masks-toxic-masculinity-covid-men-gender.html.

33 A metaphor popularized by Mussolini, "drenare la palude," and later copied by Trump.

But fascist politics can also flip it the other way and "impugn" (139) the liberal ideal: a "purported" liberation movement on the part of some group (women, Black people, striking hospital workers, you name it) can be shot down as a cynical "Trojan horse" disguising an illiberal ulterior motive. This is the self-sealing plot twist contained in every conspiracy theory narrative:

> Equality, according to the fascist, is the Trojan horse of liberalism. The part of Odysseus can be variously played — by Jews, by homosexuals, by Muslims, by non-whites, by feminists, etc. Anyone spreading the doctrine of liberal equality is either a dupe,[34] "infected by the idea of freedom," or an enemy of the nation who is spreading the ideals of liberalism only with devious and indeed illiberal aims. (88)

Recall, for example, the denunciation of Snowball by Napoleon's loyal propagandist Squealer in *Animal Farm*. It's difficult to openly say you are against *equality* and *freedom,* since as abstract nouns they enjoy generally positive connotations. But as in the dark days of the French Revolution, they both can be impugned and discredited as opening the door to evil-doers and bad outcomes that are to be feared: "The fascist project combines anxiety about loss of status for members of the true 'nation,' with fear of equal recognition of [to be] hated minority groups" (88). It remains somewhat mysterious why freedom and equality extended to others should trigger *my* anxiety about loss of status for *me* and *my* group. In other words, why the zero-sum thinking instead of considering it a win-win with all boats

---

34 For example, when asked by Bob Woodward about the legitimacy of the Black Lives Matter movement's demands for social justice, including acknowledgement of the injustice of white privilege and systemic racism, Trump scoffed, "You really drank the Kool-Aid, didn't you?" In other words, for Trump, Woodward was a dupe. Quoted in Maureen Dowd, "All the President's Insecurities," *The New York Times,* September 12, 2020, https://www.nytimes.com/2020/09/12/opinion/sunday/donald-trump-bob-woodward.html.

rising? Stanley seems to follow Payne's inequality studies which, in my retelling, follow Fromm's vulnerability studies which follow Tocqueville's observations about defensive envy echoed independently by Nussbaum. All see both the vulnerable and the powerful as susceptible to going along with narratives that demonize, disbelieve, and delegitimize a minority claimant's plea for admission and acceptance into Kant's "realm of ends." In fascist politics borders and walls matter more than Black lives or the life of any persecuted outcast or huddled masses. But does it need to be that way?

Stanley further examines the strategy of disguising one's opposition to equality and freedom in the chapter on sexual anxiety that exposes fascism's pathological obsession with strict gender borders, going so far as to make an issue out of where certain people will poop and pee (see North Carolina's "bathroom wars") as part of a wider demonization of all gender bending and nonconformity and the exaltation of "real men" and "tradwives." After reviewing fascist political tactics to ignite opposition to giving humanitarian aid to Syrian and Afghan refugees starting in 2015 on the grounds that hiding among them are untold numbers of terrorists and rapists, Stanley summarizes how the masking works in this area:

> Highlighting supposed threats to the ability of men to protect their women and children solves a difficult political problem for fascist politicians. *In liberal democracy, a politician who explicitly attacks freedom and equality will not garner much support.* The politics of sexual anxiety is a way to get around this issue, *in the name of safety*; it is a way to attack and undermine the ideals of liberal democracy without being seen as explicitly so doing. (138, emphasis added)

"Without being seen as explicitly" attacking freedom and equality, and by acting "in the name of safety" — bingo! During the French Revolution, the governmental organization responsible for issuing death sentences, among other executive functions, was called the Comité de salut public, known in English as the

Committee of Public Safety, though *salut* also means salvation. Stanley is adept at schooling his reader to recognize the masks and masking of fascist propaganda. He has clearly put in the 10,000 hours to become an expert at it himself. The trouble is that most of us have not. This lack of practice ramps up the danger and damage of the normalization of fascist politics and policies when actual fascist autocrats take power (in a government, army, business, church, hospital, school, union, or team) and begin removing enemies and appointing loyalists. Why? Because as fascism's fantasy politics becomes increasingly normal, the real pain caused by fascism's extreme practices, not just its ideas, also risks becoming normal and accepted. This is especially true when large numbers of the vulnerable come to see tolerating or endorsing the autocrat as their least bad defense mechanism ("stand by your man"), and when the autocrats themselves believe their own trumped-up propaganda about being the indispensable stable genius uniquely qualified to lead. In his epilogue, Stanley asks rhetorically, "Does anyone really want their children's sense of identity to be based on a legacy of marginalization of others?" The short answer, based on a 400-year historical record of one-party racist politics throughout the southern United States and plenty of other places, is *Yes*. Or more precisely, *Yes, but without being seen as explicitly so doing.*

It is for this reason, Stanley suggests, and I agree, that calling out these tactics with the resonant term "fascism" — instead of going along with euphemisms such as "authoritarianism," "right-wing populism," "illiberal democracy," or "alternative right," or a nationalist slogan such as "Americanism" or "America first" — may help prevent the harm of fascist practices from fading into invisibility and tacit approval. If "silence = death" and if Americans are serious about recent calls for "No more silence," whether it's about racial injustice, income inequality, sexual assault, unfair labor practices, voter suppression, whatever; in short, if "we" (democrats) do not want the pain fascism causes to become normal, then using the word fascism is a good first step for preventing that from happening, though only a first step. Stanley's discussion of the word *fascism* repeats the claim made by some in the recent George Floyd phase of the Black Lives Matter movement, such as kihana miraya ross in her June 4, 2020 *New York Times* editorial, "Call it What it Is: Anti-Blackness." The subtitle of that piece reads: "When black people are killed by the police, 'racism' isn't the right word." For ross, the "catch-all" term *racism* "oversimplifies and defangs" the violence against Black people which fundamentally, she writes, derives from "the inability to recognize black humanity." Similarly, I'm suggesting, following Stanley's observation, the irritating quality of the word *fascism* may help unmask, or "refang" if you like, and thereby trip up the normalization of fascist extremism:

> What normalization does is transform the morally extraordinary into the ordinary. It makes us able to tolerate what was once intolerable by making it seem as if this is the way things have always been. By contrast, the word "fascist" has acquired a feeling of the extreme, like crying wolf. Normalization of fascist ideology, by definition, would make charges of "fascism" seem like an overreaction, even in societies whose norms are transforming along worrisome lines. Normalization means precisely that encroaching ideologically extreme conditions are not recognized as such because they have become to seem normal. The charge of fascism will always seem extreme; normalization means that the goalposts for the legitimate use of "extreme" terminology continually move. (190)

Stanley's "wolf" and "goalposts" metaphors may be incomprehensible to some readers, but his argument is basically sound. However, since most people "don't know much about history," it would be naïve to think that the word *fascism* will permanently function as a verbal stumbling stone to denounce the extreme, the not normal, and the (hopefully) not normalizable denial of full personhood to certain humans. Paxton was already concerned that whatever "inoculation" against evil the irritating word *fascism* might provide directly after 1945, it would eventually wear off. What's troubling is that Stanley's updating of Paxton demonstrates the near ubiquity of fascist politics acting as the evil twin of liberal democracy, a performance described by Tocqueville near the end of *Democracy in America* without giving it a name. Democracy's open principle of tolerance makes it hard for it to curb the intolerant and set limits on the freedom to hate and humiliate. For fascism to hijack democracy, the hijackers have to have been allowed on the plane — and they invariably are. The trick is wresting control from them before they crash it. Rigorous vetting of politicians and platforms by the press and in policy-focused debates *before* elections take place can reduce the likelihood of disaster. But seeking zero risk would end up with democracy betraying its core values of freedom and tolerance and devolving into intolerant totalitarianism. The Tao-like nobility of democracy, which skeptics like Joseph Goebbels could only ridicule, derives from its acceptance of its own vulnerability to attack and its ability to see this acknowledgment as not a weakness but a source of strength.[35]

Stanley deliberately undermines the imagined singularity of "fascism," which he always spells lower-case as a common noun, and in so doing he joins Paxton and others, including me, who prefer to speak of "functional equivalents of fascism" and say that "fascism is as fascism does." That view is relayed by Sarah Churchwell who joined other women, predictably shot down by men as "elite hysterics," to say it's about time we call Trump a fascist.[36] Churchwell concludes with an inventory of fascism's dark

---

35 Stanley reminds his reader of the Goebbels quip by quoting it as the epigraph to his book on how propaganda works: "This will always remain one of the best jokes of democracy, that it gave its deadly enemies the means by which it was destroyed." And yet democracy has outlasted the Third Reich which endured only twelve years.

36 Sarah Churchwell, "American Fascism: It Has Happened Here," *The New York Review of Books*, June 22, 2020, https://www.nybooks.com/daily/2020/06/22/american-fascism-it-has-happened-here/. A second Cassandra is Michelle Goldberg who asked, "Can we call it fascism yet?" following Trump's deployment of paramilitary forces in the streets of Portland, Oregon: "Trump's Occupation of American Cities Has Begun," *The New York Times*, July 20, 2020, https://www.nytimes.com/2020/07/20/opinion/portland-protests-trump.html. Goldberg asked related ques-

tions six weeks after the 2020 election: "Just How Dangerous Was Donald Trump?" *The New York Times,* December 14, 2020, https://www.nytimes.com/2020/12/14/opinion/trump-fascism.html. Jennifer Szalai compares those who answer "Yes" to Goldberg's question with others (often white men) who say "No": "The Debate over the Word 'Fascism' Takes a New Turn," *The New York Times,* June 10, 2020, https://www.nytimes.com/2020/06/10/books/fascism-debate-donald-trump.html. Szalai quotes Stanley repeating the thesis advanced by Churchwell: "Fascism is not a new threat, but rather a permanent temptation." These pieces, inventoried by Spencer Bokat-Lindell, "Fascism: A Concern," *The New York Times,* July 30, 2020, https://www.nytimes.com/2020/07/30/opinion/fascism-us.html, are late assessments that stand in symmetry to a similar line of questioning about Trump and the f-word that took place in the months before and after the 2016 election. David Denby's thoughts on the subject were footnoted in the Fromm chapter. Jamelle Bouie declared early on, Yes, "Donald Trump Is a Fascist," *Slate,* November 25, 2015, https://slate.com/news-and-politics/2015/11/donald-trump-is-a-fascist-it-is-the-political-label-that-best-describes-the-gop-front-runner.html. Bouie focuses on seven items from the fourteen-point checklist offered by Umberto Eco in his essay "Ur-Fascism," *The New York Review of Books,* June 22, 1995, https://www.nybooks.com/articles/1995/06/22/ur-fascism/. Ross Douthat has answered "No" twice: first early, "Is Donald Trump a Fascist?" *The New York Times,* December 3, 2015, https://www.nytimes.com/2018/09/11/books/review/jason-stanley-how-fascism-works.html; then later, "Donald Trump Doesn't Want Authority," *The New York Times,* May 19, 2020, https://www.nytimes.com/2020/05/19/opinion/coronavirus-trump-orban.html. Mr. Douthat thinks Trump's disinterest in leading or exploiting a national response to the pandemic is proof he's not an autocrat. But let's not forget the "auto" in autocrat. Who needs Zyklon B if, by doing nothing to fight the pandemic and obstructing others' efforts, the coronavirus can disproportionately kill off more of Trump's opponents (read: minorities and "blue state," "weak" citizens) than his supporters? For the view that Trump is responsible for thousands of preventable deaths if not exactly an American genocide, see Jennifer Senior, "Trump to New York: Drop Dead," *The New York Times,* March 24, 2020, https://www.nytimes.com/2020/03/24/opinion/trump-nyc-coronavirus.html. Today's Germans explain Trump via the arsonist-fireman metaphor that they know well from their own Reichstag fire history in 1933, as Roger Cohen recalls in "American Catastrophe through German Eyes," *The New York Times,* July 24, 2020, https://www.nytimes.com/2020/07/24/opinion/trump-germany.html. In the wake of the January 6 riot at the US Capitol, the debate about Trump and the f-word heated up again with Robert Paxton swinging to the "Yes" camp. For two post-1/6 discussions of the question, see Jonah S. Rubin, "It's Time to Use the F-word: An Anti-Fascist Approach to Trump and Franco," *Society for Cultural Anthropology,* April 15, 2021, https://culanth.org/fieldsights/its-

arts that is similar to those carried out by Umberto Eco, Toni Morrison, Paxton, Stanley, and others; and equally convincing:

American fascist energies today are different from 1930s European fascism, but that doesn't mean they're not fascist, it means they're not European and it's not the 1930s. They remain organized around classic fascist tropes of nostalgic regeneration, fantasies of racial purity, celebration of an authentic folk and nullification of others, scapegoating groups for economic instability or inequality, rejecting the legitimacy of political opponents, the demonization of critics, attacks on a free press, and claims that the will of the people justifies violent imposition of military force. Vestiges of interwar fascism have been dredged up, dressed up, and repurposed for modern times. Colored shirts might not sell anymore, but colored hats are doing great.

Reading about the inchoate American fascist movements of the 1930s during the Trump administration feels less prophetic than proleptic, a time-lapse montage of a para-fascist order slowly willing itself into existence over the course of nearly a century. It certainly seems less surprising that recognizably fascistic violence is erupting in the United States under Trump, as his attorney general sends troops to the national capital to act as a private army, armed paramilitary groups occupy state capitols, laws are passed to deny the citizenship and rights of specific groups, and birthright citizenship as guaranteed under the Fourteenth Amendment is attacked. When the president declares voting an "honor" rather than a right and "jokes" about becoming president for life, when the government makes efforts to add a new question of citizenship to the decennial census for the first time in the nation's history, and when nationwide protests in

time-to-use-the-f-word-an-anti-fascist-approach-to-trump-and-franco; and Mikael Nilsson, "Trump Is a Warning That Fascism Didn't Die with Hitler and Mussolini," *Haaretz,* January 21, 2021, https://www.haaretz.com/us-news/2021-01-21/ty-article-opinion/.premium/trump-legacy-fascism-far-right-biden/0000017f-df2b-df9c-a17f-ff3b20380000.

response to racial injustice become the pretext for mooting martial law, we are watching an American fascist order pulling itself together.

Trump is neither aberrant nor original. Nativist reactionary populism is nothing new in America, it just never made it to the White House before. In the end, it matters very little whether Trump is a fascist in his heart if he's fascist in his actions.

I imagine Stanley would heartily agree, and Paxton would likely nod at Churchwell's "stages" thinking and her focus on the harm of fascist actions no matter at what stage. But reaching agreement on terminology and inventories is the relatively easy part, especially among professors and other word people. The harder task will be "surviving autocracy" (Masha Gessen), reversing global authoritarianism[37] and authoritarianization (Milan Svolik), and building democracy back better (Joe Biden). Democracy sympathizers interested in taking on that challenge will have to answer Robert Kuttner's question, *Can Democracy Survive Global Capitalism?* That key question has since been updated by Shoshana Zuboff who asks if democracy can survive global surveillance capitalism.[38]

The short answer is *No*; or, *Yes, but only with major changes to both the current functioning of today's democracies and the global capitalist system*. Why? Because over the past fifty years, it is global, financialized, internet-boosted authoritarian capitalism operating largely without accountability that has been respon-

---

37 Max Fisher, "As Dictators Target Citizens Abroad, Few Safe Spaces Remain," *The New York Times*, June 4, 2021, https://www.nytimes.com/2021/06/04/world/europe/repression-uyghurs-belarus.html.

38 Shoshana Zuboff, "The Coup We Are Not Talking About," *The New York Times*, January 29, 2021, https://www.nytimes.com/2021/01/29/opinion/sunday/facebook-surveillance-society-technology.html, adapted from her book *The Age of Surveillance Capitalism: The Fight for A Human Future at the New Frontier of Power* (New York: Hachette, 2019). Kuttner updated his diagnosis of the problem in anticipation of the 2020 US elections in *The Stakes: 2020 and the Survival of American Democracy* (Cambridge: Harvard University Press, 2019).

sible for creating a lot of the vulnerability and fear among the 99%. Five hundred years after the first European tremors caused by capitalism's emergence in the Late Middle Ages, (in Fromm's retelling), late capitalism since the dismantling of the 1944 Bretton Woods agreement starting around 1973 (in Kuttner's retelling), and accelerating in the internet age of mass surveillance and manipulation, has caused vulnerable people to once again turn away from traditional politics, which seem to have failed or betrayed them, and toward extreme experiments no matter how unlikely to succeed judged by ordinary logic and track records. "When mainstream politics does not address core concerns about people's livelihoods, voters look to the extremes."[39] The upshot is that, as with any addiction, irrational behavior (for example, electing a coastal elite from outside government to rail against coastal elites who operate outside governmental controls) then becomes oddly rational, or seems so from inside a world of pain and dependence. But the pain relief is short-lived, and the possibility of lethal overdose is all too real. There's a grain of truth in the idea "It takes a thief to catch a thief," but who in their right mind would believe a thief is interested in the rule of law or fairness?

Increasing accountability, reducing extreme inequality, and other policy recommendations to strengthen democracy were sketched out at the end of my Tocqueville book. But I did not emphasize enough that the purpose of reducing inequality is to reduce the pain of physical and psychological vulnerability caused by inequality, pain that can lead one to give up on democracy, freedom, and rational thinking altogether. A revised version of those recommendations, taking into account recent developments and with a clearer focus on vulnerability reduction and dignity enhancement, will be offered in the Conclusion.

---

39 Robert Kuttner, *Can Democracy Survive Global Capitalism?* (New York: W.W. Norton & Co., 2018), 217.

Reinventing Democracy in Vulnerable Times

RICK: Don't you sometimes wonder if it's worth all this? I mean what you're fighting for.

LASZLO: You might as well question why we breathe. If we stop breathing, we'll die. If we stop fighting our enemies, the world will die.

RICK: Well, what of it? It'll be out of its misery.

LASZLO: You know how you sound, Monsieur Blaine? Like a man who's trying to convince himself of something he doesn't believe in his heart. Each of us has a destiny, for good or for evil.

RICK: I get the point.

LASZLO: I wonder if you do. I wonder if you know that you're trying to escape from yourself, and that you'll never succeed.

RICK: You seem to know all about my destiny.

— *Casablanca* (1942)

This book has claimed that fascist politics, today euphemistically called right-wing populism, a name which serves to sidestep the opprobrium associated with the f-word, is a strong temptation in times of high vulnerability such as we are experiencing now. Near the end of his book about the harm to democracy of present-day global capitalism, Robert Kuttner also noted "a direct connection between the stress on liberal democracy and the vulnerability of citizens to economic reverses."[1] Kuttner's guiding spirit was not Alexis de Tocqueville or Erich Fromm, but the Hungarian émigré Karl Polanyi (1886–1964), a contemporary of John Maynard Keynes (1883–1946). Keynes was the main architect of the Bretton Woods agreement and a critic, along with Jacques Bainville and a few others, of the severe punishment imposed on Germany at the end of World War I in the Treaty of Versailles.[2] Polanyi's *The Great Transformation* (1944) laid out the case that Franklin Roosevelt also made for a "Second Bill of Rights" in his 1944 State of the Union Address. Both documents declared how the United States and its allies could win the peace and prevent fascism's return by avoiding punitive measures and demonization this time around and instead build democracy into something nobler, attractive, and worthy of imitation that would rest on a foundation of mutual respect, political rights *and* economic rights.[3] Kuttner examines the economic roots of fascism and how those weeds proliferate when there is too much laissez-faire and not enough supervision of financial elites. I learned a lot from Kuttner, and from Masha Gessen and Timothy Snyder, but I could not devote a full chapter to every strong intervention on this complex topic.[4]

---

1   Robert Kuttner, *Can Democracy Survive Global Capitalism?* (New York: W.W. Norton & Co., 2018), ch. 11, "Liberalism, Populism, Fascism," 258.

2   See Zachary D. Carter, *The Price of Peace: Money, Democracy, and the Life of John Maynard Keynes* (New York: Random House, 2020).

3   See Caleb Crain's review of Kuttner's book, "Is Capitalism a Threat to Democracy?" *The New Yorker,* May 7, 2018, https://www.newyorker.com/magazine/2018/05/14/is-capitalism-a-threat-to-democracy.

4   Gessen and Snyder have written and spoken extensively about authoritarian and fascist history and recent trends. Gessen's comments in *The New Yorker* and Snyder's across many news outlets are models of clear instruction. For example, on the riot at the US Capitol on January 6, 2021, see Masha Gessen, "The Capitol Invaders Enjoyed the Privilege of Not Being Taken Seriously," *The New Yorker,* January 7, 2021, https://www.newyorker.com/news/our-columnists/the-capitol-invaders-enjoyed-the-privilege-of-not-being-taken-seriously. See also Timothy Snyder's analysis based on calling out "the big lie" and a distinction between breakers and gamers of

This book has focused on the history, logic, and psychology of fascism elaborated in the work of Robert Paxton (2004), Jason Stanley (2018), and Erich Fromm (1941). Fromm's contribution received the most detailed examination because his writings, which once sold in the millions, have been neglected, one could even say repressed, in recent discussions of the attraction of right-wing populism. I believe rediscovering *Escape from Freedom* and *The Art of Loving* would be helpful medicine at this time. Fromm's analysis of the "psychology of Nazism" and "automaton conformity" helps one understand how, under the guise of promoting national unity and prosperity, fascist right-wing populism, along with exaggerated faith in "free markets," "tech," and "devices," allows one to turn away from the burden of being a free and fragile individual in a competitive, open, pluralist democratic society. While professing courage and plain speaking, right-wing populism is often a fearful turn away from adult responsibilities and an extension of childhood attitudes and evasion fantasies under a domineering parent or algorithm. Instead of being a co-participant in constructing projects and policies that advance the general public good, vulnerable citizens may choose (or fall into) codependency and sign over their creative adult role to a class of managers relaying the orders of a charismatic rescuer-leader who claims to have their interests at heart but is in fact a bullying sadist and narcissist bent on power and domination.[5] At base, fascism is the symptom and

democracy, "The American Abyss," *The New York Times,* January 9, 2021, https://www.nytimes.com/2021/01/09/magazine/trump-coup.html. Gessen's book *The Man Without a Face: The Unlikely Rise of Vladimir Putin* (New York: Riverhead, 2012) and Timothy Snyder's *Bloodlands: Europe Between Hitler and Stalin* (New York: Basic Books, 2010) are particularly useful for understanding the Russian invasions of Ukraine in 2014 and 2022. Other historians who have offered valuable commentaries of recent events include David W. Blight, Karen L. Cox, Joanne B. Freeman, Greg Grandin, Eyal Press, and Heather Cox Richardson.

5   On identifying with a powerful aggressor as a self-defense mechanism, see Joseph Nowinski on Mary Trump's memoir about her uncle Donald's relationship with his father Fred Trump: "Identifying with the Aggressor," *Psychology Today,* July 17, 2020, https://www.psychologytoday.com/us/

the aggravator of a mental health problem worsened by extreme inequality and other vulnerabilities.[6]

People are particularly susceptible to an exploitive fascist relationship in a context of high vulnerability, either because they are experiencing health issues, economic precariousness, or suffering status anxiety due to lost social standing.[7] And fear of loss can be more upsetting and a sharper spur to radicalization than actual loss, studies show.[8] Hurt people hurt people — and themselves. This was true in Weimar Germany, and it is true in many countries today, with now the added vulnerabilities caused by the Covid-19 pandemic which echoes the destabilizing epidemic of 1918 that preceded the first episodes of European fascism.[9]

Understanding the vulnerabilities that lead people to want to escape from freedom because they come to view it, and the unmapped future generally, more as a threat than an opportunity, requires delving into life histories. This is why the first two "theory" chapters were followed by six chapters devoted to non-

---

blog/the-almost-effect/202007/identifying-the-aggressor. See also Marwa Azab, "Why Would Groups Attacked by Trump Vote for Him?" *Psychology Today,* November 11, 2016, https://www.psychologytoday.com/us/blog/neuroscience-in-everyday-life/201611/why-would-groups-attacked-trump-vote-him. The short answer, Stockholm Syndrome: "identifying with the aggressor provides a temporary bandage to conceal deep scars of anxiety, feelings of inferiority and pain," writes Azab.

6 See Farida Rustamova, "Putin Rules Russia Like an Asylum," *The New York Times,* May 23, 2022, https://www.nytimes.com/2022/05/23/opinion/russia-putin-war.html.

7 Thomas B. Edsall, "Status Anxiety Is Blowing Wind into Trump's Sails," *The New York Times,* February 9, 2022, https://www.nytimes.com/2022/02/09/opinion/trump-status-anxiety.html.

8 For a survey of the most recent research on loss anxiety with international data sets and links to several studies, see Thomas B. Edsall, "The Resentment That Never Sleeps," *The New York Times,* December 9, 2020, https://www.nytimes.com/2020/12/09/opinion/trump-social-status-resentment.html.

9 Covid-19 spurred conversations about the forgotten devastation of that earlier pandemic. See John M. Barry, *The Great Influenza: The Story of the Deadliest Pandemic in History* (New York: Penguin Books, 2004), and Nancy K. Bristow, *American Pandemic: The Lost Worlds of the 1918 Influenza Epidemic* (Oxford: Oxford University Press, 2012).

fictional and fictional narratives that retell the stories of vulnerable individuals. These vulnerability studies examined the situation of particular people and the choices they make — toward freedom or unfreedom — at critical junctures of their lives. We saw how these individuals responded to their vulnerability and the fascist temptation, tilting either toward or away from the enticing but ultimately crippling authoritarian "solution" it offers.

The last three chapters examined hybrid, theory-and-practice manifestos written in urgency by two philosophers (Martha Nussbaum and Jason Stanley) and a psychologist, Keith Payne. We saw how these manifestos combine argument and evidence, reasons and stories, through an examination of words and deeds that support the overall argument about fascism's pathological harmfulness. Stanley's rhetoric of fascism is an updating of Paxton's history with recent examples of "functional equivalents" of fascist politics around the world and a more explicit account of what Paxton suggestively called fascism's "emotional lava." Nussbaum shows through many examples how the heat source of that lava is fear (of loss, inadequacy, death), and how intense fear in turn fuels three negative emotions — anger, envy, and disgust — which have been highly destructive in recent right-wing populist politics.

The two philosophers were brought into a triangular dialogue with the compilation of social science experiments discussed by Payne in *The Broken Ladder* (2017). Payne's evidence, an anthology of stories, shows how extreme economic inequality and the unavowable fear and anxiety it engenders, especially among men burdened with the expectation of being "providers," scrambles the decision-making faculties of people in specific ways. It makes the vulnerable adopt a "live fast, die young" mentality and may incline one to take a sadistic pleasure in the destruction and the suffering of others of lower status or "caste."[10] On

---

10 See Jamelle Bouie, "What 'Structural Racism' Really Means," *The New York Times,* November 9, 2021, https://www.nytimes.com/2021/11/09/opinion/structural-racism.html. Bouie's argument goes back to the work of Oliver Cromwell Cox in *Caste, Class, and Race: A Study in Social Dynamics* (Lon-

the other end, the securely wealthy tend to overestimate their merit and entitlement, underestimate their sheer good luck, and may become contemptuous and unfeeling, or downright cruel, toward those termed "weak." Like Kuttner, Joseph Stiglitz, and Paul Krugman, Payne reveals the economic roots of social polarization which is favorable terrain for the divisive politics of *us* versus *them* thoroughly X-rayed by Stanley and Nussbaum who both identify this rift as the effect and accelerant of fascism's exploitation of fear to undermine trust in democracy and in the possibility of pluralism and peaceful coexistence.

Despite their clarity and timeliness, however, these consciousness-raising exercises about what fascism was, is, or might be and how fascism works are inadequate for reducing its likelihood and the pain it causes. History lessons and logical demonstrations are necessary but insufficient tools for combatting fascism and defending, restoring, or building democracy. In addition to specific kinds of knowledge, one must mobilize and vote to decrease inequality. One must also work to increase a stock of positive experiences and memories associated with the pleasures of being equal and free — to do and to make — such that one will consistently prefer and pursue the freedom, equality, and solidarity that only creative, participatory democracy offers, and that fascism, authoritarianism, and empire always denigrate and destroy.

Key to building up that stock of positive feelings is lowering barriers to voting, to communicating, to education and lifelong learning, to healthcare including mental health services, to changing jobs and moving about, and to experimentation in general. Lowering these barriers would empower "we the people" and be a salutary force for the public good, especially now since extreme income and wealth inequality coupled with the fragilizing forces of monopolistic global capitalism and the double threat of not just climate change but epidemiological threats (Covid-19, -20?, -21?, -22?...) means that vulnerability,

---

don: Forgotten Books, 2018). See also the bestseller by Isabel Wilkerson, *Caste: The Origins of Our Discontents* (New York: Random House, 2020).

and with it paralyzing panic or rage violence, is running high on every continent. Vulnerability is generally a terrible feeling and condition though also sometimes a learning opportunity, if one lives to tell the tale.[11] Extreme vulnerability must be reduced if we are going to keep from losing our heads and repeating the destructive mistake of falling for far-right populism's alluring but ultimately always disappointing pseudo-solutions to the social, political, economic, and ecological challenges we face — "we" being everyone on the planet. Keeping our heads, and hearts, means resisting the temptation of quick fixes, especially the "sugar high" that comes with the cruel victimization of dehumanized, "otherized" outgroups and all acts of misplaced condescension, angry retaliation, defiant projection, and sterile zero-sum thinking. It requires choosing calm and inclusive, dignity-based democracy and rejecting exclusionary, circling-the-wagons fascism.

The choice for the United States and every nominally free society is clear and urgent: one can either stoke or watch as others stoke grievances and sectarianism, persecute scapegoats, and destroy solidarity and democracy[12] (or in the case of China and other unfree nations abandon all striving to rise out of authoritarianism); or one can demand that we tame global surveillance capitalism and place it back under the rule of law and the public good, as once happened in North America and Europe using the Bretton Woods agreement during the "thirty glorious years" after 1945. The latter course would strengthen democracy by making it more responsive to the material and spiritual needs of a given citizenry, and set a positive example for oth-

---

11 Near the end of his operatic memoir *Fire Shut Up in My Bones* (New York: Mariner, 2014), Charles M. Blow claims "vulnerability is the leading edge of truth" (219). But as we saw with Martha Dodd, Hélène Berr, Leslie Jamison, Offred, Philip, and Frances, many don't survive extreme vulnerability, no one goes unscarred, and few can spin it into gold.

12 See former Fox News employee Chris Stirewalt's book *Broken News: Why the Media Rage Machine Divides America and How to Fight Back* (New York: Center Street, 2022).

ers to imitate if and how they wish.[13] The former is the fascist road to authoritarian unfreedom and already the daily reality not just in Iran, Russia, and China, but for over half the world's population, according to Freedom House.[14] By joining others down that road, however, the degradation will no longer be experienced in Lyon, London, or Los Angeles from a safe distance as history, diary, memoir, fairy story, dystopian fiction, breaking news from a faraway land, or a riveting TV miniseries. It will be live — such as with the riot at the US Capitol on January 6, 2021 and the Russian invasion of Ukraine on February 24, 2022.

In the "choice theory" language of William Glasser, we only care about things in our "quality world"; and the only things in our quality world are things which we feel in our bones are meeting our primary needs: to survive, to love, feel loved and have a sense of belonging, to feel powerful, to feel free, and to have fun.[15] The European Union's regular reminder that since 1945 there has been no World War III or a repeat of the Holocaust on European soil (so long as one downplays the Balkan wars and ethnic cleansing in the 1990s) is a low bar for celebration and may be a partial explanation of why European integration and feeling "European" has advanced slowly in recent dec-

13 See, David Remnick, "A Person of the Year: Jamie Raskin," *The New Yorker,* December 16, 2021, https://www.newyorker.com/news/daily-comment/a-person-of-the-year-jamie-raskin, Remnick's tribute to Raskin, the US Congressman from Maryland's Eighth District, lead House manager during Trump's second impeachment trial, and author of *Unthinkable: Truth, Trauma, and the Trials of American Democracy* (New York: HarperCollins, 2022).

14 All countries are classified as either free, partly free, or not free at Freedomhouse.org. In 2021 President Joe Biden and the Chinese leader Xi Jinping became the faces of rival "alliances" of democracies versus autocracies in a global competition for overall social and economic superiority. Biden called it "a battle between the utility of democracies in the 21st century and autocracies [...] We've got to prove democracy works" (March 25, 2021). See Steven Lee Myers, "An Alliance of Autocracies? China Wants to Lead a New World Order," *The New York Times,* March 29, 2021, https://www.nytimes.com/2021/03/29/world/asia/china-us-russia.html.

15 William Glasser, *Choice Theory: A New Psychology of Personal Freedom* (New York: HarperCollins, 1998).

ades, though it may accelerate in the wake of Vladimir Putin's invasion of Ukraine. Just as many young people do not include school in their quality world because it is not meeting enough of their needs, so too democracy is not yet part of many Europeans' quality world. This is especially true in southern and eastern Europe where democracy has shallow roots, to use Kuttner's metaphor. However, in 2020, 2021, and 2022 a mostly democratic Europe may have edged closer to being considered a quality world, and to actually being one, than any other continent; though it would be great to witness a friendly competition for that honor, like being first in happiness or kindness, or "first in love… first in moral excellence… first in generosity,"[16] instead of watching a race to the bottom of quality of life indexes which today's global capitalism and authoritarianization continue to exacerbate.

When Secretary of State Madeleine Albright called the United States the "indispensable nation" in 1998, some may have winced or raised an eyebrow, but many grudgingly or still enthusiastically agreed.[17] So in early 2018, when Kuttner's book went to press, it was somewhat understandable that he would conclude, "Though America in the Trump era is increasingly self-isolating and not much of a beacon for anything, it is hard to imagine any other nation claiming the global mantle of political liberalism and economic equity."[18] Like Albright, he's an American, and a New Yorker to boot, rooting for the home team, and in the following pages he sketches some of the shortcomings of Europe, especially the challenges facing French president Emmanuel Macron — France being America's long-

---

16 Martin Luther King, Jr., "The Drum Major Instinct," in *I Have A Dream: Writings and Speeches That Changed the World* (New York: HarperCollins, 1992), 189. Finland often ranks first in World Happiness Reports.

17 Madeleine Jana Korbel Albright, née Marie Jana Korbelová (1937–2022), died as this book was going to press. One of her last public statements was a warning published on the eve of Vladimir Putin's invasion of Ukraine, "Putin Is Making a Historic Mistake," *The New York Times,* February 23, 2022, https://www.nytimes.com/2022/02/23/opinion/putin-ukraine.html.

18 Kuttner, *Can Democracy Survive Global Capitalism?,* 289–90.

time friendly rival.[19] Two years later, however, American dysfunction has only increased and become apparent to all with the glaring statistic that the US has less than 5 percent of the world's population but accounts for roughly a quarter of coronavirus cases and 20 percent of Covid-19 deaths.[20] Trump's deliberate lies and denials about the severity of Covid-19, redoubled by members of his base who continued to attend political rallies (often without masks) through the summer and fall of 2020 despite ample proof of the highly contagious nature of the virus — all this is common knowledge and leaves many observers shaking their heads.[21] Increasingly, with the anti-democratic and anti-science stance of one of its two major political parties, the US has become literally a sick joke, an object of pity, shame, or bewilderment, or simply ignored.[22] Foreign students were already considering other options pre-Covid when they only had to weigh the complicated United States visa process, the high cost of living in some metropolitan areas, and the open carry gun laws and school shootings. Now the country's attractiveness for international tourism, business, and diplomacy is no longer a sure thing due to health care costs and "medical deserts" (what

---

19 For a summary of Europe's strengths and weaknesses by a European, see Caroline de Gruyter, "Europe Is in Danger. It Always Is," *The New York Times,* May 2, 2022, https://www.nytimes.com/2022/05/02/opinion/european-union-macron-ukraine.html.

20 Coincidentally the same as the United States's incarceration rate: only 5 percent of world population, but 25 percent of all prisoners.

21 About Trump's candid interviews with veteran Watergate journalist Bob Woodward, Maureen Dowd remarked, "Donald Trump is his own whistleblower": "All the President's Insecurities," *The New York Times,* September 12, 2020, https://www.nytimes.com/2020/09/12/opinion/sunday/donald-trump-bob-woodward.html.

22 See Robin Wright, "To the World, We're Now America the Racist and Pitiful," *The New Yorker,* July 3, 2020, https://www.newyorker.com/news/our-columnists/to-the-world-were-now-america-the-racist-and-pitiful; Hannah Beech, "'I Feel Sorry for Americans': A Baffled World Watches the U.S.," *The New York Times,* September 25, 2020, https://www.nytimes.com/2020/09/25/world/asia/trump-united-states.html; and Roger Cohen, "How Trump Lowered America's Standing in the Word," *The New York Times,* October 29, 2020, https://www.nytimes.com/2020/10/29/opinion/trump-foreign-policy-us-allies.html.

if Jean-Pierre has a health emergency on vacation?), a workforce of questionable abilities (when the United States turns off the immigrant faucet, who's left to get the job done?), and growing distrust of US leadership given the erratic pronouncements, lies, and self-dealing of President Trump and his aides, and the polarization verging on sectarianism across the country which is plain for all to see.[23]

Europe's problems (corruption, inequality, grudges and prejudice, energy dependence, and lack of an agreed on non-mythical history and workable foreign policy) have not gone away, but there are signs of more EU solidarity and coordination, notably in their efforts both to combat Covid-19 and to collectively address the socio-economic devastation it has caused.[24] Europe's biggest problems are the drag caused by lingering pockets of antidemocracy within its borders (especially Hungary and Poland), the democracy deficit of its institutions,[25] and the possibility of the UK becoming a sponsor of more rogue

---

23 New research goes beyond "polarization" and speaks of "political sectarianism," a term usually reserved for openly violent societies such as Northern Ireland and Lebanon in the 1970s and '80s. For a review of several alarming studies, see Thomas B. Edsall's *New York Times* pieces, "America, We Have a Problem," December 16, 2020, https://www.nytimes.com/2020/12/16/opinion/trump-political-sectarianism.html, and "America Has Split, and It's Now in 'Very Dangerous Territory'," January 26, 2022, https://www.nytimes.com/2022/01/26/opinion/covid-biden-trump-polarization.html; Nate Cohn, "Why Political Sectarianism Is a Growing Threat to American Democracy," *The New York Times,* April 19, 2021, https://theoneworldnews.com/americas/why-political-sectarianism-is-a-growing-threat-to-american-democracy/; and Elizabeth Kolbert who reviews new polarization studies on the occasion of the first anniversary of the Capitol riot, "How Politics Got So Polarized," *The New Yorker,* December 27, 2021, https://www.newyorker.com/magazine/2022/01/03/how-politics-got-so-polarized.

24 Bojan Pancevski and Laurence Norman, "How Angela Merkel's Change of Heart Drove Historic EU Rescue Plan," *The Wall Street Journal,* July 21, 2020, https://www.wsj.com/articles/angela-merkel-macron-covid-coronavirus-eu-rescue-11595364124. Long term, the rescue involves combatting misinformation which the EU is pursuing, around Covid-19 and other topics, with the Digital Services Act of 2022 and Digital Markets Act of 2020.

25 Kuttner, *Can Democracy Survive Global Capitalism?,* ch. 6.

banking post-Brexit.[26] Instability and autocracy in the neighborhood is what made democratic advances in Tunisia and
Egypt so difficult after the Arab Spring. Europe's regional bullies
and troublemakers pose similar challenges, but also offer an opportunity for coming together to reaffirm shared liberal values
and goals. Another bright note: there are signs that medium-
sized Pacific rim countries from New Zealand to South Korea
are successfully "adulting" without taking their cues from the
United States, Russia, or China. Africa and Latin America are
also asserting more confidence and awareness as they negotiate
new partnerships, often with China instead of the traditional
European powers or America. Indeed, *American exceptionalism*
may have changed meanings, since in key social areas (health,
education, housing, policing, prisons, voting, the environment,
labor relations, family life, and caring for children, seniors, and
the disabled, for example) the country's policies and practices
are singled out as what not to do if one cares about the public
good.[27] America, "not much of a beacon for anything"? It didn't
have to be this way.

When the Cold War ended with the fall of the Berlin Wall in
1989, the Tiananmen Square massacre the same year, and the

---

26 See Nicholas Shaxson, "The City of London Is Hiding the World's Stolen
    Money," *The New York Times,* October 11, 2021, https://www.nytimes.
    com/2021/10/11/opinion/pandora-papers-britain-london.html. On EU
    membership, one could make the "keep friends close, enemies closer"
    argument that there are advantages to having both Hungary and Poland
    within the EU circle rather than being an anti-democratic counterforce on
    the outside like the current far-right governments of Turkey and Serbia,
    for example. Looking back with 20–20 hindsight, it may have been a
    mistake by the EU to not allow Turkey to join back in the early 2000s when
    the country's far-right party was less powerful. The case for Serbia joining,
    and one day Turkey too, might be made again in a calmer post-pandemic,
    post-war environment. Much will depend on the level of attractiveness of
    democratic life and health within the EU compared to living conditions
    outside the EU.

27 On the "dire redefinition of 'American exceptionalism,'" see the official
    endorsement of Joe Biden for president, editorial unsigned, "'The New
    Yorker' Endorses a Joe Biden Presidency," *The New Yorker,* September 28,
    2020.

collapse of the Soviet Union in 1991, the United States had an opportunity to go high and build democracy back better instead of taking a smug victory lap and doubling down on the supposed virtues of being a world leader in "financial services"— via the World Trade Organization, the North American Free Trade Agreement, and other free trade levers. It seems that after the Cold War, Americans began (some would say resumed) a second cold war with themselves starting in the early 1990s. The opening salvo was Newt Gingrich versus Bill Clinton, a Wall Street-friendly Arkansas Democrat whose "tough on crime" stance mimicked the attitude of authoritarian good ol' boys who then had to resort to a lurid smear campaign to prevent him from beating them at their own game.[28] Public spending for improved overall wellness (the word *welfare* having been poisoned by Republicans in the 1980s) verus Grover Norquist's radicalization of Reagan-era tax revolts, which turned tax avoidance into an act of smart patriotism, was the second. Mitch McConnell versus Barack Obama was the third or thirtieth. Another opportunity to force global capitalism to actually serve the people, instead of it being the reverse, came in the aftermath of 9/11; but no way could be imagined that wouldn't sound like applause for Al Qaeda or being soft on terrorism — as Mary Beard and Mary Robinson both discovered.[29] Yet another opportunity came with

---

28 Greg Grandin sees Clinton as "Reagan's greatest achievement," *The End of the Myth: From the Frontier to the Border Wall in the Mind of America* (New York: Metropolitan Books, 2019), 233–34: "He carried forward the Republican agenda by combining a postindustrial fatalism — regulation wasn't possible, austerity was unavoidable, budgets had to be balanced, crime was a condition of culture not economic policy — with a folksy postmodern optimism, offering sunny bromides touting the 'politics of inclusion' that endless growth would make possible." Clinton's rightward tack would lead to a split among Democrats in 2000, with some defecting to Ralph Nader. This split contributed to George W. Bush's narrow electoral college victory over Bill Clinton's successor, Al Gore — a scenario that repeated itself in 2016 with the Hillary Clinton versus Bernie Sanders and Jill Stein split that worked to Trump's advantage.

29 Professor Mary Beard's response to 9/11 ("11 September," *London Review of Books*, October 4, 2001, https://www.lrb.co.uk/the-paper/v23/n19/nine-eleven-writers/11-september) caused a row. Mary Robinson was the

the Great Recession of 2008–9, but President Obama swapped one slick male and pale Dartmouth grad, Hank Paulson, for another, Timothy Geithner, to direct the government's response to the housing crisis and supervise the bailout that "abandoned Main Street while rescuing Wall Street."[30] President Obama would later express sympathy for the Occupy Wall Street protests, and yet on his watch hardly any bankers were punished for their role in the financial crisis; and ows lasted barely one hundred days with the grievances of the 99% left unresolved.[31] These were two sources of resentment among others that Trump would exploit in the 2016 presidential campaign. Other world events that further deflated confidence in us democracy's ability to respond effectively to crises include the muted response to the Syrian civil war starting in 2011, especially Bashar al-Assad's use of chemical weapons on his own people while, simultane-

---

United Nations High Commissioner for Human Rights at the time of 9/11 and was pressured to resign by Bush administration officials who, wanting a free hand, refused to have those attacks be classified as a crime against humanity within a unifying human rights framework. See Mike Chinoy, *Are You With Me? Kevin Boyle and the Rise of the Human Rights Movement* (Dublin: The Lilliput Press, 2020), ch. 23.

30 Neil Barofsky, *Bailout: An Inside Account of How Washington Abandoned Main Street While Rescuing Wall Street* (New York: Free Press, 2012); Timothy Geithner, *Stress Test: Reflections on Financial Crises* (New York: Random House, 2014); and Brandon L. Garrett, *Too Big to Jail: How Prosecutors Compromise with Corporations* (Cambridge: Harvard University Press, 2016).

31 The messaging of the #Occupy movement was drowned out by billionaire donors' support for pro-*laissez faire* lobbyists, politicians, and judges. This support was epitomized by David and Charles Koch whose decades-long deregulation crusade ramped up in the wake of the anti-democratic Citizens United v. Federal Election Commission Supreme Court decision of 2010. See Jane Mayer, *Dark Money: The Hidden History of the Billionaires Behind the Rise of the Radical Right* (New York: Random House, 2016), and Christopher Leonard, *Kochland: The Secret History of Koch Industries and Corporate Power in America* (New York: Simon & Schuster, 2019). For a summary of Leonard's thesis on the eve of the Senate hearings to appoint a third Trump justice to the Supreme Court, Judge Amy Coney Barrett, see Leonard's op-ed piece, "Charles Koch's Big Bet on Barrett," *The New York Times,* October 12, 2020, https://www.nytimes.com/2020/10/12/opinion/charles-koch-amy-coney-barrett.html.

ously, President Obama ramped up deportation proceedings and extrajudicial drone strike killings; the impunity following the Russian annexation of Crimea and Putin's destabilization of Ukraine directly after the doped up Sochi Olympics in 2014; and the "nothing to see here" response in 2016 to revelations in the Panama Papers concerning tax havens and tax evasion. Meanwhile, "stakeholder capitalism," which some within the Davos financial elite now agree should replace "shareholder capitalism," has yet to materialize.[32]

Internal frustration with American democracy since 1989 sharpened during the Covid-19 pandemic. The brutal police killing of George Floyd in late May 2020 reignited a social and racial justice movement occurring simultaneously alongside the health crisis — the overlap being the disproportionate number of Covid-19 deaths among Americans of color who often lack health insurance, live in crowded housing, hold "frontline" jobs that increase their chances of infection, and present higher rates of comorbidities, such as obesity, that make them more vulnerable to complications when they catch the virus. The lack of presidential leadership, honesty, and empathy, and the refusal to call for a national day of mourning or a South African-style truth and reconciliation conversation have been lamented, including by some Republicans. As the 2020 election approached, many feared that the United States would be the next Belarus, with a stubborn autocrat "performing fascism"[33]: unwilling to al-

---

32 Peter S. Goodman, "Stakeholder Capitalism Gets a Report Card: It's Not Good," *The New York Times,* September 24, 2020, https://www.nytimes.com/2020/09/22/business/business-roudtable-stakeholder-capitalism.html. Vladimir Putin's renewed efforts to destabilize the European Union and democracy in general, first indirectly via Belarus with the manufactured immigration crisis in autumn 2021 and then with the direct military invasion of Ukraine starting shortly after the Beijing Winter Olympics of 2022, would require more commentary than can be given here since these events are still unfolding.

33 See, for example, Masha Gessen, "Donald Trump's Fascist Performance," *The New Yorker,* June 3, 2020, https://www.newyorker.com/news/our-columnists/donald-trumps-fascist-performance.

low free and fair elections to take place unobstructed; unwilling to accept the result if he lost.[34]

Could the United States — a divided country where in 2020 a segment of the population felt the need to use yard signs to remind another segment of the population that "Black Lives Matter" and "Science is Real" — still lead an international reassertion of political liberalism and economic equity that would quell the rise of right-wing populism on every continent? Maybe, but leading implies having willing teammates who believe in the leader's qualifications, not just second-string players with no better option than being part of a coalition of the coerced. Nicholas Kristof recently commented on the findings of a global Social Progress Index that ranks the United States twenty-eighth and falling in overall quality of life based on fifty metrics from education to health to the environment.[35] That wake-up call comes ten years after his *New York Times* colleague Thomas Friedman lamented "We're No. 1(1)!" according to a similar *Newsweek* index.[36] It has also been widely reported and discussed, notably by Anne Case and Angus Deaton, that not just life quality but life expectancy has fallen in the United States

---

34 After debating the suitability of the term "fascism" to describe Trump and Trumpism between 2015 and 2020, the discussion turned to the word "coup" to describe Trump's post-election behavior. See Zeynep Tufekci, "'This Must Be Your First,'" *The Atlantic,* December 7, 2020, https://www. theatlantic.com/ideas/archive/2020/12/trumps-farcical-inept-and-deadly-serious-coup-attempt/617309/, and Jamelle Bouie, "The 'Trump Won' Farce Isn't Funny Anymore," *The New York Times,* December 11, 2020, https://www.nytimes.com/2020/12/11/opinion/trump-republicans-texas-lawsuit.html. Coup or no coup, the 2020 election proved again that minority rule is firmly established in the US, and that many Republicans have abandoned democracy's rules and norms.

35 Nicholas Kristof, "We're No. 28! And Dropping!" *The New York Times,* September 9, 2020, https://www.nytimes.com/2020/09/09/opinion/united-states-social-progress.html.

36 Thomas Friedman, "We're No. 1(1)!" *The New York Times,* September 11, 2010, https://www.nytimes.com/2010/09/12/opinion/12friedman.html. Note the proximity of both these pieces to the anniversary of 9/11, in other words timed to coincide with what Americans ritually invoke as a moment of national reflection.

in recent years.[37] So, yes, the US might qualify for a G-28 meeting, if such a thing existed, but would it get to stand at the front of the room and set the agenda — especially if toxic Trumpism is not a passing interlude (as Kuttner hoped, referring to Trump already in the past tense in 2018) but instead the new normal of one of the country's political parties with millions of authoritarian-friendly followers?[38] Face it, plenty of people go from an authoritarian homelife to vertical chains of command in their church and workplace that last for decades.[39] If coercive vertical arrangements are all one has known, democracy may seem highfalutin and make one uncomfortable — doubly so if there is a social expectation that one embrace democracy and do a second civic shift as *informed voter* in addition to one's day job, a task 30 to 50 percent of Americans refuse to do. Fascism solves that problem. So does voter suppression and election subversion; and all three often go together — with or without those nametags.[40]

---

37 Anne Case and Angus Deaton, *Deaths of Despair and the Future of Capitalism* (Princeton: Princeton University Press, 2020). See also Nicholas Kristof and Sheryl WuDunn, *Tightrope: Americans Reaching for Hope* (New York: Random House, 2020).

38 Adam Jentleson, "What If Trumpism Is the G.O.P.'s Natural State?" *The New York Times,* August 18, 2020, https://www.nytimes.com/2020/08/18/opinion/trump-republican-party.html; John W. Dean and Bob Altemeyer, *Authoritarian Nightmare: Trump and His Followers* (New York: Melville House, 2020); Charles M. Blow, "Trump's Army of Angry White Men," *The New York Times,* October 25, 2020, https://www.nytimes.com/2020/10/25/opinion/trump-white-men-election.html; and Jeff Sharlet, "He's the Chosen One to Run America: Inside the Cult of Trump, His Rallies Are Church and He Is the Gospel," *Vanity Fair,* June 18, 2020, https://www.vanityfair.com/news/2020/06/inside-the-cult-of-trump-his-rallies-are-church-and-he-is-the-gospel.

39 Elizabeth Anderson, *Private Government: How Employers Rule Our Lives (and Why We Don't Talk about It)* (Princeton: Princeton University Press, 2017). The sovereign authority of church leaders is common knowledge.

40 On the historical context, purpose, and impact of new restrictive voting rules in Georgia, a democracy battleground state, see Jamelle Bouie, "If It's Not Jim Crow, What is It?" *The New York Times,* April 6, 2021, https://www.nytimes.com/2021/04/06/opinion/georgia-voting-law.html. On the preference for election subversion over upholding democratic principles,

Viewed more hopefully, perhaps the triple crisis of Covid-19, climate change and migration, and neofascist right-wing populisms will be answered by peaceful protests and decentralized but coordinated democratic movements that resist scapegoating, personality cults, and outsourcing to prostheses and proxies to do the walking, talking, and heavy lifting. In the summer and fall of 2020, two icons, one of the civil rights movement, Congressman John Lewis, the other of the women's liberation movement, Supreme Court Justice Ruth Bader Ginsburg, died of what used to be called old age. They were not cut down like 200,000 other Americans in the middle six months of 2020 by Covid-19 cruelty and incompetence.[41] Both received the country's highest funeral honors as well as moving tributes from admirers of different backgrounds. These heroes will be missed by many — as are Senator John McCain and Congressman Elijah Cummings who also died during the Trump presidency in 2018 and 2019, respectively. However, the bright side is that the passing of these outstanding public servants can serve as a call to each of us to step up, raise our game, and get more involved. It's our turn to let freedom ring or "run for something."[42] Lewis

---

see Thomas B. Edsall's inventory of recent studies, including work by Milan Svolik, "Trump Poses a Test Democracy Is Failing," *The New York Times,* April 13, 2022, https://www.nytimes.com/2022/04/13/opinion/trump-democracy-decline-fall.html: "In sharply polarized electorates, even voters who value democracy will be willing to sacrifice fair democratic competition for the sake of electing politicians who champion their interests. When punishing a leader's authoritarian tendencies requires voting for a platform, party, or person that his supporters detest, many will find this too high a price to pay [… Partisan competition] presents aspiring authoritarians with a structural opportunity: They can undermine democracy and get away with it."

41 Less than two years later, in mid-May 2022, the United States reached the grim milestone of one million Covid-19 deaths — a statistic ignored by many, but for others a number and a moment to think about. See Damien Cave, "How Australia Saved Thousands of Lives While Covid Killed a Million Americans," *The New York Times,* May 15, 2022, https://www.nytimes.com/2022/05/15/world/australia/covid-deaths.html.

42 Amanda Litman, the co-founder of Run for Something, "a group that recruits and supports young progressive candidates for office," was interviewed by *New York Times* political commentator Ezra Klein on February

even left a posthumous open letter calling on young people to do just that.[43] It seems Ginsburg left no such parting exhortation — all the better to draw people back to her sizeable body of published work and her oral arguments from which some future Rose, Rodney, or Ruth might take inspiration.

To my knowledge, no icon of class died in 2020. I'm not even sure who would qualify in the US as an icon of class of comparable stature to Lewis on race and Ginsburg on gender. It seems to be the national conversation that has not really happened yet despite the dogged efforts of some journalists, professors, and politicians such as Bernie Sanders and Elizabeth Warren.[44] I suppose some might consider America's class icon to be the "winning" billionaire Warren Buffett or even Trump, but it is hard to imagine either will one day lie in state at the Capitol. Also, despite all the talk about the importance of *intersectional-*

1, 2022. The transcript is here: https://www.nytimes.com/2022/02/01/podcasts/transcript-ezra-klein-interviews-amanda-litman.html.

43 John Lewis, "Together, You Can Redeem the Soul of Our Nation," *The New York Times,* July 30, 2020, https://www.nytimes.com/2020/07/30/opinion/john-lewis-civil-rights-america.html. For practical steps, see Alicia Garza, *The Purpose of Power: How We Come Together When We Fall Apart* (New York: Penguin Random House, 2020), and Jamar Tisby, *How to Fight Racism: Courageous Christianity and the Journey toward Racial Justice* (Grand Rapids: Zondervan, 2021).

44 The conversation from the progressive perspective is more a thousand points of light that are sometimes gathered, such as in "The Jobs We Need," *The New York Times,* June 24, 2020, https://www.nytimes.com/2020/06/24/opinion/sunday/income-wealth-inequality-america.html, or in the older but still relevant anthology Bill Keller, ed., *Class Matters* (New York: Henry Holt, 2005). Mostly the conversation occurs in spurts, such as after a crime. See May Jeong, "The Deep American Roots of the Atlanta Shootings," *The New York Times,* March 19, 2021, https://www.nytimes.com/2021/03/19/opinion/atlanta-shooting-massage-sex-work.html: "The events were also informed by class: These women, some of whom were working class, almost certainly died because they were at work. As working women of color, they existed at the terrible nexus of race, gender and class. It is, of course, often women who don't speak English or are undocumented who are locked out of traditional labor markets, or are otherwise marginalized."

ity since Kimberlé Crenshaw introduced the term in 1989[45] — a fateful year, the dawn of the Internet Age, and the bicentenary of both America's first presidential election and the start of the French Revolution — there are still few examples of a synergistic, intersectional approach to mobilizing and campaigning together for greater equality, freedom, and solidarity. Race-Class Academy is a rare exception with a clear message about how to combat dog-whistle politics[46] and all the divide and conquer strategies from Barry Goldwater, Lewis Powell, and Richard Nixon to Steve Bannon, Stephen Miller, and Trump that leave global capitalists morally unburdened, financially untaxed, and legally unaccountable.[47]

Certain politicians exploit racist rhetoric to divide and distract, while they rig government and the economy for themselves and their big money donors. They get richer, we get poorer — and the power of government is turned against communities of color. But we can fight back and win. Here's the most powerful movement-building message today: *When we come together to reject racism as a weapon of the reactionary rich, we can make sure that the government works for all of us, of every race and color.*[48]

---

45 Kimberlé Crenshaw, "Demarginalizing the Intersection of Race and Sex: A Black Feminist Critique of Antidiscrimination Doctrine, Feminist Theory and Antiracist Politics," *University of Chicago Legal Forum* 1989, no. 1 (1989): 139–67.

46 Ian Haney López, *Dog-Whistle Politics: How Coded Racial Appeals Have Reinvented Racism and Wrecked the Middle Class* (Oxford: Oxford University Press, 2014).

47 Kim Phillips-Fein, *Invisible Hands: The Businessmen's Crusade against the New Deal* (New York: W.W. Norton & Co., 2009). See also her *New York Times* guest essays, "Is Amy Coney Barrett Joining a Supreme Court Built for the Wealthy?" September 27, 2020, https://www.nytimes.com/2020/09/27/opinion/amy-coney-barrett-business-supreme-court.html, and "I Wouldn't Bet on the Kind of Democracy Big Business is Selling Us," February 1, 2022, https://www.nytimes.com/2022/02/01/opinion/corporations-democracy.html.

48 From the Race-Class Academy homepage, https://race-class-academy.com/. In brief, see Ian Haney López and Tory Gavito, "This Is How Biden

Agreed. And not only "of every race and color," but of every "religion, national origin, membership in a particular social group, and political opinion." This covers all the categories of harmful discrimination that are central to the cases of asylum seekers who must prove past persecution or well-founded fear of future harm should they be returned to their country of origin. Asylum would be worth little if, once residing in the receiving country, the asylum seeker remained vulnerable to the same kind of persecution the person had escaped from. Here one sees that national governance, like capitalism, has a transnational dimension once one enters into international agreements about *human* rights and not merely the rights of a particular subset of native or naturalized citizens. Another reason American democracy is tarnished lately is the growing international awareness that the US government is adept at promoting international agreements that expand its rights to do global trading and capital transfers; but loathe to accept agreements and institutions — such as the International Criminal Court or global climate accords — that constrain its share of responsibility to uphold the rule of law, human rights, and environmental protections. Increasingly this preference for washing dirty laundry behind closed doors while coercing an open-door trade policy and unregulated capital markets has been called out as hypocritical and thuggish. This has provoked a revolt against the so-called Washington Consensus (another dubious legacy of the 1980s) that unfortunately can

---

Should Approach the Latino Vote," *The New York Times,* September 18, 2020, https://www.nytimes.com/2020/09/18/opinion/biden-latino-vote-strategy.html. See also Jamelle Bouie's use of Oliver Cromwell Cox's early intersectional approach in Cox's *Caste, Class, and Race: A Study in Social Dynamics* (New York: Monthly Review Press, 1948): "Race prejudice," Cox writes, "developed gradually in Western society as capitalism and nationalism developed. It is a divisive attitude seeking to alienate dominant group sympathy from an 'inferior' race, a whole people, for the purpose of facilitating its exploitation." Jamelle Bouie, "What 'Structural Racism' Really Means," *The New York Times,* November 9, 2021, https://www.nytimes.com/2021/11/09/opinion/structural-racism.html.

lead to the democracy baby being thrown out with the abusive financial services bathwater.[49]

Hostility toward bossy bankers flying in from supposed democracies and "monetizing poor people" has been exploited in Venezuela, Hungary, Italy, and elsewhere in order to sell protectionist mafia-style capitalism as the lesser evil — instead of productively channeling the people's rightful indignation about the harm done by unscrupulous international businessmen into building the regulatory apparatus necessary for keeping all capitalism subordinate to a participatory, egalitarian, and honest social democracy. There is a clear historical record that shows democracy without checks and balances runs itself into the ground. The same is true for capitalism. Tocqueville and Karl Marx famously predicted it. But the historical record also shows that fascist authoritarianisms are not durable solutions but only dig the hole deeper, placing most people further away from a quality world capable of meeting their needs more consistently and reliably. Fromm and later Payne and others with various backgrounds and toolboxes have all testified to the high emotional cost, across all classes, of inequality and envious comparisons, as well as the tangle of pathologies that develop from asymmetrical vulnerabilities and the asymmetry of inequality itself — including the distortions caused by "poor logic,"[50] "class cluelessness,"[51] and "the anxieties of affluence."[52]

---

49 In her manifesto against neoliberal excess and cruelty toward women in particular, Kristin R. Ghodsee uses the same metaphor to encourage salvaging the best aspects of socialism: "There was a baby in all that bathwater. It's time we got around to saving it." Kristin R. Ghodsee, *Why Women Have Better Sex under Socialism: And Other Arguments for Economic Independence* (New York: Nation Books, 2018), 177.

50 Keith Payne, *The Broken Ladder: How Inequality Affects the Way We Think, Live, and Die* (New York: Viking, 2017), ch. 3, "Poor Logic: Inequality Has a Logic of Its Own," 57–82.

51 Joan C. Williams, *White Working Class: Overcoming Class Cluelessness in America* (Cambridge: Harvard Business Review Press, 2018).

52 Rachel Sherman, *Uneasy Street: The Anxieties of Affluence* (Princeton: Princeton University Press, 2017). For a paired review of Payne's *Broken Ladder* with Rachel Sherman's *Uneasy Street: The Anxieties of Affluence* (Princeton: Princeton University Press, 2017), see Elizabeth Kolbert, "The

There would be much more to say, but as I've said, saying more is not, alone, going to repair America's broken democracy or halt fascist experiments in other countries, because, as Congressman Lewis said, "Democracy is not a state. It is an act."[53] Only massive peaceful protests, carefully crafted messaging such as with the templates offered by Race-Class Academy, and more voting for progressive, pro-democracy candidates can reduce inequality and vulnerability and increase individual dignity, freedom, and opportunity for all. I endorse Kuttner's recommendations in his concluding "The Road from Here" chapter. Ultimately, it's of secondary importance which countries take the lead in implementing those policies so long as people take back their democracies from the hijackers. I recommend heeding the advice of Gessen and Snyder in their guidebooks for surviving autocracy and tyranny.[54] I also stand by the list of recommendations I made at the end of *Tocqueville and Democracy in the Internet Age.* Reducing inequality[55] is still job No. 1, and I still believe some paid national service should be required of everyone; however, elective office should not become a lifelong sinecure which is why I favor generous but firm term-limits, somewhere between fifteen and twenty-five years, including

---

Psychology of Inequality," *The New Yorker,* January 8, 2018, https://www.newyorker.com/magazine/2018/01/15/the-psychology-of-inequality.

53   John Lewis, "Together, You Can Redeem the Soul of Our Nation," *The New York Times,* July 30, 2020, https://www.nytimes.com/2020/07/30/opinion/john-lewis-civil-rights-america.html.

54   See also Snyder's manifesto, *Our Malady: Lessons in Liberty from a Hospital Diary* (New York: Crown, 2020).

55   At the start of 2021, the richest 1 percent of Americans held 32 percent of the nation's wealth, the highest level since records began in 1989; the bottom 50 percent held just 2 percent of the nation's wealth. Karen Petrou, "Only the Rich Could Love This Economic Recovery," *The New York Times,* July 12, 2021, https://www.nytimes.com/interactive/2021/07/12/opinion/covid-fed-qe-inequality.html, adapted from her book *Engine of Inequality: The Fed and the Future of Wealth in America* (New York: John Wiley & Sons, 2021), and Peter Coy, "Wealth Inequality Is the Highest Since World War II," *The New York Times,* February 2, 2022, https://www.nytimes.com/2022/02/02/opinion/inequality-wealth-pandemic.html.

for judges.[56] In addition to that ten-year-old list written during the Arab Spring, and the proposals sketched in the Nussbaum and Payne chapters, I add here other measures that could be the focus of public demonstrations and campaigns to support candidates who will fight for democracy-building and problem-solving initiatives. They all aim to increase a stock of good feelings such that one is more likely to include democracy in one's quality world because you feel it is truly meeting your needs.

The focus of this list is building democracy back better in the US but many of these proposals could be pursued in other countries. I recommend same-day, not staggered, primary voting and Maine-style ranked choice voting or French-style run-off elections to encourage a broader range of ideas and candidates while avoiding plurality governance and curbing extremism[57]; automatic voter registration on the rolls of one's place of residence when a citizen turns eighteen or a tax-paying foreigner obtains long-term legal resident status; expansion of early and mail-in voting and making election day a holiday; an end to gerrymandering; granting voting rights to prisoners convicted of minor offenses and a clean slate to all released prisoners who have paid their debt to society; universal broadband across rural and urban areas, affordable phone plans, and a deprivatized internet[58] that is open but also held accountable; private-public partnerships

---

56 Here I am supporting the proposal of Hendrik Hertzberg, James Lindgren, Steven G. Calabresi, and most recently Rosalind Dixon, "Why the Supreme Court Needs (Short) Term Limits," *The New York Times,* December 31, 2021, https://www.nytimes.com/2021/12/31/opinion/supreme-court-term-limits.html.

57 See Richard H. Pildes, "How to Keep Extremists out of Power," *The New York Times,* February 25, 2021, https://www.nytimes.com/2021/02/25/opinion/elections-politics-extremists.html, and Richard L. Hasen, *Election Meltdown: Dirty Tricks, Distrust, and the Threat to American Democracy* (New Haven: Yale University Press, 2020).

58 Ben Tarnoff, "The Internet Is Broken. How Do We Fix It?" *The New York Times,* May 27, 2022, https://www.nytimes.com/2022/05/27/opinion/technology/what-would-an-egalitarian-internet-actually-look-like.html, adapted from his book *Internet for the People: The Fight for Our Digital Future* (New York: Verso, 2022).

to prop up local journalism with a PBS-like business model[59] that frees journalists from over-reliance on advertising revenue; tuition-free public pre-K through PhD for citizens and long-term legal residents as well as continuing education grants and tax credits for skills evolution and career changes; encouraging double majors in a trade, business, engineering, or science *and* the humanities — especially support for the liberal arts featured in this book: history, literature, creative writing, philosophy, psychology, and political economy; encouragement of foreign language acquisition, amateur theater, music and art education, study and work abroad opportunities, and sister-city partnerships to broaden horizons and foster empathy and international understanding; ending for-profit medicine (i.e., monetizing sick bodies); guaranteeing affordable health insurance, including for teeth, eyes, and counseling, that can also be used internationally to access quality medical care wherever and whenever one needs it; early automatic issuance of a passport for travel and identification purposes, just like the routine attribution of a social security number at a young age, and then regular renewal of the passport for a nominal fee through any government post office, embassy, or consulate; elimination of barriers to unionization; raising the federal minimum wage to $15 and inciting other countries to increase theirs in order to discourage global shopping for the cheapest labor; ratification of the Equal Rights Amendment; making tax returns public to discourage cheating; passage of stronger international tax evasion penalties, higher corporate tax minimums, and banking transparency agreements. To fill knowledge gaps, break bad patterns, and discourage simply "winging it," I recommend distribution of a "Parenting 101" handbook to every adult who leaves the hospital with a newborn and an "Adulting 101" handbook to every high school graduate.[60] And finally, I support reinvesting in public goods

---

59 On American public media, see the report written by Sue Gardner, "Public Broadcasting: Its Past and Its Future," *The Knight Foundation*, 2017, https://knightfoundation.org/public-media-white-paper-2017-gardner/.

60 For inspiration, see Julie Lythcott-Haims, *How to Raise an Adult: Break Free of the Overparenting Trap and Prepare Your Kids for Success* (New

and services, what Kuttner calls "reclaiming the public realm" and "restoring the credibility of public institutions."[61] If corporations, tax cheats, and the super-rich were required to pay their fair share,[62] and America's XXL military budget could come up for scrutiny and slimming, there would be enough money to fund these peaceful and peace-building measures which in the long run would pay for themselves since peace is less costly than war.

The specific form taken by these life-affirming policies might vary from country to country depending on local conditions, imperatives, and preferences. The beauty of democracy is that it acknowledges different ways to reach the same general goal (using people power to satisfy people's needs), just as different cuisines can all constitute healthy diets.[63] The same can be said of many exercise regimens, school curricula, and forms of worship. Fascism and authoritarianism, on the other hand, have a narrowly repetitive playbook that fails to produce long-term broad prosperity and eventually ends in a death spiral that can drag thousands or millions down with it.[64] No surprise, the two

---

York: St Martin's Press, 2015), and Nora Bradbury-Haehl, *The Twentysome-thing Handbook* (Nashville: Nelson Books, 2021).

61 Kuttner, *Can Democracy Survive Global Capitalism?*, 302–6.

62 On the size of the tax fraud problem and what reducing it could then pay for, see Chye-Ching Huang, "How Biden Funds His Next Bill: Shrink the $7.5 Trillion Tax Gap," *The New York Times*, March 10, 2021, https://www.nytimes.com/2021/03/10/opinion/deficits-taxes-biden-infrastructure.html.

63 Democracy building proposals abound from The Port Huron Statement of 1962 to the newly minted report of the American Academy of Arts and Sciences, *Our Common Purpose: Reinventing American Democracy for the 21st Century* (Cambridge: American Academy of Arts and Sciences, 2020), https://www.amacad.org/ourcommonpurpose/report.

64 The death and destruction of Putinism is plain to see. Less visible is the death spiral in Narendra Modi's neofascist India. For proposals on how to break out of it, see Prabhat Patnaik, "Why Neoliberalism Needs Neofas-cists," *Boston Review*, July 19, 2021, https://bostonreview.net/articles/why-neoliberalism-needs-neofascists/. Patnaik's general claim echoes Kuttner and others opposed to neoliberal global capitalism: "The neofascist assault on democracy is a last-ditch effort on the part of neoliberal capitalism to rescue itself from crisis. The only solution is a decisive retreat from globalized finance."

countries besides the US that fell in the Social Progress Index referenced by Kristof are nations experimenting with far-right populism: Brazil and Hungary. Ignorance, force and fraud, chronic vulnerability, or a mind-scrambling crisis may lead to periodic repetition of fascist experiments in the future.[65] Liberalism, as William Dodd wrote in a letter to Roosevelt about Nazi Germany, implies giving people a chance to try their schemes. However, thanks to its checks, balances, and feedback loops, democracy makes repairable mistakes, as Tocqueville noted approvingly. Vigilant and adequately funded democratic institutions staffed by individuals with a sense of public virtue should usually be able to convince a majority that there are better alternatives to an escape from freedom; in other words, better alternatives to fascist bullying and escapism, alternatives that would be healthier in the long run because they offer more freedom, creative power, fun, and fellow feeling. Life-affirming choices in an open society all feel better than the death, destruction, codependency, and cruelty of fascism; and they offer better ways to cope with life's ups and downs and our inevitable unforeseen vulnerabilities.[66]

If democracy's feedback loops are functioning properly, mistakes can generally be identified and repaired before they get out of control. When Dodd says people must be given a chance

---

65 Recent research suggests that one's desire for democracy may fluctuate in inverse relationship to how much one is experiencing democracy at a given time. See Christopher Claassen, "In the Mood for Democracy? Democratic Support as Thermostatic Opinion," *American Political Science Review* 114, no. 1 (February 2020): 36–53.

66 For another reminder that to repair what is broken one must strike a balance between bottom-up and top-down approaches, see Yuval Levin, *A Time to Build: From Family and Community to Congress and the Campus, How Recommitting to Our Institutions Can Revive the American Dream* (New York: Basic Books, 2020). Levin summarized his thesis in "Either Trump or Biden Will Win. But Our Deepest Problems Will Remain," *The New York Times,* November 3, 2020, https://www.nytimes.com/2020/11/03/opinion/2020-election.html. He cautions against placing too much hope in being rescued, which is a shirking of personal responsibility and an escape from freedom. To rebuild their country, Americans must affirm both personal responsibility and collective responsibilities.

to try their schemes, he is repeating a central tenet of an open society. However, one should be paying close attention to the details of those schemes and to what the stated and perhaps unconscious motives might be. One of the most important things to be learned from Leslie Jamison's addiction memoir is that parents (and elected officials) need to be listening more and better to their children (and constituents) when, for example, they stuff their mouths with sticks of butter and raw macaroni. Looking on mutely or green-lighting harmful behavior with an indifferent "Go ahead" is bad parenting which is likely to only make matters worse. Listening and leadership matter. A similar lesson of broader significance can be learned from the distress signals sent out by Martha Dodd's sexual promiscuity with Nazis and other powerful men. Ditto for the self-harm of Sally Rooney's codependent duo, the bossy Bobbi and the faux-meek Frances whose skin cutting and cutting remarks, especially jokes about Irish fascism, should not be laughed off or ignored. When early warning signs of far-right populism are detected, and invariably they are unsubtle (e.g., record-high Antisemitism, the insanity of QAnon[67]), it would be wrong to simply mail off a copy of Paxton's *Anatomy of Fascism*, or Stanley's warning or Madeleine Albright's or Toni Morrison's, with a post-it slapped on saying, "Might want to rethink what you're doing," "We have seen this movie before," or "Grow up."[68] Doing so, as we've said, is what

---

67 On the QAnon conspiracy theory, which has spread from the US to Europe, see Katrin Bennhold, "QAnon is Thriving in Germany: The Extreme Right Is Delighted," *The New York Times,* October 11, 2020, https://www.nytimes.com/2020/10/11/world/europe/qanon-is-thriving-in-germany-the-extreme-right-is-delighted.html. See also Scott Wiener, "What I Learned When QAnon Came for Me," *The New York Times,* October 19, 2020, https://www.nytimes.com/2020/10/19/opinion/scott-wiener-qanon.html, especially the concluding paragraph: "If we want QAnon to go away, yes, we must increase people's media literacy and hold social media platforms accountable. But we also need to make people's lives better. That's the hard truth of 2020."

68 On the weaponization of conspiracy theories in Putin's Russia and in the US, especially Florida, and the dangers of ignoring or dismissing these tactics instead of combatting them, see Jamelle Bouie, "Democrats, You Can't Ignore the Culture Wars Any Longer," *The New York Times,* April 22,

Freud denounced as useless wild psychoanalysis.[69] It offers no pain relief and only adds insult to injury. "Deplorable" labeling and virtue signaling do nothing to stop the spread and harm of exclusionary right-wing populist rhetoric on conservative talk radio, cable news, and other outlets.[70] Such gestures throw fuel on the fire and trigger backlashes as we see with the Hillary-bashing gone wild from Rush Limbaugh and Tucker Carlson

---

2022, https://www.nytimes.com/2022/04/22/opinion/red-scare-culture-wars.html; Paul Krugman, "The Attack on Big Mouse Is Also an Assault on Democracy," *The New York Times,* April 25, 2022, https://www.nytimes.com/2022/04/25/opinion/republicans-florida-disney-conspiracy-theories.html; and Ilya Yablokov, "The Five Conspiracy Theories That Putin Has Weaponized," *The New York Times,* April 25, 2022, https://www.nytimes.com/2022/04/25/opinion/putin-russia-conspiracy-theories.html.

69 On the history of liberalism's hollow warnings from the Kerner Commission (1965) to the report on policing in Ferguson, Missouri (2015), see Jelani Cobb, "A Warning Ignored," *The New York Review of Books,* August 19, 2021, https://www.nybooks.com/articles/2021/08/19/kerner-commission-warning-ignored/.

70 It should be remembered that Rush Limbaugh (1951–2021) started his radio career in the late 1980s after the FCC's repeal of the "fairness doctrine," became a leading Hillary-basher in the 1990s, and then went on to command an audience of fifteen million, a salary of $85 million, and the admiration of Donald Trump and many Trump-supporting antifeminists and misogynists. For a summary of Limbaugh's career, see Jill Filipovic, "The Life and Death of a Woman-Hater," *The New York Times,* February 20, 2021, https://www.nytimes.com/2021/02/20/opinion/rush-limbaugh-women.html. On Limbaugh's successor who already has an audience of 8.5 million listeners per week, see Evan Osnos, "Dan Bongino and The Big Business of Returning Trump to Power," *The New Yorker,* December 27, 2021, https://www.newyorker.com/magazine/2022/01/03/dan-bongino-and-the-big-business-of-returning-trump-to-power, an adaptation from Osnos's book *Wildland: The Making of America's Fury* (New York: Farrar, Straus and Giroux, 2021). On the "infrastructure of radicalization," see Nicole Hemmer, *Messengers of the Right: Conservative Media and the Transformation of American Politics* (Philadelphia: University of Pennsylvania Press, 2016) and her intervention shortly after the Buffalo mass shooting, "What Oprah Winfrey Knows about American History That Tucker Carlson Doesn't," *The New York Times,* May 19, 2022, https://www.nytimes.com/2022/05/19/opinion/sunday/buffalo-oprah-winfrey-tucker-carlson.html.

to Dan Bongino and QAnon.[71] Listening, social justice protests, and demonstrably better progressive leadership that improves lives for the Many are what is needed to rebuild trust in democracy and each other.[72]

It would be useful now, with ongoing neofascist experiments at various stages in at least a dozen countries[73], to recall Paxton's history lesson about how France's leaders in the 1920s and '30s, including a Jewish prime minister, curbed *boulangisme,* anomie, and inchoate grievances within the Third Republic by anticipating, addressing, and solving some problems, especially those of lower-middle-class people, before things got ugly, thereby reducing the likelihood of something much worse

---

71 Michelle Goldberg, "QAnon Believers Are Obsessed with Hillary Clinton. She Has Thoughts," *The New York Times,* February 5, 2021, https://www. nytimes.com/2021/02/05/opinion/qanon-hillary-clinton.html. This piece alludes to a book by Mike Rothchild, *The Storm Is Upon Us: How QAnon Became a Movement, Cult, and Conspiracy Theory of Everything* (New York: Melville House, 2021). See also Michelle Goldberg, "Antisemitism Increased under Trump. Then It Got Even Worse," *The New York Times,* April 29, 2022, https://www.nytimes.com/2022/04/29/opinion/antisemitism-post-trump.html, and Nicholas Confessore, "How Tucker Carlson Stoked White Fear to Conquer Cable," *The New York Times,* April 30, 2022, https://www.nytimes.com/2022/04/30/us/tucker-carlson-gop-republican-party.html.

72 One measure of distrust in American democracy is the high voter abstention rate — between 30 and 50 percent in most states: Sabrina Tavernise and Robert Gebeloff, "They Did Not Vote in 2016. Why They Plan on Skipping the Election Again," *The New York Times,* October 26, 2020, https:// www.nytimes.com/2020/10/26/us/election-nonvoters.html. In Maine, which had the third highest voter turnout in 2016 at 70 percent, there were 310,445 eligible nonvoters, while Hillary Clinton's margin of victory was 22,142. Many "swing states" show even higher numbers of nonvoters combined with slim margins of victory; for example, Michigan: 2,621,344 eligible nonvoters, Trump's margin of victory: 10,704. The "record turnout" in 2020 was still only 67 percent. On the existential necessity for Democrats to improve the lives of the Many, see Ezra Klein, "Democrats, Here's How to Lose in 2022. And Deserve It," *The New York Times,* January 21, 2021, https://www.nytimes.com/2021/01/21/opinion/biden-inauguration-democrats.html.

73 For an assessment, see Fintan O'Toole, "Trial Runs for Fascism Are in Full Flow," *The Irish Times,* June 26, 2018, https://www.irishtimes.com/opinion/fintan-o-toole-trial-runs-for-fascism-are-in-full-flow-1.3543375.

than a repeat of the polarizing Dreyfus Affair.[74] Fast forward a century — leaping over the complex mix of heroism, treachery, vulnerability, luck and loss of the Vichy time that Paxton got the French, Germans, and others to start to read better — and observe how President Emmanuel Macron and his prime minister Édouard Philippe, initially blindsided and rather deaf to the Yellow Jacket grievances and protests in 2018 and 2019, became better listeners over time and took the lead in facilitating extensive and inclusive listening opportunities. They refrained from snap judgments and over simplifying — nor did they say "Go ahead" when the protests spilled over into harmful violence and other law-breaking and incivilities.[75] The police response was measured (or mismeasured, depending on your outlook), criticized, and regularly recalibrated in accordance with continuous feedback loops of internal and external scrutiny as always happens now in the era of amateur and professional video footage.[76] The results of all these interventions are still unfolding. France's more participatory democracy is young and the authoritarian reflex in this centralized, pyramidal country is ever ready.[77]

---

74 See Robert O. Paxton, *Anatomy of Fascism* (New York: Alfred A. Knopf, 2004), 68–73. Besides collaborating on a second edition of *Vichy France and the Jews* (Stanford: Stanford University Press, 2019), Robert Paxton answered the call of the daily *Le Monde* in December 2021 to again debunk the "Vichy as shield" claim that was reaffirmed with no supporting evidence by the French far-right pundit and presidential candidate Éric Zemmour, *Le Monde,* "Zemmour, Vichy, et les juifs: L'historien Robert Paxton répond (entretien exclusif)," *YouTube,* December 5, 2021, https://www.youtube.com/watch?v=ZFGDlEQ457we.

75 Anne Applebaum's *Twilight of Democracy: The Seductive Lure of Authoritarianism* (New York: Doubleday, 2020) has many strengths, but she's off base when she labels the gilets jaunes protesters "anti-establishment anarchists" (177). For a collection of points of view on that movement captured in medias res, see Joseph Confavreux, *Le fond de l'air est jaune: Comprendre une révolte inédite* (Paris: Seuil, 2019).

76 For a global perspective on policing and video footage, see Amanda Taub, "From Columbia to U.S., Police Violence Pushes Protests into Mass Movements," *The New York Times,* May 19, 2021, https://www.nytimes.com/2021/05/19/world/americas/colombia-protests-police.html.

77 For an assessment by France's foremost democracy specialist, Pierre Rosanvallon, see Simon Blin, interview with Pierre Rosanvallon, "On se

However lines of communication are at least open even if tensions and distrust remain high.[78] Still, there are few signs of the development of a parallel fascist universe in France that could give rise to a "dual state" situation like in Nazi Germany where a muscly "prerogative state" encroached upon the "normative state."[79] European Union countries lack America's permissive gun laws that open the door to vigilantism, paramilitary activity, and mass shootings. Some worry about a resurgent far-right in Germany, but isn't it preferable to have the Alternative für Deutschland be a political party playing the democracy game with members in parliament, *if* they win seats fair and square, and on mic rather than pushing toward lawlessness in streets and chatrooms and clandestine venues?[80] In the Bundestag and

rapproche d'une démocratie à tendance technocratique mâtinée d'un penchant liberticide," *Libération,* December 4, 2020, https://www.liberation.fr/debats/2020/12/04/pierre-rosanvallon-on-se-rapproche-d-une-democratie-a-tendance-technocratique-matinee-d-un-penchant-_1807550/.

78 Distrust runs deep in France dating back to the Algerian War, Vichy, and the Dreyfus Affair to name just three French national traumas, but it is not insurmountable. For one diagnosis of the problem, see Yann Algan and Pierre Cahuc, *La société de la défiance: comment le modèle social français s'autodétruit* (Paris: Editions ENS rue d'Ulm, 2008). In addition to the work of Desmond Tutu in South Africa and Kevin Boyle in Ireland, Susan Neiman's *Learning from the Germans: Race and the Memory of Evil* (New York: Farrar, Straus and Giroux, 2019) suggests a way forward for the US, France, and others.

79 Paxton, *The Anatomy of Fascism,* 121–28. Some are concerned that the white power movement in the US, frequently dog-whistled by President Trump, has the potential to become the violent paramilitary frontal edge of a "prerogative state." See Kathleen Belew's "Why 'Stand Back and Stand By' Should Set Off Alarm Bells," *The New York Times,* October 2, 2020, https://www.nytimes.com/2020/10/02/opinion/trump-proud-boys.html, published in the wake of President Trump's coded message to the Proud Boys in the first presidential debate with Democratic candidate Joe Biden; see also her book, *Bring the War Home: The White Power Movement and Paramilitary America* (Cambridge: Harvard University Press, 2018). See also Cynthia Miller-Idriss, *Hate in the Homeland: The New Global Far Right* (Princeton: Princeton University Press, 2020).

80 Some question whether European far-right parties respect democracy's norms and rules. See Katrin Bennhold, "Germany Places Far-right AfD Party under Surveillance for Extremism," *The New York Times,* March 3,

at press conferences there's a chance they can be brought around to the wisdom conveyed by General Washington to Alexander Hamilton in the hit Broadway show: "Winning was easy, young man, governing is harder." However, France — having a large immigrant population, enormous pride as "the country of the rights of man," and longstanding ambivalence about whether *fraternité* means universal solidarity or brothers versus others — is arguably the key European bellwether of neofascism.[81] So far, French experiments with far-right "identitarian" populism, fueled since the end of the Algerian War by the collective narcissism of empire nostalgics such as Jean-Marie Le Pen and his fellow ethnonationalists, including Éric Zemmour[82] and Renaud Camus,[83] seem to have leveled off short of stage 3: getting power at the national level.[84] But it would be unwise for anyone

---

202, https://www.nytimes.com/2021/03/03/world/europe/germany-afd-surveillance-extremism.html.

81 That said, British insularity, a long and checkered human rights record, large immigrant population, empire nostalgia, and extreme inequality all make the UK a hot mess ready for neofascist impulses and experimentation.

82 For a profile of Zemmour, see Adam Gopnik, "The Ultra-Nationalist Éric Zemmour Makes a Bizarre Bid for the French Presidency," *The New Yorker,* December 3, 2021, https://www.newyorker.com/news/daily-comment/the-ultra-nationalist-eric-zemmour-makes-a-bizarre-bid-for-the-french-presidency. See also the special issue, Alexandra Schwartzbrod, "'Tant de haines': Un hors-série pour comprendre l'extrême droitisation du débat," *Libération,* February 15, 2022, https://www.liberation.fr/plus/tant-de-haines-un-hors-serie-pour-comprendre-lextreme-droitisation-du-debat-politique-20220214_IPKM2CLAVRDBBASJWUKG5V2MDI/.

83 For a profile of Renaud Camus and his influence on the Charlottesville riots, see Thomas Chatterton Williams, "The French Origins of 'You Will Not Replace Us'," *The New Yorker,* November 27, 2017, https://www.newyorker.com/magazine/2017/12/04/the-french-origins-of-you-will-not-replace-us. On how in five years "replacement theory" went from fringe to mainstream in America, see Nicholas Confessore and Karen Yourish, "A Fringe Conspiracy Theory, Fostered Online, Is Refashioned by the G.O.P.," *The New York Times,* May 15, 2022, https://www.nytimes.com/2022/05/15/us/replacement-theory-shooting-tucker-carlson.html.

84 On the three-time losing presidential candidate Marine Le Pen and her rebranded neofascist party, Le Rassemblement National, see Rim-Sarah Alouane, "Marine Le Pen Is as Dangerous as Ever," *The New York Times,*

to claim victory too soon, tilt rightward preemptively, resort to heavy-handed paternalism, or stop listening to "the streets," to universities, journalists, and their own conscience — especially given the added strain on the social fabric throughout Europe, including the authoritarian temptation, caused by the unpredictable and unrelenting Covid-19 pandemic and made worse by the war in Ukraine.[85]

April 20, 2022, https://www.nytimes.com/2022/04/20/opinion/le-pen-france-election.html. On her father, Jean-Marie Le Pen, see Philip Gourevitch, "The Unthinkable: How Dangerous Is Le Pen's National Front?" *The New Yorker,* April 28, 1997. On normalizing the National Front, see Nonna Mayer, "Le mythe de la dédiabolisation du FN," *La vie des Idées,* December 4, 2015, https://laviedesidees.fr/Le-mythe-de-la-dediabolisation-du-FN.html; see also the far-right watch in the mordant French videos by Usul, for example, Mediapart, "Usul. Faut-il vraiment voter Macron?" *YouTube,* April 18, 2022, https://www.youtube.com/watch?v=MCjAbMoY8gw. Brimming with fascist tropes, Zemmour's video announcement of his presidential candidacy on November 30, 2021 was timed provocatively to upstage the "Panthéonisation," the same day, of the artist and civil rights activist Joséphine Baker. For more on President Macron's speech that day honoring Joséphine Baker, while also defending his own political vision, see France 24, "Emmanuel Macron rend hommage à Joséphine Baker lors de son entrée au Panthéon," *YouTube,* November 30, 2021, https://www.youtube.com/watch?v=-xP_T_dvncQ.

85   Just as there is "fake news," there is also the risk of fake listening. On the authoritarian temptation endemic to democracy at all times, see Michel Wieviorka, "Les deux autoritarismes," *Libération,* November 17, 2020, https://www.liberation.fr/debats/2020/11/17/les-deux-autoritaris-mes_1805862/; Frédéric Worms, "Pourquoi la lutte contre le fascisme ne cesse-t-elle de revenir?" *Libération,* October 15, 2021, https://www.libera-tion.fr/idees-et-debats/opinions/pourquoi-la-lutte-contre-le-fascisme-ne-cesse-t-elle-de-revenir-20211015_T32O6Q7EXJEXRLL53LMQAWP-NAU/; and Gaspard Koenig, "Eric Zemmour, une menace pour l'identité française," *Libération,* December 2, 2021, https://www.liberation.fr/idees-et-debats/tribunes/eric-zemmour-une-menace-pour-lidentite-fran-caise-20211202_P6GEPQJZCBEONCIREO767IQ7PM/. "The streets" can vehicle "the wisdom of crowds" (James Surowiecki) or madness and hate (Gustave Le Bon, inter alia). In France, many "anti-vaccin" and "anti-pass" demonstrations took an ugly turn, reigniting old anti-Semitic tropes. See the interview with historian Tal Bruttmann in Christophe Ayad, "Les accusations d'empoisonnement pars les juifs avaient disparu depuis le Moyen Age," *Le Monde,* August 18, 2021, https://www.lemonde.fr/societe/arti-cle/2021/08/18/les-accusations-d-empoisonnement-par-les-juifs-avaient-

In a timely editorial published just before another anniversary of 9/11 and with the Belarus popular uprising against a rigged election and aging dictator in full swing, Ivan Krastev performed a Socratic question and answer dialogue that extends the debate I was having with a group of international students in a seminar on democracy before our class was rudely interrupted by Covid-19 in mid-March 2020:

The protests in Belarus should force us to rethink the relationship between the pandemic and authoritarianism. Does the virus infect our societies with authoritarian governance or, alternatively, can it strengthen democratic immunity?

Some fear that more than any other crisis, a public health emergency like this one will impel people to accept restrictions on their liberties in the hope of improving personal security. The pandemic has increased tolerance of invasive surveillance and bans on freedom of assembly. In several Western countries — including the United States and Germany — there were public protests against mask mandates and lockdowns.

At the same time, the pandemic has eroded the power of authoritarians and the authoritarian-inclined. The instinctive reaction of leaders like Mr. Lukashenko in Belarus, Vladimir Putin in Russia, Jair Bolsonaro in Brazil and Donald Trump in the United States was not to take advantage of the state of emergency to expand their authority — it was to play down the seriousness of the pandemic.

Why are authoritarian leaders who thrive on crises and who are fluent in the politics of fear reluctant to embrace the opportunity? Why do they seem to hate a crisis that they should love? The answer is straightforward: Authoritarians

---

disparu-depuis-le-moyen-age_6091723_3224.html; see also many pieces by journalist Lucie Delaporte in *Mediapart* (e.g., August 19, 2021, "Passe sanitaire, Covid: les résurgences d'un antisémitisme virulent," https://www.mediapart.fr/journal/france/190821/passe-sanitaire-covid-les-resurgences-d-un-antisemitisme-virulent) that examine recent extremist words and deeds.

only enjoy those crises they have manufactured themselves. They need enemies to defeat, not problems to solve. The free-dom authoritarian leaders cherish most is the freedom to choose which crises merit a response. It is this capacity that allows them to project an image of Godlike power.[86]

Kuttner made a similar observation pre-Covid-19: "Trump's personal habit of dwelling in an alternative reality where up was down and truth was lie could work to get him elected. But once in office, he bumped into the real world."[87] That's a good story, but one could just as well say, if politics is storytelling: he bumped into the real world, shouted at it for not watching where it was going, and continued on his way.[88] Bruno Maçães calls this Trump's (delusional) "hyperfreedom."[89] As I write this Conclusion, Trump and others in the current crop of fascist-leaning authoritarians have yet to fully experience their come-uppance; and the final Covid-19 report cards for each nation and

---

86 Ivan Krastev, "The Pandemic Was Supposed to Be Great for Strongmen. What Happened?" *The New York Times,* September 8, 2020, https://www.nytimes.com/2020/09/08/opinion/coronavirus-dictatorships.html. The pandemic also disrupted the power of China's authoritarian Xi Jinping starting in spring 2022.

87 Kuttner, *Can Democracy Survive Global Capitalism?,* 278.

88 For a sober updating, three bumpy years later, of his views on what the French call les rapports de force, see Kuttner's elegiac piece, "Capitalism vs. Liberty," *The American Prospect,* December 1, 2021, https://prospect.org/politics/capitalism-vs-liberty/.

89 Trump's resistance to reality, even after losing to Joe Biden by seven mil-lion votes, astonished and outraged many observers. Others were less surprised. See Bruno Maçães, "How Trump Almost Broke the Bounds of Reality," *The New York Times,* November 12, 2020, https://www.nytimes.com/2020/11/12/opinion/donald-trump-reality.html. The salient phrase is this: "But the virus had a hard logic of its own and would not disappear. With a winter wave approaching, Mr. Trump was vulnerable." Trump's vulnerability increased throughout 2020 as he became cut off from his fountain of youth and power, the crowd. On this point Elias Canetti's retrospective essay would be worth rereading as Trump recedes in the rearview mirror of history. "Hitler, According to Speer: Grandeur and Per-manence," in *The Conscience of Words,* trans. Joachim Neugroschel (New York: Continuum, 1979), 145–70

for every leader in charge of managing a part of the pandemic (but also global warming, climate migration, extreme inequality and vulnerability) are not in — but they will come, and so will more comparisons which are already raging.

Krastev concludes his piece with the suggestion that the Covid-19 global crash course in problem-solving might contribute to toppling authoritarians around the world, just as, in his retelling, the 1986 Chernobyl nuclear disaster contributed to the collapse of the Soviet Union.[90] Democracy sympathizers certainly hope so, just as Black Lives Matter sympathizers are hoping that the senseless killing of George Floyd, Ahmaud Arbery, and Breonna Taylor in 2020 will spark[91] the truth and reconciliation conversation in the United States that had been sputtering and stuttering since the deaths of Trayvon Martin and Michael Brown, and all the way back to the 1955 killing of

---

90 Ivan Krastev offered a mix of censure and hopefulness in a piece published shortly after the January 6 riot at the Capitol: "Trump Has Made America a Laughingstock," *The New York Times,* January 12, 2021, https://www. nytimes.com/2021/01/12/opinion/trump-america-allies.html.

91 Historians will debate the cause-and-effect relationships for years, but my assessment is this: widespread indignation in the months following those killings contributed to narrow but incontrovertible democratic victories, by a Jew and a Black man, in two US Senate run-off elections in the traditionally conservative state of Georgia on January 5; the unavowable white rage and panic triggered by those electoral outcomes in favor of Jon Ossoff and Raphael Warnock, which also tipped majority control of the Senate from the Republicans to the Democrats, further inflamed the January 6, 2021 riot at the US Capitol — in effect a repeat, only bigger and deadlier, of the fascist marching and chanting of "You [Jews and Blacks] will not replace us!" in Charlottesville, Virginia on August 11–12, 2017. It may turn out that those two Democratic victories in Georgia, more than Covid-19 which only cost him the election, are what finally burst the bubble of Donald Trump's freedom from accountability. For two other assessments by a seasoned journalist and a Harvard history professor, see Thomas B. Edsall, "White Riot," *The New York Times,* January 13, 2021, https://www. nytimes.com/2021/01/13/opinion/capitol-riot-white-grievance.html, and Lisa McGirr, "Trump Is the Republican Party's Past and Future," *The New York Times,* January 13, 2021, https://www.nytimes.com/2021/01/13/opinion/gop-trump.html. This speculation may look quite different in two, ten, or twenty years.

Emmett Till — and lead swiftly to improved living conditions for people of color and by extension (assuming zero-sum thinking can be checked) for all Americans.[92] Mohamed Bouazizi and his fight for dignity and democracy are gone and mostly forgotten, but this time will be different we can tell ourselves.

Or do black labs matter more? And is Trump toast but the Trumpism variant of fascism going global? From where I'm standing it's hard to say.[93] I'm reminded of a line that Reagan or Philip Roth might have used: it's difficult to make predictions, especially about the future. But people who believe democracy works or can still work and who think it offers a healthier and happier way of life won't just be placing bets on how things will turn out in the next election cycle or flu season. And they won't panic or seek to escape from freedom. They will involve themselves in imagining and choosing to create alongside others — in streets, skateparks, schools, studios, forests, farms, factories, and a million other venues — the quality world they want to be a part of and leave to their children and future generations.

---

92 On the harm of zero-sum thinking and the benefit of "solidarity dividends" for all, see Heather C. McGhee, "The Way Out of Zero-Sum Thinking on Race and Wealth," *The New York Times,* February 13, 2021, https://www.nytimes.com/2021/02/13/opinion/race-economy-inequality-civil-rights.html, an adaptation from her book *The Sum of Us: What Racism Costs Everyone and How We Can Prosper Together* (New York: One World, 2021).

93 See Thomas B. Edsall's reviews of expert speculation in *The New York Times,* "Why Trump Still Has Millions of Americans in His Grip," May 5, 2021, https://www.nytimes.com/2021/05/05/opinion/trump-automation-artificial-intelligence.html, and "Trumpism without Borders," June 16, 2021, https://www.nytimes.com/2021/06/16/opinion/trump-global-populism.html.

Bibliography

The Target Texts in This Study

Atwood, Margaret. *The Handmaid's Tale.* Toronto: McClelland & Stewart, 1985.

Berr, Hélène. *Journal.* Paris: Éditions Tallandier, 2008.

Fromm, Erich. *Escape from Freedom.* New York: Henry Holt, 1969.

Jamison, Leslie. *The Recovering: Intoxication and Its Aftermath.* New York: Little, Brown and Co., 2018.

Larson, Erik. *In the Garden of Beasts: Love, Terror, and an American Family in Hitler's Berlin.* New York: Crown, 2011.

Nussbaum, Martha. *The Monarchy of Fear: A Philosopher Looks at Our Political Crisis.* New York: Simon & Schuster, 2018.

Paxton, Robert O. *The Anatomy of Fascism.* New York: Alfred A. Knopf, 2004.

Payne, Keith. *The Broken Ladder: How Inequality Affects the Way We Think, Live, and Die.* New York: Viking, 2017.

Rooney, Sally. *Conversations with Friends.* London: Faber & Faber, 2017.

Roth, Philip. *The Plot Against America.* New York: Houghton Mifflin, 2004.

Stanley, Jason. *How Fascism Works: The Politics of Us and Them.* New York: Random House, 2018.

Key Writings on Fascism, Authoritarianism, and Democracy

Adorno, Theodor, Else Frenkel-Brunswik, Daniel J. Levinson, and R. Nevitt Sanford. *The Authoritarian Personality.* London: Verso, 2019.

Albright, Madeleine. *Fascism: A Warning.* New York: HarperCollins, 2018.

American Academy of Arts and Sciences. *Our Common Purpose: Reinventing American Democracy for the 21st Century.* Cambridge: American Academy of Arts and Sciences, 2020. https://www.amacad.org/ourcommonpurpose/report.

Applebaum, Anne. *Twilight of Democracy: The Seductive Lure of Authoritarianism.* New York: Doubleday, 2020.

Arendt, Hannah. *The Origins of Totalitarianism.* New York: Meridian Books, 1962.

Ben-Ghiat, Ruth. *Strongmen: Mussolini to the Present.* New York: W.W. Norton & Co., 2020.

Delogu, C. Jon. *Tocqueville and Democracy in the Internet Age.* Ann Arbor: Open Humanities Press, 2014.

Frantz, Erica. *Authoritarianism: What Everyone Needs to Know.* New York: Oxford University Press, 2018.

Gessen, Masha. *Surviving Autocracy.* New York: Riverhead Books, 2020.

Hett, Benjamin Carter. *The Death of Democracy: Hitler's Rise to Power and the Downfall of the Weimar Republic.* New York: Henry Holt & Co., 2018.

Kuttner, Robert. *Can Democracy Survive Global Capitalism?* New York: W.W. Norton & Co., 2018.

Levitsky, Steven, and Daniel Ziblatt. *How Democracies Die.* New York: Crown, 2018.

MacWilliams, Matthew C. *On Fascism: 12 Lessons from American History.* New York: St. Martin's Press, 2020.

Roberts-Miller, Patricia. *Demagoguery and Democracy.* New York: The Experiment, 2017.

Snyder, Timothy. *The Road to Unfreedom: Russia, Europe, America.* New York: Tim Duggan Books, 2018.

Stenner, Karen. *The Authoritarian Dynamic.* Cambridge: Cambridge University Press, 2005.

Stiglitz, Joseph E. *The Price of Inequality: How Today's Divided Society Endangers Our Future.* New York: W.W. Norton & Co., 2012.

Sunstein, Cass R., ed. *Can It Happen Here? Authoritarianism in America.* New York: Dey St., 2018.

Svolik, Milan W. *The Politics of Authoritarian Rule.* Cambridge: Cambridge University Press, 2012.

Tocqueville, Alexis de. *Democracy in America; and, Two Essays on America.* Translated by Gerald Bevan. London: Penguin Books, 2003.

Wolin, Sheldon S. *Democracy Inc: Managed Democracy and the Specter of Inverted Totalitarianism.* Princeton: Princeton University Press, 2008.

Supporting Documents

"10 Warning Signs of a Frenemy." *Power of Positivity,* September 6, 2015. https://www.powerofpositivity.com/10-warning-signs-frenemy/.

Ackerman, Spencer. "How Sept. 11 Gave Us Jan. 6." *The New York Times,* September 9, 2021. https://www.nytimes.com/2021/09/09/opinion/how-sept-11-gave-us-jan-6.html.
———. *Reign of Terror: How the 9/11 Era Destabilized America and Produced Trump.* New York: Viking, 2021.

Acocella, Joan. "Counterlives: Philip Roth's 'The Plot Against America.'" *The New Yorker,* September 20, 2004. https://www.newyorker.com/magazine/2004/09/20/counterlives.

Albright, Madeleine. "Putin Is Making a Historic Mistake." *The New York Times,* February 23, 2022. https://www.nytimes.com/2022/02/23/opinion/putin-ukraine.html.

Alduy, Cécile, and Stéphane Wahnich. *Marine Le Pen prise aux mots: décryptage du nouveau discours frontiste.* Paris: Seuil, 2015.

Algan, Yann, and Pierre Cahuc. *La société de la défiance: comment le modèle social français s'autodétruit.* Paris: Éditions ENS rue d'Ulm, 2008.

Allardice, Lisa. Interview with Margaret Atwood. "I am not a prophet. Science fiction is really about now." *The Guardian,* January 20, 2018. https://www.theguardian.com/books/2018/jan/20/margaret-atwood-i-am-not-a-prophet-science-fiction-is-about-now.

Alouane, Rim-Sarah. "Marine Le Pen Is as Dangerous as Ever." *The New York Times,* April 20, 2022. https://www.nytimes.com/2022/04/20/opinion/le-pen-france-election.html.

Altan, Ahmed. *Je ne reverrai plus le monde: Textes de prison.* Arles: Actes Sud, 2019.

Alter, Adam. *Irresistible: The Rise of Addictive Technology and the Business of Keeping Us Hooked.* New York: Penguin Books, 2017.

Anderson, Elizabeth. *Private Government: How Employers Rule Our Lives (and Why We Don't Talk about It).* Princeton: Princeton University Press, 2017.

Applebaum, Anne. *Red Famine: Stalin's War on Ukraine.* New York: Doubleday, 2017.

Atwood, Margaret. "Margaret Atwood on What 'The Handmaid's Tale' Means in the Age of Trump." *The New York Times,* March 10, 2017. https://www.nytimes.com/2017/03/10/books/review/margaret-atwood-handmaids-tale-age-of-trump.html.

———. "What Art under Trump?" *The Nation,* January 18, 2017. https://www.thenation.com/article/archive/what-art-under-trump/.

Aviv, Rachel. "The Philosopher of Feelings." *The New Yorker,* July 18, 2016. https://longform.org/posts/the-philosopher-of-feelings.

Ayad, Christophe. "Les accusations d'empoisonnement pars les juifs avaient disparu depuis le Moyen Age." *Le*

Monde, August 18, 2021. https://www.lemonde.fr/societe/
article/2021/08/18/les-accusations-d-empoisonnement-
par-les-juifs-avaient-disparu-depuis-le-moyen-
age_6091723_3224.html.

Azab, Marwa. "Why Would Groups Attacked by Trump Vote
for Him?" *Psychology Today,* November 11, 2016. https://
www.psychologytoday.com/us/blog/neuroscience-in-
everyday-life/201611/why-would-groups-attacked-trump-
vote-him.

Balakian, Peter. *The Burning Tigris: The Armenian Genocide
and America's Response.* New York: Perennial, 2003.

Baradaran, Mehrsa. "The Neoliberal Looting of America."
The New York Times, July 2, 2020. https://www.nytimes.
com/2020/07/02/opinion/private-equity-inequality.html.

Barnett, Erica C. *Quitter: A Memoir of Drinking, Relapse, and
Recovery.* New York: Viking, 2020.

Barofsky, Neil. *Bailout: An Inside Account of How Washington
Abandoned Main Street While Rescuing Wall Street.* New
York: Free Press, 2012.

Barrett, Ruth Shalit. "Where's the Train Wreck? Can Leslie
Jamison Top 'The Empathy Exams' with Her Mega-memoir
of Addiction?" *Vulture,* March 18, 2018. https://www.vulture.
com/2018/03/leslie-jamison-the-recovering-addiction-
memoir.html.

Barry, John M. *The Great Influenza: The Story of the Deadliest
Pandemic in History.* New York: Penguin Books, 2004.

Bawer, Bruce. *The Victims' Revolution: The Rise of Identity
Studies and the Closing of the Liberal Mind.* New York:
Broadside Books, 2012.

Beard, Mary. "11 September." *London Review of Books,* October
4, 2001. https://www.lrb.co.uk/the-paper/v23/n19/nine-
eleven-writers/11-september.

Beech, Hannah. "'I Feel Sorry for Americans': A Baffled World
Watches the U.S." *The New York Times,* September 25, 2020.
https://www.nytimes.com/2020/09/25/world/asia/trump-
united-states.html.

Belew, Kathleen. *Bring the War Home: The White Power Movement and Paramilitary America*. Cambridge: Harvard University Press, 2018.

———. "The Long Game of White-Power Activists Isn't Just About Violence." *The New York Times,* May 17, 2022. https://www.nytimes.com/2022/05/17/opinion/buffalo-shooting-replacement-theory.html.

———. "Why 'Stand Back and Stand By' Should Set Off Alarm Bells." *The New York Times,* October 2, 2020. https://www.nytimes.com/2020/10/02/opinion/trump-proud-boys.html.

Belew, Kathleen, and Rámon A. Gutiérrez, eds. *A Field Guide to White Supremacy.* Berkeley: University of California Press, 2021.

Bellamy, Richard. "Democracy without Democracy? Can the EU's Democratic 'Outputs' Be Separated from the Democratic 'Inputs' Provided by Competitive Parties and Majority Rule?" *Journal of European Public Policy* 17 (2010): 2–19. DOI: 10.1080/13501760903465256.

Bennhold, Katrin. "Germany Places Far-right AfD Party under Surveillance for Extremism." *The New York Times,* March 3, 2021. https://www.nytimes.com/2021/03/03/world/europe/germany-afd-surveillance-extremism.html.

———. "QAnon is Thriving in Germany: The Extreme Right is Delighted." *The New York Times,* October 11, 2020. https://www.nytimes.com/2020/10/11/world/europe/qanon-is-thriving-in-germany-the-extreme-right-is-delighted.html.

Bennhold, Katrin, and Melissa Eddy. "'Politics of Hate' Takes a Toll in Germany Well Beyond Immigrants." *The New York Times,* February 21, 2020. https://www.nytimes.com/2020/02/21/world/europe/germany-mayors-far-right.html.

Berlin, Isaiah. *Two Concepts of Liberty: An Inaugural Lecture Delivered before the University of Oxford on 31 October 1958.* Oxford: Clarendon Press, 1958.

Berman, Paul. "'The Plot Against America' by Philip Roth." *The New York Times,* October 3, 2004. https://www.nytimes.

com/2004/10/03/books/review/the-plot-against-america.
html.

Bernays, Edward L. *Propaganda*. Brooklyn: ig Publishing, 2014.

Bernstein, Albert J. *Emotional Vampires: Dealing with People Who Drain You Dry*. Revised second edition. New York: McGraw Hill, 2012.

Berr, Hélène. *The Journal of Hélène Berr.* Translated by David Bellos. New York: Weinstein Books, 2008.

Blin, Simon. Interview with Pierre Rosanvallon. "On se rapproche d'une démocratie à tendance technocratique mâtinée d'un penchant liberticide." *Libération,* December 4, 2020, https://www.liberation.fr/debats/2020/12/04/pierre-rosanvallon-on-se-rapproche-d-une-democratie-a-tendance-technocratique-matinee-d-un-penchant-_1807550/.

Blow, Charles M. *Fire Shut Up in My Bones.* New York: Mariner Books, 2014.

———. "States Keep Failing Black People." *The New York Times,* May 13, 2020. https://www.nytimes.com/2020/05/13/opinion/black-people-states.html.

———. "Trump's Army of Angry White Men." *The New York Times,* October 25, 2020. https://www.nytimes.com/2020/10/25/opinion/trump-white-men-election.html.

Bokat-Lindell, Spencer. "Fascism: A Concern." *The New York Times,* July 30, 2020. https://www.nytimes.com/2020/07/30/opinion/fascism-us.html.

Baumbach, Noah, dir. *Frances Ha.* New York: ICF Films, 2012.

Bouie, Jamelle. "America Punishes Only a Certain Kind of Rebel." *The New York Times,* July 13, 2021. https://www.nytimes.com/2021/07/13/opinion/jan-6-trump-impunity.html.

———. "Can Only Republicans Legitimately Win Elections?" *The New York Times,* January 5, 2021. https://www.nytimes.com/2021/01/05/opinion/trump-georgia-senate-elections.html.

———. "Democrats, You Can't Ignore the Culture Wars Any Longer." *The New York Times,* April 22, 2022. https://www.

nytimes.com/2022/04/22/opinion/red-scare-culture-wars. html.

———. "Donald Trump Is a Fascist." *Slate,* November 25, 2015. https://slate.com/news-and-politics/2015/11/donald-trump-is-a-fascist-it-is-the-political-label-that-best-describes-the-gop-front-runner.html.

———. "If It's Not Jim Crow, What Is It?" *The New York Times,* April 6, 2021. https://www.nytimes.com/2021/04/06/opinion/georgia-voting-law.html.

———. "Maybe This Isn't Such a Good Time to Prosecute a Culture War." *The New York Times,* July 7, 2020. https://www.nytimes.com/2020/07/07/opinion/trump-mount-rushmore-culture-war.html.

———. "The Authoritarian Stamp of Jim Crow." *The New York Times,* January 21, 2020.

———. "The Republican Party Has Embraced Its Worst Self." *The New York Times,* February 7, 2020. https://www.nytimes.com/2020/02/07/opinion/sunday/senate-impeachment-acquittal.html.

———. "The 'Trump Won' Farce Isn't Funny Anymore." *The New York Times,* December 11, 2020. https://www.nytimes.com/2020/12/11/opinion/trump-republicans-texas-lawsuit.html.

———. "This Is a Crime against the Laws of Humanity.'" *The New York Times,* April 2, 2022. https://www.nytimes.com/2022/04/02/opinion/anti-lynching-law-east-st-louis.html.

———. "What 'Structural Racism' Really Means." *The New York Times,* November 9, 2021. https://www.nytimes.com/2021/11/09/opinion/structural-racism.html.

———. "Where Might Trumpism Take Us?" *The New York Times,* February 21, 2020. https://www.nytimes.com/2020/02/21/opinion/trump-authoritarian-jim-crow.html.

Bradbury-Haehl, Nora. *The Twentysomething Handbook.* Nashville: Nelson Books, 2021.

Bristow, Nancy K. *American Pandemic: The Lost Worlds of the 1918 Influenza Epidemic.* Oxford: Oxford University Press, 2012.

Brody, Richard. "The Frightening Lessons of Philip Roth's 'The Plot Against America.'" *The New Yorker,* February 1, 2017. https://www.newyorker.com/culture/cultural-comment/the-frightening-lessons-of-philip-roths-the-plot-against-america.

Brooks, David. "How Democrats Can Win the Morality Wars." *The New York Times,* May 19, 2022. https://www.nytimes.com/2022/05/19/opinion/democrats-morality-wars.html.

———. "This Is Why Putin Can't Back Down." *The New York Times,* March 10, 2022. https://www.nytimes.com/2022/03/10/opinion/putin-ukraine-russia-identity.html.

Brown, Brené. *Atlas of the Heart: Mapping Meaningful Connection and the Language of Human Experience.* New York: Random House, 2021.

Brownmiller, Susan. *Against Our Will: Men, Women, and Rape.* New York: Simon & Schuster, 1975.

Brühwiler, Claudia Franziska, and Lee Trepanier, eds. *A Political Companion to Philip Roth.* Lexington: University of Kentucky Press, 2017.

Burke, Kenneth. "The Rhetoric of Hitler's 'Battle.'" In *The Philosophy of Literary Form,* 191–220. Berkeley: University of California Press, 1973. Originally published in *The Southern Review* 5 (Summer 1939): 1–21.

Canetti, Elias. "Hitler, According to Speer: Grandeur and Permanence." In *The Conscience of Words,* translated by Joachim Neugroschel, 145–70. New York: Continuum, 1979.

Carnes, Patrick J. *Don't Call it Love: Recovery from Sexual Addiction.* New York: Bantam Books, 1991.

———. *The Betrayal Bond: Breaking Free of Exploitive Relationships.* Deerfield Beach: Health Communications, 1997.

Carr, Nicholas. *The Shallows: What the Internet Is Doing to Our Brains.* New York: W.W. Norton & Co., 2010.

Carter, Zachary D. *The Price of Peace: Money, Democracy, and the Life of John Maynard Keynes.* New York: Random House, 2020.

Case, Anne, and Angus Deaton. *Deaths of Despair and the Future of Capitalism.* Princeton: Princeton University Press, 2020.

Cave, Damien. "How Australia Saved Thousands of Lives While Covid Killed a Million Americans." *The New York Times,* May 15, 2022. https://www.nytimes.com/2022/05/15/world/australia/covid-deaths.html.

Chinoy, Mike. *Are You With Me? Kevin Boyle and the Rise of the Human Rights Movement.* Dublin: The Lilliput Press, 2020.

Chomsky, Noam. *Failed States: The Abuse of Power and The Assault on Democracy*. New York: Metropolitan Books, 2006.

———. *Requiem for the American Dream: The 10 Principles of Concentration of Wealth and Power,* edited by Peter Hutchenson, Kelly Nyks, and Jared P. Scott. New York: Seven Stories Press, 2017.

Churchwell, Sarah. "American Fascism: It Has Happened Here." *The New York Review of Books,* June 22, 2020. https://www.nybooks.com/daily/2020/06/22/american-fascism-it-has-happened-here/.

Claassen, Christopher. "In the Mood for Democracy? Democratic Support as Thermostatic Opinion." *American Political Science Review* 114, no. 1 (February 2020): 36–53. DOI: 10.1017/S0003055419000558.

Coaston, Jane. "'Virtue Signaling' Isn't the Problem. Not Believing One Another Is." *The New York Times,* April 8, 2017. https://www.nytimes.com/2017/08/08/magazine/virtue-signaling-isnt-the-problem-not-believing-one-another-is.html.

Coates, Ta-Nehisi. "The Case for Reparations." *The Atlantic,* June 2014. https://www.theatlantic.com/magazine/archive/2014/06/the-case-for-reparations/361631/.

Cobb, Jelani. "A Warning Ignored." *The New York Review of Books,* August 19, 2021. https://www.nybooks.com/articles/2021/08/19/kerner-commission-warning-ignored/.

———. "The Man Behind Critical Race Theory." *The New Yorker,* September 13, 2021. https://www.newyorker.com/magazine/2021/09/20/the-man-behind-critical-race-theory.

———. *The Substance of Hope: Barack Obama and the Paradox of Progress.* London: Walker Books, 2010.

Cohen, Michael. *Disloyal: A Memoir.* New York: Skyhorse, 2020.

Cohen, Roger. "American Catastrophe through German Eyes." *The New York Times,* July 24, 2020. https://www.nytimes.com/2020/07/24/opinion/trump-germany.html.

———. "How Trump Lowered America's Standing in the World." *The New York Times,* October 29, 2020. https://www.nytimes.com/2020/10/29/opinion/trump-foreign-policy-us-allies.html.

Cohen, Yves. *Le siècle des chefs: une histoire transnationale du commandement et de l'autorité, 1890–1940.* Paris: Editions Amsterdam, 2014.

Cohn, Nate. "Why Political Sectarianism Is a Growing Threat to American Democracy." *The New York Times,* April 19, 2021. https://theoneworldnews.com/americas/why-political-sectarianism-is-a-growing-threat-to-american-democracy/.

Coleman, Colette. "The Case for Paying All Teachers Six Figures." *The New York Times,* May 28, 2021. https://www.nytimes.com/2021/05/28/opinion/teacher-pay-covid.html.

Collins, Lauren. "Sally Rooney Gets in Your Head." *The New Yorker,* January 7, 2019. https://www.newyorker.com/magazine/2019/01/07/sally-rooney-gets-in-your-head.

Confavreux, Joseph, ed. *Le fond de l'air est jaune: Comprendre une révolte inédite.* Paris: Seuil, 2019.

Confessore, Nicholas. "How Tucker Carlson Stoked White Fear to Conquer Cable." *The New York Times,* April 30, 2022. https://www.nytimes.com/2022/04/30/us/tucker-carlson-gop-republican-party.html.

Confessore, Nicholas, and Karen Yourish. "A Fringe
 Conspiracy Theory, Fostered Online, Is Refashioned by the
 G.O.P." *The New York Times,* May 15, 2022. https://www.
 nytimes.com/2022/05/15/us/replacement-theory-shooting-
 tucker-carlson.html.
Cox, Oliver Cromwell. *Caste, Class, and Race: A Study in Social
 Dynamics.* New York: Monthly Review Press, 1948.
Coy, Peter. "Here Are Three Reasons Putin Might Fight On."
 The New York Times, March 14, 2022. https://www.nytimes.
 com/2022/03/14/opinion/putin-rational-irrational.html.
———. "Wealth Inequality Is the Highest Since World War II."
 The New York Times, February 2, 2022. https://www.nytimes.
 com/2022/02/02/opinion/inequality-wealth-pandemic.html.
Crain, Caleb. "Is Capitalism a Threat to Democracy?" *The
 New Yorker,* May 7, 2018. https://www.newyorker.com/
 magazine/2018/05/14/is-capitalism-a-threat-to-democracy.
Crawford, Alan. *Thunder on the Right: The "New Right" and the
 Politics of Resentment.* New York: Pantheon, 1980.
Crenshaw, Kimberlé. "Demarginalizing the Intersection
 of Race and Sex: A Black Feminist Critique of
 Antidiscrimination Doctrine, Feminist Theory and
 Antiracist Politics." *University of Chicago Legal Forum* 1989,
 no. 1 (1989): 139–67. https://chicagounbound.uchicago.edu/
 uclf/vol1989/iss1/8.
Cullingford, Elizabeth. *Yeats, Ireland and Fascism.* London:
 Palgrave Macmillan, 1981.
Dallek, Robert. *Democrat and Diplomat: The Life of William E.
 Dodd.* Oxford: Oxford University Press, 2012.
David-Weill, Cécile. *Parents under the Influence: Words of
 Wisdom from a Former Bad Mother.* New York: Other Press,
 2019.
Davis, Chris. Interview with Timothy Snyder. "Yale History
 Professor Timothy Snyder Told 'Insider' He Fears
 American Democracy May Not Survive Another Trump
 Campaign." *Business Insider,* January 14, 2022. https://www.
 businessinsider.com/timothy-snyder-fears-democracy-may-
 not-survive-another-trump-campaign-2022-1.

Dawe, Gerald. *In Another World: Van Morrison and Belfast.* Newbridge: Merrion Press, 2017.

de Gruyter, Caroline. "Europe Is in Danger. It Always Is." *The New York Times,* May 2, 2022. https://www.nytimes.com/2022/05/02/opinion/european-union-macron-ukraine.html.

de Man, Paul. *Allegories of Reading: Figural Language in Rousseau, Nietzsche, Rilke, and Proust.* New Haven: Yale University Press, 1979.

———. *The Rhetoric of Romanticism.* New York: Columbia University Press, 1984.

"Des Moines Speech: Delivered in Des Moines, Iowa, on September 11, 1941, This Speech Was Met with Outrage in Many Quarters." *Charles Lindberg: An American Aviator.* http://www.charleslindbergh.com/americanfirst/speech.asp.

de Tocqueville, Alexis. *The Ancien Régime and the Revolution.* Translated by Gerald Bevan. London: Penguin Books, 2008 .

Dean, John W., and Bob Altemeyer. *Authoritarian Nightmare: Trump and His Followers.* New York: Melville House, 2020.

Decèze, Dominique. *La Machine à broyer: De France Télécom à Orange, quand les privatisations tuent.* Paris: Jean-Claude Gawsewitch, 2004.

Delaporte, Lucie. "Passe sanitaire, Covid : les résurgences d'un antisemitisme virulent." *Mediapart,* August 19, 2021. https://www.mediapart.fr/journal/france/190821/passe-sanitaire-covid-les-resurgences-d-un-antisemitisme-virulent.

Delue, Steven M. *How the Liberal Arts Can Save Liberal Democracy.* Lanham: Lexington Books, 2018.

Denby, David. "The Plot Against America: Donald Trump's Rhetoric." *The New Yorker,* December 15, 2015. https://www.newyorker.com/culture/cultural-comment/plot-america-donald-trumps-rhetoric.

———. "The Three Faces of Trump." *The New Yorker,* August 12, 2015. https://www.newyorker.com/culture/cultural-comment/the-three-faces-of-trump.

Deneuve, Catherine. "#MeToo Controversy: Read Catherine Deneuve's Letter Published in 'Libération.'"

Libération, January 15, 2018. https://www.liberation.fr/
debats/2018/01/15/metoo-controversy-read-catherine-
deneuve-s-letter-published-in-liberation_1622561.

Dewey, John. *Freedom and Culture.* New York: Putnam, 1939.

Didion, Joan. *The Year of Magical Thinking.* New York: Alfred
A. Knopf, 2005.

Dixon, Rosalind. "Why the Supreme Court Needs (Short)
Term Limits." *The New York Times,* December 31, 2021.
https://www.nytimes.com/2021/12/31/opinion/supreme-
court-term-limits.html.

Dodd, William E. *Woodrow Wilson and His Work.* Garden
City: Doubleday, 1920.

Donaldson-Pressman, Stephanie, and Robert M. Pressman. *The
Narcissistic Family: Diagnosis and Treatment.* San Francisco:
Jossey-Bass, 1994.

Douthat, Ross. "Donald Trump Doesn't Want Authority."
The New York Times, May 19, 2020. https://www.nytimes.
com/2020/05/19/opinion/coronavirus-trump-orban.html.

———. "Is Donald Trump a Fascist?" *The New York Times,*
December 3, 2015. https://www.nytimes.com/2018/09/11/
books/review/jason-stanley-how-fascism-works.html.

Dowd, Maureen. "All the President's Insecurities." *The New
York Times,* September 12, 2020. https://www.nytimes.
com/2020/09/12/opinion/sunday/donald-trump-bob-
woodward.html.

Eco, Umberto, "Ur-Fascism." *The New York Review of
Books,* June 22, 1995. https://www.nybooks.com/
articles/1995/06/22/ur-fascism/.

Editorial unsigned. "Nous défendons une liberté d'importuner,
indispensable à la liberté sexuelle." *Le Monde,* January 9,
2018. https://www.lemonde.fr/idees/article/2018/01/09/
nous-defendons-une-liberte-d-importuner-indispensable-a-
la-liberte-sexuelle_5239134_3232.html.

Editorial unsigned. "'The New Yorker' Endorses a Joe Biden
Presidency." *The New Yorker,* September 28, 2020.

———. "Why does the US Military Celebrate White
Supremacy?" *The New York Times,* May 23, 2020. https://

www.nytimes.com/2020/05/23/opinion/sunday/army-base-names-confederacy-racism.html.

———. "With Coronavirus, 'Health Care for Some' Is a Recipe for Disaster." *The New York Times,* March 6, 2020. https://www.nytimes.com/2020/03/06/opinion/coronavirus-immigrants-health.html.

———. "The Jobs We Need." *The New York Times,* June 24, 2020. https://www.nytimes.com/2020/06/24/opinion/sunday/income-wealth-inequality-america.html.

Edsall, Thomas B. "America Has Split, and It's Now in 'Very Dangerous Territory'." *The New York Times,* January 26, 2022. https://www.nytimes.com/2022/01/26/opinion/covid-biden-trump-polarization.html.

———. "America, We Have a Problem." *The New York Times,* December 16, 2020. https://www.nytimes.com/2020/12/16/opinion/trump-political-sectarianism.html.

———. "How to Tell When Your Country Is Past the Point of No Return." *The New York Times,* December 15, 2021. https://www.nytimes.com/2021/12/15/opinion/republicans-democracy-minority-rule.html.

———. "Status Anxiety Is Blowing Wind into Trump's Sails." *The New York Times,* February 9, 2022. https://www.nytimes.com/2022/02/09/opinion/trump-status-anxiety.html.

———. "The Resentment That Never Sleeps." *The New York Times,* December 9, 2020. https://www.nytimes.com/2020/12/09/opinion/trump-social-status-resentment.html.

———. "Trumpism without Borders." *The New York Times,* June 16, 2021. https://www.nytimes.com/2021/06/16/opinion/trump-global-populism.html.

———. "Trump Poses a Test Democracy Is Failing." *The New York Times,* April 13, 2022. https://www.nytimes.com/2022/04/13/opinion/trump-democracy-decline-fall.html.

———. "White Riot." *The New York Times,* January 13, 2021. https://www.nytimes.com/2021/01/13/opinion/capitol-riot-white-grievance.html.

———. "Why Do We Pay So Many People So Little Money?" *The New York Times,* June 24, 2020. https://www.nytimes.com/2020/06/24/opinion/wages-coronavirus.html.

———. "Why Trump Still Has Millions of Americans in His Grip" *The New York Times,* May 5, 2021. https://www.nytimes.com/2021/05/05/opinion/trump-automation-artificial-intelligence.html.

Ehrenreich, Barbara. *Fear of Falling: The Inner Life of the Middle Class.* New York: Pantheon, 1989.

———. *Nickel and Dimed: On (Not) Getting By in America.* New York: Metropolitan, 2010.

Elster, Jon. *Alexis de Tocqueville, The First Social Scientist.* Cambridge: Cambridge University Press, 2009.

Emerson, Ralph Waldo. "Napoleon; or, the Man of the World." In *The Portable Emerson,* edited by Jeffrey S. Cramer, 354–71. New York: Penguin, 2014.

———. "Self-Reliance." In *Essays, Vol. 1,* 46–98. London: Arthur L. Humphreys.

Exposito, Linda. "6 Signs of a Co-dependent Relationship." *Psychology Today,* September 19, 2016. https://www.psychologytoday.com/us/blog/anxiety-zen/201609/6-signs-codependent-relationship

Farmer, Paul. *To Repair the World: Paul Farmer Speaks to the Next Generation.* Edited by Jonathan Weigel. Berkeley: University of California Press, 2020.

Filipovic, Jill. "The Life and Death of a Woman-Hater." *The New York Times,* February 20, 2021. https://www.nytimes.com/2021/02/20/opinion/rush-limbaugh-women.html.

Finkel, Eli J., Christopher A. Bail, Mina Cikara, Peter H. Ditto, Shanto Iyengar, Samara Klar, Lilliana Mason, et al. "Political Sectarianism in America." *Science* 370, no. 6516 (October 30, 2020): 533–36. DOI: 10.1126/science.abe1715.

Fisher, Max. "As Dictators Target Citizens Abroad, Few Safe Spaces Remain." *The New York Times,* June 4, 2021. https://www.nytimes.com/2021/06/04/world/europe/repression-uyghurs-belarus.html.

Fisher, Mark. *Capitalist Realism: Is There No Alternative?* Hants: Zero Books, 2009.

———. *Ghosts of My Life: Writings on Depression, Hauntology, and Lost Futures.* Hants: Zero Books, 2014.

———. "Why Mental Health Is a Political Issue." *The Guardian,* July 16, 2012. https://www.theguardian.com/commentisfree/2012/jul/16/mental-health-political-issue.

Fitzgerald, F. Scott. *The Great Gatsby*. London: Penguin, 2000.

Flood, Colleen M., and Vanessa MacDonnell, Jane Philpott, Sophie Thériault, Sridhar Venkatapuram, eds. *Vulnerable: The Law, Policy and Ethics of Covid-19.* Ottawa: University of Ottawa Press, 2020.

Forster, E.M. *Aspects of the Novel.* New York: Harcourt, 1985.

Foster, Roy. "Philosophy and a Little Passion: Roy Foster on WB Yeats and Politics." *The Irish Times,* June 10, 2015. https://www.irishtimes.com/culture/books/philosophy-and-a-little-passion-roy-foster-on-wb-yeats-and-politics-1.2241504.

France 24. "Emmanuel Macron rend hommage à Joséphine Baker lors de son entrée au Panthéon." *YouTube,* November 30, 2021. https://www.youtube.com/watch?v=-xP_T_dvncQ.

Frankfurt, Harry G. *On Bullshit.* Princeton: Princeton University Press, 2005.

Friedman, Lawrence J. *The Lives of Erich Fromm: Love's Prophet.* New York: Columbia University Press, 2013.

Friedman, Thomas. "America 2022: Where Everyone Has Rights and No One Has Responsibilities." *The New York Times,* February 8, 2022. https://www.nytimes.com/2022/02/08/opinion/spotify-joe-rogan-covid-free-speech.html.

———. "We're No. 1(1)!" *The New York Times,* September 11, 2010. https://www.nytimes.com/2010/09/12/opinion/12friedman.html.

———. "Who Can Win America's Politics of Humiliation?" *The New York Times,* September 8, 2020. https://eu.registerguard.com/story/opinion/columns/2020/09/11/

friedman-who-can-win-americas-politics-humiliation/5765607002/.

Friedman, Vanessa. "Why Rioters Wear Costumes." *The New York Times,* January 7, 2021. https://www.nytimes.com/2021/01/07/style/capitol-riot-tactics.html.

Fromm, Erich. *The Art of Loving.* New York: HarperCollins, 2006.

Galchen, Rivka. "The Teachers' Strike and the Democratic Revival in Oklahoma." *The New Yorker,* May 28, 2018. https://www.newyorker.com/magazine/2018/06/04/the-teachers-strike-and-the-democratic-revival-in-oklahoma.

Gallagher, Conor. "The Far Right Rises: Its Growth as a Political Force in Ireland." *The Irish Times,* September 19, 2020. https://www.irishtimes.com/news/ireland/irish-news/the-far-right-rises-its-growth-as-a-political-force-in-ireland-1.4358321.

Gardner, Sue. "Public Broadcasting: Its Past and Its Future." *The Knight Foundation,* 2017. https://knightfoundation.org/public-media-white-paper-2017-gardner/.

Garrett, Brandon L. *Too Big to Jail: How Prosecutors Compromise with Corporations.* Cambridge: Harvard University Press, 2016.

Garza, Alicia. *The Purpose of Power: How We Come Together When We Fall Apart.* New York: Penguin Random House, 2020.

Gawande, Atul. "Hellhole." *The New Yorker,* March 23, 2009. https://www.newyorker.com/magazine/2009/03/30/hellhole.
———. "Why Americans Are Dying from Despair." *The New Yorker,* March 16, 2020. https://www.newyorker.com/magazine/2020/03/23/why-americans-are-dying-from-despair.

Geithner, Timothy. *Stress Test: Reflections on Financial Crises.* New York: Random House, 2014.

Gerven Oei, Vincent W.J. van. "Lea Ypi and the Rehabilitation of Albanian Fascism." *Exit,* July 30, 2022. https://exit.al/en/2022/07/30/lea-ypi-and-the-rehabilitation-of-albanian-fascism/.

Gessen, Masha. "Donald Trump's Fascist Performance." *The New Yorker,* June 3, 2020. https://www.newyorker.com/news/our-columnists/donald-trumps-fascist-performance.

———. "The Capitol Invaders Enjoyed the Privilege of Not Being Taken Seriously." *The New Yorker,* January 7, 2021. https://www.newyorker.com/news/our-columnists/the-capitol-invaders-enjoyed-the-privilege-of-not-being-taken-seriously.

———. *The Man without a Face: The Unlikely Rise of Vladimir Putin.* New York: Riverhead, 2012.

———. "The Russian Memory Project that Became an Enemy of the State." *The New Yorker,* January 6, 2022. https://www.newyorker.com/news/news-desk/the-russian-memory-project-that-became-an-enemy-of-the-state.

Ghodsee, Kristin R. *Why Women Have Better Sex under Socialism: And Other Arguments for Economic Independence.* New York: Nation Books, 2018.

Gilbert, Sandra, and Susan Gubar. *The Madwoman in the Attic: The Woman Writer and the Nineteenth-Century Literary Imagination.* New Haven: Yale University Press, 1979.

Giroux, Henry A. *American Nightmare: Facing the Challenge of Fascism.* San Francisco: City Lights, 2018.

Gitlin, Todd. *The Sixties: Years of Hope, Days of Rage.* New York: Bantam Books, 1987.

Glasser, William. *Choice Theory: A New Psychology of Personal Freedom.* New York: HarperCollins, 1998.

Gleiberman, Owen. "The Handmaid's Tale." *Entertainment Weekly,* March 9, 1990. https://ew.com/article/1990/03/09/handmaids-tale-2/.

Godzich, Wlad. "The Tiger on the Paper Mat." In Paul de Man, *The Resistance to Theory,* ix–2. Minneapolis: University of Minnesota Press, 1986.

Goldberg, Michelle. "After Trump, America Needs Accountability for his Corruption." *The New York Times,* August 13, 2020. https://www.nytimes.com/2020/08/13/opinion/trump-corruption.html.

———. "America Is Too Broken to Fight the Coronavirus." *The New York Times,* June 22, 2020. https://www.nytimes.com/2020/06/22/opinion/us-coronavirus-trump.html.

———. "Antisemitism Increased under Trump. Then It Got Even Worse." *The New York Times,* April 29, 2022. https://www.nytimes.com/2022/04/29/opinion/antisemitism-post-trump.html.

———. "How 9/11 Turned America into a Half-Crazed, Fading Power." *The New York Times,* September 9, 2021. https://www.nytimes.com/2021/09/09/opinion/how-9-11-turned-america-into-a-half-crazed-fading-power.html.

———. "Just How Dangerous Was Donald Trump?" *The New York Times,* December 14, 2020. https://www.nytimes.com/2020/12/14/opinion/trump-fascism.html.

———. "Loneliness Is Breaking America." *The New York Times,* July 19, 2021. https://www.nytimes.com/2021/07/19/opinion/trump-covid-extremism-loneliness.html.

———. "QAnon Believers Are Obsessed with Hillary Clinton. She Has Thoughts." *The New York Times,* February 5, 2021. https://www.nytimes.com/2021/02/05/opinion/qanon-hillary-clinton.html.

———. "Trump's Occupation of American Cities Has Begun." *The New York Times,* July 20, 2020. https://www.nytimes.com/2020/07/20/opinion/portland-protests-trump.html.

Golding, William. *Lord of the Flies.* London: Faber and Faber 1954.

Goodman, Peter S. "A Fresh Look at the Apostle of Free Markets." *The New York Times,* April 13, 2008. https://www.nytimes.com/2008/04/13/weekinreview/13goodman.html.

———. "Stakeholder Capitalism Gets a Report Card: It's Not Good." *The New York Times,* September 24, 2020. https://www.nytimes.com/2020/09/22/business/business-roudtable-stakeholder-capitalism.html.

Gopnik, Adam. "The Habit of Democracy." *The New Yorker,* October 8, 2001. https://www.newyorker.com/magazine/2001/10/15/the-habit-of-democracy.

———. "The Ultra-Nationalist Éric Zemmour Makes a Bizarre Bid for the French Presidency." *The New Yorker,* December 3, 2021. https://www.newyorker.com/news/daily-comment/the-ultra-nationalist-eric-zemmour-makes-a-bizarre-bid-for-the-french-presidency.

Gottlieb, Robert. "The Novelist Who Saw Middle America as It Really Was." *The New York Times,* January 2, 2022. https://www.nytimes.com/2021/12/31/books/review/sinclair-lewis-babbitt-main-street.html.

Gourevitch, Philip. "The Unthinkable: How Dangerous is Le Pen's National Front?" *The New Yorker,* April 28, 1997.

Graff, Gerald. *Beyond the Culture Wars: How Teaching the Conflicts Can Revitalize American Education.* New York: W.W. Norton & Co., 1992.

Grandin, Greg. *The End of the Myth: From the Frontier to the Border Wall in the Mind of America.* New York: Metropolitan Books, 2019.

Grant, Adam. "The Dark Side of Emotional Intelligence." *The Atlantic,* January 2, 2014. https://www.theatlantic.com/health/archive/2014/01/the-dark-side-of-emotional-intelligence/282720/.

Green, Avishai. "Speaking Bullshit to Power: Populism and the Rhetoric of Bullshit — A Conceptual Investigation." Unpublished paper, Department of Political Science, Hebrew University, Academia.edu, 2019.

Greenberg, Gary. "In Grief is How We Live Now." *The New York Times,* May 7, 2022. https://www.nytimes.com/2022/05/07/opinion/grief.html.

———. "Leslie Jamison's 'The Recovering' and the Stories We Tell About Drinking." *The New Yorker,* April 2, 2018. https://www.newyorker.com/magazine/2018/04/02/leslie-jamisons-the-recovering-and-the-stories-we-tell-about-drinking.

———. *Manufacturing Depression: The Secret History of a Modern Disease.* New York: Simon & Schuster, 2010.

Greenhouse, Linda. *Justice on The Brink: The Death of Ruth Bader Ginsburg, the Rise of Amy Coney Barrett, and Twelve*

Months That Transformed the Supreme Court. New York: Random House, 2021.

———. "The Supreme Court, Weaponized." *The New York Times,* December 16, 2021. https://www.nytimes.com/2021/12/16/opinion/supreme-court-trump.html.

Grinspan, Jon. "What We Did the Last Time We Broke America." *The New York Times,* October 29, 2021. https://www.nytimes.com/2021/10/29/opinion/normal-politics-gilded-age.html.

Gupta, Alisha Haridasani. Interview with Anand Giridharadas. "How an Aversion to Masks Stems From 'Toxic Masculinity.'" *The New York Times,* October 22, 2020. https://www.nytimes.com/2020/10/22/us/masks-toxic-masculinity-covid-men-gender.html

Hacker, Jacob S., and Paul Pierson. *Let Them Eat Tweets: How the Right Rules in an Age of Extreme Inequality.* New York: Liveright, 2020.

Haidt, Jonathan. *The Righteous Mind: Why Good People Are Divided by Politics and Religion.* New York: Random House, 2012.

Haney López, Ian. *Dog-Whistle Politics: How Coded Racial Appeals Have Reinvented Racism and Wrecked the Middle Class.* Oxford: Oxford University Press, 2014.

Haney López, Ian, and Tory Gavito. "This Is How Biden Should Approach the Latino Vote." *The New York Times,* September 18, 2020. https://www.nytimes.com/2020/09/18/opinion/biden-latino-vote-strategy.html.

Harriet Staff, "On Auden's 'September 1, 1939.'" *The Poetry Foundation,* September 26, 2019, https://www.poetryfoundation.org/harriet-books/2019/09/on-audens-september-1-1939.

Harris, Johnny, Nicholas Kristof, and Adam B. Ellick. "America Wrote the Pandemic Playbook, Then Ignored It." *The New York Times,* September 29, 2020. https://www.nytimes.com/video/opinion/100000007358968/covid-pandemic-us-response.html.

Hasen, Richard L. *Election Meltdown: Dirty Tricks, Distrust, and the Threat to American Democracy.* New Haven: Yale University Press, 2020.

"Heads Together: The Duke and Duchess of Cambridge and Prince Harry's Campaign to End Stigma around Mental Health." *royal.uk.* https://www.royal.uk/heads-together-duke-and-duchess-cambridge-and-prince-harrys-campaign-end-stigma-around-mental-health.

Heller, Zoë. "Beyond Belief: What Makes a Cult a Cult?" *The New Yorker,* July 5, 2021. https://www.newyorker.com/magazine/2021/07/12/what-makes-a-cult-a-cult.

Hemmer, Nicole. *Messengers of the Right: Conservative Media and the Transformation of American Politics.* Philadelphia: University of Pennsylvania Press, 2016.

———. "What Oprah Winfrey Knows about American History That Tucker Carlson Doesn't." *The New York Times,* May 19, 2022. https://www.nytimes.com/2022/05/19/opinion/sunday/buffalo-oprah-winfrey-tucker-carlson.html.

Hendrix, Harville. *Getting The Love You Want: A Guide for Couples.* New York: St. Martin's Press, 2008.

Herman, Edward S. and Noam Chomsky. *Manufacturing Consent: The Political Economy of Mass Media.* New York: Pantheon, 1988.

Hessel, Stéphane. *Indignez-vous!* Barcelona: Indigène éditions, 2010.

Hidden Brain, "Romeo and Juliet in Kigali: How a Soap Opera Sought to Change Behavior in Rwanda." Hosted by Shankar Vedantam. *NPR,* April 16, 2018. https://www.npr.org/transcripts/602872309.

Higgins, Andrew. "Bound by a Sense of Victimhood, Serbia Sticks with Russia." *The New York Times,* March 30, 2022. https://www.nytimes.com/2022/03/30/world/europe/ukraine-serbia-russia.html.

Hill, Anita. *Speaking Truth to Power.* New York: Penguin Books, 1997.

Hing, Julianne. "For Trump, Cruelty Is the Point." *The Nation,* March 15, 2018. https://www.thenation.com/article/archive/for-trump-cruelty-is-the-point/.

Hofstadter, Richard. *Anti-intellectualism in American Life.* New York: Alfred A. Knopf, 1963.

Howells, Coral Ann, ed. *The Cambridge Companion to Margaret Atwood.* Cambridge: Cambridge University Press, 2006.

Hrytsak, Yaroslav. "Putin Made a Profound Miscalculation on Ukraine." *The New York Times,* March 19, 2022. https://www.nytimes.com/2022/03/19/opinion/ukraine-russia-putin-history.html.

Huang, Chye-Ching. "How Biden Funds His Next Bill: Shrink the $7.5 Trillion Tax Gap." *The New York Times,* March 10, 2021. https://www.nytimes.com/2021/03/10/opinion/deficits-taxes-biden-infrastructure.html.

Ioffe, Julia. "Europe's 9/11." *Puck News,* March 3, 2022. https://puck.news/europes-9-11/.

James, Clive. "Fatherland." *The Atlantic,* November 2004. https://www.theatlantic.com/magazine/archive/2004/11/fatherland/303564/.

Jamison, Leslie. "Since I Became Symptomatic." *The New York Review of Books,* March 26, 2020. https://www.nybooks.com/daily/2020/03/26/since-i-became-symptomatic/.

———. *The Empathy Exams.* Minneapolis: Graywolf, 2014.

———. "This Year Has Taught Me a Lot about Nostalgia." *The New York Times,* March 11, 2021. https://www.nytimes.com/2021/03/11/opinion/covid-isolation-narrative.html.

Jentleson, Adam. "What If Trumpism Is the G.O.P.'s Natural State?" *The New York Times,* August 18, 2020. https://www.nytimes.com/2020/08/18/opinion/trump-republican-party.html.

Jeong, May. "The Deep American Roots of the Atlanta Shootings." *The New York Times,* March 19, 2021. https://www.nytimes.com/2021/03/19/opinion/atlanta-shooting-massage-sex-work.html.

Jeremic, Sladjana. "Serbian Fascism in Online Comments: A Case Study of 'Small Town Philosophy' of Radomir Konstantinović ." Unpublished MA thesis, Université Jean Moulin Lyon 3, 2015.

Judt, Tony. *Ill Fares the Land: Essays on Food, Hunger, and Power.* New York: Penguin Press, 2010.

Kakutani, Michiko. *The Death of Truth: Notes on Falsehood in the Age of Trump.* New York: Tim Duggan Books, 2018.

———. "The Handmaid's Thriller: In 'The Testaments' There's a Spy in Gilead." *The New York Times,* September 3, 2019. https://www.nytimes.com/2019/09/03/books/review/testaments-margaret-atwood-handmaids-tale.html.

Kaplan, Erin Aubry. "Everyone's an Antiracist, Now What?" *The New York Times,* July 6, 2020. https://www.nytimes.com/2020/07/06/opinion/antiracism-what-comes-next.html.

Kaufman, Dan. "Scott Walker's Wisconsin Paved the Way for Donald Trump's America." *The New York Times,* July 6, 2021. https://www.nytimes.com/2021/07/06/opinion/wisconsin-act-10-trump.html.

Kaufman, Jay S. "Science Alone Can't Heal a Sick Society." *The New York Times,* September 10, 2021. https://www.nytimes.com/2021/09/10/opinion/covid-science-trust-us.html.

Keats, John. *Letters of John Keats.* Edited by Robert Gittings. London: Oxford University Press, 1970.

Keefe, Patrick Radden. *Empire of Pain: The Secret History of the Sackler Dynasty.* New York: Doubleday, 2021.

Keller, Bill, ed. *Class Matters.* New York: Henry Holt, 2005.

Kimmel Jr., James. "What the Science of Addiction Tells Us About Trump." *Politico,* December 12, 2020. https://www.politico.com/news/magazine/2020/12/12/trump-grievance-addiction-444570.

King, Jr. Martin Luther. "The Drum Major Instinct (1968)." In *I Have A Dream: Writings and Speeches That Changed the World,* 180–92. New York: HarperCollins, 1992.

Kiwan, Nadia. "A Disorienting Sense of Déjà-vu? Islamophobia and Secularism in French Public Life." *Berkeley Center for*

Religion, Peace and World Affairs, Georgetown University, Washington, DC, May 18, 2021. https://berkleycenter. georgetown.edu/responses/a-disorienting-sense-of-deja-vu-islamophobia-and-secularism-in-french-public-life.

Klein, Ezra. "Democrats, Here's How to Lose in 2022. And Deserve It." *The New York Times,* January 21, 2021. https://www.nytimes.com/2021/01/21/opinion/biden-inauguration-democrats.html.

———. "Transcript: Ezra Klein Interviews Amanda Litman." *The New York Times,* February 1, 2022. https://www.nytimes.com/2022/02/01/podcasts/transcript-ezra-klein-interviews-amanda-litman.html.

———. "Transcript Ezra Klein Interviews Margaret Atwood." *The New York Times,* March 25, 2022. https://www.nytimes.com/2022/03/25/podcasts/transcript-ezra-klein-interviews-margaret-atwood.html.

Klein, Sarah, and Tom Mason. "How to Win an Election." *The New York Times,* February 18, 2016. https://www.nytimes.com/2016/02/18/opinion/how-to-win-an-election.html.

Koenig, Gaspard. "Eric Zemmour, une menace pour l'identité française." *Libération,* December 2, 2021. https://www.liberation.fr/idees-et-debats/tribunes/eric-zemmour-une-menace-pour-lidentite-francaise-20211202_P6GEPQJZCBEONCIREO767IQ7PM/.

Kolbert, Elizabeth. "How Politics Got So Polarized." *The New Yorker,* December 27, 2021. https://www.newyorker.com/magazine/2022/01/03/how-politics-got-so-polarized.

———. "The Psychology of Inequality." *The New Yorker,* January 8, 2018. https://www.newyorker.com/magazine/2018/01/15/the-psychology-of-inequality.

Kramer, Jane. "Taking the Veil." *The New Yorker,* November 22, 2004. https://www.newyorker.com/magazine/2004/11/22/taking-the-veil.

Krastev, Ivan. "The Pandemic Was Supposed to Be Great for Strongmen. What Happened?" *The New York Times,* September 8, 2020. https://www.nytimes.com/2020/09/08/opinion/coronavirus-dictatorships.html.

———. "Trump Has Made America a Laughingstock." *The New York Times,* January 12, 2021. https://www.nytimes.com/2021/01/12/opinion/trump-america-allies.html.

Kristof, Nicholas. "If Only There Were a Viral Video of Our Jim Crow Education System." *The New York Times,* May 21, 2021. https://www.nytimes.com/2021/05/21/opinion/sunday/education-racism-segregation.html.

———. "We're No. 28! And Dropping!" *The New York Times,* September 9, 2020. https://www.nytimes.com/2020/09/09/opinion/united-states-social-progress.html.

Kristof, Nicholas, and Sheryl WuDunn. *Tightrope: Americans Reaching for Hope.* New York: Random House, 2020.

Krugman, Paul. "America's Right Has a Putin Problem." *The New York Times,* March 10, 2022. https://www.nytimes.com/2022/03/10/opinion/putin-ukraine-russia-usa.html.

———. *Arguing with Zombies: Economics, Politics, and The Fight for a Better Future.* New York: W.W. Norton & Co., 2020.

———. "'Freedom,' Florida and the Delta Variant Disaster." *The New York Times,* August 2, 2021. https://www.nytimes.com/2021/08/02/opinion/Covid-Florida-vaccines.html.

———. "The Attack on Big Mouse Is Also an Assault on Democracy." *The New York Times,* April 25, 2022. https://www.nytimes.com/2022/04/25/opinion/republicans-florida-disney-conspiracy-theories.html.

———. *The Conscience of a Liberal: Reclaiming America from the Right.* New York: W.W. Norton & Co., 2007.

Kübler-Ross, Elisabeth. *On Death and Dying.* New York: Macmillan, 1969.

Kuttner, Robert. "Capitalism vs. Liberty." *The American Prospect,* December 1, 2021. https://prospect.org/politics/capitalism-vs-liberty/.

———. *The Stakes: 2020 and the Survival of American Democracy.* Cambridge: Harvard University Press, 2019.

Lacorne, Denis. *The Limits of Tolerance: Enlightenment Values and Religious Fanaticism.* Translated by C. Jon Delogu and Robin Emlein. New York: Columbia University Press, 2019.

Laffitte, Michel. "L'UGIF, collaboration ou résistance ?" *Revue d'Histoire de la Shoah* 2, no. 185 (2006): 45–64.

Larson, Sarah. "Brené Brown's Empire of Emotion." *The New Yorker,* October 25, 2021. https://www.newyorker.com/magazine/2021/11/01/brene-browns-empire-of-emotion.

Lebow, Richard Ned. *Forbidden Fruit: Counterfactuals and International Relations.* Princeton: Princeton University Press, 2010.

Lemann, Nicholas. "The Tea Party Is Timeless." *Columbia Journalism Review,* September–October 2014. https://archives.cjr.org/second_read/richard_hofstadter_tea_party.php.

Le Monde. "Zemmour, Vichy, et les juifs: L'historien Robert Paxton répond (entretien exclusif)." *YouTube,* December 5, 2021. https://www.youtube.com/watch?v=ZFGDlEQ457we.

Leonard, Christopher. "Charles Koch's Big Bet on Barrett." *The New York Times,* October 12, 2020. https://www.nytimes.com/2020/10/12/opinion/charles-koch-amy-coney-barrett.html.

———. *Kochland: The Secret History of Koch Industries and Corporate Power in America.* New York: Simon & Schuster, 2019.

Leong, Nancy. *Identity Capitalists: The Powerful Insiders Who Exploit Diversity to Maintain Inequality.* Stanford: Stanford University Press, 2021.

Leonhardt, David. "The Monopolization of America." *The New York Times,* November 25, 2018. https://www.nytimes.com/2018/11/25/opinion/monopolies-in-the-us.html.

Leonhardt, David, and Stuart A. Thompson. "How Working-Class Life Is Killing Americans, in Charts." *The New York Times,* March 6, 2020. https://www.nytimes.com/interactive/2020/03/06/opinion/working-class-death-rate.html.

Lerner, Melvin J. *The Belief in a Just World: A Fundamental Delusion.* New York: Springer, 1980.

Levin, Yuval. *A Time to Build: From Family and Community to Congress and the Campus, How Recommitting to Our*

Institutions Can Revive the American Dream. New York: Basic Books, 2020.

———. "Either Trump or Biden Will Win. But Our Deepest Problems Will Remain." *The New York Times,* November 3, 2020. https://www.nytimes.com/2020/11/03/opinion/2020-election.html.

Levinas, Emmanuel. *Difficile liberté.* Paris: Albin Michel, 2006.

Levitsky, Steven, and Daniel Ziblatt. "Why Republicans Play Dirty." *The New York Times,* September 20, 2019. https://www.nytimes.com/2019/09/20/opinion/republicans-democracy-play-dirty.html.

Lewis, John. "Together, You Can Redeem the Soul of Our Nation." *The New York Times,* July 30, 2020. https://www.nytimes.com/2020/07/30/opinion/john-lewis-civil-rights-america.html.

Liljas, Per. "An Apology for the Rwandan Genocide, 20 Years Later." *Time Magazine,* April 17, 2014. https://time.com/66095/rwanda-genocide-keating-apology/.

Linz, Juan J., and Alfred Stepan, ed. *The Breakdown of Democratic Regimes: Europe.* Baltimore: Johns Hopkins University Press, 1978.

Lipset, Seymour. *Political Man: The Social Bases of Politics.* Garden City: Anchor Books, 1963.

Lorenz, Taylor. "'OK Boomer' Marks the End of Friendly Generational Relations." *The New York Times,* October 29, 2019. https://www.nytimes.com/2019/10/29/style/ok-boomer.html.

Louie, Sam. "I Don't See Color — Then You Don't See Me." *Psychology Today,* February 22, 2016. https://www.psychologytoday.com/us/blog/minority-report/201602/i-dont-see-color.

Lumpkins, Charles L. *American Pogrom: The East St. Louis Race Riot and Black Politics.* Athens: Ohio University Press, 2008.

Lyall, Sarah. "A Nation on Hold Wants to Speak with a Manager." *The New York Times,* January 1, 2022. https://

www.nytimes.com/2022/01/01/business/customer-service-pandemic-rage.html.

Lythcott-Haims, Julie. *How to Raise an Adult: Break Free of the Overparenting Trap and Prepare Your Kids for Success.* New York: St Martin's Press, 2015.

Mações, Bruno. "How Trump Almost Broke the Bounds of Reality." *The New York Times,* November 12, 2020. https://www.nytimes.com/2020/11/12/opinion/donald-trump-reality.html.

MacLean, Nancy. *Democracy in Chains: The Deep History of the Radical Right's Stealth Plan for America.* New York: Viking, 2017.

Malcolm, Janet "The Impossible Profession," Parts I and II. *The New Yorker,* November 24 and December 1, 1980.

Malesic, Jonathan. "How Men Burn Out." *The New York Times,* January 4, 2022. https://www.nytimes.com/2022/01/04/opinion/burnout-men-signs.html.

Manguel, Alberto, Maaza Mengiste, Valeria Luiselli, Margaret Atwood, and Colm Tóibín. "Concentration Camps for Kids: An Open Letter." *The New York Review of Books,* November 6, 2018. https://www.nybooks.com/daily/2018/11/06/concentration-camps-for-kids-an-open-letter/.

Manne, Kate. "Diet Culture Is Unhealthy. It's Also Immoral." *The New York Times,* January 3, 2022. https://www.nytimes.com/2022/01/03/opinion/diet-resolution.html.

———. *Down Girl: The Logic of Misogyny.* Oxford: Oxford University Press, 2017.

———. *Entitled: How Male Privilege Hurts Women.* New York: Crown, 2020.

Marantz, Andrew. *Antisocial: Online Extremists, Techno-Utopians, and the Hijacking of the American Conversation.* New York: Penguin Books, 2019.

———. "Does Hungary Offer a Glimpse of Our Authoritarian Future?" *The New Yorker,* July 4, 2022. https://www.newyorker.com/magazine/2022/07/04/does-hungary-offer-a-glimpse-of-our-authoritarian-future.

———. "Free Speech Is Killing Us." *The New York Times,* October 4, 2019. https://www.nytimes.com/2019/10/04/opinion/sunday/free-speech-social-media-violence.html.

Marchese, David. "Rev. William Barber on Greed, Poverty and Evangelical Politics." *The New York Times,* December 28, 2020. https://www.nytimes.com/interactive/2020/12/28/magazine/william-barber-interview.html.

Marsh, John. *Class Dismissed: Why We Cannot Teach or Learn Our Way Out of Inequality.* New York: Monthly Review Press, 2011.

Mathiot, Cédric. "Le nombre de féminicides augmente-t-il vraiment?" *Libération,* November 20, 2019. https://www.liberation.fr/checknews/2019/11/20/le-nombre-de-feminicides-augmente-t-il-vraiment_1763789.

Maxim, Chloe, and Canyon Woodward. "What Democrats Don't Understand about Rural America." *The New York Times,* May 2, 2022. https://www.nytimes.com/2022/05/02/opinion/democrats-rural-america.html.

Mayer, Jane. *Dark Money: The Hidden History of the Billionaires Behind the Rise of the Radical Right.* New York: Random House, 2016.

———. "Remembering Walter Mondale." *The New Yorker,* April 19, 2021. https://www.newyorker.com/news/postscript/remembering-walter-mondale.

Mayer, Jane, and Jill Abramson. *Strange Justice: The Selling of Clarence Thomas.* Los Angeles: Graymalkin Media, 2018.

Mayer, Nonna. "Le mythe de la dédiabolisation du FN." *La vie des Idées,* December 4, 2015. https://laviedesidees.fr/Le-mythe-de-la-dediabolisation-du-FN.html.

McCarthy, Mary. "'The Handmaid's Tale' by Margaret Atwood." *The New York Times,* February 9, 1986.

McElroy, Alex. "This Isn't Your Old Toxic Masculinity. It Has Taken an Insidious New Form." *The New York Times,* January 13, 2022. https://www.nytimes.com/2022/01/13/opinion/toxic-masculinity.html.

Mcfly et Carlito. "OK Boomer (clip officiel)." *YouTube,*
    February 27, 2020. https://www.youtube.com/watch?v=1-
    ac8jxb66U.
McGhee, Heather C. *The Sum of Us: What Racism Costs
    Everyone and How We Can Prosper Together.* New York:
    One World, 2021.
———. "The Way Out of Zero-Sum Thinking on Race and
    Wealth." *The New York Times,* February 13, 2021. https://
    www.nytimes.com/2021/02/13/opinion/race-economy-
    inequality-civil-rights.html.
McGirr, Lisa. "Trump Is the Republican Party's Past and
    Future." *The New York Times,* January 13, 2021. https://www.
    nytimes.com/2021/01/13/opinion/gop-trump.html.
McGrath, Charles. "No Longer Writing, Philip Roth Still Has
    Plenty to Say." *The New York Times,* January 16, 2018. https://
    www.nytimes.com/2018/01/16/books/review/philip-roth-
    interview.html.
Meacham, Jon. *The Hope of Glory: Reflections on the Last
    Words of Jesus from the Cross.* New York: Convergent Books,
    2020.
———. "Why Religion Is the Best Hope against Trump." *The
    New York Times,* February 25, 2020. https://www.nytimes.
    com/2020/02/25/opinion/christianity-trump.html.
Mead, Rebecca. "Margaret Atwood, The Prophet of Dystopia."
    The New Yorker, April 10, 2017. https://www.newyorker.com/
    magazine/2017/04/17/margaret-atwood-the-prophet-of-
    dystopia.
Mediapart. "Usul. Faut-il vraiment voter Macron?"
    YouTube, April 18, 2022. https://www.youtube.com/
    watch?v=MCjAbMoY8gw
Menand, Louis. "Joseph McCarthy and the Force of Political
    Falsehoods." *The New Yorker,* August 3 and 10, 2020. https://
    www.newyorker.com/magazine/2020/08/03/joseph-
    mccarthy-and-the-force-of-political-falsehoods.
———. *The Free World: Art and Thought in the Cold War.* New
    York: Farrar, Straus and Giroux, 2021.

———. "The Making of the New Left." *The New Yorker,* March 22, 2021. https://www.newyorker.com/magazine/2021/03/22/the-making-of-the-new-left.

———. "What Our Biggest Best-Sellers Tell Us about a Nation's Soul." *The New Yorker,* May 31, 2021. https://www.newyorker.com/magazine/2021/06/07/what-our-biggest-best-sellers-tell-us-about-a-nations-soul.

Mercieca, Jennifer. *Demagogue for President: The Rhetorical Genius of Donald Trump.* College Station: Texas A&M University Press, 2020.

Michaud, Jon. "The Miracle of Van Morrison's 'Astral Weeks.'" *The New Yorker,* March 7, 2018. https://www.newyorker.com/culture/culture-desk/the-miracle-of-van-morrisons-astral-weeks.

Miklashek, Greeley, "Trumpism: The Psychology of Trump Supporters." *Academia.edu,* November 8, 2020. https://www.academia.edu/70412114/Trumpism.

Miller, Geoffrey. *Virtue Signaling: Essays on Darwinian Politics and Free Speech.* N.p.: Cambrian Moon, 2019.

Miller-Idriss, Cynthia. *Hate in the Homeland: The New Global Far Right.* Princeton: Princeton University Press, 2020.

Mills, C. Wright. *The Power Elite.* Oxford: Oxford University Press, 1956.

Morrison, Toni. "Racism and Fascism." *The Journal of Negro Education* 64, no. 3 (Summer 1995): 384–85.

Muirhead, Russell, and Nancy L. Rosenblum. *A Lot of People are Saying: The New Conspiricism and the Assault on Democracy.* Princeton: Princeton University Press, 2020.

Müller, Jan-Werner. *Democracy Rules.* New York: Farrar, Straus & Giroux, 2021.

Myers, Steven Lee. "An Alliance of Autocracies? China Wants to Lead a New World Order." *The New York Times,* March 29, 2021. https://www.nytimes.com/2021/03/29/world/asia/china-us-russia.html.

Nagourney, Adam. "Was Reagan a Precursor to Trump? A New Documentary Says Yes." *The New York Times,* November 11,

2020. https://www.nytimes.com/2020/11/11/arts/television/
the-reagans.html.

Neiman, Susan. *Learning from the Germans: Race and the
Memory of Evil.* New York: Farrar, Straus and Giroux, 2019.

Newfield, Christopher. *The Great Mistake: How We Wrecked
Public Universities and How We Can Fix Them.* Baltimore:
Johns Hopkins University Press, 2016.

———. *Unmaking the Public University: The Forty-Year
Assault on the Middle Class.* Cambridge: Harvard University
Press, 2008.

Nicolaou, Elena. "The Original Book Review of 'The
Handmaid's Tale' Got it So Crazy Wrong." *Refinery29,* May
17, 2017. https://www.refinery29.com/en-us/2017/05/154866/
handmaids-tale-hulu-timing-review-mary-mccarthy.

Nilsson, Mikael. "Trump Is a Warning That Fascism Didn't
Die with Hitler and Mussolini." *Haaretz,* January 21, 2021.
https://www.haaretz.com/us-news/2021-01-21/ty-article-
opinion/.premium/trump-legacy-fascism-far-right-
biden/0000017f-df2b-df9c-a17f-ff3b20380000.

Nowinski, Joseph. "Identifying with the Aggressor." *Psychology
Today,* July 17, 2020. https://www.psychologytoday.com/us/
blog/the-almost-effect/202007/identifying-the-aggressor.

Nussbaum, Martha C. "A Cunning Adaptation of 'The
Handmaid's Tale.'" *The New Yorker,* May 15, 2017. https://
www.newyorker.com/magazine/2017/05/22/a-cunning-
adaptation-of-the-handmaids-tale.

———. *Not for Profit: Why Democracy Needs the Humanities.*
Princeton: Princeton University Press, 2010.

Obama, Barack. *The Audacity of Hope: Thoughts on Reclaiming
the American Dream.* New York: Crown, 2006.

O'Brien, Dennis. "Orwell, '1984' and the Elections." *The
Christian Science Monitor,* December 31, 1984. https://www.
csmonitor.com/1984/1231/123148.html.

O'Hara, Frank. "To the Film Industry in Crisis." In *Meditations
in an Emergency,* 3–5. New York: Grove Press, 1957.

Olds, Jacqueline, and Richard S. Schwartz. *The Lonely American: Drifting Apart in the Twenty-First Century.* Boston: Beacon Press, 2009.

Ortaliza, Jared, Giorlando Ramirez, Venkatesh, and Krutika Amin. "How Does US Life Expectancy Compare to Other Countries?" *Health System Tracker,* September 28, 2021. https://www.healthsystemtracker.org/chart-collection/u-s-life-expectancy-compare-countries/#item-le_total-life-expectancy-at-birth-in-years-1980-2017_dec-2019-update.

Osnos, Evan. "Can Mark Zuckerberg Fix Facebook before It Breaks Democracy?" *The New Yorker,* September 10, 2018. https://www.newyorker.com/magazine/2018/09/17/can-mark-zuckerberg-fix-facebook-before-it-breaks-democracy.

———. "Dan Bongino and the Big Business of Returning Trump to Power." *The New Yorker,* December 27, 2021. https://www.newyorker.com/magazine/2022/01/03/dan-bongino-and-the-big-business-of-returning-trump-to-power.

———. "How Greenwich Republicans Learned to Love Trump." *The New Yorker,* May 3, 2020. https://www.newyorker.com/magazine/2020/05/11/how-greenwich-republicans-learned-to-love-trump.

———. *Wildland: The Making of America's Fury.* New York: Farrar, Straus and Giroux, 2021.

O'Toole, Fintan. *Ship of Fools: How Stupidity and Corruption Sank the Celtic Tiger.* New York: PublicAffairs, 2010.

———. "Trial Runs for Fascism Are in Full Flow." *The Irish Times,* June 26, 2018. https://www.irishtimes.com/opinion/fintan-o-toole-trial-runs-for-fascism-are-in-full-flow-1.3543375.

Ovide, Shira. "Bogus Ideas Have Superspreaders, Too." *The New York Times,* July 1, 2020. https://www.nytimes.com/2020/07/01/technology/social-media-superspreaders.html.

Ozick, Cynthia. "Who Owns Anne Frank?" *The New Yorker,* October 6, 1997. https://www.newyorker.com/magazine/1997/10/06/who-owns-anne-frank.

Pancevski, Bojan, and Laurence Norman. "How Angela
  Merkel's Change of Heart Drove Historic EU Rescue Plan."
  The Wall Street Journal, July 21, 2020. https://www.wsj.com/
  articles/angela-merkel-macron-covid-coronavirus-eu-
  rescue-11595364124.
Pappis, Konstantinos. "Conversations with 'Frances Ha': The
  Intersection between Sally Rooney's Millennial Fiction
  and Greta Gerwig's Mumblecore Classic." *ourculture,*
  October 26, 2019. https://ourculturemag.com/2019/10/26/
  conversations-with-frances-ha-the-intersection-between-
  sally-rooneys-millennial-fiction-and-greta-gerwigs-
  mumblecore-classic/.
Patnaik, Prabhat. "Why Neoliberalism Needs Neofascists."
  Boston Review, July 19, 2021. https://bostonreview.net/
  articles/why-neoliberalism-needs-neofascists/.
Pauley, Garth. "Criticism in Context: Kenneth Burke's 'The
  Rhetoric of Hitler's "Battle".'" *KB Journal* 6, no. 1 (Fall 2009).
  https://www.kbjournal.org/content/criticism-context-
  kenneth-burkes-rhetoric-hitlers-battle.
Paxton, Robert O. "American Duce: Is Donald Trump a Fascist
  or a Plutocrat?" *Harper's Magazine,* May 2017. https://
  harpers.org/archive/2017/05/american-duce/.
———. *Vichy France and the Jews.* Stanford: Stanford
  University Press, 2019.
———. *Vichy France: Old Guard and New Order, 1940–1944.*
  New York: Columbia University Press, 1972.
Payson, E.D. *The Wizard of Oz and Other Narcissists: Coping
  with the One-Way Relationship in Work, Love, and Family.*
  Royal Oak: Julian Day, 2009.
Perlstein, Rick. *Reaganland: America's Right Turn, 1976–1980.*
  New York: Simon & Schuster, 2020.
Perraudin, Johanna. "What Is Left of the American
  Dream? — Taking Stock of America's 'Broken' Society."
  Unpublished MA thesis, Université Jean Moulin-Lyon 3,
  2021.
Petrou, Karen. *Engine of Inequality: The Fed and the Future of
  Wealth in America.* New York: John Wiley & Sons, 2021.

———. "Only the Rich Could Love This Economic Recovery." *The New York Times,* July 12, 2021. https://www.nytimes. com/interactive/2021/07/12/opinion/covid-fed-qe- inequality.html.

Philips, Patrick. *Blood at the Root: A Racial Cleansing in America.* New York: W.W. Norton & Co., 2016.

Phillips-Fein, Kim. *Invisible Hands: The Businessmen's Crusade against the New Deal.* New York: W.W. Norton & Co., 2009.

———. "Is Amy Coney Barrett Joining a Supreme Court Built for the Wealthy?" *The New York Times,* September 27, 2020. https://www.nytimes.com/2020/09/27/opinion/amy-coney- barrett-business-supreme-court.html.

———. "I Wouldn't Bet on the Kind of Democracy Big Business is Selling Us." *The New York Times,* February 1, 2022. https://www.nytimes.com/2022/02/01/opinion/ corporations-democracy.html.

Pildes, Richard H. "How to Keep Extremists out of Power." *The New York Times,* February 25, 2021. https://www.nytimes. com/2021/02/25/opinion/elections-politics-extremists.html.

Polanyi, Karl. *The Great Transformation: The Political and Economic Origins of Our Time.* Boston: Beacon Press, 2001.

Poniewozik, James. "When Democracy Dies in Daylight." *The New York Times,* September 1, 2020. https://www.nytimes. com/2020/09/01/arts/television/plot-against-america- election.html.

Porter, Eduardo. *American Poison: How Racial Hostility Destroyed Our Promise.* New York: Alfred A. Knopf, 2020.

Postman, Neil. *Crazy Talk, Stupid Talk: How We Defeat Ourselves by the Way We Talk–And What to Do About It.* New York: Delacorte, 1976.

Potter, Claire Bond. "The Only Way to Save Higher Education Is to Make It Free." *The New York Times,* June 5, 2020. https://www.nytimes.com/2020/06/05/opinion/sunday/ free-college-tuition-coronavirus.html.

———. "The Shadow of Ronald Reagan Is Costing Us Dearly." *The New York Times,* November 11, 2021. https://www. nytimes.com/2021/11/11/opinion/reagan-social-welfare.html.

Prose, Francine. "Selling Suffering." *The New York Review of Books,* May 4, 2017.

Quinn, Susan. *A Mind of Her Own: The Life of Karen Horney.* New York: Da Capo, 1988.

Raskin, Jamie. *Unthinkable: Truth, Trauma, and the Trials of American Democracy.* New York: HarperCollins, 2022.

Rayack, Elton. *Not So Free to Choose: The Political Economy of Milton Friedman and Ronald Reagan.* New York: Praeger, 1987.

Remnick, David. "An American Tragedy." *The New Yorker,* November 8, 2016. https://www.newyorker.com/news/ news-desk/an-american-tragedy-2.

———. "A Person of the Year: Jamie Raskin." *The New Yorker,* December 16, 2021. https://www.newyorker.com/news/ daily-comment/a-person-of-the-year-jamie-raskin.

———. "Is Donald Trump an Anti-Semite?" *The New Yorker,* December 21, 2021. https://www.newyorker.com/news/ daily-comment/is-donald-trump-an-anti-semite.

Renkl, Margaret. "Thank God for the Poets." *The New York Times,* April 5, 2021. https://www.nytimes.com/2021/04/05/ opinion/poets-poetry-month.html.

Rich, Frank. "In 2008, America Stopped Believing in the American Dream." *New York Magazine,* August 5, 2018. https://medium.com/new-york-magazine/in-2008-america-stopped-believing-in-the-american-dream-2d493c7ae7f3.

Rich, Motoko, and Hikari Hida. "As Pandemic Took Hold, Suicide Rose Among Japanese Women." *The New York Times,* February 22, 2021. https://www.nytimes. com/2021/02/23/world/as-the-pandemic-took-hold-suicide-rose-among-japanese-women.html.

Robin, Corey. *The Enigma of Clarence Thomas.* New York: Henry Holt, 2019.

Romeo, Nick. "The M.I.T. Professor Defining What It Means to Live." *The New York Times,* December 28, 2021. https://www. nytimes.com/2021/12/28/opinion/living-wage-calculator. html.

Rooney, Sally. *Normal People.* New York: Crown, 2018.

Roosevelt, Franklin D. "State of the Union Message to Congress, January 11, 1944." *Franklin D. Roosevelt Library and Museum.* https://www.fdrlibrary.org/address-text.

Rosanvallon, Pierre. "Interview: Emmanuel Macron est devenu la figure centrale de la droite française." *Libération,* March 30, 2022. https://www.liberation.fr/idees-et-debats/ pierre-rosanvallon-emmanuel-macron-est-devenu- la-figure-centrale-de-la-droite-francaise-20220330_ HPVFRPUZIJC5TO3S2QW6E32WCQ/.

Rosen, Madeleine. "Democracy in Name Only." *Amor Mundi,* December 22, 2017. https://medium.com/amor-mundi/ democracy-in-name-only-c0e8aa5a661a.

Ross, Janell. "Obama Revives His 'Cling to Guns or Religion' Analysis — For Donald Trump Supporters." *The Washington Post,* December 21, 2015. https://www.washingtonpost.com/ news/the-fix/wp/2015/12/21/obama-dusts-off-his-cling-to- guns-or-religion-idea-for-donald-trump/.

ross, kihana miraya. "Call It What It is: Anti-Blackness." *The New York Times,* June 4, 2020. https://www.nytimes. com/2020/06/04/opinion/george-floyd-anti-blackness.html.

Roth, Kenneth. "The Age of Zombie Democracies." *Foreign Affairs,* July 28, 2021. https://www.foreignaffairs.com/ americas/age-zombie-democracies.

Rothchild, Mike. *The Storm Is Upon Us: How QAnon Became a Movement, Cult, and Conspiracy Theory of Everything.* New York: Melville House, 2021.

Rothstein, Richard. *The Color of Law: A Forgotten History of How Our Government Segregated America.* New York: Liveright, 2017.

Rubin, Jonah S. "It's Time to Use the F-word: An Anti-fascist Approach to Trump and Franco." *Society for Cultural Anthropology,* April 15, 2021. https://culanth.org/fieldsights/

its-time-to-use-the-f-word-an-anti-fascist-approach-to-trump-and-franco.

Rustamova, Farida. "Putin Rules Russia Like an Asylum." *The New York Times,* May 23, 2022. https://www.nytimes.com/2022/05/23/opinion/russia-putin-war.html.

Santiáñez, Nil. *Topographies of Fascism: Habitus, Space, and Writing in Twentieth-Century Spain.* Toronto: University of Toronto Press, 2013.

Sargent, Greg. "For Trump, the Cruelty Is the Point. But It's Actually Worse Than That." *The Washington Post,* April 9, 2019. https://www.washingtonpost.com/opinions/2019/04/09/trump-cruelty-is-point-its-actually-worse-than-that/.

Sarson, Steven. *Barack Obama: American Historian.* London: Bloomsbury Academic, 2018.

Scheppele, Kim Lane. "What Donald Trump and Ron DeSantis Are Learning About the Politics of Retribution." *The New York Times,* May 24, 2022. https://www.nytimes.com/2022/05/24/opinion/trump-desantis-viktor-orban.html.

Schwartz, Alexandra. "A New Kind of Adultery Novel." *The New Yorker,* July 31, 2017. https://www.newyorker.com/magazine/2017/07/31/a-new-kind-of-adultery-novel.

———. "Improving Ourselves to Death." *The New Yorker,* January 8, 2018. https://www.newyorker.com/magazine/2018/01/15/improving-ourselves-to-death.

Schwartz, Herman. *Right Wing Justice: The Conservative Campaign to Take Over the Courts.* New York: Nation Books, 2004.

Schwartz, Madeleine. "How Should a Millennial Be?" *The New York Review of Books,* April 18, 2019. https://www.nybooks.com/articles/2019/04/18/sally-rooney-how-should-millennial-be/.

Schwartzbrod, Alexandra. "'Tant de haines': Un hors-série pour comprendre l'extrême droitisation du débat." *Libération,* February 15, 2022. https://www.liberation.fr/plus/tant-de-haines-un-hors-serie-pour-comprendre-

lextreme-droitisation-du-debat-politique-20220214_
IPKM2CLAVRDBBASJWUKG5V2MDI/.

Schwendinger, Herman, and Julia Schwendinger. *Homeland Fascism: Corporatist Government in the New American Century.* Earth: punctum books, 2016.

Scott, A.O. "Once Upon a Timeline in America." *The New York Times,* April 20, 2020. https://www.nytimes.com/2020/04/20/arts/television/plot-against-america-alternate-history.html.

Senior, Jennifer. "Rod Rosenstein Was Just Doing His Job." *The New York Times,* October 15, 2020. https://www.nytimes.com/2020/10/15/opinion/rod-rosenstein-family-separation.html.

———. "Trump to New York: Drop Dead." *The New York Times,* March 24, 2020. https://www.nytimes.com/2020/03/24/opinion/trump-nyc-coronavirus.html.

Serwer, Adam. "The Cruel Logic of the Republican Party, before and after Trump." *The New York Times,* June 26, 2021. https://www.nytimes.com/2021/06/26/opinion/trump-republican-party.html.

———. "The Cruelty Is the Point." *The Atlantic,* October 3, 2018. https://www.theatlantic.com/ideas/archive/2018/10/the-cruelty-is-the-point/572104/.

———. *The Cruelty Is the Point: The Past, Present, and Future of Trump's America.* New York: Random House, 2021.

———. "The First Days of the Trump Regime." *The Atlantic,* February 19, 2020. https://www.theatlantic.com/ideas/archive/2020/02/trump-regime/606682/.

Sharlet, Jeff. "He's the Chosen One to Run America: Inside the Cult of Trump, His Rallies Are Church and He Is the Gospel." *Vanity Fair,* June 18, 2020. https://www.vanityfair.com/news/2020/06/inside-the-cult-of-trump-his-rallies-are-church-and-he-is-the-gospel.

Shaxson, Nicholas. "The City of London Is Hiding the World's Stolen Money." *The New York Times,* October 11, 2021. https://www.nytimes.com/2021/10/11/opinion/pandora-papers-britain-london.html.

Sherman, Rachel. *Uneasy Street: The Anxieties of Affluence.*
Princeton: Princeton University Press, 2017.

Shklar, Judith N. "Putting Cruelty First." *Daedalus* 111,
no. 3 (Summer 1982): 17–27. https://www.jstor.org/
stable/20024800.

Shpancer, Noam. "Rape Is Not (Only) about Power: It's (Also)
about Sex." *Psychology Today,* February 1, 2016. https://www.
psychologytoday.com/us/blog/insight-therapy/201602/rape-
is-not-only-about-power-it-s-also-about-sex.

Silverstein, Shel. *The Giving Tree.* New York: Harper & Row,
1964.

Sinclair, Upton. *I, Candidate for Governor, and How I Got
Licked.* Berkeley: University of California Press, 1994.

Smail, David. "Power, Responsibility and Freedom."
Unpublished manuscript, 2005.

Snyder, Timothy. *Bloodlands: Europe Between Hitler and Stalin.*
New York: Basic Books, 2010.

———. "Europe's Dangerous Creation Myth." *Politico,* May
1, 2019. https://www.politico.eu/article/europe-creation-
project-myth-history-nation-state/.

———. *On Tyranny: Twenty Lessons from the Twentieth
Century.* New York: Tim Duggan Books, 2017.

———. *Our Malady: Lessons in Liberty from a Hospital Diary.*
New York: Crown, 2020.

———. "The American Abyss." *The New York Times,* January
9, 2021. https://www.nytimes.com/2021/01/09/magazine/
trump-coup.html.

———. *The Road to Unfreedom: Russia, Europe, America.* New
York: Tim Duggan Books, 2018.

———. "The War in Ukraine Is a Colonial War." *The New
Yorker,* April 28, 2022. https://www.newyorker.com/news/
essay/the-war-in-ukraine-is-a-colonial-war.

———. "The War on History Is a War on Democracy." *The
New York Times,* June 29, 2021. https://www.nytimes.
com/2021/06/29/magazine/memory-laws.html.

Sonic Youth. "Kool Thing." On *Goo.* DGC Records, 1990.

Sorkin, Andrew Ross. "A Free Market Manifesto that Changed the World, Reconsidered." *The New York Times,* September 11, 2020. https://www.nytimes.com/2020/09/11/business/dealbook/milton-friedman-doctrine-social-responsibility-of-business.html.

Staff, Harriet. "On Auden's 'September 1, 1939.'" *Poetry Foundation,* September 26, 2019. https://www.poetryfoundation.org/harriet/2019/09/on-audens-september-1-1939.

Stanley, Jason. "America Is Now in Fascism's Legal Phase." *The Guardian,* December 22, 2021. https://www.theguardian.com/world/2021/dec/22/america-fascism-legal-phase.

———. *How Propaganda Works.* Princeton: Princeton University Press, 2015.

Staub, Ervin. "Reconciliation after Genocide, Mass Killing, or Intractable Conflict: Understanding the Roots of Violence, Psychological Recovery, and Steps toward a General Theory." *Political Psychology* 27, no. 6 (December 2006): 867–94. https://www.jstor.org/stable/20447006.

Stevens, Stuart. "I Hope This Is Not Another Lie about the Republican Party." *The New York Times,* July 29, 2020. https://www.nytimes.com/2020/07/29/opinion/trump-republican-party-racism.html.

———. *It Was All a Lie: How the Republican Party Became Donald Trump.* New York: Penguin Books, 2020.

Stewart, Katherine. "Christian Nationalism Is One of Trump's Most Powerful Weapons." *The New York Times,* January 6, 2022. https://www.nytimes.com/2022/01/06/opinion/jan-6-christian-nationalism.html.

———. *The Power Worshippers: Inside the Dangerous Rise of Religious Nationalism.* New York: Bloomsbury, 2020.

———. "Trump or No Trump, Religious Authoritarianism Is Here to Stay." *The New York Times,* November 16, 2020. https://www.nytimes.com/2020/11/16/opinion/trump-religion-authoritarianism.html.

Stirewalt, Chris. *Broken News: Why the Media Rage Machine Divides America and How to Fight Back.* New York: Center Street, 2022.

Stokes, Melvyn. *D.W. Griffith's "The Birth of a Nation."* Oxford: Oxford University Press, 2008.

Sullivan, Margaret. *Ghosting the News: Local Journalism and the Crisis of American Democracy.* New York: Columbia Global Reports, 2020.

Szalai, Jennifer. "The Debate over the Word 'Fascism' Takes a New Turn." *The New York Times,* June 10, 2020. https://www.nytimes.com/2020/06/10/books/fascism-debate-donald-trump.html.

Szalavitz, Maia. "Opioids Feel Like Love. That's Why They're Deadly in Tough Times." *The New York Times,* December 6, 2021. https://www.nytimes.com/2021/12/06/opinion/us-opioid-crisis.html.

Tarnoff, Ben. *Internet for the People: The Fight for Our Digital Future.* London: Verso, 2022.

———. "The Internet Is Broken. How Do We Fix It?" *The New York Times,* May 27, 2022. https://www.nytimes.com/2022/05/27/opinion/technology/what-would-an-egalitarian-internet-actually-look-like.html.

Taub, Amanda. "From Columbia to U.S., Police Violence Pushes Protests into Mass Movements." *The New York Times,* May 19, 2021. https://www.nytimes.com/2021/05/19/world/americas/colombia-protests-police.html.

———. "How Autocrats Can Triumph in Democratic Countries." *The New York Times,* April 18, 2017. https://www.nytimes.com/2017/04/18/world/europe/how-autocrats-can-triumph-in-democratic-countries.html.

Tavernise, Sabrina, and Robert Gebeloff. "They Did Not Vote in 2016. Why They Plan on Skipping the Election Again." *The New York Times,* October 26, 2020. https://www.nytimes.com/2020/10/26/us/election-nonvoters.html.

"The Mail." *The New Yorker,* September 5, 2016.

The New York Times. "Why These Disneyland Employees Can't Afford Rent | NYT Opinion." *YouTube,* September 5, 2018. https://www.youtube.com/watch?v=3P8fsrWg6No.

Thurman, Judith. "Philip Roth E-Mails on Trump." *The New Yorker,* January 30, 2017. https://www.newyorker.com/magazine/2017/01/30/philip-roth-e-mails-on-trump.

Tisby, Jamar. *How to Fight Racism: Courageous Christianity and the Journey toward Racial Justice.* Grand Rapids: Zondervan, 2021.

Tolentino, Jia. "Margaret Atwood Expands the World of 'The Handmaid's Tale.'" *The New Yorker,* September 5, 2019. https://www.newyorker.com/magazine/2019/09/16/margaret-atwood-expands-the-world-of-the-handmaids-tale.

Toobin, Jeffrey. *Too Close to Call.* New York: Random House, 2001.

Tooze, Adam. "What If the Coronavirus Crisis Is Just a Trial Run?" *The New York Times,* September 1, 2021. https://www.nytimes.com/2021/09/01/opinion/covid-pandemic-global-economy-politics.html.

Trump, Mary L. *Too Much and Never Enough: How My Family Created the World's Most Dangerous Man.* New York: Simon & Schuster, 2020.

Tufekci, Zeynap. "How Millions of Lives Might Have Been Saved from Covid-19." *The New York Times,* March 11, 2022. https://www.nytimes.com/2022/03/11/opinion/covid-health-pandemic.html.

———. "'This Must Be Your First.'" *The Atlantic,* December 7, 2020. https://www.theatlantic.com/ideas/archive/2020/12/trumps-farcical-inept-and-deadly-serious-coup-attempt/617309/.

———. "Where Did the Coronavirus Come From? What We Already Know Is Troubling." *The New York Times,* June 25, 2021. https://www.nytimes.com/2021/06/25/opinion/coronavirus-lab.html.

Turkle, Sherry. *The Empathy Diaries: A Memoir.* New York: Penguin Books, 2021.

Veblen, Thorstein. *The Theory of the Leisure Class.* New York: Modern Library, 2001.

Waldman, Amy. *The Submission.* New York: Farrar, Straus & Giroux, 2011.

Warzel, Charlie. "I Talked to the Cassandra of the Internet Age." *The New York Times,* February 4, 2021. https://www.nytimes.com/2021/02/04/opinion/michael-goldhaber-internet.html.

Wells, Paul. "Donald Trump Is Stuck in the 80s." *Maclean's,* April 9, 2017. https://www.macleans.ca/culture/books/donald-trump-is-stuck-in-the-1980s/.

Werb, Dan. "To Understand the Wuhan Coronavirus, Look to the Epidemic Triangle." *The New York Times,* January 30, 2020. https://www.nytimes.com/2020/01/30/opinion/wuhan-coronavirus-epidemic.html.

Whitman, James Q. *Hitler's American Model: The United States and the Making of Nazi Race Law.* Princeton: Princeton University Press, 2017.

Wiener, Scott. "What I Learned When QAnon Came for Me." *The New York Times,* October 19, 2020. https://www.nytimes.com/2020/10/19/opinion/scott-wiener-qanon.html.

Wieviorka, Annette. *Auschwitz expliqué à ma fille.* Paris: Seuil, 1999.

Wieviorka, Michel. "Les deux autoritarismes." *Libération,* November 17, 2020. https://www.liberation.fr/debats/2020/11/17/les-deux-autoritarismes_1805862/.

Wilkerson, Isabel. *Caste: The Origins of Our Discontents.* New York: Random House, 2020.

Wilkinson, Richard, and Kate Pickett. *The Spirit Level: Why More Equal Societies Almost Always Do Better.* London: Allen Lane, 2009.

Williams, Joan C. *White Working Class: Overcoming Class Cluelessness in America.* Cambridge: Harvard Business Review Press, 2018.

Williams, Paige. "Reading Philip Roth after the Pittsburgh Massacre." *The New Yorker,* November 12, 2018. https://www.

newyorker.com/magazine/2018/11/12/reading-philip-roth-after-the-pittsburgh-massacre.

Williams, Thomas Chatterton. "The French Origins of 'You Will Not Replace Us.'" *The New Yorker,* November 27, 2017. https://www.newyorker.com/magazine/2017/12/04/the-french-origins-of-you-will-not-replace-us.

Williamson, Marianne. *A Return to Love: Reflections on the Principles of a Course in Miracles.* New York: HarperCollins, 1992.

Wilson, Sharon R., Thomas B. Friedman, and Shannon Hengen, eds. *Approaches to Teaching Atwood's "The Handmaid's Tale" and Other Works.* New York: Modern Language Association, 1996.

Wood, Amy Louise. *Lynching and Spectacle: Witnessing Racial Violence in America, 1890–1940.* Chapel Hill: University of North Carolina, 2009.

Workman, Nancy V. "Sufi Mysticism in Margaret Atwood's 'The Handmaid's Tale.'" *Studies in Canadian Literature* 14, no. 2 (1989). https://journals.lib.unb.ca/index.php/scl/article/view/8103/9160.

Worms, Frédéric. "Pourquoi la lutte contre le fascisme ne cesse-t-elle de revenir?" *Libération,* October 15, 2021. https://www.liberation.fr/idees-et-debats/opinions/pourquoi-la-lutte-contre-le-fascisme-ne-cesse-t-elle-de-revenir-20211015_T32O6Q7EXJEXRLL53LMQAWPNAU/.

Wright, Lawrence. *The Plague Year: America in the Time of Covid.* New York: Alfred A. Knopf, 2021.

Wright, Robin. "Madeleine Albright Warns of a New Fascism — and Trump." *The New Yorker,* April 24, 2018. https://www.newyorker.com/news/news-desk/madeleine-albright-warns-of-a-new-fascism-and-trump.

———. "To the World, We're Now America the Racist and Pitiful." *The New Yorker,* July 3, 2020. https://www.newyorker.com/news/our-columnists/to-the-world-were-now-america-the-racist-and-pitiful.

Wu, Tim. *The Curse of Bigness: Antitrust in the New Gilded Age.* New York: Columbia Global Reports, 2018.

Wyman, David S. *The Abandonment of the Jews: America and the Holocaust 1941–1945.* New York: Pantheon, 1984.

Yablokov, Ilya. "The Five Conspiracy Theories That Putin Has Weaponized." *The New York Times,* April 25, 2022. https://www.nytimes.com/2022/04/25/opinion/putin-russia-conspiracy-theories.html.

Ypi, Lea. *Free: Coming of Age at the End of History.* London: Allen Lane, 2021.

Zaretsky, Robert. "How French Secularism Became Fundamentalist." *Foreign Policy,* April 7, 2016. https://foreignpolicy.com/2016/04/07/the-battle-for-the-french-secular-soul-laicite-charlie-hebdo/.

Zarum, Lara. "Mary McCarthy Was Wrong: 'The Handmaid's Tale' Is Scary Because It's True." *Flavorwire,* April 13, 2017. https://www.flavorwire.com/603492/mary-mccarthy-was-dead-wrong-the-handmaids-tale-is-scary-because-its-true.

Zelizer, Julian E. *Burning Down the House: Newt Gingrich, the Fall of the Speaker, and the Rise of the New Republican Party.* New York: Penguin Press, 2020.

Zimmerman, Jonathan. "What Is College Worth?" *The New York Review of Books,* July 2, 2020. https://www.nybooks.com/articles/2020/07/02/what-is-college-worth/.

Zuboff, Shoshana. *The Age of Surveillance Capitalism: The Fight for A Human Future at the New Frontier of Power.* New York: Hachette, 2019.

———. "The Coup We Are Not Talking About." *The New York Times,* January 29, 2021. https://www.nytimes.com/2021/01/29/opinion/sunday/facebook-surveillance-society-technology.html.

Zucman, Gabriel. *The Hidden Wealth of Nations: The Scourge of Tax Havens.* Translated by Teresa Lavender Fagan. Chicago: University of Chicago Press, 2015.

Zygar, Mikhail. *All the Kremlin's Men: Inside the Court of Vladimir Putin.* New York: PublicAffairs, 2016.

———. "How Vladimir Putin Lost Interest in the Present." *The New York Times,* March 10, 2022. https://www.nytimes.com/2022/03/10/opinion/putin-russia-ukraine.html.

www.ingramcontent.com/pod-product-compliance
Lightning Source LLC
Chambersburg PA
CBHW071727270326
41928CB00013B/2588